STRIKE UP THE BAND

Also by Scott Miller

From Assassins to West Side Story:
The Director's Guide to Musical Theatre

Deconstructing Harold Hill:
The Insider's Guide to Musical Theatre

Rebels with Applause:
Broadway's Groundbreaking Musicals

Let the Sun Shine In:
The Genius of HAIR

In the Blood
a novel

STRIKE UP THE BAND

*A New History of
Musical Theatre*

S C O T T   M I L L E R

HEINEMANN
Portsmouth, NH

Heinemann
361 Hanover Street
Portsmouth, NH 03801–3912
www.heinemanndrama.com

Offices and agents throughout the world

Library of Congress Cataloging-in-Publication Data
Miller, Scott, 1964–
    Strike up the band : a new history of musical theatre / Scott Miller.
        p. cm.
    Includes index.
    ISBN-13: 978-0-325-00642-0
    ISBN-10: 0-325-00642-3
    1. Musicals—United States—20th century—History and criticism.   I. Title.

ML1711.5.M55 2006
792.60973—dc22   2006029094

Editor: Lisa A. Barnett
Production: Vicki Kasabian
Cover design: Night & Day Design
Typesetter: Techbooks
Manufacturing: Jamie Carter

Printed in the United States of America on acid-free paper
Sheridan 2019

To Joan Zobel and Don Miller, my parents, who ignited my love for musicals long before I can now remember, raising me on a healthy diet of *The Music Man*, *Carousel*, *Hello, Dolly!*, *Camelot*, and *My Fair Lady*; to the Muny in St. Louis, the amazing outdoor theatre where I was an usher for eight years and got an incomparable education in the literature of musical theatre; to Judy Rethwisch, my high school drama teacher, who cultivated my love of musicals and encouraged me to write my first musical; to Anne Dhu Shapiro and Peter Lieberson at Harvard, who took my passions seriously and taught me how to understand theatre music in depth; to my college roommate and fellow musical theatre lover David Flores for all those late nights deconstructing musicals; to Lisa Barnett, who decided to publish my first book on musicals and opened dozens of doors for me; and to Greg Redford, who emailed me one day and asked me where he could find a good musical theatre history book. . . .

Contents

Overture   1

1 An Era Exploding: 1900–1919   9

2 I Want to Be Happy: The 1920s   19

3 Anything Goes: The 1930s   32

4 Oh, What a Beautiful Morning: The 1940s   44

5 Something's Coming: The 1950s   60

6 Let the Sun Shine In: The 1960s   85

7 In Comes Company: The 1970s   116

8 Do You Hear the People Sing? The 1980s   156

9 Songs for a New World: The 1990s   179

10 An Era Exploding, a Century Spinning: The New Millennium   221

Index   239

Overture

The best musicals have everything the best plays have—great words, great characters, great emotions, great drama and comedy, timeless themes, universal truths. But musicals also have *music*. And no matter how you slice it, words alone can never have the dramatic power or intensity of emotion that music possesses. The great director and teacher Konstantin Stanislavski said that the abstract language of music is the only direct way to the human heart. And in this modern world where emotions—particularly *big* emotions—are often considered inappropriate, inconvenient, even impolite, where the expression of full-bodied emotion has been "civilized" out of most of us, the extreme, unapologetic emotionalism of musical theatre offers audiences a much needed release. Only in musical theatre can those big emotions be adequately expressed. Of course, it's this emotionalism that makes some people, inculcated with a fear of emotion, so uncomfortable.

Martin Gottfried wrote in his book *Broadway Musicals*, "Ultimately, the Broadway musical is a metaphor for the ecstasy we are capable of creating and experiencing; it offers us an emotional orgasm. The Broadway musical is not a passive theater. Its audiences are transformed as they are being made love to."

It's fair to argue that no spoken monologue by itself could ever achieve the power of Sweeney's "Epiphany" in *Sweeney Todd*, Floyd's "How Glory Goes" in *Floyd Collins*, Edgar's "Apology to a Cow" in *Bat Boy*, Collins' eulogy for Angel in *Rent*, or, for that matter, the finales of *Hair*, *Hedwig and the Angry Inch*, *Sunday in the Park with George*, *A New Brain*, *The Cradle Will Rock*, *Man of La Mancha*, *Company*, or dozens of other musicals. Why is emotion so important in the theatre? Because emotion is what makes us human.

In the November 2003 issue of *American Theatre*, performance artist Tim Miller wrote:

> As I watched the national Tony broadcast last June, savoring the folks singing and dancing their way through numbers from the nominated musicals, I was struck by how cheerfully utopian it all felt. These shows and the people who made them seemed to manifest a clear, alternative political vision of our country—one where

gay couples are smoochingly visible; where the short fat girl wins; where people of different races boogie together; where progressive politics is everywhere you look. The Tonys conjured up an America I wish actually existed.

It's easy for people, even theatre people sometimes, to malign musicals as a kind of guilty pleasure—superficial, reactionary fluff; a bad habit, like bingeing on bonbons. But I believe the legacy of the musical theatre is infinitely more complicated and subversive and admirable.

Miller declared that musicals taught him everything he ever needed to know about life, love, politics, and America itself. The musical theatre is America's mythology, a chronicle not just of America's times, people, and events, but even more of America's dreams, legends, national mood, politics, and its extraordinary muscle and resilience. As Ian Bradley writes in his book *You've Got to Have a Dream,* "Is it escapism or is it rather their strangely spiritual, almost sacramental quality which makes musicals deal in dreams, possibilities, and visions of what might be if only we lived in a better world?"

Just like good plays, good musicals are about important issues, either on the surface or in the subtext. Musical theatre isn't some ancient, dusty, irrelevant invalid; it is, *right now,* a thriving, vigorous art form that gives us an exciting forum in which to talk about the issues of our world and to make sense of the chaos of our lives. Just take a look at some of the really interesting shows of the last decade: *Songs for a New World* (1995), *Floyd Collins* (1996), *Bring in 'da Noise, Bring in 'da Funk* (1996), *Rent* (1996), *Avenue X* (1997), *Ragtime* (1998), *Parade* (1998), *A New Brain* (1998), *Hedwig and the Angry Inch* (1998), *Bright Lights, Big City* (1999), *Bat Boy* (2001), *Urinetown* (2001), *The Last Five Years* (2002), *Avenue Q* (2003), *Hairspray* (2003), *The Light in the Piazza* (2003), *Caroline or Change* (2004), *Spelling Bee* (2005), and so many others—some of the most exciting theatre we've seen in many years.

Perhaps part of why some people think musical theatre is dead is because Broadway has become so commercialized that it's nearly impossible for innovative new work to get produced there. Stephen Sondheim's last show, *Bounce,* never made it to New York. Only a few of the shows listed above made it to Broadway. But dozens of brilliant new musicals are being produced around the country in regional theatres every year, many of them too edgy and too honest for Broadway. Musical theatre is more daring and more vigorous than ever, just not necessarily on the Great White Way.

And then there are the older commentators and historians who claim musical theatre is dead because they wish musicals still looked like *Carousel* and *My Fair Lady,* believing that the musical theatre should have stopped evolving around 1964. They bemoan the conceptual work of Hal Prince, Bob Fosse, and Tommy Tune; they whine about the use of microphones and the inferiority of rock and pop music; they hate that this vigorous art form continues to evolve and change in ever more surprising ways, leaving them and their dusty, vinyl cast albums to the history books. But an art form can't stand still, and any attempt to force it into stagnation is doomed.

In the December 2003 issue of *American Theatre*, director Molly Smith wrote, "The seriousness I embraced in dramatic form during my early career, I have now rediscovered—to my delight—in the content of musicals. For me, this robust, craggy art form is in the bones of American culture. It is unpretentious, earthy, forward-looking and optimistic. At the same time, it is full of conflict and contradiction." She finished with, "As you can tell, I've been smitten by my rediscovery of this most robust of American art forms. Moreover I envision a future in which the American musical is the 'serious' theatre I so revered beginning in my twenties."

Admittedly, there are some people who just don't think serious issues have any place in musicals because they insist that musical theatre is such a *silly* and *trivial* art form. The anti-naturalism of characters breaking out into song is more than they can handle, so they just stay away from the "ridiculous" conventions of musicals altogether. You have to wonder if those people ever went to see any of the *Star Wars* movies.

What all these folks don't understand is that *all* art is artificial. God makes lousy theatre, as the saying goes. Art makes order out of the chaos of the real world. Art arranges and edits real life so that it's easier to see and understand certain moments and ideas. Musical theatre engages major political and social issues just as readily as any other form of art. Singing is just the language of musical theatre the way iambic pentameter is the language of Shakespeare, the way special effects are the language of sci-fi, fantasy, and horror films, the way paint is the language of Da Vinci, Monet, and Degas. The conventions of musical theatre are no more ridiculous than any other art form. Movies have romantic montages that telescope time. Many plays have narrators that speak directly to the audience. And have you ever known people in the real world who talk the way they do in a Neil Simon play, a David Mamet play, or a Woody Allen movie?

Some people also confuse realism with naturalism. Naturalism is a style of theatre or film in which everything feels as if it's actually happening for the first time, like a documentary, a style in which people mumble, lines overlap each other, in which the artists try to *imitate* life exactly. Robert Altman makes naturalistic films like *Nashville*, *Ready to Wear*, and *M*A*S*H*. Realism, on the other hand, is not necessarily about style; it's about content. Realistic plays and films are those that portray human life as it really is, no sugar coating, no ignoring of the darker, more complex side of things. George Furth and Stephen Sondheim's *Company*—as unnaturalistic as a show can get—is also one of the most realistic musicals ever written because it deals honestly with the complexity, the difficulty, the messiness of human relationships. Its central character Robert doesn't get a fully happy ending because people in the real world don't get fully happy endings.

And then there's the issue of the acting style. Because musical theatre generally (though not always) requires a bigger, broader, more expressive acting style, some people assume it's also a less nuanced, less disciplined, less skilled kind of acting. On the contrary, to portray genuine emotions and subtle nuances within a broad style is one of the greatest challenges any actor can face. The acting required in a play without music often doesn't compare in its complexity and difficulty with the acting required in shows like *Bat Boy*, *March of the Falsettos*, *The Cradle Will Rock*, *Chicago*, or *Company*. In fact, *Bat Boy*'s co-author and original director Keythe Farley coined a phrase that describes this challenge: "the height of expression, the depth of sincerity." The canvas is bigger, the colors richer, the brushstrokes more expansive, but the image is no less true, the details no less real, the textures no less subtle. Many big-name "legitimate" actors have tanked in Broadway musicals because they were unable to walk the dangerous acting tightrope that musicals require. Acting well in a musical is a very special and very specialized talent that is often underappreciated and misunderstood. It's tougher than it looks.

On the whole, musical theatre deserves more respect than it often gets and that's the purpose of this book, to look in a new way at the continuing miracle of American musical theatre, at its evolution over the twentieth century, at the bold, outrageous—and quite often successful—experiments that have taken the form forward in giant leaps every decade or so. Modern American musical theatre is what opera composer Richard Wagner meant when he talked about *Gesamtkunstwerk*, a "total theatre" using all the art forms to create a powerful, unified work of art in an accessible, populist form. American musical theatre has grown as much in one century as other art forms have grown in several centuries. What other art form could have produced something as mature as *Show Boat* in the third decade of its existence? It's as if the art form was born almost fully grown, as if it shot from infancy to adolescence overnight. And its success and its sophistication is due not only to the brilliant artists, some of them geniuses, who move the art form forward but also to the audiences who were—*and still are*—adventurous enough to embrace the experiments, to buy the tickets and encourage producers to keep trying new things. How else can one explain the hit status of *Urinetown*, *Avenue Q*, or *The 25th Annual Putnam County Spelling Bee*?

In fact, musical theatre—or musical comedy, as it was usually called up until the 1940s—is one of the few indigenous American art forms. Some scholars believe the only truly American art forms are musical comedy, comic books, the murder mystery, and jazz, all forms that have impacted nearly every corner of the civilized world. American musicals overshadow British musicals even in London, even though the British have contributed mightily to the art form over the years. In Germany and other parts of Europe, as well as in Japan, audiences give standing ovations to even the most run-of-the-mill American musicals simply because they are American. They just can't get enough of that muscle. Composer Leonard Bernstein once called musical theatre "an art that arises out of American roots, out of our speech, our tempo, our moral attitudes, our way of moving."

But musicals aren't just American. They are also political, some more wholly political like *Assassins*, *Camelot*, *Cabaret*, or *Hair*; some only partly so like *Purlie*, *Li'l Abner*, *Finian's Rainbow*, *Hairspray*, or *Ragtime*; and some even subliminally political like *Man of La Mancha*, *West Side Story*, or *The Rocky Horror Show*. But once you look for politics, you find it everywhere. For instance, in *Annie Get Your Gun*, the fierce sexism of the plot and the songs "The Girl That I Marry" and "You Can't Get a Man with a Gun" are disturbing enough from a modern perspective, but the idea that Annie has to *lose on purpose* in order to win Frank couldn't be more abhorrent today. You might argue that we shouldn't look at old shows through a modern lens, but it was a *political* choice to tell that story that way with that ending. It mirrored and reinforced the dominant view of gender in America. *Kiss Me Kate* swam in the same politics, juxtaposing a fictional, past, male-dominated world against a real world in which women were becoming increasingly uncontrollable. Both shows came at a time when America was trying to wedge women back into their old, prewar subservience. Just a couple years later, women in musicals would start to get stronger, in *South Pacific*, *Guys and Dolls*, *The King and I*, and a revival of *Pal Joey*, among others.

Political trends have been present in almost all musical theatre storytelling over the years. Casts became integrated as America became integrated. Female characters became overtly sexual (in shows like *On the Town* and *Pal Joey*) when American women became overtly sexual. Musical comedy morality became more ambiguous as mainstream American culture moved away from the certainties of traditional organized religion. Every choice made by writers, directors, and designers was political, and each choice either reinforced or challenged prevailing social and political values. *No, No, Nanette* was about wealth and its implications. *Anything Goes* was about American culture's preoccupation with celebrity. *Gentlemen Prefer Blondes* was about America's reinvigorated postwar hypermaterialism. It was all political, as well as a heck of a lot of fun.

Musical theatre had no precise beginning. Music was used in theatre by the classical Greeks and Romans, by Shakespeare, and by most other dramatists. Theatre had *always* used music; that's all there was to it. It was only in the 1800s that the distinction emerged (and still survives today, unfortunately) between "legitimate" theatre and musical theatre. Up to that point, the idea of a piece of theatre without music was absurd, and audiences did not believe, as some do today, that theatre using music was less legitimate. They thought theatre without music was incomplete. And today, in a world in which our entire lives are set to music—car stereos, piped-in music in stores, streaming audio on the Internet, TV commercials, MTV and VH1, cell phone rings, iPods, families singing "Happy Birthday"—it seems even more unnatural now than ever before to have theatre without music. Human lives *are* musical.

And yet for the art form to get where it is now from where it was a century ago, lots of things had to happen. Audiences had to crave characters and plots in their musicals that reflected their real lives and issues; lyricists and bookwriters had to learn to write in the language of everyday people; composers had to learn to write in a style accessible to their audiences and to create original scores that didn't just scavenge existing pop music or old, worn-out European traditions but actually offered up something fresh; and directors and actors had to discover the very American style of acting and staging we now recognize (even if unconsciously) as musical theatre—fast, brash, energetic, intense, emotional, and presentational.

Musical theatre as we define it today, the art form of Stephen Sondheim, Bob Fosse, Hal Prince, Andrew Lloyd Webber and Tim Rice, John Kander and Fred Ebb, Richard Rodgers and Oscar Hammerstein, was invented in America, it was largely developed in America, and in the estimation of many (perhaps biased) theatre people, it is still done best by Americans. There are British authors who declare categorically that the Brits invented musical theatre, but they're talking about operetta, ballad opera, and other such things. There are German authors who will claim *their* country invented the form. But musical theatre as we know it today is a uniquely American art form, even though it is now often practiced by non-Americans. And it stands as a perfect metaphor for the melting pot heritage of America's immigrant nation, with bits and pieces from almost everywhere, all coming together so completely melded, so fully integrated, that the result is something entirely original.

Musical comedy appeared on the scene around the turn of the last century. The musicals of George M. Cohan were like nothing anyone had ever seen before. They were not a mere evolution; they were genuinely new. A few history books will claim that *The Black Crook* in 1866 was the first musical, but don't be fooled; it was just an accident that combined a bad play with a ballet troupe. It wasn't a musical in any way we know it today. Some people try to trace musical theatre's history back that far perhaps because they can't believe it just appeared as suddenly as it did.

It is true that there were a few American shows in the late 1800s in which certain elements of musical comedy appeared in very early, protoplasmic form, shows like *Evangeline* (1874), *The Brook* (1879), *A Trip to Chinatown* (1890), *In Town* (1892), *Clorindy* (1898), and *A Trip to Coontown* (1898), but most of them wouldn't be recognizable to today's audiences as musicals. They were built on haphazard, mindless stories and used songs and dances entirely unconnected to the script. There was virtually no structure, no integration, no reason for the songs to be there and no reason for the audience to care. Even the most insubstantial of twentieth-century musicals would look Shakespearean next to these shows. In reality, musical comedy appeared on Broadway around 1900 (even though the label was invented a short while earlier), nearly unheralded, pretty much unprecedented.

Still, despite the stature they should enjoy, musicals have gotten the short end of the PR stick over the years. A definition of "musical comedy" didn't appear in the highly respected *Grove Dictionary of Music and Musicians* until 1980. Today, too many people have seen the older shows—*Carousel, Show Boat, The King and I, The Music Man, Hello, Dolly!*—done by schools or churches or community groups in which enthusiasm exceeds skill, in which the directors are lucky to get the show opened, much less communicate subtle nuances about character and relationships to their actors, most of whom have families and day jobs to contend with. And then there are directors who just don't respect musical theatre, who butcher scripts and scores, who add jokes and comic *schtick*, cut songs, rewrite dialogue, add things from movie versions, things they'd *never* do to a play without music.

As a result, audiences sometimes see spirited but uninformed productions of complex shows like *Carousel* or *The King and I* or *Chicago*, the subtlety and depth of which get lost in the shuffle, and those audiences think the shows themselves are lacking. Or people see shows done by touring companies in three- or four-thousand-seat touring houses in which an audience member may well be three city blocks from the actors (an unfortunate economic necessity of the road) and there's no hope of any real emotional connection, no hope of seeing subtle facial expressions, and no way for the actors to do any real acting that will still reach the upper balcony. Perhaps worst of all, people see lousy movie versions of shows like *Carousel* or *Annie* or *A Chorus Line* or the unfortunate television remake of *The Music Man*, assume they are accurate representations of their source material, and therefore assume the source material sucks.

This book is an attempt to right some of those wrongs. It is a tour of musical theatre history that presents not just what happened but, more important, why it matters. It's arranged chronologically, not by Broadway opening dates but by when shows were created or first performed, even when that happens years before a show's Broadway debut. The point of the chronology is to examine shows in context, to compare and contrast them with other contemporaneous work. It took years for *Rent* and other shows to reach full professional productions, but this survey looks at the historical and artistic context of the *creation* of important work. Likewise, this is a book about an art form, not geography, so the focus is not just on Broadway, but also off Broadway, off off Broadway, American regional theatre, and European theatre.

The list of shows discussed is an eclectic one, including shows many people have probably never heard of, even some that failed commercially but were important artistically, and shows that never made it to Broadway because they're just too smart or too edgy for the tourist trade. The list leaves out many shows some people consider classics but that contributed nothing to the evolution of the art form. So don't look for *Brigadoon* or *The Sound of Music* here—those are perfectly nice shows, but they played no part in the evolution of the musical theatre. There are plenty of hit musicals discussed—*Cats, Hello, Dolly!, Cabaret,*

Show Boat, My Fair Lady, Les Miz, Rent—but also plenty of shows you may never have heard of, like *The Ballad of Little Mikey, Avenue X, Rainbow, The Nervous Set,* and others. You'll also encounter here many shows that get left out of other histories, shows by and about African Americans, Asian Americans, Latinos, women, gays, and people with disabilities, shows that had an impact on the art form and have been ignored in the past. The history of musical theatre is *not* just about white men (though they did dominate the art form for much of its history), it's not just about America, and it's *really* not just about Broadway.

1

An Era Exploding
1900–1919

And there was distant music,
Skipping a beat, singing a dream,
A strange, insistent music,
Putting out heat, picking up steam,
The sound of distant thunder
Suddenly starting to climb . . .
It was the music
Of something beginning,
An era exploding,
A century spinning.
In riches and rags
And in rhythm and rhyme . . .

These lyrics by Lynn Ahrens from the contemporary Broadway musical *Ragtime* (1996) were written to describe America, the country and the culture, at the beginning of the twentieth century, as immigrants poured onto its shores, as cultures mixed and clashed, as music mixed and melded, as cities filled, and women, African Americans, and the working classes stood up for the first time and said loudly and decisively that they would *not* go quietly into the night, that their voices would be heard.

But these lyrics also describes the American musical theatre itself, a new art form to describe a new era. Never before had the world seen anything like American musical comedy. And never before had the world seen what American musical comedy would become, the muscle of George M. Cohan, the deep emotion of Rodgers and Hammerstein, the sociological insights of Kander and Ebb, the rich human complexity of Stephen Sondheim. It truly was the music of something new beginning—not something old that had been altered—something wholly new, wholly original, and it would change the face of world theatre forever.

Some called George M. Cohan the man who invented musical comedy. Cohan wrote, composed, directed, choreographed, and starred in most of his shows. The astonishing part is that he was pretty good at all those jobs. His first musical comedy, based on a vaudeville sketch he had done with his performing family, was called *The Governor's Son*, opening in 1901. The show didn't do very well, but Cohan learned valuable lessons from this first attempt, and within a few short years, he would be the king of the art form.

Historian Cecil Smith described Cohan as "the apostle of breeziness, of up-to-dateness, of Broadway brashness and slang. Speed, directness, and 'ginger' were the chief ingredients of his musical plays." One of his famous directions to his cast before the curtain of a Cohan musical was, "Speed! Speed! And lots of it! Above all, speed!" Cohan gave the musical comedy its tempo, its attitude, its fierceness, its sheer, aggressive American-ness. Years later, playwright Albert Innaurato said of these times, "Theater must be a paradox to succeed, and this was ferocious fluff, deadly uproarious political theater that was also tons of fun."

Yet when he first burst onto the Broadway scene, Cohan caused more bafflement than celebration. The critics were outraged and the public sometimes confused by his slang, his (what was then considered) vulgarity, his arrogance, his jokes, and his dismissal of anything that wasn't New York. They were baffled by his characters directly addressing the audience, blithely ignoring the cherished "fourth wall" (the imaginary wall between actor and audience, the quaint and curious notion that the audience is eavesdropping on "reality"). In a Cohan show, everybody involved admitted plainly and openly that they were making the very artificial art form of musical comedy. The once cherished "suspension of disbelief" was irrelevant. Of course, that part wasn't *really* new—Shakespeare's characters talked to the audience all the time. Moliere did it. The classical Greeks did it. Theatre had been doing it since the beginning, and only in the mid-1800s had the absurd concept of the "fourth wall" become the norm, about the same time that music had been forcibly divorced from theatre.

Cohan was merely "repairing" the art of live theatre in every way, turning commercial theatre on its ear. But soon enough, his brand of muscular, brash, rough-and-tumble American musical caught on. Critic Brooks Atkinson has said that Cohan's songs were "sublimations of the mood of their day. They said what millions of people would have said if they had Cohan's talent." Oscar Hammerstein II would later say, "Never was a plant more indigenous to a particular part of the earth than was George M. Cohan to the United States of his day. The whole nation was confident of its superiority, its moral virtue, its happy isolation from the intrigues of the old country, from which many of our fathers and grandfathers had migrated."

Cohan continued with *Running for Office* (1903), *Little Johnny Jones* (1904)—his first hit, the one that debuted the songs "Give My Regards to Broadway" and

"Yankee Doodle Dandy"—*Forty-Five Minutes from Broadway* (1906), *George Washington Jr.* (1906), *The Honeymooners* (1907, a reworking of *Running for Office*), *Fifty Miles from Boston* (1908), *The American Idea* (1908), and *The Man Who Owns Broadway* (1909). His song "You're a Grand Old Flag," in *George Washington Jr.*, became the first song written for a musical to sell more than a million copies of sheet music.

In *Forty-Five Minutes from Broadway*, Cohan made the unprecedented move of starting his show with a lone male voice singing a cappella offstage. Everybody thinks Rodgers and Hammerstein were the first to do that with *Oklahoma!* but Cohan did it first. He wrote a total of twenty-one musicals and twenty plays during his career. His plots were slight but still coherent and dramatic. His life story (much of it fictionalized) was told in the 1942 film *Yankee Doodle Dandy*, which recreated the climactic song and dance from *Little Johnny Jones*. A musical revue of Cohan's songs that also told his life story was created in 1968 called *George M*, and it gave many of his songs new life, introducing his legacy to a whole new generation.

Little Johnny Jones (1904), one of Cohan's better shows, was inspired by Tod Sloane, a real American jockey in London for the English Derby. But in Cohan's show, the jockey Johnny Jones is framed on bogus charges of fixing the race by an unscrupulous American gambler. Strangely enough, this story occupied only the first two acts, while Act III moved to San Francisco's Chinatown where Jones' fiancée is kidnapped. Of course, the kidnapper is the same guy who framed poor Johnny in London. Johnny Jones would soon become the prototype for all musical comedy heroes, brash, cocky, funny, slangy, and charming as hell, the base upon which stood later leading men like MacHeath in *The Threepenny Opera*, Billy Crocker in *Anything Goes*, Larry Foreman in *The Cradle Will Rock*, Joey Evans in *Pal Joey*, Curly McLain in *Oklahoma!*, Woody Mahoney in *Finian's Rainbow*, Sky Masterson in *Guys and Dolls*, Harold Hill in *The Music Man*, and so many more.

Just eleven days before *Little Johnny Jones* premiered, the New York City subway system opened its newest station at Times Square, just a block from *Little Johnny Jones*, in effect giving birth to the Broadway theatre district as we now know it. The show ran only 52 performances in its initial New York run, but Cohan kept fiddling with the show as he took it on tour, and when he brought it back to Broadway, it clocked in an impressive 200 additional performances, quite a run for that time. As coincidence would have it, both Johnny Jones and George M. Cohan were born on the Fourth of July (or so Cohan claimed—it's never been settled). And as if Cohan wasn't patriotic enough on his own, consider that his first monster hit song, "The Yankee Doodle Boy," contained quotations from "The Star-Spangled Banner," "Dixie," "The Girl I Left Behind Me," and of course, "Yankee Doodle."

The *Milwaukee Press* said of Cohan's work, "All the froth, the humor, the fatalism, the philosophy, compounded of Epicureanism, cynicism, and opportunism, characteristic of the futile little rialto world are perfectly reflected by Mr. Cohan in his songs and slang dialogue." He had started the ball rolling.

In 1903, after a seven-month tour, the legendary black actor Bert Williams made it to the big time with his and George Williams' Broadway musical *In Dahomey*, the first full-length black musical comedy to play a major Broadway theatre. The plot, a bit silly but well structured and well integrated (meaning the lyrics and script worked together rather than independently), involved two black men going to Africa for treasure, but it also introduced one of America's greatest character actors to Broadway audiences. Usually wearing baggy pants, oversized shoes, and an old top hat, Williams created an enduring character that was both sad and funny, and seventy-two years later, he provided the inspiration for the song "Mr. Cellophane" in the Broadway musical *Chicago*, a number based on one of Williams' most famous numbers, "Nobody." *In Dahomey* signaled a step forward in black entertainment, its songs focused less on racial stereotypes and more on love and other more universal sentiments.

It was shocking for white audiences to see a show that suggested that black folks felt all the same things white folks did. One measure of the quality and popularity of the score is that it was published in its entirety, a rare honor for musical comedies at that time. Most of the praise centered on Bert Williams, and though the New York production ran only 53 performances, the show went on to a healthy run of 251 performances in London, including a command performance at Buckingham Palace, after which it returned to New York for another run.

Also in 1903, in response to a popular (though not very good) stage musical version of *The Wizard of Oz*, with lyrics by L. Frank Baum himself and direction by the brilliant, quickly-going-deaf Julian Mitchell, composer Victor Herbert opened his own musical comedy *Babes in Toyland*. This show was also directed by Mitchell, the first artist to supervise *all* movement in a musical, a practice that wouldn't be commonplace for decades. Both shows had kids in the leads, adults as villains (the witch in *Oz*, the murderous and greedy Uncle Barnaby in *Toyland*), a terrible storm (*Toyland*'s hurricane transparently ripping off *Oz*'s tornado), a journey through the woods, and an eventual arrival at a magical city. Sure, *The Wizard of Oz* had a better story and more interesting characters, but its score (no relation to that of the later MGM film) was awfully weak. And Herbert, a composer of great stature, wrote a beautiful and sophisticated score for *Babes in Toyland*, which ran 192 performances. Laurel and Hardy appeared in the first film version of *Babes in Toyland* in 1934, and the Disney Studios made an antiseptic, musically inferior version in 1961.

Babes in Toyland was such a hit, Herbert went on to write more musical comedies, all but abandoning his operetta roots, with *Babette* (1903), *It Happened in Nordland* (1905), and *Mlle. Modiste* (1905), though not all with the success of *Babes in Toyland*. All in all, he wrote twenty-three full scores for musical comedies and operettas between 1900 and 1915, including *The Red Mill* (1906) and *Naughty Marietta* (1910), the latter produced by Oscar Hammerstein the first.

In August 1906, black producer and writer Bob Cole, his vaudeville partner J. Rosamund Johnson, and Johnson's brother James wrote *The Shoo-fly Regiment*, an all black musical that broke quite a few rules. The story focused on Hunter Wilson, an educated black man just graduated from the Lincolnville Institute (a fictionalized version of the real Tuskegee Institute) who decides to fight for his country in the Spanish-American War. The biggest change was the nature of the main characters. Hunter Wilson was an educated, articulate, brave, patriotic young black man—a character never before seen on a Broadway stage. Also, the show depicted serious, sincere romance between Wilson and his fiancée Rose. No black musical had ever done such a thing before for fear of offending white audiences. The very notion of equating African Americans with Americans of European descent was revolutionary and decidedly subversive. If blacks thought and felt and loved just like whites, how could white audiences justify thinking of them as "lesser" humans, a point of view still widely held at the time?

Some critics were outraged that black artists would dare appropriate the conventions of a "white" art form. The critic for *Theatre* wrote that Cole and Johnson "have much to learn before they can instruct or entertain our public." Notice that it's *our* public, not *the* public. The review went on, "They may reach a certain standard, but, for the present, such performances are futile. If they are to advance, they must advance in a direction of their own. In the direction of imitation they will accomplish nothing, or nothing that is worth while, and by means of which they can attain to any dignity of their own." The show opened at New York's Grand Opera House, ran only a week, went on tour through Ohio and Pennsylvania, and then returned two months later to the Bijou Theatre in New York, where it ran another two weeks.

But Cole and the Johnson Brothers' time would come. New York's *Dramatic News* thought their next show, *The Red Moon*, in 1909, about blacks and Native Americans, was "brilliant." They were finally being taken seriously as dramatic artists.

At the end of 1914 producer Charles Dillingham made a big and important change in America musical comedy. He offered the first "syncopated musical show," *Watch Your Step*, with a score by the very young Irving Berlin, written for the famous ballroom dancers Vernon and Irene Castle. It was the first Broadway musical with a score written entirely in the style of syncopated dance music, most notably the foxtrot, the standard model for show tunes for decades to come. The magnitude, the daring, the *scandal* of creating the first "ragtime musical" was profound. *It just wasn't decent!* But though the show appropriated African American music and dance forms, not a single black performer could be found in its cast. It ran an impressive 175 performances on Broadway and was a success in London as well.

Beginning in 1915, musical comedy took a big step forward with the Princess shows, mounted in the unusually intimate, 299-seat Princess Theatre, built in 1912 with a stage that could hold only about sixteen actors at a time and an orchestra pit that could hold only about a dozen musicians. These were intimate, necessarily small-cast little musical comedies with scores by Jerome Kern and, later on, books by Guy Bolton and P. G. Wodehouse (pronounced WOOD-house). The most valuable attribute Wodehouse brought to the team was an almost complete ignorance of the conventions of musical theatre. Because he didn't know the conventions, he didn't use them and the result was a new kind of musical. Legendary composer Richard Rodgers would later say, "Before Larry Hart, only Wodehouse had ever made any assault on the intelligence of the song-listening public."

In a Princess show the laughs relied on character and situation, not on one-liners. The songs sat comfortably on the story, and the audience identified with the characters and situations onstage. After writing more than two hundred songs to interpolate into other composers' shows over a period of about ten years (generally to Americanize imported British shows), Kern was finally writing his own scores and getting to show what he could do. Kern wrote four Princess shows in 1915, all of which did well, convincing the producers that these small shows could be profitable. But it wasn't until the fourth show, *Very Good Eddie* in December 1915, that Kern (with lyricist Schuyler Greene) hit pay dirt, the show running 314 performances and going on to London. The book, by Bolton and Philip Bartholomae (based on his 1911 play *Over Night*), told of two honey-mooning couples, both accidentally separated, each husband with the other's wife, plus a third young couple not yet actually coupled.

More than its plot or its lovely score, the important thing, historically speaking, was that the Princess shows had found a style with *Very Good Eddie*, and it shared a lot with George M. Cohan's style—speed, brashness, and high energy. And more so, perhaps, than in any other musical comedy that had gone before, the acting was as good as in a play that lacked music, the characterizations and plot just as important as the songs. The show signaled a real shift in the priorities of musical comedy, although the old habits would take a while to die completely. One critic wrote, "Unlike most musical comedies, it has a connected story with laughable situations following one another in rapid succession." Many historians have declared that the "integrated" musical, in which songs served the characters and story, didn't appear until *Show Boat*, and then not again after that until *Oklahoma!*, but that's just not true. The Princess shows were integrating their scores long before *Show Boat*, though admittedly not with the sophistication or skill of later efforts. A full ten years before *Show Boat*, audiences were seeing the beginnings of modern musical theatre.

And then everything changed again. Once America got involved in World War I, popular affection began to evaporate for German/Austrian operetta—or anything that felt even vaguely Germanic—on American stages. It may be that if not for World War I, some of America's greatest musical theatre writers—Richard Rodgers and Larry Hart, Irving Berlin, Cole Porter, and George and Ira Gershwin, the men who would shape the nature of the musical theatre (what many people think of today when they hear the word *Broadway*)—might never have gotten their shot. And America might never have developed one of its most enduring and internationally beloved indigenous art forms, one of its greatest gifts to the world. Historian John McGlinn says, "German operettas were no longer popular in 1914. A patriotic spirit made people want American music. America was no longer bound by an artistic inferiority complex, right about the time Kern started [with the Princess shows]. At that time, Kern is the older generation in music. He was the father figure and mentor to Gershwin, Rodgers, and Cole Porter. He was just older enough that all these younger composers looked up to him and suddenly there is an explosion of American songwriters about the time of World War I and there was a forum for them on Broadway."

The sometimes rabid patriotism stirred up by World War I had made it to Broadway, and audiences—even London audiences, curiously enough—wanted American product. The more populist, more accessible, more aggressively American form of musical comedy that Cohan had essentially invented was pushed to the forefront not necessarily because it was better but because America was at war. This gave musical comedy the breathing room it needed to get its footing, to evolve, to experiment, to mature, probably more so than it would have otherwise if audiences had retained a choice between the still more primitive musical comedy and the more sophisticated forms of operetta and opera. It was a whole new ball game now and musical comedy had to serve both ordinary and elite audiences. Its artists saw that, like Shakespeare had, they now needed to appeal both to the uneducated lower classes and *also* to the educated upper classes. Musical comedy was given a new job description and it would quickly rise to the challenge.

In February of 1917, the Princess shows hit their full stride with *Oh Boy!*, yet another show with lots of mismatches and mistaken identities and a really terrific score. The critics went nuts over it. The *New York Sun* wrote, "If there be such things as masterpieces of musical comedy, one reached the Princess last night." The *New York Times* wrote, "You might call this as good as they make them if it were not palpably much better." *Oh Boy!* ran 463 performances, the longest Princess run yet. After *Oh Boy!* opened, Guy Bolton wrote in the *Dramatic Mirror* that the public wanted realism in acting and that *Oh Boy!* depended "as much on plot and character development for success as on the music." Dorothy Parker famously wrote, "Bolton and Wodehouse and Kern are my new favorite indoor sport."

By the end of 1918, the Princess shows (and their imitators) were done. Unbelievably, the series had only lasted four and a half years and included just seven shows (this is counting the two Kern shows of the time that weren't actually at the Princess Theatre—*Leave It to Jane* and *Have a Heart*), but the impact of the Princess shows would be felt throughout the rest of the century. Their intimacy, their humor, their reliance on character and situation changed American musical comedy forever.

In late 1919, the lessons of the Princess shows were solidified in the musical *Irene*, with a book by James Montgomery (based on his play), music by Harry Tierney, lyrics by Joseph McCarthy, and direction and choreography by Edward Royce. It was one in a long line of musicals loosely based on the Cinderella legend, but it was the first one to do it well. And it was the beginning of a trend toward putting women at the center of musicals, rather than staging traditional male-based stories. But musicals were still almost entirely written by men, and so these female-centered stories were sometimes a bit condescending and misogynistic. *Irene* would be followed by almost duplicate plotlines in *Poor Little Ritz Girl* (1920), *The Right Girl* (1921), *Two Little Girls in Blue* (1921), *The O'Brien Girl* (1921), *Good Morning, Dearie* (1921), *Suzette* (1921), *Sue, Dear* (1922), *Daffy Dill* (1922), *Poppy* (1923), *Mary Jane McKane* (1923), *Lollipop* (1924), and the list goes on. . . .

But *Irene* came first. It told of a poor New York upholstery shop girl who makes a delivery to the rich Marshall family estate on Long Island, where the dashing young Donald instantly falls in love with her. He gets her a job in the upscale dress shop of Madame Lucy (a male designer who uses this name to impress his customers) and though Irene's lowly status is revealed, she eventually charms his family at a big party with her openness and genuineness, and everything ends happily. Like the Princess shows, *Irene* told a story about realistic people in the real world, taking on issues of poverty, hypocrisy, and class distinctions, and the score used elements of jazz in its harmonies and rhythms. American musicals were starting to grow up, not by taking a giant leap ahead, no, but by moving slowly and emphatically forward. Most important of all, audiences embraced *Irene* lovingly. It even spawned a popular hit in its first song, "Alice Blue Gown." *Irene* ran a whopping 675 performances, running until June 1921. It set a new record for a long run on Broadway (beating out *A Trip to Chinatown*) and held that record for twenty-five years, until *Pins and Needles* outran it. *Irene* ran a respectable 399 performances in London, before going on to Australia and Hungary.

On June 16, 1919, one of America's greatest temples to the musical theatre, situated in historic Forest Park, site of the 1904 World's Fair, began its life in St. Louis, Missouri. The city fathers, led by Mayor Kiel, had decided St. Louis needed a municipal theatre. After some outdoor performances on a hill in Forest Park, a semi-permanent seating area and stage had been erected. Soon dubbed the St. Louis Municipal Opera Association, or more commonly The Muny, the theatre opened that June night with a performance of Reginald De Koven's operetta *Robin Hood* for an audience of four thousand. But just a week after the opening, a torrential rainstorm overflowed the banks of River Des Peres, which ran under and behind the Muny stage, and it literally washed away the sets, orchestra instruments, pretty much everything. Kiel and his buddies chased it all down, dried everything off, brought it back, and reopened the next night.

But it was a wet summer and attendance was sparse. Someone jokingly suggested that Mayor Kiel go peddle tickets door to door. So he did. He approached nearly every businessman in St. Louis, asking them to buy blocks of tickets. Many of them did, and the first official season was salvaged. Over the years, the Muny was outfitted with revolutionary "outdoor air conditioning"; a world class stage with a natural proscenium arch of giant trees and a ninety-foot revolve (the world's largest), which could make a scene change in less than a minute; the most powerful stage lights ever created; a state-of-the-art sound system; and permanent seating for more than thirteen thousand, including about fifteen hundred free seats (a tradition from the beginning), making it the largest outdoor legitimate theatre in the world.

In the early 1930s, J. J. Shubert (of the famous New York family of theatre producers) was named productions director of the Muny, and he said the theatre "offers hope for the development of a true national theater. Because it is fundamentally a project of the community, it is a direct expression of the people's artistic desires and ambitions. Because it is of the people, it automatically makes high standards of performances available to all."

The Muny became one of the nation's showplaces for musical theatre, at first mostly opera and operetta, then later primarily Broadway musicals, at its peak running an eleven-week summer season, with a new show each week and performances seven nights a week. During the 1960s and 1970s, some Broadway shows actually closed down for a week and brought the entire production, stars and all, to St. Louis to play a week at the Muny. So many Broadway musicals brought their original casts to the Muny: Ethel Merman and *Call Me Madam*, Zero Mostel and *Fiddler on the Roof*, Pearl Bailey, Cab Calloway, and *Hello, Dolly!*, Jerry Orbach and *Promises, Promises*, Joel Grey and *Cabaret*, Lauren Bacall and *Applause*, Yul Brynner and a revival of *The King and I*, and the entire original cast of Stephen Sondheim's *Follies*. The Muny also sometimes serves as a pre-Broadway tryout for shows like *Sugar Babies*.

The Muny still stands today, now the St. Louis Municipal Theatre Association, as a place for the community to come together on a summer's night, a place where families can bring their children without fear of content, and a place where future artists can not only learn about but actually see onstage the great musicals of the past, the literature of the art form, everything from *The Desert Song* and *Show Boat* to *Cats* and *Miss Saigon*. Because of its enormity, the Muny has never been about dramatic subtlety or cutting-edge work. It is about spectacle and special effects, about gigantic choruses and full-sized Cotton Blossoms when *Show Boat* plays there. It is by its very nature mainstream and "safe," but it is the greatest repository of Broadway's musical past ever created and an invaluable training ground for tomorrow's musical theatre performers, directors, writers, and producers. There is nothing else like it.

Back in 1919, Broadway was changing. Social issues had been slowly, subtly creeping into the scripts of Broadway musicals, but after a major actors strike in 1919, one of the hottest issues of the day had landed squarely on Broadway's doorstep and its way of doing business would be forever changed. Producers weren't too worried at first; business was great. After World War I, the U.S. economy boomed and so did American theatre. The public was thirsty for entertainment and producers had more money to risk than ever before. Any show with even the slightest chance at success could be mounted, and even if an occasional show was awful, there would be an audience for it. In the decade that followed, there would be too many theatres that needed shows to fill them, and to satisfy that need, too many untrained and untalented writers and actors joined the industry. That meant there were a lot of bad shows opening.

But it also meant that musical comedy and its more talented practitioners now had more time, money, and space than ever before to experiment and learn, more than they ever would have gotten under other circumstances. American audiences now craved pleasure, revelry, and novelty like never before, and they found it in their jazz, their speakeasies, and their musical comedy. The thirst for novelty meant anything was possible. The revue became popular during this time, thanks to *The Ziegfeld Follies*, *The Passing Shows*, *George White's Scandals*, *The Greenwich Village Follies*, and others, all breezy, spectacular, sensory-stimulating, and empty-headed. And though the revue had little influence on musical theatre as a dramatic art form, it gave first opportunities and paychecks to some of the men who would go on to polish the first generation of real American musical theatre—George and Ira Gershwin, Irving Berlin, Cole Porter, Jerome Kern, Richard Rodgers and Larry Hart, and others.

America and its theatre were poised for the development of the musicals that would become the great classics, the shows that would live on long after they closed on Broadway, long after their creators had died. In the 1920s the art form would be developed and codified. In the 1930s the first true geniuses of the form would emerge, and in the 1940s the so-called Golden Age of musical theatre would begin. Everything was ready.

2

I Want to Be Happy
The 1920s

The 1920s brought several innovations to the musical theatre. First, dance began to take on more and more importance and American musical comedies started incorporating—and sometimes inventing—major dance crazes like the Charleston, the foxtrot, the shimmy, the one-step, the two-step, the Boston, the tango, and more. This emphasis on dance would eventually mature in the 1930s and 1940s, leading to the great choreographic innovations of *On Your Toes* and *Oklahoma!*

Second, writing teams began writing the songs as the book was being written or in some cases *after* the book. Since songs had been written before the script in the past, the story always had to contort and twist itself to lead up to them. Now theatre songs began to feel more directly integrated and to do more of the heavy lifting when it came to character and plot. More than that, musical comedy scores finally found their stylistic voice in the 20s, embodying more than any other art form the incredible energy, fizz, and smart-alecky joy of the Jazz Age. Near the end of the decade, everything would change with *Show Boat*.

Other things were going on too. The Broadway theatre was exploding, with more than two hundred shows opening each season in the 1920s. Operetta, after nearly dying in America during World War I, made something of a comeback during the 20s, with its settings now mostly in America, then took its last dying breath and keeled over, rarely to be seen again. Still, during this decade, the list of longest running shows included several operettas, including *The Student Prince* in the top spot.

Some history books declare that Noble Sissle and Eubie Blake's 1921 musical *Shuffle Along* doesn't really qualify as a musical because it was only a revue of songs. True, it was based on a vaudeville sketch, but it was expanded into a full-blown musical comedy, with a book by Flournoy Miller and Aubrey Lyles (both also starred in the show). The show told the story of a mayoral race in Jimtown, somewhere in the American South, between the corrupt Steve Jenkins and the virtuous Harry Walton (inspiration for the show's biggest hit song, "I'm Just Wild About Harry"). Although no black musicals had opened in years, partly because Broadway producers were sure white audiences wouldn't buy tickets, *Shuffle Along* ran 504 performances, and a survey by *Variety* found that the *Shuffle Along* audience was about ninety percent white. Also, the show offered midnight shows on Wednesdays nights, when all the theatre folks from other shows would come to see *Shuffle Along*, so it also became the time for gawkers and stargazers to come not only for the performance but also for celebrity sightings. *Shuffle Along* proved that black shows were commercial and it paved the way for many more, although most of them were plotless revues rather than genuine musicals. Evidence of this movement can be found in the title of a song from the *Ziegfeld Follies of 1922*— "It's Getting Dark on Old Broadway."

Composer Noble Sissle wrote, "The proudest day of my life was when *Shuffle Along* opened. At the intermission all those white people kept saying, 'I would like to touch him, the man who wrote the music.' Well, you got to feel that. It made me feel like, well, at last, I'm a human being." The great black poet and author Langston Hughes maintained that *Shuffle Along* was responsible for initiating the great Harlem Renaissance in the 1920s. It also marked the tentative beginning of the end of segregation in Broadway audiences. But now largely back in the hands of white producers and fashioned for white audiences, black musicals had to conform to certain artistic and social stereotypes. Unfortunately, *Shuffle Along* conformed to these comfortable (for white audiences) stereotypes, and its huge success locked black musicals into these stereotypes for years afterward.

In 1924, Broadway welcomed a now forgotten musical called *I'll Say She Is!*, one of the biggest hits of the season, with admittedly pedestrian music by Tom Johnstone and book and lyrics by Will B. Johnstone. The slight plot concerned several brothers applying to a talent agency and meeting a beautiful girl, called simply "Beauty" in the program. Beauty is a thrill seeker, and as the show continues, she visits an opium den, is arrested, tried, and acquitted, then tries hypnosis and goes back to a previous life as Napoleon's Josephine. What made the show such a hit were the actors playing the brothers—Groucho, Chico, Harpo, and Zeppo Marx. Their first show out of vaudeville, they debuted their brilliant brand of comic anarchy, only occasionally sticking to the dialogue as written. Largely on the talent of the Marx Brothers, the show ran 313 performances. It set the brothers up for certain stardom and it set the musical theatre up to accept satire.

In December 1924 came one of the first hits from the Brothers Gershwin, *Lady, Be Good*, starring Fred and Adele Astaire, and cementing George's insistent, driving style of jazz in the ears of the theatregoing public, taking up where the black composers of earlier years had left off and moving the jazz idiom in American theatre forward. There was nothing else in the theatre like his use of jazz and blues harmonies and melodies and his penchant for throwing in the most unexpected rhythms. He also loved to work in bits of melody from one song into the accompaniment of another, to lend greater musical unity to the score and to build one melody on the general shape of another, related song, often subtly enough that an audience wouldn't consciously notice. This was something classical composers did in symphonies and Gershwin was bringing these ideas to Broadway.

The show contained several hit songs, like "Lady, Be Good," "Fascinating Rhythm," and "Little Jazz Bird." It was intended by producers Alex Aarons and Vinton Freedley to continue in the spirit of the Princess musicals, to consciously move the art form forward. Fred Astaire later said, "We were trying to do something that hadn't been done before." Astaire called the Gershwin sound an "outlaw idiom." One of George's greatest inventions was the melody to "Fascinating Rhythm," a repeating melodic phrase that shifted its rhythmic position each time it was heard. No one had ever toyed with rhythm so brashly or had subverted audience expectations so boldly.

The plot centered on siblings Dick and Susie Trevor, both financially strapped and each attempting a money making scheme that ends with problems and ultimately, of course, romance. The Astaires received as many raves as the Gershwin score. New York critic Alexander Woolcott wrote, "I do not know whether George Gershwin was born into this world to write rhythms for Fred Astaire's feet or whether Fred Astaire was born into this world to show how the Gershwin music should really be danced. But surely they were written in the same key, these two." American theatre music was changing, even if the musical's dramaturgy was still less ambitious. *Lady, Be Good!* ran 330 performances, plus a run of 326 performances in London and a modest tour of Australia. The Gershwins were laying the groundwork for profound innovations in the 1930s.

In 1925, the first of the genuine classics of musical comedy appeared on Broadway, *No, No, Nanette*, with a book by Otto Harbach and Frank Mandel (based on Mandel's play *His Lady Friends*), music by Vincent Youmans (then only twenty-six), and lyrics by Harbach and Irving Caesar (then only twenty-nine). The show was directed by producer Harry Frazee and choreographed by Sammy Lee, who would later choreograph *Show Boat*. Youmans was hired as the composer only because his mother made a sizeable investment in the show and demanded Frazee hire her son, but he proved himself an outstanding composer. Youmans employed the kind of harmonic sophistication and experimentation equaled only by George Gershwin at the time, along with a genuine gift for melody.

Everything about the show was built on threes, just as Sondheim's *A Little Night Music* would be decades later. With an old-fashioned three-act, one-set-per-act structure, the story focused on three couples: Jimmy and Sue Smith, Billy and Lucille Early, and the young lovers Tom and Nanette. Because Sue is so tight with the millions Jimmy has made selling Bibles, Jimmy "adopts" three pretty young women and finances their various enterprises. Jimmy, his lawyer Billy, and his niece Nanette (another trio) all go to Atlantic City to meet the three girls who are now threatening to blackmail Jimmy. Lucille catches Billy with the girls; Tom and the rebellious, looking-to-raise-some-hell Nanette fight; everyone gets confused; and it looks like no one will get a happy ending. But sure enough, everything gets explained and after some hits songs like "Tea for Two" and "I Want to Be Happy," along with the sensual "Where Has My Hubby Gone Blues," all is forgiven. In fact, the majority of songs in *Nanette*'s score became pop hits. The plot was light, no question, but once again, every moment and every song supported the plot and relationships and unlike most shows that had come before it, *Nanette* had something to say.

Behind the antics, this show was about money and American greed. Nearly every character in the show had some interesting relationship to money. Jimmy was a millionaire who loved giving people money just to make them happy, and the three gold-diggers were there just to con him into giving them generous handouts. Jimmy's wife Sue was thrifty and hated the idea of spending money foolishly. Sue's best friend Lucille was a compulsive shopper, buying things just for the sake of buying them and to keep her husband on a leash by making him work like crazy to pay her bills. Nanette felt imprisoned because she had no money of her own and thus, no independence. The maid Pauline even had a song early in the show to set up this theme, "Pay Day Pauline." Money, *Nanette*, was telling us, is a weapon, a source of power, a prison, and a sure road to victimization. And lest we forget, Jimmy had made his fortune as a Bible publisher, a subtle reminder of the Bible's position on the love of money. America in 1925 and its rampant consumerism were right there on stage to be laughed at, sure, but also to be slyly and accurately commented on. After all, this was an age of unprecedented wealth in America.

Unlike other shows, *Nanette* didn't start on Broadway. It first opened in Detroit in April 1924, then went on to Chicago in May 1924 for a six-month run, where it underwent repeated emergency surgery. (Only after its run in Detroit did its songwriting team write the show's two biggest hits, "Tea for Two" and "I Want to Be Happy.") Each time the show was changed, the critics were invited back, and each time they liked it a bit more. Still, by the end of the Chicago run, producer Frazee had lost about $75,000. A second *Nanette* company was sent to Philadelphia and the eastern seaboard. Another company was sent west. The rights to a London production were sold while it toured and so it opened in London in March 1925, a full six months before its Broadway debut. In fact, it ran longer in London than on Broadway—665 performances in London, and only 321 performances on Broadway. In April 1926, the show opened in France, with much more spectacle and much more dance. Then the London production toured to Berlin, Vienna, and Budapest.

Nanette was filmed twice, once in 1930 with a greatly reworked plot, and once in 1940 with Anna Neagle (the original London Nanette) and only two songs, neither film much worth watching. Jackie Gleason appeared in an abbreviated version on television in March 1951, as part of the *Musical Comedy Time*

series. *Nanette* was revived in 1971, the script ransacked, the score fiddled with and overorchestrated, the whole thing overproduced and gaudy, but it ran 861 performances, fully eclipsing the original production and sadly losing much of the insightful social satire that made it so subversive and so much fun.

In the last days of 1926, composer Richard Rodgers and lyricist Larry Hart started to show their experimental colors with *Peggy-Ann*, with a book by Herbert Fields. The show was an expressionistic, absurdist story set in a young girl's decidedly Freudian dreamworld. In some ways, it was a practice run at the fully Freudian *Lady in the Dark*, which Ira Gershwin, Moss Hart, and Kurt Weill would bring us in 1941. Here in *Peggy-Ann*'s subconscious, she experienced a trip on a yacht, her own wedding, getting thrown overboard during a ship's mutiny, and seeing the horse races in Havana. Within this dreamworld, policemen had pink moustaches, fish talked, and Peggy-Ann's family wore huge, oversized hats. The show was all about breaking rules. Costumes and sets were changed in full view of the audience without benefit of blackouts. The first song didn't come until fifteen minutes into the show. The beginning and end of the show were both played in virtual darkness. Amazingly, this wild, weird musical was a hit and ran 333 performances. This was only the fourth Rodgers and Hart musical on Broadway, but it already showed their impatience with the conventions of musical comedy. Rodgers, first with Hart but later with Hammerstein, would continue to break rules for much of his career.

To be blunt, Richard Rodgers would never be a truly transcendent composer among the ranks of Gershwin, Kern, Sondheim, Bernstein, or even his grandson Adam Guettel, but he was a brilliant dramatist and one of the most groundbreaking musical theatre artists in history. Strangely, he almost always broke ground in dramatic terms but rarely in musical terms. Rodgers never developed the rhythmic or harmonic adventurousness of Gershwin or Kern, and he never explored the complexity of form and structure that Sondheim or Bernstein would. He worked pretty much in one style with Hart, and then in a second, nearly unrelated style with Hammerstein, largely because with Hart he wrote the music first, but with Hammerstein he set music to existing lyrics. There were certainly jazz influences in his work with Hart (which completely disappeared with Hammerstein) but only a taste of it, never the kind of gutsy immersion and experimentation that could be seen in his contemporaries like Gershwin and Arlen. Still, what he did dramatically and what he chose as source material were often gutsier than anyone else at the time.

The first Great American Musical, the show against which all others would forever be measured, opened two days after Christmas 1927, Jerome Kern and Oscar Hammerstein's *Show Boat* (Kern's thirty-first complete Broadway score), based on Edna Ferber's mammoth, epic novel. Populated with a racially mixed cast—unusual for the time—the show was directed by Hammerstein (uncredited) with help from stage manager Zeke Colvan, dances by Sammy Lee, and lavish sets by Joseph Urban, Ziegfeld's favorite designer. *Show Boat* was not just a serious show about real people, real problems, and large social issues, it was also built with a kind of sophistication Broadway had not seen before. Robert Coleman in the *Daily Mirror* called it "a work of genius" and went on to say with tremendous foresight, "It shows that managers [producers] have not until now realized the tremendous possibilities of the musical comedy as an art form."

Show Boat was produced, paradoxically, by the great revue impresario Florenz Ziegfeld, the great supplier of spectacle, scantily clad girls, and empty calories to the Great White Way; not unexpectedly, *Show Boat* boasted a chorus of ninety-six. Critics just couldn't believe Ziegfeld (who was in the midst of personal bankruptcy proceedings) would produce such a substantial, and more important, such a *depressing* musical. Ziegfeld himself was deeply worried about the gigantic commercial risk he was taking, but he also said at the time that he knew it was the greatest opportunity of his life. It was widely known that he was a compulsive gambler who had lost his entire fortune more than once at the gaming tables in Monte Carlo, so in retrospect, maybe taking a chance on something as wildly risky as *Show Boat* was completely in character. Then too, the charges that all producers at this time were unconcerned with art and only concerned with profit isn't entirely fair. First, they were running businesses, so profit was not an inappropriate aim. But second, innovations *were* happening during the teens and twenties. This was a brand-new art form and for us today to expect it, with our twenty-twenty hindsight, to have sprung fully grown from the ether is unfair. The producers making musicals in the twenties were looking to please audiences, and Americans have *always* been interested in what's New and Improved. As *Show Boat*'s success and the success of the Princess Theatre shows prove, there *was* innovation and audiences ate it up. Even in revues, innovation was happening on a regular basis; how else could you get audiences back time after time to see the next *Ziegfeld Follies*?

Show Boat took the best from the musicals that had gone before it—the pacing, the girls, the laughs, the song forms, the comic second couple, the American settings and characters, the slangy dialogue, even a couple interpolated songs and celebrity impressions—and to that mix it added important, complex social issues; tragic, flawed, *real* characters; complex relationships; an integrated, dramatic score; a muscular, profoundly American sound; and an epic scope like no musical had ever achieved before. *Show Boat* blended the best of American drama with the best of musical comedy and created a new animal: the American musical drama, the kind of show that would eventually just be called "a musical." During the process of writing and rewriting, Hammerstein did build some scenes based on the old models of gags and clichés, but he just as quickly discarded them. He even went so far as to eliminate the curtain call from the original production, believing that this would give the show even more weight.

As he wrote the book and lyrics for *Show Boat*, and then as he directed it, Hammerstein matured, seemingly overnight, from a competent romantic comedy writer into a gifted, innovative dramatist who would change the face of musical

24

comedy. For the first time, music was used as a dramatic device. It was used as subtext. For the first time, music was used the way the greatest dramatists had always used words, and though Hammerstein wasn't writing the music, he was at the center of this sea change.

Show Boat dealt most centrally with race-related issues, with various forms of racism, with laws against interracial marriage, with blacks "passing" for white, the oppression of African Americans, and the appropriation of black culture by whites. It showed how these issues directly affected, and often destroyed, people's lives. It raised race issues out of the abstract for its white audiences and gave them human faces. The show began with a "Negro" chorus on stage telling us that the "niggers" do all the backbreaking work of the riverfront while the white folks all live lives of leisure—potent, subversive political content. The show introduced the character of Julie early in Act I, got the audience to love her, then sprung the surprise that she was of mixed race and that her marriage to her husband was illegal for no reason other than the color of her ancestors' skin. The legal term was "miscegenation." Unlike the musicals that had gone before it, *Show Boat* put center stage two strong women taking control of their own destinies, Julie LaVerne and Magnolia Hawks Ravenal, one of them (technically) a black woman.

Still, the fact can't be ignored that the black characters disappeared as the story progressed, no matter how important they were at the beginning. And Queenie, a major black character (at least in Act I), was played not by a black actor but by Tess Gardella, a white actor famous for her blackface character Aunt Jemima, and that's how she was listed in *Show Boat*'s program. Some African American critics were not happy about Paul Robeson taking the role of Joe in *Show Boat*, because they saw the show itself as racist.

Show Boat also explored issues of compulsive gambling, alcoholism, divorce, and single parenting. Perhaps *Show Boat* reduced some of its plot lines to the level of melodrama, but it was more honest than any musical had ever been before about difficult, real issues. And more than that, it was written with tremendous intelligence, craft, artistry, and as much racial sensitivity as could be expected at the time. The score was built on important musical themes and motifs that identified ideas and characters and foreshadowed events, reminding the audience of relationships and past deeds. And with the story covering eighty years, Kern enjoyed the challenge of using musical styles to anchor the various scenes in their unique time periods, something Sondheim would do sixty-three years later with *Assassins*. The show jump-started the use of extended musical scenes moving seamlessly back and forth between singing and spoken dialogue with music underneath (the best example is the "Make Believe" scene).

More than any other lyricist who had gone before, Hammerstein wrote in the voices of his characters. Every lyric seemed to come organically from the mind and mouth of the character who was singing. Unlike Larry Hart, Ira Gershwin, and most of the other lyricists of the 1920s and 30s, Hammerstein did not invent words to make a rhyme, he didn't invert sentences to make a rhyme, and he didn't mangle grammar to make a rhyme. His lyrics didn't sound like song lyrics. They sounded like dialogue that just happened to rhyme. He wrote the most naturalistic lyrics Broadway had yet seen—and they would get even better in his work with Rodgers—learning important lessons from George M. Cohan's songs but doing it even better. No one would dispute the genius of Hart or Ira Gershwin as lyricists, but even at their peaks they didn't compare with Hammerstein as dramatists. As he would do with Rodgers in the years to come, Hammerstein approached lyric writing not as a songwriter but as a storyteller. Years later, he was quoted as saying, "There are few things in life of which I am certain, but I'm sure of this one thing: that the song is the servant of the play, that it is wrong to write first what you think is an attractive song and then try to wedge it into the story."

Show Boat was a hit, despite its initial running time of well over four hours in its Washington, DC, tryout, easily an hour or more too long, even back when most musicals were longer than they are now. By the time the show got to Philadelphia, eight songs were gone, then one was added in Pittsburgh. Unfortunately, one of the lost songs was also one of the strongest; "Mis'ry's Comin' Around" not only underscored the tragedy coming in the plot but also underlined the difference between the way blacks saw the world and the way whites saw the world. No matter that it was one of the most important songs thematically, it had to go. The show ended up about three hours long by the time it got to New York. There the critics loved it and it ran 572 performances. It went on to London the following year (350 performances) and then Paris (115 performances) but the rest of Europe wasn't all that interested in this deeply American story. The European producers continued to tinker with the score, adding songs and replacing songs from the New York version. Three years after the original production, Ziegfeld revived it on Broadway with most of the original cast.

Although Show Boat was a monster hit in the States, there were no immediate imitators. The great rule of innovation in the theatre is that breaking new ground only matters if it's a hit. An innovative new masterpiece means nothing if it's a flop because no one will copy it and its innovations will die on the vine. But hits get imitated. Historians have argued for years over why Show Boat didn't spawn imitations. Perhaps it was the Great Depression and its choke hold on America coming less than two years later, making it impossible for many people to afford tickets to a show and making those with money desperate for lighthearted, escapist pabulum. Whatever the reasons, Show Boat would matter greatly in the evolution of the form, but we only know that in retrospect.

Both script and score continued to change as the show was revived and toured for decades. Racially charged words like *nigger* were replaced (with *darkies*, then later with *colored folks*), orchestrations were changed to reflect the tastes of the times, songs were dropped or reinstated, and dance sequences were added. There were three film versions, first in 1929, originally shot as a silent film but then recut with audible dialogue scenes and songs and an added prologue featuring some of the original Broadway cast.

The second film, directed by James Whale (*Frankenstein*), was released in 1936, with a screenplay by Hammerstein and with nine of the original sixteen songs intact, plus three new songs. The cast included members of the original Broadway cast, the original London cast, and the first national tour, including Helen Morgan (the original "Julie"), Charles Winninger (the original "Captain Andy"), Sammy White (the original "Frank"), and Paul Robeson, who was supposed to be the first "Joe" on Broadway but ended up debuting the role in London. The film's other leads, Irene Dunne and Allan Jones, had played their roles before as well. Of the various film versions, this screenplay comes closest to the stage script and the original style of the show. It preserves the humor and joy of the original production alongside its weighty social issues, something the 1951 version couldn't—or wouldn't—come close to accomplishing. The only drawback of the 1936 version is an unfortunate interpolated blackface number.

The third version was released in 1951 by MGM, with awfully pretty scenery and lots of dance, but also a heavily, awkwardly rewritten plot. This screenplay mangled the original script, cutting, inventing, and reordering scenes and songs until too much was lost. It cut entirely the scene in which Queenie wonders why Julie knows the black folk song "Can't Help Lovin' Dat Man," the most important foreshadowing the stage script offered. It also cut Queenie and Joe's verses of the song and the important interaction between Magnolia and the black workers. MGM didn't want to deal with race issues any more than they absolutely had to. The MGM version was the least intelligent of the various film versions (they even used the wrong kind of boat—real show boats were barges, not paddle wheelers), and the least respectful of the original, and it has left us with an unfortunate legacy. Ever since 1951, most stage productions follow MGM's lead in making the songs (notably "Ol' Man River" and "Can't Help Lovin' Dat Man," but others too) *way* too slow, too self-indulgent, more about lush orchestrations than about characters and relationships. Like MGM, these less thoughtful stage productions take all the sense of perpetual motion out of "Ol' Man River" and they replace the playfulness and irony of "Can't Help Lovin' Dat Man" with weepy melodramatic romance. They turn a smart, well-crafted musical drama into just another silly piece of fluff. (For an idea of the tempos Kern intended, check out the 1936 film version.)

In 1988, historians Miles Kreuger and John McGlinn reassembled the original script and score, and perhaps most important, the original orchestrations for *Show Boat* and made the first-ever complete recording of the score as it was presented in 1927, as well as several songs and musical scenes cut or added later. The show has been revived in New York many times and has become a staple of regional theatres. Harold Prince directed a revival in 1993 in Toronto that took an entirely new look at the show, revising, trimming, tightening the script, coming at it fresh, renewing its seriousness *and* its playfulness, its emotion, its intensity, putting back "Mis'ry's Comin' Around." He cut the World's Fair scene, he added two dance montages to clarify the time frame, and he even gave the nonsinging character Parthy a song. He discarded some of the musical comedy conventions from 1927, restoring the gravity and social impact the show must have had in its original production. With more than a half hour of the show cut (much of which was dialogue no longer needed to cover more technologically advanced scene changes), this production moved to Broadway in 1994 and used more music written for the show than any other production ever to play New York, including the original. It also boasted a cast of seventy-one, a pit orchestra of thirty, and nearly five hundred costumes.

But there were protests about the racial portrayals. Prince had, like those before him, cut the word *nigger* from the opening number, but he kept it in dialogue scenes. At producer Garth Drabinsky's insistence, Prince met with black leaders, but there was still a picket line on the first day of rehearsals and at the first preview. Finally, James Earl Jones agreed to be the production's unofficial spokesman and he helped to quell the outrage.

With this production, Prince ushered the first Great American Musical happily into the age of dark postmodernism in the musical theatre—even including controversy—and it proved that *Show Boat*'s prescient genius was even more at home among the sophisticated offerings of the 1990s than among the musical comedies of the 1920s. For this show, Prince won his twentieth Tony Award; the production also won Tonys for best revival, best choreography, and best costumes.

Show Boat's greatest legacy—one which is largely overlooked today—is that it proved once and for all that audiences *don't* only like what they already know, that audiences *aren't* afraid of innovation and experimentation and of being challenged. *Show Boat*, along with later shows like *Pal Joey, Oklahoma!, West Side Story, Company,* and many others proved over and over again that audiences like what's *good.* Even today, theatres across America believe that audiences will buy tickets only to innocuous, empty-headed shows that don't ask too much of them. But the people running these theatres forget that in 1927 *Show Boat* was radical. It was outrageously new, and audiences found it utterly thrilling. Audiences today are no different.

Show Boat should have marked the boundary between old and new, straddling the old way of making musical comedy and the new way, even using old songs like "After the Ball" and "Hot Time in the Old Town Tonight" to help establish the ever shifting period. As it traced its eighty-year story, it also traced (perhaps unconsciously) the evolution of musical theatre. It should have been the gateway to Everything New, but because no one followed or imitated it right away, Broadway just kept getting the silly stuff.

But half a world away, in Berlin in 1928, one of the most important musicals of the twentieth century opened. John Gay's 1728 ballad opera *The Beggar's Opera* had been revived in London a few years earlier for a run of more than three and a half years, and was then reworked and presented in Austria. Then, in Berlin, the controversial genius playwright and director Bertolt Brecht co-wrote with Elizabeth Hauptmann a new, contemporary, sociopolitical, satirically savage updating of the show called *The Three-Penny Opera*, with a ground-breaking, darkly jazz-influenced score by Kurt Weill (pronounced *Wile* by Weill himself, but usually pronounced *Vile* by others). Black author Stanley Crouch has said that artists who want to express adult emotions, who want to move beyond adolescent emotions, use jazz. Historian Cecil Smith later wrote, "It proves that a small musical show can be both engrossing and magnificently entertaining without sacrificing high imagination, acute intelligence, superbly unified and thoroughly artistic production, and an underlying sense of purpose." Certainly, *Three-Penny* was a lot more adult than much of what had come before it. The show opened at the Theater am Schiffbauerdamm in August 1928. It was such a hit, additional companies were opened in Vienna, Budapest, Frankfurt, and Hamburg.

The satirical plot focused on the career criminal MacHeath who plans to marry the innocent Polly, daughter to Mr. Peachum, the King of the Beggars, with the help of Mack's friend Tiger Brown, the Chief of Police. Peachum threat-ens to organize London's beggars to ruin Queen Victoria's coronation unless Tiger Brown arrests and hangs MacHeath. Of course, at the last minute, the Queen pardons Mack, makes him a Baron and bestows a pension on him. Lots of double crosses and skullduggery combined into a scathing indictment of the dishonesty and cruelty of "polite society."

Bertolt Brecht was already forging a new kind of theatre in the early part of the twentieth century. He didn't like the way most plays involved their audi-ences emotionally but not intellectually. Audiences laughed and cried but never *thought* about what was happening in the story. He wanted to create a theatre of ideas, a theatre of issues, and in order to encourage an audience's intellectual involvement, he began to develop ways to continually remind the audience that they were in a theatre, to keep them from being too swept away by the story, to keep them from getting "lost" in the fictional reality that most other playwrights strove to create and maintain. He would have actors step out of scenes to talk directly to the audience, and he would use songs that commented on what had just happened or was about to happen (again addressing the audience directly), rather than using songs that sprang organically from the action. Today, this idea is not so revolutionary but when Brecht began to make theatre this way, it was bizarre. Today, concept musicals like *Company, Follies, Kiss of the Spider Woman, Chicago, Assassins,* and perhaps most of all, *Sweeney Todd,* are extremely Brecht-ian in their construction and presentation.

Dark, aggressive, and unrelenting in its social commentary, *The Three-Penny Opera* was a political satire for a new age and for a Germany on the brink of fas-cism and Nazism. It also found success touring Europe, playing an estimated 10,000 performances over five years. A German film version was made, *Die*

3groschenoper, directed by Georg Wilhelm Pabst and starring original cast member Lotte Lenya (wife of the composer and, not incidentally, a former prostitute) as the whore Jenny. The film was an interesting preservation of the piece but not a great film; disjointed, too stagey for film and too filmic to be just a recording of the stage play, it ended up wandering somewhere in the middle. Still, some considered it a masterpiece and the German government thought it might be good anticapitalist propaganda. The film's editor, Jean Oser, said in an interview, "*Three-Penny Opera* was a very hot property at the time: it had come out as a big theatrical hit; in fact in was almost phenomenal how much it influenced a complete generation. It formed the entire pre-Hitler generation until 1933; for about five years every girl in the country wanted to marry a man like Mackie. Apparently, the ideal man was a pimp." The French made a film version, *L'Opéra de Quat'Sous*, filmed at the same time as the German film and on the same sets. In 1933, Weill and Lenya were tipped off that they were on a list of Jewish intellectuals about to be arrested by the Gestapo. They escaped to Paris, and then to the U.S. Meanwhile, Hitler decided that *Three-Penny* was an attack on wholesome German family values and it was banned. In Hitler's Museum of Degenerate Art, one room played songs from *Three-Penny* on an endless loop so that wholesome Germans could be outraged by them. But so many people came to listen to the great songs that the exhibit was hastily closed down.

The stage version of *Threepenny* (the hyphen now gone) came to New York in 1933 in a reproduction staging by Francesco von Mendelssohn, but New York was not yet ready for Brecht and it ran only twelve performances on Broadway. It did better in Paris in 1937, in London in 1940, and in Milan in 1956. Desmond Vesey's English translation of the show was performed in America in 1945 and 1948, and later in a dual translation with Eric Bentley. But it wouldn't be until 1954, in a new English translation by Marc Blitzstein—after Brecht's death—that it would become a monster hit off Broadway in New York, running 2,706 performances and six years, causing a sea change in the philosophy of serious musical theatre in America. It also gave the world one of its greatest pop hits, "Mack the Knife" (called "Moritat" in the show). Unfortunately, stage censorship at the time prevented Blitzstein from being entirely faithful to Brecht. Blitzstein's version was also produced in London in 1956, and around the world since then, becoming the preferred translation. In 1962 an anemic film version was made called *The Three Penny Opera* (the title of each version seems to have its own spacing and punctuation). It starred Sammy Davis Jr. but didn't do at all well.

Threepenny would return in 1976, starring Raul Julia, in a much grittier translation—free of 1950s censorship—for another 306 performances. An excellent 1989 film version, *Mack the Knife*, starring Raul Julia, rock singer Roger Daltry, Richard Harris, and Julie Waters didn't do well either, but in many ways, this version was closest to Brecht's philosophy and theories on theatre, his "alienation effect."

One of the most interesting musicals of the 1920s was a big flop. It was called *Deep Harlem* and it opened in 1929, with a score by Joe Jordan, Homer Tutt, and Henry Creamer and a book by Tutt and Salem Whitney. It attempted to tell the story of the African race from ancient Abyssinia to the contemporary American South and it took this subject far more seriously than anyone had yet done in a Broadway musical. The *Herald-Tribune* said that Whitney "had the air throughout his work of being somewhat a philosopher and of letting his more or less solemn thoughts about his race come to the front as much as he thought practicable in a musical show on Broadway." Another critic, Arthur Ruhl, wrote, "It was interesting nevertheless because of its attempt to make something out of what wide awake Negro minds have been thinking of as possibilities for genuine black drama, and in its very ingenuousness there was a kind of charm which is generally quite drowned out by the hullabaloo and brassy cocksureness that Broadway has come to expect and demand from black shows."

But now the movies were taking a bite out of Broadway. Audiences were flocking to movies in records numbers, sixty to seventy-five million a week in 1929, and several New York theatres converted from live performances to films. As the decade came to a close, Wall Street crashed and the Great Depression hit America and subsequently the world. The front page headline of *Variety* famously screamed, "WALL STREET LAYS AN EGG." The Great Experiment that was *Show Boat* suddenly—pretty much overnight—lost all its appeal. For the most part, audiences didn't want to think about racism, compulsive gambling, or alcoholism. They wanted nothing but pure, aggressive escapism. And this unfortunate accident of history stalled the development of the musical theatre for several years.

3

Anything Goes
The 1930s

Despite the Depression, the 1930s began with one of the most substantial black musicals so far and one of the few black book musicals in a long time, *Brown Buddies*, by Carl Rickman, Joe Jordan, and Millard Thomas and starring Bill "Bojangles" Robinson and Adelaide Hall. It told the story of black soldiers stationed in St. Louis during World War I. They are sent overseas and experience the very real horrors of war but are sent back home to St. Louis by the end of the show, arriving the day before Prohibition begins. The show received strong reviews and ran 111 performances at a time when Broadway was otherwise not doing so well.

1927 had brought us the first of George and Ira Gershwin's three political musicals, *Strike Up the Band*, the first overt sign of liberal politics, social conscience, and political awareness in musical theatre, a focus less on personal interaction and more on social, political, and economic issues and a palpable distrust of the government. The show had started its life in 1927, with pre-Broadway stands in New Jersey and Philadelphia, but it closed in Philly after only two weeks. Retooled, the Gershwins opened it again in 1930 and it ran 191 performances. The critic for *The World* wrote, "I don't remember ever before in a musical comedy having noticed or understood what it was all about. Here all is not only clear but really startling. Of all things in the world, here is a bitter, rather good, satirical attack on war, genuine propaganda at times, sung and danced on Broadway, to standing room only." A relatively hardhitting satire of big business, international politics, and war, it was the kind of thing Gilbert and Sullivan would have written if Sullivan had known about jazz.

In its original 1927 version, the show told the story of American cheese mogul Horace J. Fletcher and his suggestion that the U.S. declare war on the Swiss who have protested a ridiculously high tariff on their cheeses. Once the war is underway, his daughter's fiancé threatens to expose Fletcher's corrupt business practices, so Fletcher reverses himself and becomes a very vocal pacifist. But he's suspected of treason when he's discovered wearing a Swiss watch. Once the Americans decode the Swiss yodeling code, they win the war. And it's been such fun, the U.S. decides to impose a tariff on caviar so they can go to war with the Russians next. The show was about government corruption, the inappropriate influence of Big Business on the government, and rabid patriotism sparking waves of intolerance and jingoism, all issues America still faces today. In one scene, *The Swiss Family Robinson* is removed from libraries in deference to the war, in a striking parallel to the 2003 real-world episode in which the U.S. Congress renamed french fries in the congressional cafeteria "freedom fries" to express displeasure at the French for not supporting the American war in Iraq. Though critics enjoyed the 1927 version, audiences did not, and the leads seemed to be going through a revolving door, either leaving the show or being fired, as the show continued not to work right.

But less than three years later, after Morrie Ryskind revised and de-fanged George S. Kaufman's original script, the show was back, now setting the whole adventure as a dream that teaches the eventually reformed Fletcher a lesson about being a nice guy. *Yawn*. Swiss cheese was inexplicably changed to Swiss chocolate, and despite the softening of some of the hard edges, some of the satire remained, though it was considerably less strident. Interestingly, the second version of the show, with its plot centered on outrageous tariffs on foreign goods, opened just as the U.S. Congress was legislating exactly the same thing. The score lost eight songs in the revision, including the now classic torch song "The Man I Love." And it picked up thirteen new songs (one of which got cut before opening), including breakout hits like "I've Got a Crush on You" and "Soon."

Most of the rest of the 1930s actually took a step backward in terms of the evolution of the musical. Even the Gershwins retreated and chose for their next project the empty-headed (though hit-laden) *Girl Crazy*. It would be seventeen years before the revolution that began with *Show Boat* would take its next step with *Oklahoma!*

But meanwhile, there were exceptions. . . .

The Gershwins' masterpiece *Of Thee I Sing* hit Broadway in 1931 and went on to become the first musical to win a Pulitzer Prize for drama (beating out Eugene O'Neill's *Mourning Becomes Electra*) and the longest-running book musical of the thirties. Unfortunately, the Pulitzer committee awarded the prize to George Kaufman, Morrie Ryskind, and Ira Gershwin, but *not* to George. Apparently, music wasn't the purview of the Pulitzer Prize for drama and the committee didn't understand the inextricable integration of the modern musical. In the *New York American*, Gilbert Gabriel wrote of the show, "It was a new genre for a new decade. We first nighters were in at the liberation of musical comedy from twaddle and treacle and garden-party truck. We were laughing gratefully at a new date in stage history." In a very depressed season, *Of Thee I Sing* ran a strong 441 performances. It also became the first musical to have its script published and commercially released.

The show both told a conventional musical comedy love story and also ridiculed that love story, standing with one musical foot in the 1920s and one in the future. What other show would present an old-fashioned love song as a cynical election slogan? Here in the midst of the Great Depression, *Of Thee I Sing* railed angrily and despairingly (though oh so cleverly) at the triviality, insincerity, and uselessness of American politics and politicians. The story told of the handpicked, easily manipulated presidential candidate John P. Wintergreen (William Gaxton) who runs on a platform of Love, holding a nationwide beauty pageant and promising to the winner a proposal of marriage in every state of the union and a wedding at the inauguration. Of course, Wintergreen instead falls in love with the Simple Girl, Mary Turner, and spurns the contest winner, almost causing an international incident—and war, of course—with France. The winner Diana Devereux is, we discover, the illegitimate daughter of an illegitimate son of an illegitimate nephew of Napoleon. As Wintergreen is about to be impeached, Mary announces that she's pregnant and all is forgiven. So Vice President Throttlebottom (Victor Moore) assumes the President's duties as the Constitution dictates and *he* marries Diana. In a last touch of satiric genius, the Supreme Court decides the sex of John and Mary's baby—and it's a split decision so they end up with twins.

The very first moments of the show made clear exactly what kind of evening this was going to be. As the curtain went up, the audience heard the deliciously silly campaign song "Wintergreen for President," while the campaigners hold up bitingly satiric signs: "A Vote for Wintergreen Is a Vote for Wintergreen," "Vote for Prosperity and See What It Gets You," "Wintergreen—The Flavor Lasts," and "Even Your Dog Likes Wintergreen." Meanwhile, the song teeters uncertainly between major and minor, between hopefulness and sheer (comic) despair, a kind of choral moan following every exhortation of "Wintergreen for President," and interpolations of one overly American song after another ("The Red, White and Blue," "Sidewalks of New York," "Hail, Hail, The Gang's All Here") to ingratiate the candidate with our inbred but easily manipulated patriotism. The title song is at once a love song, a campaign song, and a conventional musical comedy Title Song; and by being all these, it also comments comically on all three types of song. That Wintergreen's love song to his future wife serves double duty as a campaign song cheapens it, and that both also do duty as an old-fashioned musical comedy Title Song trivializes the whole thing. It's both dramatically brilliant and brilliantly funny.

As with *Strike Up the Band*, the Gershwin brothers wrote extended musical sequences, songs of unusual structure and length, and long musical scenes, *finalettos*, to close each act. George integrated well-known songs into the show's numbers, pointing up the absurdity of the plot and of American politics and the insincerity of the central characters. The brothers paid homage to the creators of modern comic operetta, Gilbert and Sullivan, in several patter songs and ensemble numbers. Wintergreen's acquittal comes in a song called "Posterity Is Just

Around the Corner," a nasty jibe at Hoover's famously failed promise that *prosperity* was just around the corner. The ballads made fun of ballads. The waltzes made fun of waltzes. And the self-referential absurdity reached its zenith when in Act II the French ambassador entered to the tune of Gershwin's own "An American in Paris." *Of Thee I Sing* was granddaddy to contemporary shows like *Urinetown*, in its sass, its satire, and its brilliance.

The Gershwins, their collaborators, and their stars all returned in 1933 for a sequel called *Let 'Em Eat Cake*, in which Wintergreen loses his reelection and instead leads an American worker's revolution, but it ran only three months. *Of Thee I Sing* was revived in 1952 and flopped. Luckily, though there was no original cast album in 1931, historians restored the original orchestrations and recorded the full scores for *Of Thee I Sing* and its sequel *Let 'Em Eat Cake* in 1987.

In November 1934, Cole Porter's *Anything Goes* hit Broadway like a locomotive, starring the powerhouse trio of Ethel Merman, William Gaxton, and the hilariously stoic, trembly-voiced comedian Victor Moore, with direction by Howard Lindsay and choreography by Robert Alton. Merman, who had burst upon the scene in the Gershwins' *Girl Crazy*, was the first in a long line of musical theatre women who rejected the practice of singing in their head voice like opera singers, and instead "belted" their songs, in a strong, aggressive, chest voice, an entirely new sound for Broadway. Critic John J. O'Connor later wrote about her performance style, "Standing on stage as if she would slug the first numbskull who tried to move into her territory, Miss Merman simply belts away. The gestures are all marvelously perfunctory, the presence has all the subtlety of a block of marble, but the voice is still thrilling and always unforgettable." She changed forever the way women sing in musicals. In fact, some historians argue that she wasn't just a performing icon but actually her own song style, a style mastered only by Cole Porter and, later, Irving Berlin. Porter literally invented the fiercely American "Merman" number with songs in *Anything Goes* like "Blow, Gabriel, Blow," "I Get a Kick Out of You," and the title song.

Anything Goes wasn't Porter's first show—he had already written scores for *See America First* (1916), *Within the Quota* (1923), *Paris* (1928), *Wake Up and Dream* (1929), *The New Yorkers* (1930), *Gay Divorce* (1932), and *Nymph Errant* (1933)—but *Anything Goes* was his best thus far. Nearly every song in the show would become an American standard, and the show's success and popularity would never diminish.

But not everything about the show was conventional. The Broadway musical had begun by consciously rejecting tales of rich folks and royalty in favor of stories of common people, average Joes and Janes. As one of the only gentiles writing Broadway scores at the time, as a native of Peru, Indiana, as the heir to a considerable fortune, and as a relatively open gay man, Porter wasn't interested in immigrants or in common people. He had spent time in Paris alongside other great artists like Ernest Hemingway, F. Scott Fitzgerald, Pablo Picasso, and Gertrude Stein. So Porter wrote *his* shows about smart, glamorous, rich, sophisticated, and often slightly naughty people. His lyrics were dripping with French phrases, references to high society names, exclusive nightclubs, trans-Atlantic cruises, and time spent in Paris. And he and his collaborators dared to put forth the theory that the *real* immorality in America wasn't among the poor or even the criminal classes, but among the very wealthy, where money replaced morality as the Ultimate Good. Marc Blitzstein and others would take up this theme in the coming years, but none would have as much fun with it as Porter. The show's title and its title song were direct comic jabs at those who were sure America was in a vast moral decline (not unlike some folks today).

Originally, the show was called *Hard to Get*, then *Bon Voyage*, written mainly by Guy Bolton, with comic embellishments by P. G. Wodehouse, and it told a wacky tale of a trans-Atlantic crossing aboard a luxury liner, a wedding to be stopped, a bomb scare, a disgruntled screenwriter concocting wacky disruptions and romantic obstacles, and of course, mismatched lovers. (The first script was *not* about a shipwreck as many history books claim.) But then the real life ship-wreck of the *Morro Castle*, killing 132 people, hit the headlines right before the show went into rehearsal, and producer Vinton Freedley decided making a musi-cal comedy including a fake bomb on board a luxury liner was no longer a good idea. So Freedley introduced the director, Howard Lindsay, to the columnist and press agent Russel Crouse and asked them to write a new book. Lindsay and Crouse would go on to become one of the most successful playwriting teams in American theatre. The team fashioned their new script around Porter's already completed score, reportedly retaining less than a dozen lines from the earlier ver-sion, this time about less subversive romantic hijinks aboard a luxury liner (the ship setting had to remain since sets were already built) and no fake bombs. They did salvage a few devices from the original, including the missionary and his Chi-nese converts, now more integrated into the plot.

The most interesting character, though not the most central, was Reno Sweeney (played by Ethel Merman), an evangelist turned nightclub singer, a wicked double-satire of pop evangelist Aimee Semple McPherson and the famous speakeasy hostess Texas Guinan, the model much later for Velma Kelly in *Chicago*. In 1934, the notion of combining jazz and God was awfully provoca-tive stuff, but that had never stopped Porter before. Reno is best friends with, and secretly in love with, Billy Crocker (William Gaxton), a junior Wall Street broker, who's in love with Hope Harcourt, a debutante, who's engaged to Sir Eve-lyn Oakleigh, a British aristocrat, who's taken a fancy to Reno. Also on board is Moonface Martin (Victor Moore), Public Enemy Number Thirteen, and his girlfriend Bonnie. Moonface's pal, Snake Eyes Johnson, Public Enemy Number One, was supposed to escape with them but he misses the boat; this little plot tidbit came from the constant real world rumors that John Dillinger was escap-ing aboard trans-Atlantic ships. The plot was constructed on the familiar build-ing blocks of mistaken identity, misunderstandings, and surprise (and ridiculous) revelations before the final curtain, along with dozens of satiric swipes at contemporary celebrities.

But what made this show click was the amazing Porter score, including "Anything Goes," "You're the Top," "All Through the Night" (replacing "Easy to Love"), "I Get a Kick Out of You," and other great songs. (When "I Get a Kick Out of You" was recorded by pop singers, a line mentioning cocaine could not be sung on the radio and Porter had to write an alternate line.) Songs written for *Anything Goes* but cut (though fewer than for most other Porter scores) included "Thank You So Much, Mrs. Lowsborough-Goodby," "Kate the Great" (which Merman refused to sing because of its sexual content), and "Waltz Down the Aisle." During out-of-town tryouts, they also cut "There's No Cure Like Travel," "What a Joy to Be Young," and "Buddie Beware," the last of which was replaced by a reprise of "I Get a Kick Out of You."

The *New York Times* called *Anything Goes* "a thundering good show," and "hilarious and dynamic entertainment." The *Boston Post* wrote, "It opened fast, it raced along; in liveliness and beauty, wit and humor, it weaved a spell of genuine enjoyment that far exceeds anything the stage has given us in many a season." And Porter invented a new kind of show tune: the list song. He had already written a couple of list songs, most notably "Let's Do It," the famous song unmistakably about sexual intercourse that had brought him his first fame. But "You're the Top" raised the list song to an art form. No one would ever do it as well as Porter, but because of him, it became a staple of musical comedy for years to come. Even as recently as *Rent*'s "La Vie Bohème" in 1996, the list song lives on. *Anything Goes* ran 420 performances, the fourth-longest run of the decade, and 261 performances in London in 1935. A bad film version was made in 1936 with Merman and Bing Crosby that used six of Porter's songs and six new songs by other writers. A shortened TV version was aired on NBC in 1954 with Merman, Frank Sinatra, and Bert Lahr, with some of the original score and other Porter songs added. A 1956 film was made that had nothing to do with the show except the title and a few songs.

Anything Goes was revived off Broadway in 1962 with a revised script by Guy Bolton and interpolated songs from other Porter shows and it ran 239 performances. Then it hit London again in 1969 but only ran 15 performances. The show returned to Broadway in 1987 for an impressive 804 performances, and London once more in 1989. The 1962 version rewrote the script, moving the entire story onto the ship, and the 1987 version sported a new script by John Weidman and Timothy Crouse, based on the original and including more of the original score, including some cut songs. It was revived again in London in 2002, directed by Trevor Nunn.

After a not always pleasant stint in Hollywood, Rodgers and Hart returned to New York by the mid-1930s. Hollywood usually paid songwriters a lot more than Broadway did, but Broadway offered a kind of artistic freedom Hollywood would not. Lyricists like Larry Hart, Ira Gershwin, and Cole Porter were much freer to write more adult, more sophisticated, and often, more sexually explicit lyrics for the more sophisticated New York audiences.

Still, despite their disenchantment, Rodgers and Hart were interested when RKO contacted them about an idea for a movie musical for Fred Astaire. So the team came up with a comedy about a vaudeville "hoofer" and a ballet star—a kind of dancer's *Romeo and Juliet*. RKO rejected their idea, so the team decided to turn it into a stage musical. The Shubert Brothers took an option on the show, but kept delaying actual work on it. Finally, the Shuberts let the option lapse, and Rodgers and Hart went to another producer, Dwight Deere Wiman, who would go on to produce several other Rodgers and Hart shows. Finally, in 1936, work could begin and Rodgers and Hart decided that, for the first time, they would write not only the score but the script as well for their new musical, *On Your Toes*. Director George Abbott came on board, and comedian and dancer Ray Bolger (soon to be the world famous Scarecrow in MGM's *Wizard of Oz*) was hired as the hoofer. Two extended ballet sequences were planned, "Princess Zenobia," a spoof of classical ballet, and "Slaughter on Tenth Avenue," a dark, jazz ballet that would be the climax of the story.

No one had done it before, but Rodgers and Hart were ready to try another wild experiment. For the first time ever, they would work ballet into the very fabric of their story. They would make dance inextricably integrated into their musical comedy. In the story, the ballet dancer's ex-boyfriend and dance partner is so furious that she's fallen for the hoofer that he hires two gangsters to kill the hoofer. The gangsters show up during the climactic ballet "Slaughter on Tenth Avenue"—a self-reflexive story about love and murder—and the hoofer has to keep dancing until the gangsters can be caught and arrested. If he leaves the stage, he dies. So not only does the ballet figure in the story but it also comments on the plot as well. There had been ballets before on Broadway but never used like this. Rodgers and Hart hired the brilliant Russian choreographer George Balanchine, a star with the Ballet Russe who had just moved to the United States, making him the first artist to ever receive a "choreographer" credit (before then, it was usually "dances by"). Who better to parody classical ballet intelligently than one of the top classical ballet choreographers in the world? Balanchine's wife Tamara Geva played the ballet dancer. The "Slaughter" ballet has since entered the regular repertoire of several ballet companies around the world, including New York City Ballet. In 1990, the Stuttgart Ballet premiered *On Your Toes* as its very first musical.

Theatre Arts magazine said "We may have come unknowingly upon a successor to the old musical form, a musical show that is not a comedian's holiday, but a dancer's." The show opened in April 1936, with George Abbott—the inheritor and disciple of George M. Cohan's distinctive, fast-paced, uniquely American style—as director and script doctor. In the *New York Times*, Brooks Atkinson wrote, "If the word *sophisticated* is not too unpalatable, let it serve as a description of the mocking book, the songs, and the performances." It ran

315 performances, then crossed The Pond to London where it ran another 123. It was revived in 1954 for 64 performances, and again in 1983 for 505 performances, this time with Abbott back at the helm at age 106.

By the mid-1930s, though, America was a country in crisis. Thousands of Americans were joining the communist party and it's not hard to see why. Everything had been fine, everybody loved democracy, and all was right with the world; then one day, out of the blue, the stock market crashed, people lost their life's savings, and unemployment skyrocketed from less than half a million to about four million in two months, eventually reaching a whopping sixteen million within a few years. So many people lost everything they had, money, businesses, families. The suicide rate leapt. Many people stopped believing in democracy; it had failed them. The promises of communism—the redistribution of wealth, expansive rights for workers—were very seductive. Some historians believe that if it hadn't been for Roosevelt's New Deal programs, the American communist party would have grown even stronger than it did. Many famous artists, actors, directors, writers, composers, and poets were members of the party and began to create aggressively leftist art.

Into this world came the firebrand Hallie Flanagan. Under the leadership of Flanagan, the groundbreaking, history-making Federal Theatre Project hit the ground running. The Federal Theatre was part of the vast U.S. government emergency relief program during the Depression called the Works Progress Administration (WPA). The purpose of the WPA and the Federal Theatre Project—as far as the government was concerned—was to create jobs to put unemployed Americans back to work. But the project's director, Hallie Flanagan, had two other goals as well. She wanted to create theatre that was closer to the real lives of ordinary Americans, theatre that dealt with real issues and presented realistic portrayals of everyday Americans. She also wanted to create a "national theatre" that would reach millions of people across the country who had never seen live theatre before.

Perhaps the most famous piece the Federal Theatre produced was Marc Blitzstein's 1937 concept musical *The Cradle Will Rock*, both a fascinating piece of political musical theatre and a remarkable piece of theatre history, produced by John Houseman and directed by a very young Orson Welles. Blitzstein called his show "a labor opera composed in a style that falls somewhere between realism, romance, vaudeville, comic strip, Gilbert and Sullivan, Brecht, and agitprop." It laid the groundwork, in its politics and its episodic construction, for later shows as varied as *Cabaret, Hair, Pippin, Chicago, Assassins*, and *Rent*.

It was the first musical comedy Marc Blitzstein ever wrote, even though he was already, at age thirty-two, an internationally respected classical composer and music commentator. Completed in only five weeks, its subject matter was very serious and yet it lived in a world of cartoon characters and melodrama. It was one of the funniest musicals of the 1930s, but even though the audience laughed at all the characters, Blitzstein created an emotional investment that paid off in the show's very passionate, very dramatic ending. Its politics were communist and unionist, yet it was unmistakably an American musical comedy and it still holds a place of honor in musical theatre history.

On the morning of June 16, opening night of *The Cradle Will Rock*, the Federal Theatre Project office began calling the press, announcing the cancellation of the show—the official reason was budgetary but the political motivations were clear. Armed guards (Houseman referred to them as "Cossacks") were posted at the theatre to make sure no one removed sets, costumes, props, or anything else paid for by the Federal Theatre Project. Houseman spent the day calling the press, telling them the show would indeed open in another theatre, which he still had not found. Actors' Equity, the actors' union, informed Welles that as long as the actors in *Cradle* were employees of the Federal Theatre Project, they could not appear on any stage that wasn't officially sanctioned by the Project. The musicians' union then told Welles that if they moved to another theatre, they could no longer pay the musicians the reduced rate allowed for the Federal Theatre Project. Welles and Houseman would have to pay the musicians full union scale, as well as back pay for rehearsals, and they would have to hire more musicians in accordance with the standard Broadway contract. There was no way Welles and Houseman could afford this.

So Welles came up with a plan—the actors would come to the new theatre (wherever it might be), sit in the audience, and when the time came, perform their roles from the house. Of course, many of the actors were not comfortable with this plan, fearing that they might lose their jobs with the Federal Theatre Project. Still, Welles and Houseman insisted the show could go on, without sets, without lights, without an orchestra, perhaps even without some of the cast. They planned to put Blitzstein onstage at a piano (he was not a member of the musicians' union) to play the whole score and even sing some of the parts if necessary. They sent an assistant, Jean Rosenthal (destined to become a major Broadway lighting designer), to go find a piano and a truck and just keep driving around Manhattan until they could book another theatre. By late afternoon, the press and hundreds of ticket holders began gathering outside the theatre. Some of the cast came outside and performed for them to keep them occupied. A few minutes before eight o'clock, a theatre was found, the Venice, twenty-one blocks uptown, for a rental fee of $100. They sent Rosenthal up there with the piano, and they led the crowd, now swelling to even greater numbers, on a twenty-one block march uptown to the Venice, picking up hundreds more along the way. The show began at 8:50 P.M., with Blitzstein alone on stage, a single follow spot focused on him.

As Blitzstein began singing the first song, he heard a small voice begin to sing along out in the house, and the follow spot swung out into the audience to illuminate Olive Stanton, a novice actress in her first show, who was playing the role of Moll. Slowly, one by one, the actors stood when their cues came and ended up playing the whole show in and among the audience, never venturing onstage. As historian Ethan Mordden described it, "Blitzstein would bang out his music alone on the Venice's empty stage as his play rose up to join with him in the electric air of bootleg theatre." Though most of the cast had come to the Venice, Blitzstein sang eight of the roles that night, while some of the actors doubled up on other roles. Occasionally during the evening, the one musician who had come along, an accordion player, would stand up where he sat and play along with the solo piano. After the finale the audience went wild, cheering and screaming for what seemed like forever. Not only had New York seen the premiere of an exciting new musical by a gifted writer and composer, these lucky people had witnessed the birth of a theatrical legend.

The Cradle Will Rock ran nineteen performances like that at the Venice Theatre (although the Federal Theatre Project kept telling callers that the show was not running anywhere), all done with the actors out in the audience. The *New York Times* said the show was "written with extraordinary versatility and played with enormous gusto, the best thing militant labor has put into the theatre yet." The *New York Post* called it "a propagandistic tour de force." Hallie Flanagan defended this controversial show by saying that "the theatre, when it's good, is always dangerous."

Welles resigned from the Federal Theatre Project over the attempted closing of *Cradle* and Houseman was fired for insubordination. Unfazed, they formed the Mercury Theatre and went back to work. During the summer of 1937, they produced *Cradle* all over New York, in outdoor auditoriums, amusement parks, and other unlikely locations, as well as touring to the steel districts of Pennsylvania, Ohio, and elsewhere. In the fall of 1937, Welles and Houseman put together a series of Sunday night performances (to enable original cast members now in other shows to participate). This time, Welles put the actors onstage sitting in three rows of chairs. With the solo piano still on stage, they used the piano as a prop, as a drugstore counter or a judge's bench. Of these performances, *Stage* magazine said, "Remarkable how, in an entertainment world drugged with manufactured glamour, they conjure Steel Town out of thin air, set it raw and terrible before your eyes." The critics again praised it, even those who had hated it just a few months before. Still, some held out. George Jean Nathan wrote that it was "little more than the kind of thing Cole Porter might have written if, God forbid, he had gone to Columbia instead of Yale."

In December, Welles presented a radio production of the show. The show opened for a proper Broadway run on January 3, 1938 and ran 108 performances. Although still using only solo piano, the producers were forced by the musicians union to pay ten musicians *not* to play each night. Blitzstein chose ten of his neediest friends for the job. Though *The Band Wagon* had been the first musical to record a cast album, *Cradle* was actually the first cast album to be released.

The show was revived in New York in 1947 in a concert presentation at City Center (the first time the orchestrations were used), conducted by Leonard Bernstein and with several of the original leads. It was then produced later that year on Broadway starring Alfred Drake as Larry Foreman and Vivian Vance as Mrs. Mister, running a mere 34 performances. It was revived again by the New York City Opera in February 1960, staged by Howard DaSilva, who had created the role of Larry Foreman. In November 1964, it was revived off Broadway in a production starring Jerry Orbach and directed again by DaSilva. It was revived again Off Broadway in 1983, this time with Patti LuPone as Moll and directed by John Houseman. This production toured the United States, played the Old Vic in London, and was videotaped for PBS.

Another unionist musical appeared in New York in the mid-thirties called *Pins and Needles*, produced by the International Ladies Garment Workers Union (ILGWU) with a score by Harold Rome and a script by Marc Blitzstein and a stable of other writers. Inspired by contemporary headlines, by the work of Bertolt Brecht, and by the aggressive politics of Berlin cabaret in the late 1920s and early 1930s, it premiered in June 1936 at the famous Princess Theatre, now renamed the Labor Stage. The show was the brainchild of Louis Schaffer, the cultural director of the ILGWU, who was looking for a project for the union. The original version of the show was peopled exclusively by union members—cutters, dressmakers, pressers—who rehearsed for a full year, three evenings a week (because the whole cast was working full time), and then only performed on weekends at the outset. It officially opened in November 1937, after *Cradle* had already stunned New York. After a year, it moved uptown to Broadway and eventually moved back to the Labor Stage. During its five-year run, Rome continued to update and add new songs to comment on new issues and events, creating four separate "editions" of the show. By the time it closed in 1941, it had run 1,108 performances, outrunning both *Show Boat* and *Irene*, becoming the longest-running Broadway musical to date.

Like *The Cradle Will Rock*, *Pins and Needles* was a concept musical, without a linear plot but with a strong central concept that raised it out of the random compilation of most revues. Its most famous song was "Sing Me a Song of Social Significance." Other songs included "Doing the Reactionary," "Four Little Angels of Peace" (Hitler, Mussolini, Tojo, and Chamberlain), "Chain Store Daisy," and "It's Not Cricket to Picket." Later editions included "It's Better with a Union Man," "Sitting on Your Status Quo," and other similar numbers. *Pins and Needles* was revived in 1967 at the Roundabout Theatre and ran an additional 214 performances. Harold Rome would go on to write the score to the 1962 satirical book musical *I Can Get It for You Wholesale* about corruption in New York's garment industry.

Rodgers and Hart were back in 1938 with some slightly groundbreaking fun in the form of *The Boys from Syracuse*, the first musical comedy based on Shakespeare. Dozens of musical adaptations of the Bard have come along since then, but Dick and Larry were first. Having been a big Shakespeare fan all his life, Hart observed one day that no one had made a musical comedy out of Shakespeare and this tidbit so fascinated Rodgers that they quickly settled on *The Comedy of*

Errors as the source material for their next show. The other tidbit was that Hart's performer brother Teddy looked almost exactly like comedian Jimmy Savo. And since *The Comedy of Errors* is about two sets of identical twins, they had a head start in casting. The script by director George Abbott retained only one line from Shakespeare's original but stayed true to the story. The show's title was an insider's joke, making a sly reference to the all-powerful Shubert Brothers, the powerful producing clan who came from Syracuse, New York.

The show was a respectable hit, running 235 performances. It was revived in 1963, running 502 performances, then moved to London for another 100 performances. The show returned to Broadway in 2002 but managed only a short two month run. More significantly, a hip-hop version of the show called *Da Boyz* appeared at the London Fringe Festival in 2003.

As the 1930s were winding down, America's "Good Neighbor Policy" often inspired the stunt casting of Latinos on Broadway and on film. Carmen Miranda made her first Broadway appearance in June 1939 in a mediocre revue called *The Streets of Paris*, beating Desi Arnaz to the Rialto by just a few months. Arnaz's big break came with Rodgers and Hart's *Too Many Girls* in October 1939. The flimsy script by George Marion Jr. (script-doctored by George Abbott) centered on a rich girl whose father has secretly hired four football players to accompany her to college as bodyguards. (Sound familiar? Try Elvis Presley's 1965 *Girl Happy.*) As luck would have it, she falls in love with one of them—*not* of course, God forbid, the Latino, played by Desi Arnaz. Still, Arnaz, formerly a band singer, got to shine in several scenes, and the score included several pseudo-Latin numbers, "All Dressed Up (Spic and Spanish)" (*no kidding*), "She Could Shake the Maracas," "Babalú," and the now painful "Give It Back to the Indians." Then Arnaz headed straight for Hollywood to recreate his role for the film version in November 1940. One critic, Gustavo Péres Firmat, said of the film years later, "To be sure, *Too Many Girls* is a modern multiculturalist's nightmare."

4

Oh, What a Beautiful Morning
The 1940s

The 1940s was the decade in which Richard Rodgers left lyricist Larry Hart for lyricist Oscar Hammerstein II, and in a strange way, Rodgers' move mirrored the musical theatre itself as it too moved away from (for the most part) wacky, light-weight plots with (it was hoped) hit tunes chock full of trick rhymes and inverted sentences, and instead toward a new kind of integrated, more mature musical theatre. Once World War II began to rescue the American economy from the throes of the Depression, the experiment that was *Show Boat* would finally be continued in the forties with *Pal Joey*, *Oklahoma!*, and the shows that followed their lead.

The 1940s became the decade in which the Classic Musical was born, the kind of show that would be revived over and over, forever after. The only shows written before 1940 that are still revived today with any frequency are *Show Boat* and *Anything Goes*. Other early shows had great scores, but their scripts were just too slight for the now more sophisticated audiences. But after 1940, there was *Pal Joey*, *Oklahoma!*, *Carousel*, *The King and I*, *South Pacific*, *Annie Get Your Gun*, *Brigadoon*, *On the Town*, *Kiss Me Kate*, *Finian's Rainbow*, *Guys and Dolls*, *The Pajama Game*, *Damn Yankees*, and many others.

As the 1940s began, musical comedy was mostly still about escapism. There had been a few exceptions in the 1930s—*The Cradle Will Rock*, *Pins and Needles*—but the majority of musicals on Broadway were still lightweight comedies about young love and catchy tunes, either with or without more substantial content under the surface. Looking back, musical theatre historian Ethan Mordden wrote, "With *Pal Joey* . . . we find something even more unlikely than fantasy: real life."

Rodgers and Hart's 1940 musical *Pal Joey* was about casual sex, predatory men, and promiscuous women. Sex had been lurking in musical comedy for a long time, especially in the bawdy songs of Cole Porter, but never before had a musical tack-led real sex, recreational sex, sex worth regretting, cheerfully adulterous sex. This was something new. And though musical comedy had always been about romance, never before had a musical been so clearly and exclusively about copulation. Both leading characters in *Pal Joey* wanted very little besides sexual intercourse. It might be fair to say that musical comedy hit puberty with *Pal Joey*, and it would hit maturity three years later with *Oklahoma!*

Other musicals had already featured less than heroic heroes, like Gaylord Ravenal in *Show Boat*, but Ravenal wasn't *Show Boat*'s central character. Until *Pal Joey*, no musical comedy had centered on a genuine scoundrel. Describing the show's characters, Rodgers said in an interview, "They were all bad people. Except the girl. And she was stupid."

John O'Hara originally wrote his "Pal Joey" stories for the *New Yorker*, as a series of short pieces in the form of letters written to "Pal Ted," a fictional New York bandleader, from "Pal Joey," a cheap, usually down on his luck singer. O'Hara approached Rodgers and Hart about turning his stories into a musical. Like Wodehouse before him, O'Hara knew virtually nothing about musicals, and he had no idea how utterly wrong his stories were for a musical comedy. Joey was a heel, a cad, a user and a loser, not the kind of guy that headlined musicals. Also luckily, Rodgers and Hart were very interested in O'Hara's idea. Years later, Rodgers wrote, "Not only would the show be different from anything we had ever done before, it would be different from anything anyone else had ever tried. This alone was reason enough for us to want to do it. . . . It seemed time to us that musical comedy get out of its cradle and start standing on its own feet. Looking at the facts of life."

So O'Hara wrote a new story about Joey (with uncredited help from producer-director George Abbott), using the *New Yorker* pieces only as backstory, as a prelude to the action of the musical. A few details remain in the show that refer to O'Hara's *New Yorker* stories (like the banker's daughter in Columbus) and this ready-made backstory gave Joey a full, real life, a detailed past that most musical comedy characters didn't have at the time.

Pal Joey first opened in 1940, starring Gene Kelly and Vivienne Segal, with direction by George Abbott and brilliant choreography by Robert Alton, and it ran a respectable 374 performances. *Pal Joey* ran the season, closed for the summer (as shows usually did before air conditioning), ran three more months, then went on tour until 1942. But many of the reviews were very negative. Broadway was not ready for Joey quite yet.

Ten years later, the song "Bewitched" was rediscovered by dance bands and seven different versions of the song made it to the top of the charts. Also, perhaps because of the song's newfound popularity, Columbia Records producer Goddard Lieberson decided to record the whole score for the first time, with Vivienne Segal and Harold Lang. In 1951, composer Jule Styne saw future choreographer Bob Fosse play Joey in a summer stock production and decided to produce a revival of the show. The next year, *Pal Joey* opened again on Broadway with Harold Lang (and Fosse as his understudy) and Vivienne Segal, this time running 540 performances, easily beating out the original production. By now, audiences were more sophisticated; four Rodgers and Hammerstein shows had opened, and two were still running, *South Pacific* and *The King and I*. Walter Kerr wrote in the *New York Herald-Tribune* that *Pal Joey* was "one of the shrewdest, toughest, and in a way most literate books ever written for musical comedy." In the *New York Post*, Richard Watts said the show was "revolutionary in its toughness and scorn for musical comedy sentimentality. To tell the truth, it shocked people because it took as its central figures a kept man and rich woman who kept him, and it didn't molest him with moral disapproval."

After a 1954 London production, a film was made in 1957 with Frank Sinatra, Kim Novak, and Rita Hayworth (both women's voices were dubbed). The filmmakers rewrote the show a great deal, cut eight of the score's fourteen songs, and added four other Rodgers and Hart songs. A few years later, Bob Fosse twice recreated the role at New York's City Center, first in 1961 and again in 1963. In 1995, New York's *Encore!* series presented the show in concert and made a new recording with Patti LuPone, Peter Gallagher, and Bebe Neuwirth. In 1999, playwright Terrence McNally revised the script for a proposed Broadway revival and submitted it to the producing organization Livent right before the company went out of business. The production never happened.

Today, *Pal Joey* may seem old-fashioned in some respects, but we have to see it in its original context—a musical comedy (*before* the Rodgers and Hammerstein revolution) that dealt with a hustler and thief, adultery, premarital sex, blackmail, and other fun things. A musical comedy centered on an antihero is something we're used to now, but it was pretty subversive in 1940.

Broadway's next black musical was in some ways like many of the black musicals before it—written and produced by mostly white men. *Cabin in the Sky* had a book by Lynn Root, a score by John LaTouche and Vernon Duke, direction by George Balanchine and Albert Lewis, choreography by Balanchine and Katherine Dunham (the only African American on the team), and sets by Boris Aronson. The show told the Faustian fable of a morally weak man, Little Joe, whose soul is the object of a battle between "the Lawd's general" and "Lucifer Jr.," all while Joe's wife Petunia prays for his redemption. The cast included Todd Duncan (recently the star of the Gershwin opera *Porgy and Bess*), Rex Ingram, Ethel Waters, and Katherine Dunham. Though it still fed some of the stereotypes of black men as lazy gamblers, it boasted a strong book and score. Brooks Atkinson in the *New York Times* called it "original and joyous in an imaginative vein which suits the theatre's special genius." Finally here was a black musical that rejected what Atkinson had called "Broadway's Negro formula: hot dancing, hot singing, dark-town comedy about poker playing and fried chicken." Sure, it was still musical comedy—and a fantasy story at that—but it addressed real issues with real emotion and real understanding. Ethel Waters' character Petunia had an intelligence, patience, and sense of faith that had been rarely seen in black shows. It ran 156 performances.

In January 1941, three of the biggest talents in musical theatre—bookwriter Moss Hart, lyricist Ira Gershwin, and composer Kurt Weill—got together and wrote the first psychoanalysis musical, *Lady in the Dark*. Hart himself had suffered a nervous breakdown and he credited his psychoanalysis for his recovery. This show was important to him. It focused on this latest trend in mental health in New York and California, and it contrasted the real world with the dream world come to life on the psychiatrist's couch. Liza Elliott (played by British mega-star Gertrude Lawrence) was a successful magazine publisher who was unhappy and unfulfilled. Except for the end of the show, the musical numbers only appeared in the four extended dream sequences, staged by modern dancer Albertina Rasch—one a Ziegfeld-style show, one a wedding, one a circus, and the last a childhood dream. The show was unusual because the admittedly unnatural act of breaking into song was confined to dream sequences (with one well-motivated exception). Finally, Liza figures out who she really loves and what she really wants, and all is well. By today's standards, the psychology of the work may have been simplistic, but it was remarkable for its time, and it presaged the use of psychological themes and dream sequences in *Oklahoma!* and other shows.

Lady in the Dark called itself a "musical play" instead of a "musical comedy" as was the norm. The show ran 467 performances. After a national tour, the show came back to Broadway in 1943 for another 83 performances. A movie version was made in 1944.

By the early 1940s, composer Richard Rodgers, famous for his jazzy, urbane Broadway scores, had been enjoying a string of hit musical comedies with his partner Larry Hart (*Babes in Arms, On Your Toes, Pal Joey,* and many others), but Hart was becoming harder and harder to work with as his alcoholism and self-loathing over his looks and his homosexuality began more and more to get in the way. Theresa Helburn, one of the directors of the highly respected Theatre Guild, saw a summer stock theatre production of Lynn Riggs' cowboy play *Green Grow the Lilacs,* a play the Theatre Guild had produced on Broadway in 1931. The show had been a big flop originally but after seeing this new production ten years later with even more folk songs than the original had included, Helburn realized the more music the play had the better it became. She brought composer Richard Rodgers to see it and he agreed that what it needed was an original score to make it into a true musical.

When Larry Hart declined to work on *Oklahoma!*, Rodgers asked Oscar Hammerstein II, now in the midst of a major career slump, who agreed only after making sure he wasn't coming between Rodgers and Hart. This wasn't the first time Rodgers and Hammerstein had worked together; back in 1920 when the eighteen-year-old Rodgers was a student at Columbia University, he and Larry Hart had written the score for the Columbia Varsity Show and alumni Oscar Hammerstein had contributed lyrics to a few of Rodgers' melodies. But by this time neither man was a novice; Rodgers had already written thirty musicals and

Hammerstein had written twenty-seven, and both men had been pushing the artistic envelope in various ways.

Now, twenty-three years after their college collaboration, the two formed what was to be one of the longest-lasting partnerships in the American theatre. Hammerstein began writing some of the best lyrics of his career and he brought out a new side of Rodgers, a lush, romantic, emotional side that Rodgers had rarely explored before. Their partnership became a turning point in American musical theatre, changing everything that came after. They would go on to write other masterpieces, most notably *Carousel* and *The King and I*, that would change forever the way people wrote musicals. Hammerstein really knew how to fashion a musical script out of the sketchy material of Riggs' play, and he opened up whole new areas of drama. In the play Ado Annie had been a very minor character and Will Parker was mentioned once but never appeared onstage. It was Hammerstein's idea to create two mirroring romantic triangles. For the first time in a popular musical, neither the stars nor the songwriters were the stars of the show; this time the real star of the show was the *plot*.

And so in 1943 Broadway welcomed what was perhaps one of the most important accidents to happen in the history of musical theatre, Rodgers and Hammerstein's *Oklahoma!*, with choreography by Agnes de Mille and direction by Rouben Mamoulian, the first director to be given, contractually, entire control over the entire production in all its details. No one could have foreseen the impact this unimposing, impossibly and intentionally "unsophisticated" little show would have on the future of the art form. No one could have guessed that for decades to come almost all musicals would be written in the Rodgers and Hammerstein style, that *Oklahoma!* was not only breaking the old rules but also making all new ones, that silly, frothy musicals would forever more be considered old-fashioned.

Poet Carl Sandburg said *Oklahoma!* was like "hay mown up over barn dance floors, stepping around like an apple-faced farmhand and rolling along like a good wagon slicked up with new axle grease." It was a show about love and community, sure, but it was also about survival in an inhospitable environment, about the American Spirit in pre-urbanized America, about the kind of men and women who built America. And it was about the rule of law, how it came to America's frontier, and why it mattered. The central backdrop of the show, the ongoing dispute between the farmers and the ranchers for control of the land not only mirrored the central love triangle—with Curly the rancher and Judd the farmer competing for the love of Laurie—but it also described the central tenet of American law, that there will always be legitimate but competing interests in America and that they must be settled by compromise and by the rule of law, not by violence.

In 1998, the *London Daily Mail* said of Trevor Nunn's revival of *Oklahoma!*, "It's not just a classic American musical but—and this is the real surprise—a truthful, touching and gripping drama about growing up and falling in love, about dreams and nightmares." In 1999 the *New York Post* said, "Rogers and Hammerstein are truly up there with Eugene O'Neill as the great American theatre creators." As the twentieth century came to a close, the New York Drama League voted *Oklahoma!* the best musical of the century.

Many years later, Hammerstein's protégé Stephen Sondheim would comment, only half-jokingly, that *Carousel* is about life and death while *Oklahoma!* is about a picnic. But really, that's not far from the truth. *Oklahoma!* is mostly about the mundane, everyday lives of territory folk in 1906 Oklahoma, just before it became a state. These were the people who in a few years' time would be living in the middle of the Dust Bowl and would be driven from their homes. These are real lives full of real hardships and real tragedies, and *Oklahoma!* never once shies away from that reality.

So how did it start a major revolution in the American musical theatre, after the more substantial *Show Boat* couldn't do it in 1927? There are a lot of reasons. First, it's true that the main action of *Oklahoma!* is centered on the seemingly trivial tension over which man Laurey will choose to take her to the box social and which of them will win her basket in the auction. But it's also about attempted murder and attempted rape. This is *not* a Princess musical or a Cole Porter musical about mistaken identities, wacky plot twists, or surprise resolutions. This is the stuff of heavy, intense, truthful drama. Jud is a murderer and he collects pornography. Whether or not Laurey goes to the social with him really *is* a big deal. It is genuinely dangerous for Laurey to be alone with Jud, to be his "date." His advances on the way to the social are leading to rape, and he may be waiting to finish the job after the auction—which is why it's so important that Curly win Laurey's basket, which brings with it her company. And underneath all this, the show is also about responsibility to the community, a serious theme Sondheim would explore more thoroughly forty-four years later in his musical *Into the Woods.* Though it may not have been a conscious "statement," the overture of *Oklahoma!* even starts with "The Farmer and the Cowman," the show's one song specifically about responsibility to the community, underlining the importance of that theme.

True, *Show Boat* dealt in serious human issues too, but not as fully or confidently or—and here may be the key—as *subtly* as *Oklahoma!* And *Show Boat* had the disadvantage of opening right before the Depression, when its influence would be blunted, even obscured, until years later.

The second reason *Oklahoma!* was so revolutionary is that, though dance had been integrated into the plot in Rodgers and Hart's musical comedies *On Your Toes* (1936) and *Pal Joey* (1940), *Oklahoma!* used dance as a fully formed narrative language, just like the words and music, instead of merely as a plot device. Before de Mille, theatre dance was largely tap and ballroom; after de Mille, it was ballet, modern, jazz, ethnic, and yes, still some ballroom and tap. All these forms came together in a choreographic melting pot, creating not a new mix of dance types but an entirely new dance form: Broadway dance. Forever more, Broadway dance would be a unique form unto itself, one that existed to communicate story, character, and most radical of all, psychology. (De Mille had been through psychoanalysis and found it quite illuminating.) Though *Pal Joey* had a dream ballet in 1940, *Oklahoma!*'s dream ballet went deeper and further. Without words, Agnes de Mille's choreography gave us deep, clear insight into Laurey's most secret feelings, hopes, and fears. De Mille gave her leading lady a *sex drive*, perhaps the most revolutionary thing of all, and something which would be explored further in shows like *West Side Story*, *Man of La Mancha*, and *Cabaret*. And more than any other single element, de Mille's dream ballet (or more accurately, "nightmare" ballet) made *Oklahoma!* a serious piece of theatre. It gave the show balls.

Also for the first time, a choreographer demanded that dance music be written to her dances, rather than the other way around. De Mille and her dance arranger Morgan "Buddy" Lewis composed the music for Laurey's dream ballet, not Rodgers or the show's orchestrator, as in times past. And because the show was such a hit, for years after *Oklahoma!* every new serious musical had to have a dream ballet, even if there was no real need for it. Even *West Side Story* in 1957 and *Contact* in 2000 used dream ballets.

The third reason the show was so revolutionary is that, though *Oklahoma!* retained a few old-fashioned devices, it also broke lots of rules. While other shows opened with big chorus numbers and pretty girls, *Oklahoma!* opened with an old woman sitting alone on stage churning butter as the audience heard a solo male voice singing a cappella and offstage. The audience didn't see girls until forty-five minutes into the first act! While most musicals had a secondary comic couple, *Oklahoma!* had a secondary comic *triangle*, which balanced and foreshadowed the more dangerous primary love triangle. While most hit musicals lined up the stars—Ethel Merman, Al Jolson, Eddie Cantor—before a single note was written, *Oklahoma!* did not have even one big name in the cast. Also, the vast majority of musicals at the time were about contemporary New York. Certainly, most of Cohan's shows were, as well as most of the Gershwins', most of Cole Porter's, and most of Rodgers and Hart's. And even when the shows weren't set in New York, they were often still about New Yorkers, as in *Girl Crazy* and *Anything Goes*.

Oklahoma! shouldn't have had a prayer.

Perhaps what *Oklahoma!* did that no other show had done before was to take all the innovations, experiments, and surprises that had shown up in numerous separate musicals over the previous twenty years, put them all together in one show, and integrate them seamlessly and thoughtfully into the drama of the story—much the way *Rent* did more than fifty years later. *Oklahoma!* took the social issues of *Show Boat*, the long-form musical scenes of *Show Boat* and the Rodgers and Hart movie musical *Love Me Tonight*, the ordinary people of *Porgy and Bess*, a murder over love from *Rose Marie* and *Porgy and Bess*, the dramatic use of dance in *On Your Toes*, the psychological content of *Lady in the Dark*, a dark, frank view of sexuality and a psychological dream ballet from *Pal Joey*, and a cast of talented unknowns, as in *Babes in Arms* and *The Boys from Syracuse*. It took all these previous innovations and it made them all work *together* for the very first time. Not surprisingly, most of the shows just mentioned were written by either Rodgers or Hammerstein with other partners, so these two were the perfect team to bring it all together in a unified whole, maybe the only two people who could.

Most surprising of all—especially to its creators—the rule-busting *Oklahoma!*, with a budget of $180,000 (well over two million in today's dollars), became a monster hit, running more than five years and 2,212 performances on Broadway, becoming the longest-running show of all time. During the run Richard Rodgers' longtime partner Larry Hart died, as did Hammerstein's former partner Jerome Kern. It was officially a new era.

The national touring company of *Oklahoma!* ran uninterrupted for almost ten years. The show opened in London in 1947 and ran 1,500 performances, followed by Berlin in 1951 and Paris in 1955. The U.S. army and navy requested a USO tour of the show during World War II to play for more than a million and a half troops in the Pacific. At one point, sheet music sales for "People Will Say We're in Love'" topped 9,000 copies a day and sales for "Oh, What a Beautiful Mornin'" topped 4,000 a day. It took less than a year to sell more than a million pieces of *Oklahoma!* sheet music. The original cast album sold 800,000 copies during the Broadway run. The show won a special Pulitzer citation for excellence, two Oscars (the Tony Awards weren't around yet), then a special Tony Award in 1993, a London Evening Standard Award in 1998, an international Emmy Award in 1999, and four Olivier Awards (the British Tony Awards) in 1999. Today, the show is done in about six hundred theatres across the United States every year.

Rodgers said in his autobiography, "The chief influence of *Oklahoma!* was simply to serve notice that when writers come up with something different and it has merit, there would be a large and receptive audience waiting for it. From *Oklahoma!* on, with only rare exceptions, the memorable productions have been those daring to break free from the conventional mode." *Oklahoma!* taught musical theatre artists a lesson: audiences *don't* only like the familiar; they like an *adventure*.

Producers had been trying for years to recast classic operettas and operas with all-black companies, with mostly mediocre results and medium to short runs— *The Swing Mikado*, *The Hot Mikado*, *The Mikado in Swing*, *Swinging the Dream* (based on *Midsummer Night's Dream*), and others—but it took Oscar Hammerstein, now at the beginning of a hot streak, to make it work. Even the critics who had not liked *Porgy and Bess* all seemed to love *Carmen Jones*, Hammerstein's 1943 resetting of Bizet's opera *Carmen* in a parachute factory in South Carolina during World War II. Hammerstein had been wanting to modernize *Carmen* for years, and his success with *Oklahoma!* gave him the clout to do it.

He used the original libretto by Prosper Merimée only as a rough guide, renaming all the leading characters and cutting out all the recitative, converting the show from an opera into a musical. But Hammerstein and his collaborators were having a hard time finding a black cast with the proper training for the challenging music. On top of that, the decision was made early on to cast all the leads twice, so that they wouldn't have to sing Bizet's music eight shows a week. So Hammerstein and company recruited John Hammond to help. Hammond had made a career out of recording and preserving some of the great black American vocalists of the first half of the century, and he seemed to be the perfect man to find the talent *Carmen Jones* needed.

Hammond toured the country on his quest, visiting more than twenty-five black colleges. By the time he was through he had cast the show, but mostly with performers who had never stepped foot on a stage before. Still, the show was a major hit. Howard Barnes in the *New York Herald-Tribune* wrote, "*Carmen Jones* is something more than a major theatrical event. It opens infinite and challenging horizons for the fusion of the two art forms"—opera and musical comedy.

A film version was released on 1954, directed by Otto Preminger and starring Dorothy Dandridge, Harry Belafonte (both dubbed by white singers), Pearl Bailey, and Diahann Carroll—the same year America took a big step forward with the landmark Supreme Court decision in *Brown v. the Board of Education*, outlawing segregation in public schools. *Time* magazine wrote about the film, "The rattle of cash registers does not often serve as the drum roll of social progress. With this picture it may." Noted African American author and commentator James Baldwin had a lot of problems with *Carmen Jones*, but admitted that it was "one of the most important all-Negro musicals Hollywood has yet produced." Dandridge became the first black women nominated for a leading actress Oscar.

Then, in April 1945, Rodgers and Hammerstein struck gold again, with *Carousel*, again with direction by Rouben Mamoulian and choreography by Agnes de Mille. Today, *Carousel* is sometimes foolishly dismissed as silly sentimentality when in fact it's Rodgers and Hammerstein's most psychological, most insightful, and most disturbing musical. It also cemented a change in how musicals were staged. With *Oklahoma!* and *Carousel*, Mamoulian rejected the artificial conventions of the past, in which actors came down to the edge of the stage to deliver songs. Instead Mamoulian staged these shows just as a nonmusical would be staged and other directors took note.

Based on Ferenc Molnár's tragic 1909 French play *Liliom* (which had played Broadway in 1921), *Carousel* told the tragic story of a naive young girl, a violent, sexual boy, and their doomed marriage. By the middle of the second act, the girl is pregnant, the boy has bungled a robbery attempt and committed suicide. The show is about sex, violence, spousal abuse, the indistinguishable line between good and evil, and the cruelty of fate. *The Sound of Music* it ain't. Yet

Richard Rodgers said on several occasions it was his favorite of all the musicals he wrote. The score uses many of the conventions of opera but in the vocabulary of the American musical comedy. Entire scenes are set to music. It includes two major dance sequences, the sixteen-minute "Carousel Waltz," a kind of prologue to the action, and a lengthy Act II ballet. Rodgers and Hammerstein had reached the pinnacle of musical theatre writing, in their ability to sustain musical and lyrical interest for long spans of time while still maintaining musical unity and cohesion and dramatic intensity. *Carousel* ran on Broadway 890 performances and won the New York Drama Critics Circle Award.

Unfortunately, *Carousel's* classic status has made us too familiar with its story, its lyrics, its popular tunes, so that we tend to ignore the fascinating insights into the complexity of human nature that lie beneath its surface. If we look at the show with a fresh eye, the lyrics to "If I Loved You" aren't clichéd, they're heartbreaking—every line shows us two people very much in love (or at least deeply attracted to each other) who find it impossible to express that emotion, a problem that will plague their marriage and ruin their lives. It's both tragic and touching. And then there's the immense, almost uncomfortable emotion and redemption of "You'll Never Walk Alone." But we've stopped listening. Only with conscious effort can we look at the show as if for the first time—as director Nicholas Hytner did with the dark, dangerous, sexually intense 1994 revival—and see the beauty, the subtlety, and the profound relevance to our contemporary lives.

With *Carousel*, Rodgers and Hammerstein displayed even greater disinterest than before in the rules of musical comedy. This morality play sets up unconquerable obstacles for its central characters and then moves unflinchingly toward tragedy. Billy Bigelow, the show's hero, is not only an antihero—arrogant, violent, inarticulate—he also commits suicide, leaving behind a pregnant wife. How did Rodgers and Hammerstein think they could get away with this in 1945? Some producers even today would find this story inappropriate for a musical. It's also important to keep in mind that when the show opened, many women across the country had been widowed by World War II; this was a play that dealt with the sorrow of real life head on. All the drama of the show is internal. The plot hinges on whether or not Billy and Julie will learn to express their love and heal their marriage and whether or not Billy will forsake his ego and get an honest job to support his wife and child. The conflict and resolution of the show happen entirely inside the characters' hearts and minds, again not the usual kind of story for a musical in 1945.

One of the major themes in *Carousel* is that of community. The morals, opinions, and presence of the community is felt in every important event in the show. In Jeffrey Sweet's excellent playwriting book *The Dramatist's Toolkit*, he talks about the nature of community in traditional musicals. According to Sweet, the members of the chorus represent a community that shares words (lyrics sung in unison) because it shares values; in essence the community is a character in and of itself. The central character of a show (in this case, Billy Bigelow) sings different words and sings alone, because he does not share those values; he doesn't fit in. This creates a conflict that can be resolved in one of two ways: either the two parties come to an accommodation in which the hero learns to become a part of the community (as in *Brigadoon, The Music Man, Company, A New Brain*) or the individual is removed from the community by death or banishment (as in *Sweeney Todd, Evita, Jesus Christ Superstar, Bat Boy,* or *Hair*). They can't continue to live in conflict.

This construction paralleled the real, specifically immigrant experience lived by almost all the creators of early musical theatre, a microcosm of the American Melting Pot, for both better and worse. So many of the Jews working on Broadway had anglicized their names, had done everything to erase their Jewishness, to fully assimilate. This was the dark side of the melting pot; not just an eclectic array of groups melding together, but also the accompanying loss of individuality in the process. That fear that immigrants must assimilate or perish laid the groundwork for the dramatic arc of hundreds of American musicals, past, present, and future.

In *Carousel*, Billy resolves that conflict in the only possible way; he leaves the community by committing suicide. But even after his death, the conflict is not resolved; now Julie and Louise are in conflict with the community because of Billy's actions. With Billy's help from beyond the grave, Julie and Louise are brought into an accommodation with the community and finally sing along with them. Appropriately, the community in *Carousel* gets its own songs, like any other character, including "June Is Busting Out All Over," "This Was a Real Nice Clambake," and "You'll Never Walk Alone." The clambake is an important representation of this community, but Billy and Jigger use this tradition, this ritual, to commit robbery—to betray the community.

Rodgers and Hammerstein acknowledged the evil and danger in the world—death, despair, loss, cruelty—without sugar-coating it and yet at the same time, implied that there is a goodness that can overcome the bad. Certainly today as much as in 1945 postwar America, this is a message we need to hear. Hammerstein believed that though there is pain in the world, there is also healing. Especially as politicians lash out against the entertainment industry for destroying the moral fabric of our country, *Carousel* has become an interesting example of a unflinching look at what's wrong with our society—but also, what's *right*. Not even *Show Boat* and *Oklahoma!* were this extreme in their overturning of the conventions of the American musical comedy. But as they did with *Oklahoma!*, audiences embraced *Carousel* and it has stood the test of time.

In September 1945, a fascinating new black musical opened called *Carib Song*, by William Archibald and Baldwin Bergersen. Dancer Katherine Dunham conceived and choreographed the show after studying indigenous dance in the Caribbean islands as part of her degree program in anthropology at the University of Chicago. The show's director was a friend of Dunham's, another anthropology student, Mary Hunter. Though many critics didn't like the book, which involved a romantic triangle, it was the first time in a long time a musical had taken black characters and culture this seriously, and black artists on Broadway found in the show some reason for hope, even though it ran only thirty-six performances. Unfortunately, black musicals still could not, or at least would not, address race relations in America directly. Instead they told stories in exotic locales and might only hint at the racial problems going on at home. It would be another year and a half before these issues found their way onto the Broadway stage in *Finian's Rainbow* and then in *South Pacific*.

America was changing now—in many ways—heading into a new era of postwar prosperity, which translated into newly acquired disposable income and the resulting increase in ticket buyers for Broadway shows. The second half of the 1940s and most of the 1950s and 1960s was a time of too much mediocrity on Broadway, a time when workmanlike, relatively bland shows could run for a while, could even make back their investments much of the time. It was also a time when everybody writing musicals wanted to be Rodgers and Hammerstein. Unfortunately, Rodgers and Hammerstein had almost reached their peak—some would argue they had already passed it—and imitations would only move the art form forward so far. They were the second team approached to write *Annie Get Your Gun* (after Jerome Kern and Dorothy Fields), but Rodgers and Hammerstein declined; instead they produced it and offered the score to Irving Berlin, who also declined at first because he preferred revues to book musicals.

Annie Get Your Gun opened in May 1946, directed by Joshua Logan, and though it had a strong (if extremely conventional) score by Berlin that would become a classic, it proved just how backward the Broadway musical still could be and how easy it was now for a Broadway musical to make some money. Not only was the show profoundly sexist, its central plot based on the assumption that a strong woman must degrade herself and pretend to be less than she is in order to get a man, but it was also deeply racist in its portrayal and discussion of Native Americans. But the Europeans didn't care about that and the show did well there, even in France where it was retitled *Annie du Far-West*. It was also only barely connected to actual events even though the characters were based on real people. The show was flawed enough that it cannot be revived today without attempting wholesale revisions and discarding several songs. A badly botched attempt at giving the show a new book crippled the 1999 revival with Bernadette Peters.

But late-1940s Broadway was ready to make up for *Annie*. In January 1947, a new kind of musical appeared: Burton Lane, E. Y. Harburg, and Fred Saidy's *Finian's Rainbow*, a political fantasy about the intersection of American greed and racism, long before the civil rights movement became headline news. In the midst of a funny romantic comedy, the show managed to address issues like the abuse of Southern sharecroppers, racist poll taxes, bigotry in politics, atomic energy, the Tennessee Valley Authority, and the long-term economic outlook for America. It was also a dyed-in-the-wool, old-fashioned musical comedy, though helmed by a serious director from the nonmusical theatre, Bretaigne Windust, having a go at his first musical. The innocent-seeming musical comedy was the perfect form behind which to hide this fierce satire, a genre that had been pretty much off limits during the rabid patriotism of World War II.

In the show, Finian McLonergan, inspired by tales of the gold "buried" at Fort Knox, steals a leprechaun's pot of gold in Ireland and brings it to the American south—the fictional Rainbow Valley, Missitucky—where he plans to bury it so it'll grow as big as the gold reserves at Fort Knox. Along the way, his daughter Sharon falls in love with the American labor organizer Woody (named for Woody Guthrie). And the gold's promised three wishes get used up accidentally by people who happen to be standing where Finian buried it. Meanwhile, the leprechaun Og (modeled on A Midsummer Night's Dream's Puck), owner of the gold, has followed Finian to Rainbow Valley to reclaim his treasure. As a result of one of the accidental wishes, the bigoted Senator Billboard Rawkins is turned into a black man and learns what racism is like firsthand, echoing Bottom's transformation in A Midsummer Night's Dream. The Rawkins character was an obvious—at least at the time—parody of two racist Mississippi politicians, Senator Theodore Bilbo and Congressman John Rankin.

The music and lyrics were the very best kind of rowdy, playful, romantic, sensual, smart, dramatic tools, moving plot and character forward, developing textual themes, landing big laughs with consummate skill. Some of the songs became standards, including "That Old Devil Moon" and "How Are Things in Glocca Morra?" And Harburg continued the wild, inventive rhyming he'd been using in The Wizard of Oz and other musicals, most audaciously in the song "Something Sort of Grandish." Back in the twenties, this kind of comic word mangling, rhyme twisting, and adjective inventing was the stock in trade for Larry Hart, Ira Gershwin, and their ilk, but by the forties, that kind of trick lyric writing had gone out of favor. Now lyrics had to sound like the characters singing them. They had to function under the same rules as dialogue. But Harburg could get away with it here, in a fantasy with a leprechaun singing most of the crazy rhymes. And he didn't just indulge to impress; his verbal anarchy had direct dramatic purposes.

Black critic Miles Jefferson wrote in Phylon, "For the first time in this reviewer's memory intolerance in the Deep South has been subjected to light, but peppery, spoofing in a musical show, and this has been accomplished in the best of taste and with great style." Louis Kronenberger wrote in PM, "It is, in fact, a musical with a social conscience, with message in its madness." The show was definitely ahead of its time.

The show ran 725 performances, proving that satire can be commercial. Tonys were won for best choreographer (Michael Kidd) and best supporting actor (David Wayne as Og). It was revived on Broadway in 1960 and made into a (much maligned) film by Francis Ford Coppola in 1968 starring Fred Astaire as Finian, Petula Clark as Sharon, and Tommy Steele as Og.

In October 1948, just a few months after the closing of Rodgers and Hammerstein's experimental, only moderately successful *Allegro*, composer Kurt Weill and lyricist/bookwriter Alan Jay Lerner opened the most experimental musical yet on Broadway, *Love Life*, directed by nonmusical director Elia Kazan and choreographed by Michael Kidd. This surrealistic musical followed a married couple through a hundred and fifty years of American history, using the marriage and its disintegration and growing cynicism as a metaphor for the birth, growth, and decay of American culture. The show was billed as a "vaudeville" (as *Chicago* would be in 1975) and used vaudeville-style songs and acts placed outside the action, breaking the fourth wall, to comment on the action (like *Chicago* would). Despite the fact that it was created by major Broadway artists and ran an acceptable 252 performances, it never toured, was never recorded, never published, and never made available for amateur productions.

Love Life had very little linear plot or development, only interconnected vignettes tracing the never-aging couple and their two children from 1791 to 1948. As life in America becomes more complex, so too does the family begin to experience a strain on their relationships. Robert Coleman in the *Daily Mirror* called it "an exciting study of the rise, demise, and rebirth of standards." Though Coleman loved it, other critics found it depressing, cold, hard to understand, and hostile to its audience, accusations also thrown at *Company* in 1970. Brooks Atkinson wrote in the *New York Times*, "*Love Life* is cute, complex, and joyless—a general gripe masquerading as entertainment. *Love Life* is an intellectual idea about showmanship gone wrong." But German critic Friedrich Luft was in New York to review some American theatre, and he called *Love Life* "the most beautiful and most powerful evening of theatre. . . . Such a combination of music, lighting, dance, and wit could hardly be produced with such nonchalant precision at home, today or in the foreseeable future."

Far more conventional was Cole Porter's *Kiss Me, Kate*, which opened in December 1948, directed by John Wilson and choreographed by modern dancer Hanya Holm. The story of a traveling troupe of actors presenting a musical version of Shakespeare's *Taming of the Shrew*, it was based fairly explicitly on the infamous battles between married stage stars Alfred Lunt and Lynn Fontanne. The show was a standard-issue, show-within-a-show, art-imitates-life musical comedy, but it marked Cole Porter's rebirth as a theatre composer. After two major flops, *The Seven Lively Arts* (1944) and *Around the World in Eighty Days* (1946), conventional wisdom said that Cole Porter had lost his talent, that he just couldn't write like he used to. Porter proved conventional wisdom wrong and *Kiss Me, Kate* ran 1,077 performances. It opened in London in 1951 and ran 400 performances. It also ran in Frankfurt, Budapest, Vienna, and Paris. It was revived in New York in 1952, 1956, 1965, and 1999.

In 1949, Rodgers and Hammerstein, now on a relative winning streak with *Oklahoma!* and *Carousel* (and the fascinating but muddled *Allegro*), embarked on a new project very unlike their others. It was *South Pacific*, based on James

Michener's collection of short stories *Tales of the South Pacific*. As he had done with *Show Boat*, Hammerstein was faced with the daunting task of taking source material with an epic scope and carving it down to fit inside a musical. The script for a musical is much shorter than that of a play because music takes up more playing time than dialogue; a musical's bookwriter has to say everything that needs saying with fewer words. Director Joshua Logan came aboard, and because he had served in World War II, he helped Hammerstein remain true to the real story. The show eventually focused on just two of Michener's stories, "Our Hero-ine," about the nurse Nellie Forbush and the much older French planter Emile DeBecque, and "Fo' Dolla'," about the Polynesian entrepreneur Bloody Mary and the romance between her daughter Liat and the American lieutenant Joe Cable. The character of Luther Billis was taken from a third story, "A Boar's Tooth." Both main stories focused on issues of race (Emile has two biracial children by a Polynesian woman), one of Hammerstein's favorite themes. Bloody Mary and Liat were North Vietnamese, though they were called "Tonkinese" at the time since the French still occupied Vietnam. Little did Hammerstein know that Vietnam would figure so prominently in American history and American musi-cals in the 1960s.

South Pacific condemned racism in the strongest terms, despite its own (clearly unconscious) racism, the kind of racism that also surfaced in *The King and I* and *Flower Drum Song*. Certainly Hammerstein was progressive in his views on race, but by today's standards, he still had many racist preconceptions, and his "ethnic" dialogue is more than a little embarrassing today. Still, as proof of *South Pacific*'s progressive stance on race, its antiracism message was controver-sial enough that in 1951 the Georgia state senate officially condemned the show as propaganda.

South Pacific ran 1,925 performances and won eight Tony Awards, for best musical, best director, best book, best score, and for four of the actors. It also won the New York Drama Critics Circle Award, and the Pulitzer Prize for drama. It had the biggest advance sale up to that point and became the second longest running Broadway musical after *Oklahoma!* The show sold more than a million cast albums and more than two million dollars worth of sheet music. It ran 802 performances in London and toured the United States for five years. It remains one of the most revived American musicals, though it does not reach the artis-tic heights of *Oklahoma!*, *South Pacific*, or *The King and I*.

Lost in the Stars, featuring Todd Duncan, with book and lyrics by Maxwell Anderson and music by Kurt Weill, ended the decade on Broadway. A show explicitly about black-white race relations, it was set in South Africa and was only implicitly about America. Directed by Rouben Mamoulian, the show got mixed reviews but still ran a respectable 273 performances and sent out a national tour. Kurt Weill explained their intentions in an interview: "We wanted to treat the race problem as part of the human problem. The tragedy through which we are living is the tragedy of all men, white or black, rich or poor, young or old."

The show was produced by the New York City Opera in 1958 and was revived on Broadway in 1972. A film version was made in 1974.

One theatregoer, Ted Wofford, saw the national tour in St. Louis as a kid. He says, "It literally changed my life in many ways. The old American Theatre in St. Louis was segregated, and Todd Duncan took enormous heat from his own community for performing this show under those conditions—pickets and all. I was taken by his comment to the press in his defense, that he was fully aware of the problem, found it demeaning and distasteful, but felt that no one—even the most bigoted—could leave the production unchanged. The story unfolded in an almost cinematic flow of abstraction, imagination, movement, almost operatic music with a seamlessness I had never witnessed before. I watched its power take over the audience, its almost entirely black cast overwhelm the white audience with their multifaceted talents, and the quietly underplayed yet stunning performance of Todd Duncan melt the barriers so much a part of St. Louis at that time. At the end, a very white audience who had probably never looked at a black person as a *person* was shedding tears of sympathy for a black man. The message of hope and the eventual end of apartheid seemed very distant indeed. Very soon Jim Crow died in the city, and I believe that this production helped— *real social theatre*."

5

Something's Coming
The 1950s

As the 1950s got underway, the still new medium of television was changing the way people experienced musicals. Now they came right into your living room. A new series, *Musical Comedy Time*, premiered on NBC in October 1950, bringing Broadway musicals and operettas to the masses for the first time. True, Hollywood had frequently borrowed from Broadway, but the film versions of Broadway musicals were rarely faithful to the originals, and some film versions had literally nothing to do with the stage shows (*Strike Up the Band*, *Anything Goes*, and *The Band Wagon*, for instance). *Musical Comedy Time* presented these shows basically the way they had been presented on stage, though unfortunately cut down to an hour in length.

Though the series lasted only one season, ending in March 1951, it presented *Anything Goes* with Martha Raye; *Whoopee!* with Nancy Walker; *The Chocolate Soldier*; *Rio Rita*; *The Merry Widow*; *Hit the Deck* with Jack Gilford; *Babes in Toyland* with Dennis King; *Miss Liberty* with Kenny Baker, Doretta Morrow, and Gloria DeHaven; *Louisiana Purchase* with Victor Moore; *Mlle. Modiste*; *Revenge with Music* with John Raitt; *No, No, Nanette* with Jackie Gleason; and *Flying High* with Bert Lahr. The Broadway musical was an integral part of American cultural life like it would never be again after the 1950s

Back on Broadway, after moderate success with his first Broadway score for *Where's Charley?* in 1948, composer-lyricist Frank Loesser hit the jackpot with his next show, *Guys and Dolls*, opening in November 1950. The show many people today consider one of the most perfect musical comedies ever written had a book by Abe Burrows (the twelfth bookwriter the producers had hired for this project), direction by playwright-director George S. Kaufman, and athletic choreography by Michael Kidd. In so many ways, the show returned musical comedy to its roots, the rough-and-tumble, New York–centric, streetwise musicals of George M. Cohan.

But it also broke a big rule of musical comedy, choosing ironic detachment instead of emotional attachment. This wasn't entirely new; *The Cradle Will Rock* and *Pal Joey* had done it earlier. But it was still unusual, quite surprising for a show that would become the "perfect musical comedy" in the minds of many. British writer Norman Lebrecht said the show . . .

> is superficially a comic romance between two reformed gangsters and their everloving molls. Except it never was. The Damon Runyon tales on which the musical is founded are unblushing glorifications of mob rule in Prohibition Noo Yawk. Runyon's apologists claim that he identified with the little guy, the outsider. But his little guys were criminal hustlers and Runyon, a night-desk newspaper hack, worshipped the power of thugs like Arnold Rothstein and Al Capone whose whim sent men to sleep in cement waistcoats. . . . What Frank Loesser did in his music and lyrics in November 1950 was to take a long step back from the material, allowing viewers to choose their own level of involvement with the people on stage. . . . To appreciate how far ahead this was of its times you have only to set Guys and Dolls beside its immediate rivals, South Pacific and The King and I. Both of those classics demand an emotional response to the love story; without it, they fail. Loesser in Guys and Dolls throws the emotions into neutral: feel what you like, he tells audiences, it's your show as much as mine. Loesser's detachment anticipates Beckett and Pinter. It is the quintessence of modernity.

Guys and Dolls was based on three of author Damon Runyon's short stories, "The Idyll of Miss Sarah Brown," "Pick the Winner," and "Blood Pressure," although some of the characters in the show came from other Runyon stories. The central plot line focused on Sky Masterson who makes a bet he can make Salvation Army "doll" Sarah Brown fall in love with him; of course, in the process—it's musical comedy; opposites attract—Sky falls in love with her too. The secondary plot focused on Sky's pal, Nathan Detroit, Nathan's itinerant crap game, and his showgirl fiancée Miss Adelaide, who's been engaged to Nathan for fourteen years (later in his life, Runyon would actually marry a showgirl like Miss Adelaide). The continual postponement of their wedding gives the dumb but sincere Adelaide myriad comic, psychosomatic illnesses, described in one of the theatre's most perfect character songs, "Adelaide's Lament."

Guys and Dolls is often held up as a sterling example of the "integrated" musical, in which the book, music, and lyrics speak with one unified voice. In fact, Loesser first wrote his score to Joseph "Jo" Swerling's much more serious, much less effective script, and when the producers decided it didn't work, they called in Abe Burrows to write an entirely new script around the (mostly) already completed songs (paralleling the revisions of *Anything Goes*). It is a tribute to Loesser's faithfulness to his source material and to Burrows' skills that the result was the integrated musical we now bow down before. Burrows explained the show's success: "Nothing is in there that doesn't belong. There are no love ballads which are written in a different language from the dialogue. When a mug sings a love song, it's a mug type love song. The dances are strictly in character. There's a crap game ballet that looks like a crap game. A real Runyon crap game. In this show we didn't care about how a single number or scene would go. We were about the whole show and nothing went in unless it fit." And yet even with that in mind, it's still possible to see the vast variety of song forms Loesser used in his score— love songs, comedy numbers, a fugue, a hymn, a gospel number, an Irish ballad, even some recitative, and the stunningly beautiful art song, "My Time of Day."

According to some sources, producers Cy Feuer and Ernest Martin had hoped to land Ethel Merman to play Sarah Brown and Tony Martin to play Sky. When Merman was unavailable, they tried for Cyd Charisse. When Martin was unavailable, they tried to lure Frank Sinatra to Broadway. (He would later star in the film and would battle continuously with Loesser.) They didn't get any of them, ending up with Robert Alda as Sky, Isabel Bigley as Sarah, Sam Levene as Nathan, Vivian Blaine in her star-making role of Adelaide, and Stubby Kaye as Nicely-Nicely Johnson. Jerome Robbins was originally announced as chore-ographer, then replaced by Michael Kidd. *Guys and Dolls* ran 1,200 performances and won Tonys for best musical, best actor (Alda), best actress (Bigley), best director, best book, best producer, best composer and lyricist (although, strangely, *Call Me Madam* won best score), and best choreographer. The show also won the New York Drama Critics Circle Award and the Outer Critics Circle Award for best musical. It had been selected for the Pulitzer Prize for drama, but the committee ultimately decided not to award a prize in drama that year—rumor had it that the committee felt giving it to a musical two years in a row (*South Pacific* was the 1950 winner) would somehow cheapen the award.

John Chapman raved in the *Daily News*, "The big trouble with *Guys and Dolls* is that a performance of it lasts only one evening, when it ought to last about a week. I did not want to leave the theatre after the premiere last night and come back here and write a piece about the show. I wanted to hang around, on the chance that they would raise the curtain again and put on a few num-bers they'd forgotten—or, at least, start *Guys and Dolls* all over again. For here is New York's own musical comedy—as bright as a dime in a subway grating, as smart as a sidewalk pigeon, as professional as Joe DiMaggio, as enchanting as the skyline, as new as the paper you're holding. In all departments, *Guys and Dolls* is a perfect musical comedy."

Though the milieu of *Guys and Dolls* was very specific, it spoke volumes about America in 1950. Frank Loesser said about the song "Marry the Man Today" in a *New York Times* interview, "All this says is what every woman is always teaching her daughter: get the man. Marry him. Then worry about him. But you can't do anything with him until you marry him first." This is exactly the mindset that was starting to disintegrate in America, the idea that women *had* to find a husband and be a Good Wife. It was also the mindset that the Beat Generation would aggressively reject, a rejection that would find voice later in the decade in the Beat musicals *The Nervous Set* (1959) and *The Fantasticks* (1960).

Guys and Dolls went to London in 1953 where it ran 555 performances. A somewhat mangled movie version was made in 1955 that redeemed itself by preserving several of the original performances, including Vivian Blaine and Stubby Kaye. The show was revived at New York's City Center in 1955, 1965, and 1966. Laurence Olivier tried to put the show up in London with himself as Nathan, but unexpected surgery scuttled his plans. In 1976, it was revived in an all-black, re-orchestrated, funked-up version, which ran 239 performances. In 1982, it was finally produced in London to rave reviews. Then in 1992, it was revived on Broadway again and ran 1,143 performances. In 2005, the show was revived in London with film star Ewan McGregor to raves once again.

In March 1951 Rodgers and Hammerstein opened their next masterpiece, *The King and I*, a show of enormous power whose stature has only grown over the years to become perhaps even more powerful now than when it opened. Today, at the dawn of a new millennium, many of the leaders and intellectuals of mainland China are wondering how their country can continue to modernize, to compete with the Western nations, while still maintaining its cultural identity and traditions. Many wonder if it is even possible. Shanghai, for instance, is a city split between the cultural pride and traditions of China and the developments and economic pressures of the West. All of China faces difficulties in this area, as young Chinese covet designer consumer goods from the West and the yuppie lifestyle they see portrayed on American television, while the older generation worries about the decay of traditional morality and ethics. This friction between East and West has resulted in a generation and culture gap in China far wider than anything America has ever faced. But this is not a new problem in Asia. In fact, this is exactly the problem King Mongkut of Siam faced in the 1860s. How could he join the company of civilized nations, become respected and competitive among them, without losing the rich history and culture of his beloved Siam (now Thailand), without alienating his people who were not prepared to discard their simple but treasured way of life?

In the 1860s, Anna Leonowens, a widowed British schoolteacher was hired by King Mongkut to come to his country and teach his wives and children the English language and Western culture. She wrote of her (mostly fictionalized) experiences in a two-volume memoir. Later, Margaret Landon turned Anna's story into a novel called *Anna and the King of Siam*. A film version was made starring Irene Dunne as Anna and Rex Harrison as the King. British stage star Gertrude Lawrence saw the film and decided the story would make a great musical, with her as Anna. Rodgers and Hammerstein, after some initial objections, agreed to write the show, now called *The King and I*. Though Lawrence was supposed to be the lead, Yul Brynner became an immediate star playing the King when the show opened on Broadway in 1951. Though John van Druten's direction of the nonmusical scenes would not be remembered, choreographer Jerome

Robbins did his usual brilliant work, specifically in creating the sixteen-minute political ballet "The Small House of Uncle Thomas," with music not by Rodgers but by dance arranger Trude Rittmann, a piece commenting directly on the show's central issues through the use of dance and literary allusion.

Like other Rodgers and Hammerstein musicals, *The King and I* is a classic and that has become its greatest handicap. American directors and actors bring too much baggage and too much reverence to the piece, too many recollections of past productions and of the movie, of pop singers' overly (pseudo) soulful renditions of the "hit tunes." As with *Carousel*, it took a foreign director to find again (or perhaps for the first time) the substance, intelligence, and undeniable sexuality of this incredible work.

When Rodgers and Hammerstein wrote and produced the show in 1951, their writing was too far ahead of the moralistic and artistic limitations of contemporary musical theatre. Though musicals could by then tackle weighty subjects, the conventions and traditions of musical comedy, the inadequate dramatic training of musical comedy performers, and the moral climate of the country still got in the way. Actors were still *performing* songs rather than *acting* them (which wouldn't change until the early 1960s), even in serious musicals. Songs still needed choreography even when there might be nothing to dance about ("Getting to Know You," for example). Most actors and directors hadn't yet figured out that all the principles of serious drama could (and should) be applied to serious musical theatre.

Hammerstein was a passionate and very vocal critic of racism in any form (as evidenced by the song "You've Got to Be Carefully Taught" in *South Pacific*). So it was surely unintentional that Hammerstein's book and lyrics were a bit condescending toward the culture and people of Siam. The Siamese were treated as primitive, ridiculous, and ignorant throughout the show, with no acknowledgment of the racism, arrogance, and dismissal of Siamese traditions by the intrusive Westerners. Forty-five years after its debut, Australian director Christopher Renshaw came at the story from a different perspective. He had lived in Thailand for a while and genuinely understood and respected the Thai traditions and culture. He insisted that the costumes, set decorations, and other visual elements for the 1996 revival be as authentic as possible. He also began the show with a Thai prayer ceremony to establish for the audience the seriousness with which this culture would be treated. He even cut one song that seemed condescending, "Western People Funny."

Renshaw also made a significant change to the King's death scene. Instead of setting it off to the side or in back as usual (which was supposed to show how the King is no longer the center of power, having passed that on to the crown prince), Renshaw placed the King down front. Renshaw explained in several interviews when the revival opened that the Thai people believe everyone has two souls. One of those souls is the "kwan," a person's sense of self, his confidence, his self-respect. They believe that you can lose your kwan through the top of your head, which is why they all wear their hair in top knots (and why the King should *never* be played *bald!*), to keep the kwan in. When the King has finally lost his self-confidence, largely through Anna's doing, he has lost his kwan and therefore he dies. That's why Lady Thiang and the Kralahome try so hard to get Anna to stop her attacks on the King's beliefs and traditions; they worry that he will lose his kwan. His death scene is extremely significant and consistent with Thai beliefs, and Renshaw didn't think it should be minimized. In a way, the King has sacrificed himself so that his country may move forward; but also, in a way, Anna has killed him.

Despite our expanded understanding in the 1990s of Thai culture and people, and despite our twenty-twenty hindsight, we can't forget that Rodgers and Hammerstein were still taking great strides and risking commercial success by creating this amazing musical, the most subtextual love story the musical theatre had ever seen. Not a single direct word is ever spoken about the central love story (perhaps the team were hedging their bets with the secondary romantic couple Tuptim and Lun Tha), and the lead couple didn't even get a real love song, though they came close with "Shall We Dance." This is a show about the complexity of real love, not the idealized, simplified love usually found in musical comedies of the 1920s and 1930s. This was an impossible love, an adult, intellectual, and political *Romeo and Juliet*. This was not entirely new territory for Rodgers and Hammerstein, after *Carousel* and *South Pacific*. But the team generally dealt with American themes, and this was the first time one of their shows was almost entirely about another culture, something they had touched on in *South Pacific*.

It's a little sad to realize that less than a decade into their partnership, *The King and I* was Rodgers and Hammerstein's last great work. None of their later shows would ever equal the artistry, intelligence, or power of *Oklahoma!*, *Carousel*, *The King and I*, or the only slightly lesser *South Pacific*.

The original production of *The King and I* ran 1,246 performances. The stage version won five Tonys, including best musical, best actress (Lawrence) and best supporting actor (Brynner). A film version was released in March 1956, retaining ten of the show's thirteen songs, and starring Brynner and Deborah Kerr (dubbed by everybody's favorite dubber, Marni Nixon). In another example of unintentional racism, the film starred Rita Moreno, a Puerto Rican actor, as Tuptim, a Burmese slave. Perhaps the producers thought audiences wouldn't notice that a Latina actor was playing an Asian, that one ethnic "other" is pretty much like any other ethnic "other"? The film was nominated for nine Oscars, winning six, including best actor for Brynner. By the time Brynner died of lung cancer (he made the film with only one lung), he had played the role of the King on stage 4,625 times.

The King and I has been revived in New York in 1956, 1963, 1964, 1967, 1977 (with Brynner), 1985 (Brynner's farewell performance after a long tour), and 1996. The 1996 revival, directed by Renshaw and starring Donna Murphy and Lou Diamond Phillips, was a radical reexamination of this show that was intelligent, sexy, and for many people, a genuine revelation. Renshaw had directed the show in Australia with Hayley Mills, a production Mary Rodgers and others from the Rodgers and Hammerstein organization saw and asked him to bring to New York. This production garnered seven Tony nominations and won four Tonys, including best revival of a musical and best actress in a musical for Murphy.

Back in the early 1950s, some musical theatre writers were still trying to pull Broadway back into the past with shows like *Kismet*; others were aggressively trying to push it forward with shows like *The Most Happy Fella*. But Marc Blitzstein went both ways at once. After composer Kurt Weill's death in 1950, fellow composer and lyricist Blitzstein decided to write a new translation of *The Threepenny Opera*, the German political musical that had been such a huge flop on Broadway in 1933. He had already worked on a few isolated songs from the score. With some strong nudging, Weill's wife Lotte Lenya agreed to allow a new production of Blitzstein's adaptation. But Blitzstein wanted her to recreate her original role of Pirate Jenny, and at age fifty-five, she didn't feel confident she could pull it off. Eventually she agreed and became the cast's stylistic advisor, teaching them Weill's special style of speak-singing, talking about the original production, about Weill and Brecht's original intentions, and more. The new *Threepenny*, directed by Carmen Capalbo, opened at the Theatre de Lys off Broadway in March 1954 using New York's first thrust stage. 1950s Commie Hunter Senator Joseph McCarthy called *Threepenny* "a piece of anticapitalist propaganda which exalts anarchical gangsterism and prostitutes over democratic law and order." The show got mixed reviews but began selling out. But then the show was kicked out of its theatre after twelve weeks because of a prior booking. The public clamored for its return and so, a few months later, it came back to off Broadway in September 1955, where it ran 2,611 performances, becoming the first off Broadway megahit.

In March 1956, Alan Jay Lerner and Frederick Loewe's unquestioned masterpiece *My Fair Lady* opened on Broadway. In this thoroughly entertaining and at the same time potent social commentary, Lerner and Loewe (and George Bernard Shaw before them in the source play *Pygmalion*) explored and satirized the lines drawn between social classes. The idea that merely by learning to *sound* upper class Eliza Doolittle can *be* upper class—and our realization that Eliza actually has a lot more "class" than Higgins—said a lot about the standards upon which class distinctions are based. The show's title, an invocation of the children's song "London Bridge Is Falling Down," acted as a comic metaphor for the collapse of class barriers that Higgins' experiment implies.

The show also explored the emotionally explosive relationship between teacher and student. In the original Pygmalion myth, Pygmalion brings the statue of Galatea to life by loving her; in Shaw's *Pygmalion* and Lerner and Loewe's *My Fair Lady*, Higgins brings Eliza to life by *not* loving her. In other words, it is by ignoring Eliza that Higgins provokes the anger in her that pushes her to become an independent woman, capable of standing on her own two feet; and it is this new, strong, self-reliant woman with whom Higgins finally falls in love. Though Shaw's play has a decidedly nonromantic ending (Eliza leaves to marry Freddy, whom she does not love), in *My Fair Lady*, the ending is ambiguous but allows for an odd kind of romance-truce between Eliza and Higgins left hanging in the air.

My Fair Lady ran 2,717 performances, about six and a half years, becoming one of the longest running shows ever on Broadway, such an instant hit that it paid back its investors in only thirteen weeks. It won the New York Drama Critics Circle Award, and was nominated for twelve Tonys, winning them for best musical, best actor, best director, best book, best score, best producer, best conductor, best sets, and best costumes. It opened in London in 1958, running for five and a half years, then went on to Berlin, Vienna, and Budapest. The cast album stayed on the Billboard Top 40 charts for 292 weeks and in the Top 100 for 480 weeks, more than nine years. No rock album has ever equaled that.

The film version of *My Fair Lady* was released in October 1964, with original cast members Rex Harrison and Stanley Holloway, but Audrey Hepburn replaced Julie Andrews as Eliza. Andrews got her revenge by winning the best actress Oscar that year for *Mary Poppins*. Cary Grant was offered the role of Higgins but turned it down. Ironically, Harrison would be credited for inventing a kind of talk-singing in the role that would later be adopted by Richard Burton in *Camelot*, among others, a practice that had first been perfected by George M. Cohan at the beginning of the century.

The next really interesting musical had a long gestation period. Back in 1953, author Lillian Hellman and Leonard Bernstein had been discussing writing an opera about the life of Eva Peron but had decided against it. Then Hellman suggested musicalizing Voltaire's satirical masterpiece, the novel *Candide*. Making fun of the trendy philosophies of his time, Voltaire told the hilarious story of an innocent young man bouncing around the world encountering horror after horror (often on the receiving end) but still hanging on to his schoolmaster's idiotic philosophy that since there can be only one world, it must be the best of all possible worlds and, therefore, everything that happens here must be for the best. It seemed like a fun idea—corrupt politicians, earthquakes, sinking ships, the mythical El Dorado, a Grand Inquisitor, a woman with one buttock—so they set to work.

They brought on poet John LaTouche as lyricist, but by the end of 1954, they fired him. Dorothy Parker wrote one lyric for the show, then poet Richard Wilbur was hired. All but two of LaTouche's lyrics were cut, and even they were touched up by Wilbur. The original Broadway production of *Candide*, directed by the legendary Tyrone Guthrie, opened at the Martin Beck Theatre on Broadway in December 1956, with a book by Hellman and "lyrics by Richard Wilbur, additional lyrics by John LaTouche, Dorothy Parker, and Leonard Bernstein."

This wasn't the only musical at the time that approached opera. Frank Loesser's *The Most Happy Fella*, which opened just before *Candide*, also told its tale in somewhat operatic language with an opera singer in the lead. But *Candide* received mixed reviews and closed after only 73 performances, while *Most Happy Fella* ran 676 performances. Hellman's *Candide* script just wasn't funny. The lyrics were all over the map, some wonderful, some hilarious, some awkward, some dreadful. Tyrone's direction was heavy-handed and pompous. The humor of Bernstein's glorious music got lost in the mess. Still the *New York Times* liked it, calling it "a brilliant musical satire." John Chapman in the *Daily News* called it "an evening of uncommon quality" and even "a work of genius." Musical comedy writer Michael Stewart was called in to lighten up Hellman's script for the London production, but it didn't work. It ran in London for only sixty performances.

But like its dimwitted hero, *Candide* the musical soldiered on, thanks in large part to the popularity of its cast album. It would be back in 1973 in a completely new form. And meanwhile, Bernstein was already working on *West Side Story*.

Certainly the oddest musical of the 1950s must be *shinbone alley*, a jazz musical with a book by Joe Darion and (later on) Mel Brooks, lyrics by Joe Darion, and music by George Kleinsinger. Based on the "archy" poems by onetime newspaper man Don Marquis, this show was unique for two reasons. First, it was written as a serious, adult jazz opera/musical. Second, its heroes were the poet cockroach Archy and his pal, the randy alley cat Mehitabel. Not surprisingly, the show ran only forty-nine performances. But it was trying to expand Broadway's musical vocabulary, trying to make way for the jazz musicals to come, like *The Nervous Set*, *The Fantasticks*, *I Love My Wife*, and *City of Angels*. It would take a long time before Broadway would be comfortable with modern jazz.

Don Marquis had been writing in the voice of Archy since 1916, the fictional cockroach that used Marquis' newsroom typewriter at night to write his own free verse poems. Since Archy couldn't possibly use the shift key, everything was written in lowercase. And there was virtually no punctuation; it was just too hard. According to DonMarquis.com, "Archy's appearance came at a time of great public interest in the supernatural: Sherlock Holmes creator Arthur Conan Doyle had recently claimed to see fairies, and spiritualists held sway at elaborate séances. Marquis used Archy to poke fun at this latest fad, and also at free verse poetry, which then was spreading like influenza through New York's Greenwich Village."

Darion and Kleinsinger had first presented their musical at New York's Town Hall in December 1954 with tenor Jonathan Anderson as Archy and soprano Mignon Dunn as Mehitabel. At about the same time they produced a studio album called *archy and mehitabel: a back-alley opera* that featured the voices of Carol Channing as Mehitabel and Eddie Bracken as Archy. *Theatre Arts* magazine wrote, "Bracken is every inch a cockroach, and Miss Channing is perfection as the female feline who chose Shinbone Alley over the comforts of domestication."

Two years later the authors returned to their show and teamed up with the young, not yet famous Mel Brooks to help with the show's script. Now called *shinbone alley* (usually in all lowercase), it opened on Broadway in April 1957 with Bracken as Archy and Eartha Kitt as Mehitabel. John Chapman of the *Daily News* wrote, "It brightens the musical comedy scene like a lightning bug. It is original, it is witty, and it bubbles over with the happiest score in town. *Shinbone Alley* is as un-stereotyped as a show can get." Walter Kerr of the *Herald-Tribune* didn't think it worked, but "the possible form of a possible show hovers suggestively, and fleetingly, over the stage." Perhaps *shinbone alley* belonged in a smaller, off Broadway theatre in order to succeed. It would not be the last time that greed or simple misjudgment would open a show in the wrong arena and bring about its downfall.

Despite its failure on Broadway, *shinbone alley* was produced for television with Tammy Grimes as Mehitabel. In 1971, an animated film version of the show was made with Carol Channing and Eddie Bracken in the lead roles again, alongside John Carradine as an aging theatre cat (a precursor to Gus from *Cats?*), and Alan Reed Sr. (Fred Flintstone) as Mehitabel's tomcat boyfriend. *New York Times* film reviewer Vincent Canby panned the film, but he understood Mehitabel—"a *toujours gai* old dame with the soul of Cleopatra, the airs of Emma Bovary, the artistic longings of Isadora Duncan, the hangovers of Dorothy Parker's Big Blonde, and the sexual resolve of *Trash*'s Holly Woodlawn."

And then everything changed again. Opening on Broadway September 26, 1957, *West Side Story* was the next Great American Musical, and one of the American theatre's few great tragedies, appearing just when American cinema and theatre were discovering social-problem stories, just when America was beginning to reengage with its greatest evils. *West Side Story* told a story about hatred and prejudice in which a happy ending is not possible, in which love cannot triumph over all. The story went miles beyond its source material, Shakespeare's *Romeo and Juliet*. When director-choreographer Jerome Robbins, composer Leonard Bernstein, and bookwriter Arthur Laurents first discussed this story (lyricist Stephen Sondheim wouldn't be joining them until later), it focused on tensions between Catholics and Jews and it was called *East Side Story*. That this group of rich, white, Jewish, gay men eventually changed the focus to Anglo-Americans and Puerto Rican Americans, that the team recognized the profound racial prejudice in America (and especially New York) against Latinos may excuse the awkwardness and minimal, unintentional racism in their final product.

That racism is clear in hindsight, particularly in the stage lyrics for "America" (initially, Bernstein and Sondheim were *co*-writing the lyrics but Bernstein eventually relinquished his lyric credit), which were considerably softened for the film, and in the collective characters of the two gangs, the "cool," controlled

Jets and the "hot-blooded," stomping, yelling Sharks. Everybody knows Latinos dance and stomp and yell and snap their fingers, right?—well, on Broadway in 1957 they did. Sondheim made the mistake of having his Puerto Rican characters call the United States "America." But Puerto Ricans considered themselves—and Brazilians and Mexicans and Chileans—*all* inhabitants of the Americas. They called New York's homeland "the United States." Another amusing contradiction surfaced in 1985, when Leonard Bernstein assembled a group of opera singers to record a "definitive" *West Side Story* cast album. He hired Spaniard José Carreras to sing the role of Tony, and everybody went crazy because they thought Carreras' Spanish accent ruined the portrayal of the Anglo-American Tony. Yet nobody had complained in 1957 when Anglo-American Carol Lawrence played the Puerto Rican Maria with a fake accent.

In 1999, Amherst Regional High School in Massachusetts canceled a production of *West Side Story*, branding the show as racist and responding to complaints by Latino students and parents. Rallies and petitions followed, and the American Civil Liberties Union got involved. Ultimately, the school replaced *West Side Story* with *Crazy for You*—exchanging unintentional racism for intentional sexism and misogyny.

Despite all this, one could argue that *West Side Story* was a fable, not a documentary, and in 1957 it was still a huge leap forward from the embarrassing Latin musicals MGM had turned out in the 1930s and 40s. Latin music had been represented on Broadway even before then, with the token "exotic" number in shows like *Anything Goes, Panama Hattie*, and *Jubilee*. But in the years since then, Latinos were rarely represented on Broadway or on film, and virtually never represented respectfully, but instead burdened with absurd accents and dressed in ridiculous "ethnic" costumes no one would dare wear on the streets of any Latin country. The press loved to report on Carmen Miranda's mispronunciations, implying that foreigners—especially nonwhites—were somehow primitive and ignorant. Even in *West Side Story*, was Anita really all that different from the cartoon character Chiquita Banana? And wasn't Bernardo everything "regular" Americans already feared?

But to its credit, strictly as a work of art and ignoring its flaws as a social document, *West Side Story* is certainly a perfect blend of the many disciplines that make musical theatre; more than most musicals, the book, music, lyrics, and staging come together as a perfectly unified whole, speaking with one voice. Musical theatre is by its nature a collaborative art form but rarely do the many parts make such a consistently crafted statement. Driven by the vision of the often tyrannical Jerome Robbins, the greatest talents on Broadway created a musical that is specific yet universal (as Robbins would do again with *Fiddler on the Roof*), a show as current as today's headlines yet also timeless. It is a Broadway fable whose final curtain brings not hope for tomorrow but inconsolable grief over today; what little hope the final moments may imply, we still know that hatred does not die. In a country where hate crimes multiply exponentially each year and gang warfare has turned our urban streets into war zones, *West Side Story* is still heartbreaking and also deeply cathartic.

There's an argument to be made that *West Side Story* is actually a better piece of drama than *Romeo and Juliet*. Yes, *Romeo and Juliet* is a classic, but could it be that Stephen Sondheim's truthful, aching, emotional poetry may equal or even surpass Shakespeare's, particularly when Sondheim's words meet Leonard Bernstein's jagged, sensual, evocative, emotional music? And to be honest, *Romeo and Juliet* has some pretty big plot holes that bookwriter Arthur Laurents fixed in *West Side Story*. In the musical, the all important message about the rendezvous doesn't reach Tony in Act II because of racial hatred—the central theme of the story—rather than the silly accident in Shakespeare's play. And the fact that Tony dies at the end of *West Side Story* but Maria does *not* is far more tragic than Shakespeare's ending. Maria must now live the rest of her life without her great love *and* her big brother, knowing that racial hatred killed them both. Plotwise, *West Side Story* is simply more dramatic, more romantic, more tragic, more suspenseful, more resonant, and more emotional.

West Side Story was a big shock to the Broadway audiences of 1957, with its intricately integrated dance (co-choreographed by Peter Gennaro), its dissonant, driving, jazz-inspired score, its gritty, simple sets, its assault on the well-protected sensibilities of theatregoers. It was not a major hit. Lyricist Stephen Sondheim wasn't even mentioned in the generally positive *New York Times* review, though critic Brooks Atkinson did see the innovation and brilliance of the show. The creators were threatened with a picket by Latino groups over the song, "America," but the picket line never materialized.

The critics guardedly applauded the show, though audiences favored the concurrently running *The Music Man*, which swept the Tony Awards that year. Produced by fledgling producer and soon-to-be-famous director Harold Prince, *West Side Story* ran 732 performances, and was nominated for five Tonys, including best musical, but won only for choreography. The show then went on tour and returned to Broadway again in 1960. It opened in London in 1958 and ran 1,039 performances, followed by healthy runs in Paris, Vienna, and Budapest. The film version opened in 1961 and won ten Oscars, including best picture. The film's soundtrack album stayed in the number-one slot on the Billboard Top 40 album charts for an astounding fifty-four weeks.

It wasn't until the release of the film version that *West Side Story* finally captured the hearts of the public, along with the familiarity created by subsequent New York revivals in 1964, 1965, and 1980, which helped enhance the show's reputation with audiences, who were now presumably better equipped to deal with its unconventionality and its attack on serious social problems. Still, the filmmakers continued to play to America's prejudices, insisting that all the Sharks—including Puerto Rican actor Rita Moreno—wear dark brown face and body makeup that today looks almost as artificial and embarrassing as blackface. When Josie de Guzmán, a Puerto Rican actor, played Maria in the 1980 revival she also was deemed not Latin enough and was forced to wear dark makeup and hair coloring.

There had been serious musicals before—*Show Boat, Carousel, South Pacific,* and many others—but few with the in-your-face anguish of *West Side Story.* Here was a musical with the unheard of message that love not only *will not* triumph over all, it *cannot.* This was a show with more violence and death than any other musical before or since. The Act I curtain fell on two dead bodies, both of them leading characters. The audience went out into the lobby for intermission knowing that there could not be a happy ending.

There were twelve major dance sequences in the show, providing most of the exposition: Tony and Maria's meeting, the deaths of Riff and Bernardo, Anita's foiled attempt to deliver the message to Tony, and other important moments. The show had one of the shortest books ever written for a musical, leaving much of the plot and characterization to the songs and dance. But this was not an act of egotism on the part of director-choreographer Robbins; this story demanded it. These characters were inarticulate kids. They could not express their love, their anger, their fears through words; but all that and more could be expressed through dance.

The Music Man, which opened on Broadway in December 1957, was *West Side Story*'s polar opposite in many ways. It is one of the greatest of all American musicals, although it is not the sweet slice-of-life, all-American musical we think it is. It is the story of a con man in 1912 Iowa who seduces an innocent young woman merely to keep her from mucking up his plan to swindle the honest, hardworking people of a small town, including the young woman's troubled little brother, who's mourning the premature death of his father. Who could call that old-fashioned musical comedy with a straight face?

Along the way, the show also takes gleeful potshots at most of what Americans hold dear—small town generosity, family values, representative government, education, the Fourth of July, Caucasian Americans' view of Native American culture, classical Western culture, and the great (and often misplaced) hope of so many parents that their child might have the talent to play a musical instrument.

The show has an unusually profound sense of unity among its elements because the book, music, and lyrics were all written by one man, Meredith Willson, who was himself born in Iowa, in 1902. He studied at the Julliard School of Music and played for a while with the John Philip Sousa Band and the New York Philharmonic Orchestra. He was the music director for several radio shows in the 1930s, 40s, and 50s, and wrote the popular hit song "May the Good Lord Bless and Keep You." After *The Music Man,* Willson went on to write three other musicals, *The Unsinkable Molly Brown* in 1960, a moderate hit that ran a little over a year; *Here's Love* in 1963, based on *Miracle on 34th Street,* a critical flop that ran eight months and lost money; and *1491,* which closed out of town in 1969.

The script and score of *The Music Man* were savagely funny, occasionally touching, filled with wonderfully eccentric characters, and also expertly constructed. The leading man is a genuine scoundrel, yet we like him and we root for him to win the leading lady, even though he only pursues her to ensure that his con is successful. Part of that misplaced loyalty on our part may be due to the uncanny charm and humor of Robert Preston, who originated the role of Harold Hill on Broadway and on film, and whose spirit still hovers about any production. The score is full of memorable songs, not a single one of which is extraneous. Every song adds to characterization (of the people or the town) or furthers the plot. Music is used in this show not just as a dramatic language (as in most musicals), but also as conscious plot devices—the marching band, the harmonizing board members, Marian's piano lessons, and the rhythm of a great salesman's pitch—which is why the show's title is so clever in its simplicity. Music is an integral part of our country's everyday life, and Harold Hill, the "Music Man," uses that fact to his advantage in executing his con. As with *The Sound of Music*, music itself becomes a character. And the device of building Harold's signature tune ("76 Trombones") and Marion's signature tune "(Goodnight My Someone")" on the same melody gave their eventual union a sense of inevitability that audiences probably didn't even consciously register, but still felt emotionally.

Directed by Morton Da Costa and choreographed by Onna White, *The Music Man* swept the Tony Awards that year, and ran 1,375 performances, almost twice as long as *West Side Story*. It also won the New York Drama Critics Circle Award for best musical. It went on to run 395 performances in London. The 1962 film version starred Robert Preston and Shirley Jones.

The plot of *The Music Man* has also been adapted into two other stories for the screen: the Steve Martin film *Leap of Faith*, which transforms Harold Hill into a faith-healing con man, still romancing a young woman with a younger brother with a disability; and even more faithfully, *School of Rock* starring Jack Black in the Harold Hill role, complete with an uptight virgin as an obstacle (combined here with the Mayor Shinn character), a bunch of listless kids, an extended con by a wannabe musician, outraged parents, a chase, and ultimately a magical transformation—through the healing power of music—that brings joy to the community. This is a real American myth, one of which George M. Cohan would've been quite proud.

Rodgers and Hammerstein had struck gold with *Oklahoma!* in 1943, *Carousel* in 1945, *South Pacific* in 1949, and *The King and I* in 1951. But they had also had their flops and near-misses, *Allegro* in 1947, *Me and Juliet* in 1953, and *Pipe Dream* in 1955. By the time 1958 rolled around, Rodgers and Hammerstein had pretty much lost their brilliance. The score for *Flower Drum Song* was mostly just Rodgers and Hammerstein rehash—yet another Clash of Cultures story—nothing new, nothing surprising, another unintentionally racist plot, poorly integrated songs, and on top of it all, Rodgers' music did a lousy job of imitating Asian music. The lyrics were cute to an extreme, and Hammerstein's script just did not understand Asian American culture in general or these characters specifically.

The story, based on the novel by Chin Y. Lee, focused on the clash between traditional Chinese elders and their Americanized children growing up in San Francisco. There was a mail order bride, two mismatched romances, and a standard-issue happy ending that audiences could see coming a mile away. The novel had been about Wang Chi Yang, an older Chinese immigrant who refused to assimilate his Chinese culture into American culture and whose refusal distanced him from his family, in particular, from his son. But the musical chose to focus almost entirely on two romances, turning a provocative, interesting story into just another old-fashioned Broadway musical. To ensure some razzle-dazzle—and unintentionally overwhelm the real story—they created Sammy Fong, a decadent nightclub owner, a character not found in the novel. The central themes remained but they were covered up by *schtick*.

As with most of the black musicals, this "Asian" show was created entirely by Caucasians—Rodgers and Hammerstein, co-writer Herbert Fields, director Gene Kelly, and choreographer Carol Haney. *Flower Drum Song* was important for bringing an Asian story to Broadway and using Asians in the cast (though only a few were actually Chinese), but its creators did cast the African American Juanita Hall as the Asian aunt (just as she had played Vietnamese in *South Pacific*), not for reasons of "nontraditional casting" but because at the time, everybody who was nonwhite still seemed pretty much the same to white audiences. And most embarrassing of all was the decision to cast the very Caucasian Larry Blyden (replacing the very Caucasian Larry Storch) as one of the central Asian characters, Sammy Fong.

Today, we might be outraged at casting like this, but we also have to remember that in 1958, there were very few professional Asian actors, and even fewer that could act, sing, *and* dance. There were no opportunities for Asians in mainstream theatre, so why would they train for it? This would still be a problem in the mid-1970s when Hal Prince and Stephen Sondheim were casting *Pacific Overtures*.

Hammerstein was very ill during the creation process of *Flower Drum Song*, due to advancing cancer, and it's difficult to know how much of the script he wrote. Much of it may have been written by fellow bookwriter Joseph Fields. Hammerstein would not write the script for their next show, *The Sound of Music*, because of his health, and it would turn out to be one of their weakest shows. Still, *Flower Drum Song* ran 600 performances on Broadway, a national tour was sent out, and in 1961, a film version was made. In the *New Yorker*, Kenneth Tynan described the original production as "a stale Broadway confection wrapped up in spurious Chinese trimmings."

Much about the original was offensive to Asian Americans. A production in San Francisco in the 1980s was picketed by Asian Americans. Playwright David Henry Hwang said, "There was great interest at the time in portraying the social ills of Chinatown, instead of doing what one Asian scholar called *State Fair* in yellow face. The show was perceived as this very cheesy look at what was ostensibly an Asian American community, when that community was trying to rid itself of its false image. So it was a logical thing for us to react against."

In 2002, *Flower Drum Song* became the first Rodgers and Hammerstein show to undergo a fully sanctioned, complete rewrite. Hwang took the original score and wrote an entirely new script around the songs, retaining the main themes of cultural assimilation and generation gaps but changing virtually everything else. *American Theatre* said the show "went much farther than nip-and-tuck revisionism. It was a sincere attempt at an intricate operation: a major makeover that aimed to honor the spirit of the original work, while completely rethinking it." Hwang said in an interview, "From the beginning there was always this notion of representing the clash of cultures theatrically by juxtaposing a very traditional dramatic form, like Chinese opera, with this very American genre of musical comedy. It seemed to me that the collision between the two could symbolize some of the central issues and disputes in the piece." But Hwang had never written a musical before, so director Robert Longbottom came on board to help adapt the piece. Veteran music arranger David Chase wrote new arrangements of many of the songs, giving them a more legitimately Asian sound and also giving some of them a jazzier edge. They also added two songs, "My Best Love," cut from the original, and "The Next Time It Happens," from *Pipe Dream.*

The new *Flower Drum Song* opened at the Mark Taper Forum in Los Angeles, then moved to Broadway for a brief run. Ben Brantley wrote in the *New York Times* of the central character of Mei-Li, "Never mind that in shedding her old passivity and stock picturesqueness she has also given up all evidence of a personality to call her own. The same can be said of most of what surrounds her onstage." He went on, "Certainly you can feel the honorable intentions behind the creative team's effort to resuscitate a work regarded as terminally out of date. But equally evident is the strain in transforming cute and cozy ethnic types from the Broadway production of 1958 into a set of positive Asian role models that might be introduced into a public school presentation in 2002."

By the 1950s, the horrors of World War II visited upon the British people had greatly changed British entertainment, much of it far darker now than it had been before the war. The same thing would happen in America, but not until the 1960s when Vietnam took its toll on American optimism. This delay was obvious nowhere more than in the musical theatre. The British would turn musical theatre dark and cynical with shows like *Expresso Bongo* (1958), *Fings Ain't Wot They Used T'Be* (1959), *Oliver!* (1960), *Oh, What a Lovely War!* (1963), and *Marat/Sade* (1964). It wouldn't be until *Cabaret* (1966), *Viet Rock* (1966), and *Hair* (1967) that America would find its way to a wholly new kind of ultradark, adult musical theatre.

At the beginning of all this, in March 1958, the new musical *Expresso Bongo* opened at the Theatre Royal in London, with a book by Wolf Mankowitz and

Julian More, based on a story by Mankowitz, with lyrics by More, pop songwriter Monty Norman, and David Heneker, and music by Heneker and Norman. (The same team would go on to adapt the French musical *Irma La Douce* for the English stage.) The show's authors knew both London's East End and SoHo intimately, and that knowledge gave their show a palpable sense of authenticity. In many ways a precursor to *Bye Bye Birdie* (which some considered to be a cheap kind of *Expresso Bongo* Lite), and also the expressionistic film *Absolute Beginners*, *Expresso Bongo* was a ruthless, dark-hued satire of the world of British pop music. Just as *Bye Bye Birdie* would later be based loosely on Elvis Presley and Conway Twitty, and *Dreamgirls* would be more directly based on the Supremes, so too *Expresso Bongo* was loosely based on the ascension to stardom of pop and stage star Tommy Steele. The film version of the show even used the real club where Steele had been discovered.

The story of *Expresso Bongo* focused on a sleazy agent named Johnnie who discovers the musician Herbert Rudge playing bongo drums in a SoHo expresso coffee bar (the hot new trend in London) and signs him to a management contract. Renamed "Bongo" Herbert and fitted out with a loud, rhythmic pop song called "Expresso Party," the boy quickly becomes a pop sensation. The first act charts the new star's climb to the top; in the second act Bongo abandons Johnnie, leaving him right where he started. But as the show ends, Johnnie has already found a new future star to nurture and exploit.

The show transferred to the Saville Theatre in London's West End a month after opening and ran 316 performances. Critic Milton Shulman called the show "a raucous, rhythmic paean of disgust aimed at the shoddy side of the entertainment business. In its misanthropic tour of the gutters of the West End, it washed up an unsavory flotsam of sharp agents, talentless artists, love-starved women, greedy managers, shady café proprietors, and dim debutantes. If they had a redeeming virtue among them, it would be stolen off their backs." He also said "As a much needed antidote to the slushy wholesomeness of the *Salad Days* ilk of musical, I hail the sardonic maturity of *Expresso Bongo*. [It] ought to become the first successful adult British musical since the end of the war."

A film version was made in 1959, with Cliff Richard as Bongo, but after its initial release some of the songs were cut. Britain's *Monthly Film Bulletin* wrote, "The recent history of British musicals is so disheartening that it would be easy to overestimate any film which breaks out of the rut of wishy-washy gentility. Certainly there is nothing genteel about *Expresso Bongo*. It is loud, brash, and vulgar. Its vitality is its most endearing quality, but even this cannot hide a split in the film's personality. In broadening the humour of his original play and watering down some of its more savage satire, presumably in the hope of appealing to a mass audience, Wolf Mankowitz has fallen between two stools. The satire is still sharp enough to alienate a 'pop' audience, but the sentiment will blunt its edge for the sophisticated."

Most important, *Expresso Bongo* beat *Bye Bye Birdie* to the punch by bringing rock and roll to the musical stage first. And in truth, *Birdie*'s rock wasn't the real thing. *Bongo*'s was.

Another cultural phenomenon lay at the heart of the next noteworthy musical of the 1950s. *The Nervous Set* was a jazz musical describing the world of the Beats, a generation of young artists in post–World War II, pre-Vietnam America, swimming in disillusioned angst and apathy. It was funny, biting, outrageous, despairing, and brilliantly witty. But more than that, it was truthful, a serious social document. It was a loving evocation of the Beat writers, with all their warts and contradictions, all their nihilism and their earth-shattering realignment of modern literature and poetry.

The Nervous Set first opened in St. Louis in March 1959, in a club called the Crystal Palace, in the heart of the Gaslight Square entertainment district, the proving grounds for yet-to-be-stars like Woody Allen, Lenny Bruce, Barbra Streisand, Phyllis Diller, Mike Nichols and Elaine May, the Smothers Brothers, and others. Strangely enough, for a few years in the late fifties and early sixties, Gaslight Square was an international mecca for Beat writers, up-and-coming comedians, and jazz musicians. Artists from around the world descended on St. Louis to meet and learn from each other, and at the center of the storm were Jay and Fran Landesman, owners of the Crystal Palace, generally acknowledged stars of Gaslight Square, and, some claim, founders of the Beat culture.

Jay Landesman had written a novel—never published—called *The Nervous Set*, loosely based on his own life in New York in the early 1950s, his friendship with writers Jack Kerouac and Allen Ginsberg, and his relationship with his wife Fran. Later, when it was suggested that it would make a good musical, Jay and director Theodore Flicker wrote the script, Fran wrote lyrics, and the house music director at the Crystal Palace, Tommy Wolf, wrote the music, suffused through with the heartbeat of real 1950s jazz.

In the spring of 1959, producer Robert Lantz saw the show in St. Louis and decided to bring it to Broadway. In a moment of supreme miscalculation, Lantz decided to run the show in St. Louis until May 2, then open it on Broadway on May 12, with major revisions and only one week to transfer and re-stage the show. This meant no time for advance sales, no time to sell it to theatre parties, no time to create word of mouth or court the New York press. Lantz apparently believed the show would only be topical for a very short time, not recognizing the Beat culture's growing popularity and mainstreaming. Lantz also wanted to change the show's title to *Like Tomorrow*. Maybe the show was just too weird for Broadway, with its smartly cynical, literary, abrasively intellectual script, its existential angst, its four-piece jazz combo onstage, its lack of choreography, and its general lack of interest in any of the conventions of the Broadway musical. Maybe Lantz's changes killed it. Whichever, it was a big flop.

Lantz had demanded songs and scenes cut, the show's structure made more conventional, the very sad, very adult ending changed, and more. He told the

Landesmans that Broadway wasn't ready for a musical that ended with a suicide. Of course, this was two years after *West Side Story*, which ended Act I with two deaths and ended Act II with the hero's death. And it was more than a decade after *Carousel* had killed its hero in the middle of Act II. In fact, Lantz didn't decide how he wanted the show to end until three days before opening. At each of the previews, the show had a different ending. Lantz had stripped this exciting, new, experimental musical of everything that made it special. Perhaps had it opened ten years later—even in its emasculated state—it would have run longer. But in 1959, it could only eke out twenty-three performances, essentially robbing it of a further life in regional and community theatres. Today it may not seem as radical at it once did, but imagine a show like this opening in a season with *Once Upon a Mattress*, *Destry Rides Again*, *Gypsy*, *Fiorello!*, and *The Sound of Music*. At the time, Jay Landesman said, "Some [of the audience] hated the subject, hated beatniks, and it colored their reaction. Some who liked the idea wanted us to go into a serious, psycho-socioeconomic analysis of the beatnik attitude. Our idea was simply a fun show. But I don't think the average New York paying audience is as sophisticated as the ones we had at the Crystal Palace. They didn't seem to get half the satire."

A Parisian producer invited the Landesmans to bring *The Nervous Set* on a tour of Iron Curtain countries, but the tour never happened. Richard Rodgers called the Landesmans to congratulate them after seeing the show. Jay later wrote, "Rodgers was extremely generous and complimentary to Fran and Tommy Wolf, the composer. He told them this show would be remembered for years for its talent, and if it didn't do anything else, it had brought a talented team of songwriters to Broadway. He insisted on composer Leonard Bernstein coming to see it." Bernstein hated it.

Tommy Wolf's music was genuine, full-flavored 50s club jazz, a sound rarely heard on Broadway. But the musical's big showstopper, the torchy "Spring Can Really Hang You Up the Most" had already been recorded by jazz artists and couldn't be included in the Broadway production because Lantz refused to pay the song's publisher to use it. Another song from the score, "The Ballad of the Sad Young Men" had some life outside the show as well, but "Spring" became a jazz standard and is still performed today.

The Nervous Set told a distinctly uneasy tale. Brad, the editor of a literary magazine called *Nerves* (based on Landesman's real magazine *Neurotica*), meets a rich girl named Jan. Though they come from different worlds, they marry and have a very rough time making it work. Meanwhile, an overbearing bore named Yogi comes into Brad's life and takes over *Nerves*, nearly running it into the ground—and destroying Brad and Jan's marriage—before Brad gives him the boot. In the novel and in the early versions of the show, the story ended with Jan attempting suicide while Brad is out at a party. Along the way, Brad's Beat buddies Bummy and Danny also have their own adventures in their own interlocking orbits. Bummy was based on Jay's friend, the novelist Jack Kerouac, who would eventually become the poster boy for the Beats. In the show, Bummy finds unexpected commercial success for one of his novels, mirroring the real-world phenomenon of Kerouac's *On the Road*. Danny was based on Ginsberg.

Critical reception was decidedly mixed. Brooks Atkinson in the *New York Times* wrote, "In both words and music it has a shrewd slant on contemporary attitudes. It is a cartoon on the beatniks that comes to us from St. Louis, where it happily shook the chandeliers in the Crystal Palace until a fortnight ago. Nothing on the local music stages this season has been so acid and adult as the wry portrait of Greenwich Village beatniks it offers when the show begins." He went on, "No doubt the well-being of the nation requires a wholesome resolution to the story. But the ending cannot hold a candle to the impudence of the first act, written in the wild argot of the civilized beatnik and tightened by the ominous jazz rhythms of the music. In their opening numbers, the composer and the lyricist write with tongue in cheek. 'The Stars Have Blown My Way' is an intimidated romance. 'Fun Life' is a happy elegy. 'Rejection' is an exuberant hymn to mental sickness. 'Night People' is an ode to dissipation. 'New York' is the most caustic comment on our loose civilization since *On the Town*."

The *New York Daily News* called the show "the most brilliant, sophisticated, witty and completely novel production of the past decade." But Frank Ashton in the *World-Telegram & Sun* called it "a weird experience. Something exclusively for the beat, bop, and beret brigade." Fran Landesman and Tommy Wolf would go on to write one more show, *A Walk on the Wild Side*, set in a whorehouse, but even the audiences at the Crystal Palace weren't ready for that and it closed quickly. It's interesting to imagine what else they might have written if Broadway had been ready for *The Nervous Set* and had welcomed it more warmly. The show has only been produced twice since then, in 1985 and in 2004, both times in St. Louis.

In 1959, some of the creative gang from *West Side Story* came back together to create another masterpiece of the musical theatre (though a more conventional show), the "musical fable" *Gypsy*, about the world-famous stripper Gypsy Rose Lee and her monstrous mother, which opened on Broadway in May 1959 starring Ethel Merman as the mother, Rose. *Gypsy*'s lyricist Stephen Sondheim once paid bookwriter Arthur Laurents a high compliment by telling him *Gypsy*'s book was so strong it could survive without the score—something most musicals' books could not do. Laurents disagreed. He believed that the characters, particularly Rose, were so big that they could never live in a nonmusical play. Laurents is probably right. Rose is truly Bigger Than Life and it is her grotesque yet captivating personality that drives the show. This was certainly the most sophisticated and electric music ever written by composer Jule Styne (who had composed the far lesser *Funny Girl* score), and with Sondheim's hilarious, subtextually loaded lyrics and a first-rate book, *Gypsy* elevated the musical comedy antihero to a new level. Rose is a monster of mythic proportions who exploits and torments everyone around her, yet we actually *like* her.

In writing about the 2003 revival with Bernadette Peters, Frank Rich wrote in the *New York Times*, "*Gypsy* has less to do with *My Fair Lady* and *The Music Man* than it does with the mid-20th century canon that includes not only Eugene O'Neill's dark autobiographical exorcism but *The Glass Menagerie* and *Death of a Salesman*. Together they form a coherent repertory of blood-letting plays about paired siblings, problematic mothers and vanishing (or vanished) fathers. Fall in love with them when you are young, and they can become lifelines that help tether a childhood. But once you've grown up, they will come back and rope you in again, this time tightening the noose."

The original production ran 702 performances and received eight Tony nominations but lost them all to the terminally bland, sticky-sweet *The Sound of Music*. The *Gypsy* script and score weren't even nominated. Walter Kerr wrote in the *Herald-Tribune*, "I'm not sure whether *Gypsy* is new-fashioned, or old-fashioned, or integrated or non-integrated. The only thing I'm sure of is that it's the best damn musical I've seen in years." Some commentators have blamed Merman for *Gypsy*'s tepid success, claiming she rarely performed the show at full energy once the critics had seen it. The show then opened in London in May 1973 with Angela Lansbury (Laurents' favorite Rose) and that production returned to Broadway in 1974, where it ran another 120 performances, winning a Tony for Lansbury. It was revived again in 1989 with Tyne Daly in the lead, and again in 2003 with Bernadette Peters.

Back in early 1959, London's premier alternative theatre director Joan Littlewood and her touring People's Theatre Workshop took up residence at the Theatre Royal, Stratford East. Littlewood was looking for her next show and she read a script that had been sent to her, Frank Norman's *Fings Ain't Wot They Used T'Be*, a raucous forty-eight-page play about thieves, whores, corrupt policemen, gays, and other denizens of SoHo, a play written by a man who had never before seen a live stage performance. Like John O'Hara with *Pal Joey*, Norman didn't have to break rules, because he had no idea what the rules were.

The plot centered on a formerly big-league, now semi-retired criminal, Fred Cochran. Lil Smith, Cochran's live-in girlfriend, longs for respectability and keeps a marriage license on hand just in case (with a nod, conscious or un-, to *Guys and Dolls*). The club Fred owns is home to an odd, created family, Paddy the gambler, Tosher the ponce (pimp) and his girls Betty and Rosey, Redhot, and others. When Fred wins big on the horses it seems the gang may be back in business. Fred redecorates his place, and at the reopening the Horrible Percey Fortesque comes to gamble and a rival leader, Meatface, is beaten in a razor fight. At the end, Lil and Fred give up crime to go straight and get married. They hand the club over to the constable on the beat who has for a long time wanted to go crooked.

The script was full of delicious, truthful portrayals of life in SoHo among the disenfranchised. It would be the first time real Cockney would be spoken on stage. (No, *My Fair Lady* did not traffic in *real* Cockney.) At its heart, *Fings* was a British music hall lament for the loss of community in modern times. Little-wood liked it and set to work on it with her improvisation-oriented company. The story goes that as they began, she said to her actors, "This script's no good. We'll make it up." Frank Norman later admitted that the final published script owed much to the improvisation that took place during rehearsals by the Theatre Workshop.

But Littlewood decided it needed music. So Lionel Bart came on board, still a couple years before writing his big hit *Oliver!* but already semi-famous for writing some hit songs. Like Norman and Joe Orton, Bart had no interest in convention or rules. He wrote *his* way. Bart had come from fiercely humble beginnings himself and knew these characters. Bart wrote a score far superior to his later score for *Oliver!*, perhaps more inspired by this material—more aggressive, more exciting, more emotionally honest. Full of rowdy group numbers, bitingly satiric comedy numbers, an aching ballad or two, even a proto-rock-and-roll number, this was an outstanding, forward-looking, progressive theatre score, and an outstanding show as well, at a time when the British musical had been largely in hibernation. Some of the songs were literally improvised on the spot, in the middle of rehearsals, by a suddenly inspired Bart. Littlewood and Bart were changing how musical theatre was made. Andrew Lloyd Webber would declare in 1999 that Bart was the father of the modern British musical.

The newly reconstituted musical version of *Fings* opened in February 1959 for a six-week run. It did so well, they brought it back in April for two more weeks. By now pop singer Max Bygraves had discovered the title song, cleaned it up considerably, and recorded it. Soon it was fifth on the London pop charts, so Littlewood revised the show and brought it back again in December for an eight-week run. Within a week of its first opening, eight or nine commercial producers were making offers to transfer it to the West End. It did transfer, and it ran for two years and 897 performances. Soon, the influence of SoHo (or at least what British musical comedy *thought* was SoHo) gripped the British stage.

Back in America, off Broadway was becoming an incubator for unusual musicals that would never work on Broadway. *Threepenny Opera* had been the first really popular off Broadway musical, but it was *The Fantasticks* that made theatre history. Another musical theatre outgrowth of the Beat Generation, the story of *The Fantasticks* began with Edmond Rostand's 1890 French play *Les Romanesques*, a kind of reverse *Romeo and Juliet*, in which two fathers and best friends concoct a fake feud in order to get their rebellious kids to meet behind their backs, fall in love and marry. Its cynical view of love and marriage was right in sync with the mood of America's youth in 1959. From 1954 to 1956, writer Tom Jones (*not* the pop singer) had worked on a musical version of *Les Romanesques* with composer J. Donald Robb, creating a kind of Rodgers and Hammerstein rip-off called *Joy Comes to Dead Horse*. They reset the story with two Texan families and a Mexican co-conspirator named El Gallo (pronounced GAH-yo). An uneasy mix of *Our Town, Finian's Rainbow, Zorro*, and various

81

Shakespearean comedies, the collaborators decided it was an unsalvageable mess and they parted company. Jones went to his friend composer Harvey Schmidt and asked him to join the project. So they went to work, still intending it to be a major, large-scale, Rodgers and Hammerstein style Broadway musical.

In June 1959, actress Mildred Dunnock offered director Word Baker the opportunity to present an evening of three one-acts at the Minor Latham Theatre, way uptown in Manhattan. Baker called Schmidt and Jones and told them if they'd condense *Joy Comes to Dead Horse* into a one-act, he'd include it in his show. They'd have to do the show very minimalistically and they'd have to have the new version done in four weeks. (In an early reading, The Boy was played by Gerry Ragni, who would go on to co-write and star in *Hair*.) They discarded all the Rodgers and Hammerstein baggage and allowed into the piece their joint sense of Beat poetry and cynical whimsy, which had been struggling to get into the piece all along. The horses were gone. *Commedia dell'arte* was now the governing style. Jones' rhyming Beat-inspired dialogue and Schmidt's dissonant, polytonal jazz vocabulary came to the fore, especially with their new orchestration, scored now for just piano and harp. They went back to the source and found another translation of *Les Romanesques*, one called *The Fantasticks*. They had found their title. But even though the story was no longer set in Texas, the narrator/bandit was still named El Gallo (which is Spanish for The Cock or The Rooster).

The one-act version of *The Fantasticks*—essentially what we know today as Act I—opened in August 1959. Lore (pronounced LORE-ee) Noto saw it and offered to produce it off Broadway. Now charged with re-expanding the show into a full-length musical, Schmidt and Jones went back to work. They dubbed the romantic Act I "In the Moonlight" and they went to work on Act II, "In the Sunlight," exploring what happens to the two families and the new marriage in the light of day. As El Gallo says:

> Their moon was cardboard, fragile.
> It was very apt to fray,
> And what was last night scenic
> May seem cynic by today.
> The play's not done.
> Oh no—not quite,
> For life never ends in the moonlit night;
> And despite what pretty poets say,
> The night is only half the day.
> So we would like to finish
> What was foolishly begun.
> For the story is not ended
> And the play is never done
> Until we've all of us been burned a bit
> And burnished by the sun!

Act II was the Beat's answer to the traditional romantic Broadway musical, a kind of gentler companion piece to *The Nervous Set*, also commenting, though more urbanely, on the increasingly unhealthy isolationism and insularity of suburban America during the Eisenhower years.

In Act I of *The Fantasticks*, Matt and Luisa found a traditional Broadway-musical "Happily Ending," but it was tainted—predicated on a deception—like much of mainstream American life at the time. In Act II, the disillusionment sank in and they found that love cannot be built on false romanticism. The Happily Ever After they had been promised all their lives ran smack up against the reality of Reality. As with many young people in postwar America, they found that Marriage Is Hard. All the lovely lies of the American establishment, the Happily Ever Afters the end of World War II had promised, that mythical American Dream that only a *few* Americans actually got to enjoy, was revealed to be false, cardboard, very apt to fray. Act II of *The Fantasticks* told us that life was complicated, difficult, confusing, but that it was possible for clear-eyed realists to navigate this decidedly un-musical-comedy terrain.

The Fantasticks was the beginning of the end of the Rodgers and Hammerstein revolution, looking back to some of the great elemental myths but also looking forward to the concept musicals to come, not only rejecting the pseudonaturalism of Rodgers and Hammerstein's musicals but also the false romanticism and optimism their later musicals propagated. It was the end of romanticism and the embrace of cynicism. Like many of Schmidt and Jones shows, it used the changing of seasons as both a structural device and a central metaphor—birth, growth, death, renewal, regeneration—and like their other shows, it was also built on the battle between the generations, again reaching back to the great myths of the ancients. It was everything the Beats believed in. And it paved the way for shows like *Anyone Can Whistle*, *Cabaret*, *Company*, and *Promises, Promises*.

Jerry Orbach, who had been wowing audiences in *The Threepenny Opera*, was hired to play El Gallo, along with up-and-comers Rita Gardner, Kenneth Nelson, William Larson, Hugh Thomas, and Thomas Bruce (a stage name concocted for Tom Jones). Noto rented the tiny Sullivan Street Playhouse, a theatre so small the audience had to literally walk over the stage to get to their seats.

The show opened in May 1960, still with only its signature piano and harp accompaniment. Unfortunately, audiences and critics did not embrace the odd, unconventional show. Brooks Atkinson's review in the *New York Times* was mixed, but he said, "Harvey Schmidt's simple melodies with uncomplicated orchestrations are captivating, and the acting is charming." Walter Kerr wrote in the *Herald-Tribune*, "The jazz figures that composer Schmidt has insinuated beneath tunes that have the essential flavor of tea roses climbing a trellis help mightily to give the proceedings a contemporary wink." *Cue* magazine understood the sophisticated Beat sensibility that the more mainstream critics missed. *Cue* wrote, "The mood is martini-dry, uncommitted, upper-Bohemian, with the main enemy the cliché. I suggest you head to Sullivan Street to catch the brightest young talents on display."

Still, the reviews were mixed enough and the raves so few that the investors urged Lore Noto to close the show after opening night to minimize losses. Noto refused. Instead he used the last of his life savings to save *The Fantasticks*. Soon, word of mouth began to spread and celebrities started showing up at performances, even though some nights the cast still outnumbered the audience. Then another happy accident occurred. Producer Conrad Thibault, who ran a theatre in East Hampton, New York, a popular summer retreat, asked Noto to produce a show there. Instead of a new show, Noto closed the Sullivan Street Theatre and moved *The Fantasticks* to East Hampton for a week. All the rich and famous of Manhattan—folks who'd never go to an *off Broadway* theatre—were more than happy to see the same show while on vacation in the Hamptons. And finally, all the Right People were seeing the show, including Bob Fosse, Anne Bancroft, Elia Kazan, Jerome Robbins, and Agnes de Mille. By now the cast album was out as well. Years later, Noto said, "By the time we returned to Sullivan Street we were transformed from an endangered artistic success with an uncertain future to a commercial enterprise which has since endured."

The show won the Obie Award for best musical. In the *thirty-second* year of its run, in 1992, the show won a special Tony Award and Schmidt and Jones won the prestigious Richard Rodgers Award in 1993. The team was inducted into the Theatre Hall of Fame in 1999. To date there have been more than eight hundred foreign productions in sixty-nine countries, and more than twelve thousand productions in the United States. A Japanese-language production opened in the early 1970s and ran for years. In 1988, with Schmidt on piano and Jones back in the role of the Old Actor, an American company of *The Fantasticks* went to Japan with an English-language production and toured to nine cities. They went back in 1990 and again in 1992 for an even bigger tour. A less-than-stellar thirtieth anniversary American tour went out with Robert Goulet as El Gallo, with a full orchestra overwhelming the show's special simplicity, and a new song, "A Perfect Time to Be in Love." The song "It Depends on What You Pay" was replaced in the interest of over-zealous political correctness.

The show has returned more than ten thousand percent on its initial investment, and it eventually ran 17,162 performances at the Sullivan Street Playhouse before closing in January 2002, after an almost forty-two year run (more than twice as long as *Cats*), becoming the longest-running show in American history.

Musical theatre was ready for the tumult of America in the 1960s.

6

Let the Sun Shine In
The 1960s

As the tumult of the 1960s began, Broadway audiences were demanding more substantive musicals and off Broadway started producing groundbreaking musicals with a vengeance. The artists of off Broadway—and *off* off Broadway—were complaining that the "professional theatre" (in other words, Broadway) was dead, and even worse, that it was *boring*. They saw that the tightly ordered, regimented, safe, compartmentalized commercial theatre had no worthwhile relation to the chaotic real world of the 1960s. A theatrical revolution was afoot.

In 1962, Broadway composer Jerry Bock (*Fiddler on the Roof, Fiorello!, She Loves Me*) wrote, "Shortly it will happen. The American musical will shed its present polished state and become an untidy, adventurous something else. Shortly it will exchange its current neatness and professional grooming for a less manicured appearance, for a more peculiar profile. It will swell beyond or shrink from the finesse that regulates it now. It will poke around. It will hunt for. It will wander and wonder. It will try and trip. But at least it will be moving again, off the treadmill, out of the safety zone, crossing not at the green, but in between." He couldn't have been more right. Change was coming.

Bock predicted quite accurately that as the musical changes, "More of the book will be in the score. Much more. There will be less competition among the collaborative elements. Everybody will be on more intimate terms melding and molding together. Producer, director, costumer, scenic designer, author, composer, lyricist will get to know each other's craft and art and work more closely, more tightly, relinquishing a part of their theatrical sovereignty for a unity, for a common good that will be most uncommon." He finished his essay by saying, "The new musical may not take place between 41st and 54th street east or west of Broadway. That is, not at first. It may start in San Francisco or Chicago or Minneapolis. Or Lincoln Center. It may come from London or Paris or Rome or Johannesburg. Or the Village. It will probably be viewed and noted with greater interest. We will be less provincial about protecting the American-Broadway-musical-image. We will eliminate the high tariff against vigorous ideas not coming from The Street. We will join the common market of the theatrical world. Our eyes will stray, our ears will sharpen. And what we see and hear from everywhere will prepare us, will help us make our own new statement. Broadway may become one of many alternatives. It may, along with the musical, change its spots. And we may desert it now and then in search of something else. It won't mesmerize as much. Nor will it strangle. Its monopoly days are numbered. Nothing more exciting in the theatre will happen than this new musical."

Bock wasn't just seeing a few years ahead; he was seeing long past the turn of the millennium. He saw that off Broadway and regional theatres were going to develop many of the musicals of the future. He knew that shows like *Cats* and *Phantom* would come from London, and that shows like *Les Miz* would come from Paris. The musical theatre was changing forever, and Broadway was no longer the only place to make musical theatre art.

In December 1960, *Camelot* opened on Broadway, a magnificent though conventional work of the musical theatre, certainly flawed in some ways, but a show that would become a true classic. The critics were divided over *Camelot*, the story of King Arthur and his Round Table, based on *The Once and Future King*. And though it ran two years and a very respectable 873 performances, it couldn't compare with Lerner and Loewe's previous masterpiece *My Fair Lady*, which was still running and would close only after a staggering 2,717 performances.

Camelot had a very difficult development process. Before it had opened, director Moss Hart had had a heart attack and lyricist Alan Jay Lerner had developed ulcers and had been put on medication for depression. Costume designer Adrian died in the middle of the design process. Actors Richard Burton and Robert Goulet both got sick during previews, a chorus girl ran a needle through her foot, the costume mistress' husband died, and the master electrician was hospitalized. Moss Hart died a year after the show opened, and composer Frederick Loewe never wrote another stage musical. But there were also artistic troubles.

Perhaps the show's main problem was in trying to tell a story that was just too big for a single show. Its first public performance ran four and a half hours. They had to eliminate the equivalent of a *full musical*! By the time all the cuts were made, the show was missing the two most important elements in the story— the development of Arthur and Guenevere's relationship and the development of Guenevere and Lancelot's relationship. But *Camelot* is more than just a tragic love story, with an underlying subtext of great violence and unfettered sexuality that gives the show a very rich texture. Alan Jay Lerner wrote that at its core it contains the aspirations of mankind, and despite its shortcomings, *that's* what keeps the show from crumbling.

The critics complained that the show's creators tried to hide the material's inadequacies in the original production's expensive sets and costumes. But today, relatively free from the memory of the original, perhaps the trick to capturing all that is genuinely wonderful and provocative about *Camelot* is *not* to hide the book and score behind sets and costumes but instead to meet the material head on, engage it, conquer it, and make it work. It *can* work. In fact, Alan Jay Lerner tells a story of the last rehearsal before the first Broadway preview. Lerner thought it would be good to run the show once on a bare stage with no sets or costumes, and he wrote in his autobiography, "Free of the trimmings and trappings, the company was unprepared for the rediscovery of intimacy and intention. When I think of *Camelot* today, it is that performance that remains most vividly in my mind."

Perhaps inspired by that quote, a few productions in recent years have stripped *Camelot* down to its essentials. Strangely enough, these productions have shocked and amazed audiences, even though nothing has been rewritten, nothing added, nothing greatly "reconceptualized." Sometimes with a cast of only a dozen or so, these productions, in St. Louis and elsewhere, have put the focus back where it belongs, on Arthur, Guenevere, and Lancelot, putting back into the show the sexuality and violence that have been there all along but have been forgotten or ignored for too many years. This "innovative" approach has been merely to trust the script and to put on stage all the complexity and human drama found there. "The Lusty Month of May" can be finally really *lusty* again after forty years. "Fie on Goodness" can be genuinely violent and dangerous again. In these productions, Arthur has been played in the first scene as the twenty-five-year-old he is, rather than by a fifty-year-old star. Guenevere is played in the first scene as a seventeen-year-old because that's how old she's supposed to be. And most astonishing of all, both Arthur and Guenevere *change* and *age* in these productions over the thirteen years that the show covers. In short, the basic rules of working on a play are applied to this classic musical and the result has been astonishing to many people who have seen it. But it shouldn't be. That should be how every production of every musical is approached.

It's interesting to look at *Camelot* in the context of Lerner and Loewe's other musicals. The theme of impossible or nearly impossible love is a theme they returned to over and over throughout their collaboration. In their first hit, *Brigadoon*, in 1947, the leading lady lived in a town that appears only once every hundred years, and the leading man is an outsider. If he stays in Brigadoon, he can never leave. If she leaves, the miracle will end for the whole town. It seems they can't ever be together. Of course, *Brigadoon* being an old-fashioned musical, a last-minute change of heart saves the day and they do end up together. In the stage version of *Paint Your Wagon*, in 1951, the impossible love is an interracial relationship in 1850s California. In the film version of *Paint Your Wagon*, the impossible love is a three-way marriage that gets very difficult until one of the husbands finally leaves. In *My Fair Lady*, the leading man is an older misogynist who finds himself falling in love with a young girl but won't admit it. In *Gigi*, the age difference takes center stage, as an older man finds himself falling in love with a young girl he watched grow up. He sees her only as a child until the last-minute revelation. And in *Camelot*, the impossible love is a romantic triangle, in which each player loves the other two deeply, and an adulterous affair threatens to destroy Camelot.

It seems one or both of the collaborators were preoccupied with the idea of seemingly insurmountable obstacles to romantic happiness. One clue to this may be found in Alan Jay Lerner's difficulty in sustaining a relationship of his own. Not only did he constantly stray from Fritz Loewe professionally, while Loewe (who also had lots of trouble with women) remained completely "faithful" to Lerner, but Lerner also went through eight marriages in his lifetime. Perhaps both Lerner and Loewe were looking for answers as fervently as their characters were. Whatever the reasons, we can be grateful for the team's romantic difficulties because they inspired some of the most interesting dramatic situations ever written for the musical stage up until that time.

But the other important aspect of *Camelot* is its connection to the American zeitgeist. Like *Pippin* would be a decade later, *Camelot* was more about America than it was about its literal setting. Like America in 1960, *Camelot* straddled two worlds, one foot in the idealism of postwar America, one foot in the disillusionment that was quickly gaining ground thanks to the Beat writers and artists. *Camelot* was about a paradigm for a perfect world, but it was a paradigm that could not survive in a real world. It's not a surprise that John F. Kennedy fell in love with *Camelot*, that he loved to listen to the cast album, that he saw himself as an Arthur figure. Like Arthur's dream, Kennedy's Camelot would not survive either. And within a few years, much of American musical theatre would turn dark and cynical to match the national mood. In too many ways, *Camelot* marked the end of an era, both in musical theatre and in America.

By 1961, Broadway was ready to welcome back satire. The director Antonin Artaud once said that the theatre "causes the mask to fall, reveals the lie, the slackness, baseness, and hypocrisy of our world." The American musical theatre had braved the waters of satire for the first time in 1931 with the Pulitzer Prize–winning *Of Thee I Sing*. Only a few American musicals since then have successfully trod the dangerous path of satire. With a masterful score by Frank Loesser, *How to Succeed in Business Without Really Trying* won a Pulitzer Prize for drama, the best musical Tony, and the New York Drama Critics Circle Award for best musical. Critic Walter Kerr wrote, "Not a sincere line is spoken in the new Abe Burrows–Frank Loesser musical, and what a relief that is. It is now clear that what has been killing musical comedy is sincerity. *How to Succeed* is crafty, conniving, sneaky, cynical, irreverent, impertinent, sly, malicious, and lovely, just lovely." It's hard to imagine a critic writing that at any time before 1960.

The show opened in October 1961, and it took on one of America's great icons, Big Business, in a slightly skewed retelling of the *Faust* story, arguing that only by selling his soul can a businessman rise to the top of the game. Shepherd Mead had published the book on which the show is based in 1952, and it became a huge bestseller. Jack Weinstock (a neurosurgeon) and Willie Gilbert wrote a stage version of the book, but according to most sources, it was pretty awful.

Producers Cy Feuer and Ernie Martin decided it should be a musical and they brought in Abe Burrows (who had helped them on *Guys and Dolls*) to fix the book; apparently virtually none of the original version survived. Burrows also directed with choreography by Bob Fosse (who replaced Hugh Lambert).

The pundits say satire is never commercially viable, but *How to Succeed* is one of those exceptions, a searing satire that was also a big popular success. It's a bigger-than-life, wacky musical that is intentionally artificial, using freezes and other theatrical devices, allowing its hero Finch to break the fourth wall from time to time, and casting the same actor for both Mr. Twimble and Wally Womper, representing the bottom and top of the corporate ladder (as well as mirroring our hero's humble beginnings and outrageous final success). The show dishes out a savage indictment of the world of big business, complete with the grumbling, inept boss, lecherous executives, secretaries who really run the company, and a generous dose of lying, cheating, and stealing.

The central premise involves J. Pierrepont ("Ponty") Finch, a window washer who has taken as his bible a book called *How to Succeed in Business Without Really Trying*. The book offers a simple step-by-step process for moving up the corporate ladder without any genuine effort or talent. The book's introduction (read by an offstage voice) says: "If you have education and intelligence and ability, so much the better. But remember that thousands have reached the top without any of these qualities." And from that point until the final curtain, we see a parade of executives who don't, in fact, have any of those qualities. The show sets up a corporate structure so complicated and so large that it's possible to lie and cheat without ever getting caught. Finch learns from the book that his greatest advantage is the knowledge of what a lumbering giant the modern corporation is. Everyone at World Wide Wickets is a monster, an incompetent, or both. Finch is in many ways just as big a monster as the executives he tramples, but because those he dupes are unprincipled jerks, we enjoy seeing them get what we think they deserve. Finch is amoral and unethical, but we still love watching his triumphs. He is a cheerfully amoral successor to Harold Hill.

John Chapman wrote in the *Daily News*, "What goes on here is murder—murder by stiletto, by poison, by decapitation." John McClain wrote in the *Journal-American*, "It is gay, zingy, amoral, witty, and shot with style. It comes very close to being a new form in musicals." *How to Succeed* ran 1,417 performances, winning Tonys for best musical, best actor (Robert Morse as Finch), best featured actor (Charles Nelson Reilly as Frump), best director, best producers, best book, and best conductor. The only Tony it lost was for best composer, which Loesser lost to Richard Rodgers for *No Strings*. *How to Succeed* also won the New York Drama Critics Circle Award, a Grammy, and the Pulitzer Prize for drama. A relatively faithful film version with a few songs cut was released in 1967. A tepid, defanged revival was mounted in 1995 and ran 548 performances.

In March 1962, Richard Rodgers opened his thirty-eighth musical, the first for which he wrote both music *and* lyrics, *No Strings*, with direction by Joe Layton.

Rodgers' longtime collaborator Oscar Hammerstein had died a year and a half earlier, just a year after the opening of their last show together, *The Sound of Music*. The book of *No Strings* by Samuel Taylor told the story of a young American model living in Paris who meets and falls in love with an older American writer. The stage show introduced Diahann Carroll alongside Broadway veteran Richard Kiley, and though the dialogue never explicitly mentioned the issue, they played an interracial romantic couple. The couple's decision at the end that they could never return to America if they married carried with it the unmistakable pang of American racism. In Paris an interracial couple drew no stares; in America, it was a far different story in 1962. The fact that the show didn't mention it engendered disparate opinions. Some people thought it was very progressive for the racial aspect to be so matter-of-fact. Others thought it showed a reluctance on the part of Rodgers and Taylor to honestly address the racism in America, as Rodgers' former partner Hammerstein had done in more than one show.

In fact, the creators were planning a film version, and decided to use the Asian Nancy Kwan instead of Carroll, who was furious when she heard. She gave an interview about the decision to Earl Wilson, who wrote about it in his column and turned it into a nationwide debate—and all this in 1962! There was talk of boycotting the film and its studio, Warner's–Seven Arts. Soon, the film had been indefinitely postponed. It was never produced.

The very premise of the show spoke volumes about the times. An African American high-fashion model at the top of the profession didn't strike anyone as odd only *because she was in Paris*, not in America. As if anyone needed proof of that, Carroll recounted in her autobiography the story of how the show's opening night cast party in Detroit was canceled because the hostess was afraid for her kids to see a black person who wasn't a servant. According to Carroll, Rodgers found this very amusing, and he went to a party at the woman's house anyway. There were very few protests about the interracial romance in New York, but the tour had to shut down early because of such protests on the road.

As Rodgers had done earlier in his career (though not in a while), he broke new ground with *No Strings* that would affect everything that came after it. Director Layton had actors changing sets instead of stagehands in blackouts. He put the orchestra upstage behind the scenery, and he used selected musicians onstage to act as mute, musical characters, interacting with the speaking characters. *I Love My Wife* would follow this lead in the 1970s. Rodgers wrote, "I want the orchestra on stage because I am trying to blend the orchestral sounds with the other elements so completely that they will seem to be an integral part of the proceedings, just as much as the dialogue, the lyrics, or the action. I want the sounds of the orchestra to provide as much point and comment as those of a choral group." And toward that end, Rodgers lived up to his show's title and used no strings in his orchestra. Not only did this give the score a fresh, new sound, it also took away from it the Broadway musical's favorite source of sentimentality: soaring strings. Rodgers wanted to create an adult, real-world kind of romance, and dumping the violins was a big step in that direction. As noted before, his contribution here was not so much in the songs he wrote but in his theatrical innovation. Unlike most of his earlier shows, only one song in *No Strings* ever had much life outside the show, the opening duet "The Sweetest Sounds."

No Strings opened in March 1962 at the 54th Street Theatre on Broadway and ran 580 performances. The critics were hotly divided, and John Simon wrote in *Theatre Arts* that the script was "a concoction guaranteed to give ptomaine poisoning the moment one takes in the situation."

The show was nominated for eight Tony Awards, for best musical, best actor, best actress, best director, best music, best scenic design, best costume design, and best choreographer (also Layton). Diahann Carroll won her best actress Tony (a first for a black woman), and Joe Layton took home two. Also that year, Rodgers won the best composer Tony and was awarded a special Tony for his work with young people and for "taking the men of the orchestra out of the pit and putting them on stage."

Another black musical, Richard Adler's *Kwamina*, had opened in 1961 and told the story of an African man who falls in love with a white British woman and has to battle the traditions of his father, a tribe chieftain. Again, some people thought the interracial romance was too timid; others found it offensive. The theme of interracial romance returned in 1964 in *Golden Boy*, this time with the addition of a character who was a civil rights activist. It may be hard now to understand the enormity of all this. But we have to remember that the first interracial kiss on television didn't happen until 1966 on *Star Trek*. And it wasn't until 1967 that the U.S. Supreme Court finally struck down state laws against interracial marriage. Until then, it was illegal in many states for blacks to marry whites. But it should also be noted that *Kwamina*, *No Strings*, and *Golden Boy* were all written by white men. Black artists had not yet reclaimed black-themed Broadway musical theatre.

In 1964, one of the musical theatre's biggest hits and most lasting classics opened on Broadway: *Hello, Dolly!*, produced by the "abominable showman" David Merrick, with a score by Jerry Herman, a book by Michael Stewart, and direction and choreography by Gower Champion. (Hal Prince says Merrick offered him the gig first and he turned it down.) But *Dolly*'s story was not a new one. The story had begun as John Oxenford's 1835 nonmusical British farce *A Day Well Spent*, which was translated and adapted into the Viennese farce *Einen Jux Will er Sich Machen*. *A Day Well Spent* was also (loosely) adapted in 1890 into the musical *A Trip to Chinatown*. Most famously, it was the source for Thornton Wilder's 1938 stage comedy *The Merchant of Yonkers*, which was expanded in 1954 into the full-length play *The Matchmaker*, which in turn was the source for *Hello, Dolly!* Wilder was the first to insert the matchmaker character into the story, apparently inspired by Moliere's 1668 farce *The Miser* and its matchmaker character Frosine. Later on, Tom Stoppard used *A Day Well Spent* as the source for his (nonmusical) comedy *On the Razzle*. Before Wilder's versions with the Dolly Levi character, all the meetings and mix-ups in the story happened purely by chance; after Wilder, it was always because of that "damned exasperating woman."

Wilder's *Matchmaker* was very successful, but no version of the story has ever reached the heights of popularity of *Hello, Dolly!* It opened in January 1964 and ran 2,844 performances and almost seven years. Much of the success was due to Champion's highly stylized, high-energy staging and overall production style. Champion once again returned the musical comedy to its wacky, fast-paced roots in his neo-Cohan-ian production. The cast was sensational—Carol Channing in what became her signature role, David Burns, Eileen Brennan, Charles Nelson Reilly, and Jerry Dodge.

A big part of the show's success was that, despite the fact that it was an old-fashioned musical comedy, it was a smart one. Dolly Levi was a rich, compli-cated, fascinating, unpredictable character, a street-smart widow scratching out a living for herself, far more confident on the outside than on the inside, a char-acter with a distinct dark side, a woman who was supremely independent and yet tired of making her own way in a man's world. Her brief speech before the Act I finale, "Before the Parade Passes By" lent a kind of *gravitas* to the show that other shows like it seemed to lack. Alone on stage, Dolly looked heaven-ward and spoke to her dead husband:

> *Ephraim, let me go. It's been long enough, Ephraim. Every evening for all these years, I've put out the cat, I've locked the door, I've made myself a little rum toddy, and before I went to bed, I said a prayer thanking God that I was indepen-dent, that no one else's life was mixed up with mine. Then one night an oak leaf fell out of my Bible. I placed it there when you asked me to marry you, Ephraim. A perfectly good oak leaf but without color and without life. And I suddenly realized that I was like that leaf. For years, I had not shed one tear nor had I been filled with the wonderful hope that something or other would turn out well. And so, I've decided to rejoin the human race, and Ephraim, I want you to give me away.*

Carol Channing, comedian extraordinaire, proved her chops as a serious actor in that one small moment. And Gower Champion proved his skill as a director by letting the moment be small and personal and free from excess.

Jerry Herman, after a moderate success with his first show, *Milk and Honey*, wowed Broadway with his charming, extremely tuneful musical comedy songs. Only Cole Porter and Richard Rodgers had ever turned out this many standards in one show: "Hello, Dolly!," "Put On Your Sunday Clothes," "It Only Takes a Moment," and others. One song, "Come and Be My Butterfly," was cut early in the run and replaced by the Polka contest. Some sources say songwriter Bob Merrill wrote the show's Act II opener, "Elegance" and "The Motherhood

March" and that Charles Strouse and Lee Adams wrote an early version of "Before the Parade Passes By," but Herman swears the score is entirely his.

But *Hello, Dolly!* was not altogether old-fashioned. Herman's score reflected the changes happening in musical theatre in the early 1960s. Some subtle but pointed satire was found in the song "It Takes a Woman," taking well-aimed pot shots at all-American sexism, and in "Elegance," taking aim at the class divide in America. "The Motherhood March" satirized mindless patriotism, an issue that was about to boil over in America. And oddly enough, the show's two real love songs went to the second lead couple, Irene and Cornelius, not to Dolly and Horace. (Herman attempted to right this "wrong" by giving Dolly the almost *anti*-romantic love song "Love Is Only Love" in the film version.) Irene's "Ribbons Down My Back" was a mature, melancholy romantic ballad intentionally set in a minor key, in which Irene dreams of perfect romance just minutes before she plans to accept a marriage proposal from a man she doesn't love.

The reviews weren't all raves, but they were generally positive. Howard Taubman wrote in the *New York Times*, "It's the best musical of the season thus far. It could have been more than that. Were it not for the lapses of taste, it could have been one of the notable ones. But Mr. Champion, whose staging and choreography abound in wit and invention, has tolerated certain cheapnesses. It is a pity." Richard Watts Jr. wrote in the *New York Post*, "The fact that it seems to me short on charm, warmth, and the intangible quality of distinction in no way alters my conviction that it will be an enormous popular success." The show won Tonys for best musical, best composer, best book, best director, best choreographer, best producer, best actress (Channing), best sets (Oliver Smith), best costumes (Freddy Wittop), and best musical director (Shepard Coleman). It also won the New York Drama Critics Circle Award.

The irascible but brilliant producer David Merrick proved his chutzpah and inventiveness once again with this show. When Channing left the show, he replaced her with one star after another: Ginger Rogers, Betty Grable, Phyllis Diller, Martha Raye, and others. Merrick even talked to Jack Benny about playing Dolly in drag opposite George Burns. (It never happened.) Mary Martin played the lead in London and then in Saigon for U.S. troops. Some commentators have mused that *Hello, Dolly!* was the last of the nonironic, guilelessly innocent American musicals, and yet it did have its little ironies here and there, a smattering of social satire, and the slightest sheen of proto-feminism about it. When the central couple in a musical like *Dolly!* marries at the end of the musical for reasons *other* than love, one might be tempted to ask how innocent it really is. No, *Dolly* and 1960s America were inextricably linked. Once America had become embroiled in Vietnam, it would never recapture the innocence that *Dolly* had so slyly satirized, and musical theatre would never be the same.

When any other show would have closed, Merrick brought *Dolly* back from the brink in 1967 by recasting the entire show with African Americans, headlined by Pearl Bailey and Cab Calloway. Allen Woll wrote in his book *Black*

Musical Theatre, "On the one hand the new *Dolly* possessed remarkable symbolic value for the age. It answered a long-expressed desire of Actors' Equity in its demonstration that blacks could portray 'white' roles without the slightest harm or distortion occurring to the theatrical property. . . . The notion of *Dolly* as a new symbol of race relations in the 1960s was embraced by both Lyndon and Lady Bird Johnson, who greeted Bailey when she brought the show to Washington, D.C." But some people still believed the ideal situation would have been an *integrated* cast, not an all-black cast. Bailey and Calloway's share of the original run was 889 performances.

Ethel Merman (Champion's original first choice for Dolly, according to some sources) took over the lead in 1970—with an all-white cast again—and two songs originally written for Merman were put back in, "World Take Me Back" and "Love, Look in My Window."

A film version was made in 1969 starring Barbra Streisand (who was far too young to play the widowed Dolly), Walter Matthau, Michael Crawford (who was not yet known in America), and a very young Tommy Tune. Gene Kelly directed, with Michael Kidd choreographing. They added two new songs, the new opening, "Just Leave Everything to Me," and "Love Is Only Love" (originally written for *Mame* but cut), and they cut "The Motherhood March." They made one of the biggest, splashiest, dancing-est movie musicals in years, with 3,700 extras and a twenty-four million dollar budget. But the movie musical was dead. Or at least dormant. The film almost bankrupted Twentieth Century Fox studios.

The all-black version returned to Broadway in 1974 after touring, again with Pearl Bailey. In 1978, Carol Channing returned to recreate her role, and then came back *again* to tour it in 1994 and reopen it on Broadway in 1995.

In 1964 came *Anyone Can Whistle,* an absurdist social satire about insanity and conformity (among a dozen other things), probably the bravest show Stephen Sondheim wrote, at least until *Assassins.* It was also a spectacular flop when it first hit Broadway in April of that year, running only nine performances before closing. But leading lady Angela Lansbury later said in a 1979 interview in *Horizon* magazine, "Right then and there, I fell in love with Steve's work and, although the show folded after nine performances, it was one of the most exciting theatrical experiences I've ever had."

After writing lyrics for *West Side Story* and *Gypsy,* Sondheim had made his Broadway debut as a composer in 1962 with *A Funny Thing Happened on the Way to the Forum,* but it was with *Anyone Can Whistle* two years later that the world saw the first glimpse of Sondheim's rebel genius. The show had a script by Arthur Laurents, who had written the scripts for *West Side Story* and *Gypsy,* but *Whistle*'s plot was too unconventional and too wickedly satiric to find an audience while elsewhere on Broadway people could see more pleasant, more conventional, less threatening shows like *Hello Dolly!* and *Funny Girl.*

Sondheim's score for *Whistle* was a quirky blend of the kind of dissonant, electrifying music he later used more confidently in *Company* and other shows, along with a deft takeoff of traditional show tunes used to point up the insincerity and shallowness of certain characters. Unfortunately, since it ridiculed the people in the audience, as well as the kind of show tunes they most enjoyed, the show met with more hostility than excitement. The *New York Times* began its review with the statement, "There is no law against saying something in a musical, but it's unconstitutional to omit imagination and wit." And nothing could make up for a bad review in the *Times* at that point. It closed a week later.

Yet because of a cast album recorded after the show had already closed, *Anyone Can Whistle* became a cult favorite over the years. Sondheim has admitted it has serious flaws, despite its considerable charm and humor. The show tells the story of a town that's gone bankrupt because its only industry is manufacturing something that never wears out. In order to revive her town Mayoress Cora Hoover Hooper and her town council fake a miracle—water flowing from a rock—to attract tourists. When patients at the local mental hospital, the Cookie Jar, escape and mix with the townspeople and tourists, chaos ensues. Somehow, Sondheim and Arthur Laurents managed to shoehorn a love story in as well, between J. Bowden Hapgood, a psychiatrist who isn't really a psychiatrist, and Fay Apple, a nurse at the Cookie Jar who disguises herself as a miracle verifier sent from Lourdes. In addition to the outrageous subject matter and painfully fierce social commentary, the three-act show also included a groundbreaking, endlessly complex, thirteen-minute integrated musical sequence that ended the first act, winkingly titled "Simple." *Whistle* was not just breaking the rules of traditional musical comedy, it was throwing rotten fruit at them and, unfortunately, also at its audience.

Meanwhile, in Berlin, German musical theatre was asking similar questions about what a musical can be and taking the answer even further. German playwright Peter Weiss had written a new musical called *The Persecution and Assassination of Jean-Paul Marat as Performed by the Inmates of the Asylum at Charenton Under the Direction of the Marquis de Sade*, forever after to be referred to as *Marat/Sade*. In May of 1964, British director Peter Brook and his Royal Shakespeare Company decided to produce the show. The show was adapted into English by Adrian Mitchell, and new music was composed by Richard Peaslee, written for Weiss' odd mixture of instruments—harmonium, guitar, flute, drums, and trumpet. Peaslee's music drew upon French influences as well as American blues and other eclectic styles.

The show dramatized the goings on at a progressive insane asylum in France, whose superintendent believes that theatre is good therapy. So, the infamous Marquis de Sade writes a musical for the inmates to perform, a musical about the murder of French revolutionary Jean-Paul Marat (pronounced MAH-rah; the British pronounce the final *T*, the French do not). *Marat/Sade* mixed class politics, revolution, sex, murder, and musical comedy into a show like no other. The actors went to asylums to study people who were mentally ill, learning their behavior patterns, their physicality, trying to understand how they perceived the

95

world and how they attempted to interact with it. The *Complete Review* wrote, "A profound meditation on the nature of revolution, on power and its abuses, means and ends, *Marat/Sade* is also great theater. Weiss has written a marvelous drama here, both entertaining and thoughtful. It is, undoubtedly, one of the great works of the 1960s." Lee Alan Morrow wrote, "Brook's finest touch came when, as the play ended, the actors fought, smashing through toward the audience. Suddenly all noise and movement stopped, and the audience sensing the natural ending, applauded. Slowly, insanely, the actors applauded back." (Stephen Sondheim and Arthur Laurents used a similar device in the Act I finale of *Anyone Can Whistle*.) Director Brook said of the ending, "If we had conventional curtain calls, the audience would emerge relieved, and that's the last thing we wanted."

In his introduction to the published script, Brook wrote, "Starting with the title, everything about this play is designed to crack the spectator on the jaw, then douse him with ice-cold water, then force him to assess intelligently what has happened to him, then give him a kick in the balls, then bring him back to his senses again." The show became a big hit, running two years in London.

It traveled to Broadway in December 1965, running only 145 performances despite four Tonys, including awards for best show and best director, and despite the voyeuristic draw of nudity on a Broadway stage a full two years before *Hair*. It also won the New York Drama Critics Circle Award. The *New York Times* called it "a vivid work that vibrates on wild, intense, murmurous, and furious levels. It is sardonic and impassioned, pitiful and explosive. It may put you off at times with its apparent absurdity, or it may shock you with its allusions to violence and naked emotions. But it will not leave you untouched." Elizabeth Hardwick wrote in the *New York Review of Books*, "The harsh idealism of Marat and the soul-destroying naturalism of the Marquis de Sade, the insane in their tub-gray institutional smocks, all spoke of the deepest sexual fantasies of our time, of our suppressions, our madness, our suffering, our cruelties." The show returned to Broadway in January and February 1967 for another 55 performances. A film version was made in 1966 with much of the original cast.

The same group of creators followed this with another unusual musical in 1966, this one called *US*, about the Vietnam War, opening in London roughly the same time as *Viet Rock* opened in New York. *US* never came to New York.

More to the liking of mainstream audiences, *Fiddler on the Roof* opened in September 1964, with a script by Joseph Stein, music by Jerry Bock, lyrics by Sheldon Harnick, direction and choreography by Jerome Robbins, and starring Zero Mostel and Maria Karnilova. Based on stories by Sholom Aleichem, *Fiddler* told the tale of the Russian Jewish milkman Tevye in 1905 Czarist Russia, trying to keep his family together and hold on to his traditions in an ever changing, ever more dangerous world. One by one, he discards or modifies each of his deeply held beliefs until he finally can't go any further and he disowns one of his daughter for marrying a gentile, just as the family is forced out of their home and heads for America.

It was charming, funny, uplifting, emotional, tragic, and very Jewish. It was only the second fully, proudly Jewish mainstream Broadway musical, after 1961's *Milk and Honey*. Whereas earlier generations of Jewish writers in Hollywood and New York had been raised to hide, or at least downplay, their ethnicity, a new generation had now come forth. Sheldon Harnick said in an interview, "We had come through World War II and had a whole different attitude toward being Jewish than our parents. Before the war, even during it, my father would always tell me, 'Keep a low profile. Fight for social justice, but keep a low profile.'" Now that the horrors of the Holocaust were finally being openly acknowledged, now that Adolph Eichmann had been tried and convicted of war crimes, with Jewish films and novels finding success, it was a new era. And it is a long acknowledged fact of drama that the more specific a work is, the more universal it becomes.

The show's central metaphor of a fiddler on a roof—a man always in danger of falling, just like Tevye's precious traditions—resonated with its 1960s audience, as rock and roll was taking over pop music, as the civil rights movement grew ever bigger, as the women's movement and hippie movement were being born, as America was on the verge of the Vietnam War. There in the midst of the Teenage Revolution, parents felt all too keenly Tevye's fear of losing his traditions and losing control of his children. Americans were feeling just as unsteady as that metaphoric fiddler.

Sheldon Harnick wrote in 2003, "I am part of a generation of theatre writers whose sensibilities were shaped by the Great Depression and World War II. With those experiences in our backgrounds, it was natural for us to want to address serious issues in our work. We enthusiastically followed the footsteps of writers who had created such issue-driven musicals as *Show Boat, Pins and Needles, Of Thee I Sing, Lost in the Stars,* and *South Pacific.*" He went on, "When I began writing for the musical theatre, I firmly believed that what I chose to put onstage had the potential of changing people's lives."

The testament to *Fiddler*'s quality and the skill and artistry with which it was created is illustrated by a story. Harnick and Bock couldn't figure out how to start the show. Finally, Robbins sat them down and asked them what one idea their show was *about*. They talked about it at length and concluded the show was, above all, about tradition. Their new opening number "Tradition" was the result of that conversation, one of the strongest opening numbers in the history of the art form. From then on, they had a measuring stick for their work; any moment that wasn't about tradition, that didn't serve the central theme, was cut. Robbins imposed upon the material and the production a profound sense of unity, the sense that one mind had written and designed every moment, exactly what Rodgers and Hammerstein had been working toward. Like he had done with *West Side Story*, Robbins made *Fiddler* his own. He established once and for all the idea of "integration" in musical theatre as an indispensable given, the idea that every element is in perfect synch with every other element. A few reviews at the time complained that the material wasn't as strong as the production or the performances, but due to Robbins' sure hand, audiences embraced the show the world over. Still, after *Fiddler*, Robbins retired from Broadway at age 46 and spent the rest of his life in the ballet world, where he had more control over his work and fewer collaborators.

But *Fiddler* was not just a Rodgers and Hammerstein style musical, though its structure was fairly conventional. Once Harnick and Bock had written the show's opening number, "Tradition," *Fiddler* was raised to the level of concept musical. Instead of merely telling a story, now every element of the show and every moment in it served a central metaphor. It didn't *feel* like a concept musical but it was one, albeit in early, protoplasmic form. *Fiddler*'s producer Harold Prince would, within a few years, be one of the primary architects of the modern concept musical and we can see those roots in *Fiddler on the Roof*.

It ran for seven years and nine months, 3,242 performances, the longest run ever on Broadway—until *Grease* broke *Fiddler*'s record in 1979. *Fiddler* won the New York Drama Critics Circle Award, and nine Tony Awards, including best musical, best score, best book, best director, and best choreographer. The show opened in London in 1967 and ran 2,030 performances, before moving on to Hamburg, Vienna, Paris, and Budapest. A film version was made in 1971. It ran a full three hours, but was cut down for its rerelease in 1979. An uninspired revival was mounted in 2004.

Many theatre historians and commentators define the golden age of the American musical as the years between 1943 and 1964, or even more specifically, from *Oklahoma!* to *Fiddler on the Roof*. The traditionalists see the 1960s as a period of decline for the musical theatre. But they are wrong. The 1960s were a time of expansion and explosion and deconstruction, a time when musical theatre artists (and some who had never worked in musical theatre at all) began experimenting with the form, finding new ways to use music in theatre. It was no longer always the same AABA song structure of the so-called golden age, nor the same scene-song-scene-song plot structure of the Rodgers and Hammerstein musicals, and the possibilities for subject matter blew wide open. Musical theatre didn't decline during the 1960s; the art form entered its most exciting, most daring, most thrilling time in decades. How could a golden age *not* include brilliant works like *Man of La Mancha, Cabaret, Hair, Jacques Brel, Company, Follies, A Little Night Music, A Chorus Line, Sweeney Todd, Assassins, Rent, Hedwig and the Angry Inch, Ragtime, Sunday in the Park with George*, and many others? Some artists argue we're *still* in the golden age of musicals—or that the 1980s were the dry times and we're now in a *second* golden age.

The first really important musical not considered part of the golden age was the richly imaginative, deeply emotional *Man of La Mancha*. Today, *La Mancha* is considered by many to be a masterful, deeply moving piece of alternative theatre; others who don't pay attention to the complexity and subtlety of the writing see only sentimentality. But the show does not traffic in unabashed optimism or sentimentality, as its critics have charged; in fact, the show demonstrates quite vividly that mindless optimism leads only to pain, despair, even death. The world is a dung heap, treacherous to navigate, *La Mancha* tells us; but it also shows us the good in people that is too often beaten down and squashed, its language that of pure, naked human emotion, as extreme as Stephen Sondheim's *Passion*, which also made audiences uncomfortable.

In a sense, modern audiences are like *La Mancha*'s Dr. Carrasco, afraid to expose their emotions for fear of being laughed at. Because the song "The Impossible Dream" (listed as "The Quest" in the show's program) was embraced by every two-bit crooner in the 1960s and 70s, the song—and its lyric—became a joke. But the song *doesn't* argue that we should all wear rose-colored glasses. No, it argues something quite different: that only those who go too far will ever find out how far they can go, that we must, all of us, attempt the impossible on a regular basis, leave our comfort zone, scare ourselves with new challenges, live a gutsy, engaged life. The song never argues that we *can* reach that unreachable star or achieve that impossible dream, but it asks that we try anyway. As we must with shows like *Carousel* and *Show Boat*, we have to look at *Man of La Mancha* with fresh eyes, see the sophistication, experimentation, and truth in it, and give it another chance. There is much to admire and enjoy in this show if we only let ourselves.

In the novel *Don Quixote*, on which *Man of La Mancha* is loosely based, author Miguel de Cervantes plays with the form of the novel and with the nature of reality, he riffs on the nature of narrative and on the relationship between writer and reader, performer and audience. *Man of La Mancha* does much the same thing in theatrical terms. In *Man of La Mancha*, we have three authors (bookwriter Dale Wasserman, lyricist Joe Darion, and composer Mitch Leigh), who have created a fictional character based on a real person (Cervantes), who plays a fictional man (Quijana) who thinks he's a real knight (Quixote); the other fictional characters in the musical (the prisoners) play still *other* fictional characters in Cervantes' play (the innkeeper, Aldonza, Carrasco). Going one level deeper, when Aldonza finally sees the beauty in Quixote's view of the world, she takes on the new role of the Lady Dulcinea.

Wasserman wrote about Cervantes, "What sort of man was this—soldier, playwright, actor, tax collector, and frequent jailbird—who could suffer unceasing failure and yet in his declining years produce the staggering testament which is *Don Quixote*? To catch him at the nadir of his career, to persuade him toward self-revelation, which might imply something of significance concerning the human spirit—*there*, perhaps, was a play worth writing." The strange relationship between reality and unreality, the many interlocking levels of reality, are what writing—and theatre—are all about. What is a novel (or a play or movie) but unreality commenting on reality, unreality acting on reality, unreality *posing as* reality? The challenge is always the same: how extreme an unreality can an artist take and dress up as reality without the reader/audience objecting? Or, how close to reality can the writer shape that unreality, still keeping the two separate?

The roots of the show lie in the golden age of television, a time in the 1950s when serious drama was the *lingua franca* of live television, before sitcoms, before prime time soaps. Some of the greatest American playwrights wrote for the Philco Playhouse, Playhouse 90, the U.S. Steel Hour, General Electric Theatre, Lux Video Theatre, Kraft Television Theatre, the Hallmark Hall of Fame, and the Dupont Show of the Month. Brilliant writers like Paddy Chayevsky, Rod Serling, and others wrote some of the most interesting work ever broadcast, dealing with potent issues like racism, alcoholism, mental illness, and more. It was the Dupont Show of the Month that produced the first, nonmusical version of *Man of La Mancha*. Though playwright Dale Wasserman had chosen this title, the network brass didn't think their audience was smart enough to understand it, so it was changed to *I, Don Quixote*, missing entirely the point that the show wasn't about Quixote; it was about Cervantes. The network also demanded the deletion of any references to the Inquisition because it might offend their Catholic viewers. So the prison became a secular one. The original cast included Lee J. Cobb as Cervantes, Eli Wallach as Sancho, and a young Colleen Dewhurst as Aldonza. The stage manager was Joe Papirofsky, who would later become the world-famous producer and director Joe Papp. The show was broadcast live on November 9, 1959.

Soon after the broadcast, director Albert Marre approached Wasserman (as others already had) about turning his teleplay into a stage musical, and this time, Wasserman agreed. Soon the team swelled to include composer Mitch Leigh (mostly because Leigh was rich and put up the initial investment), and poet W. H. Auden. Soon, the others realized Auden wrote great poetry but not great lyrics, and that he was writing a different show, a more cynical, more blatantly anachronistic show. They learned the lesson that in almost all cases, poetry makes lousy lyrics. Poetry carries its own music; adding literal music to it only makes it too dense. Next, they called lyricist Joe Darion, who had recently written lyrics for *shinbone alley*. By June 1964, the new team had a first draft, now titled *Highway to Glory*. The show was now the first of its kind—a musical inside a nonmusical play, in which the outer framing device (the prison) is not a musical and no one sings there until the very end, but the interior reality (the Quixote story) is a full-blooded musical. And the climax of the show comes when Cervantes brings music out into the nonmusical world of the prison. Like Harold Hill in *The Music Man*, like Maria in *The Sound of Music*, Cervantes brings (metaphorical) music to the gray lives of his fellow prisoners, giving them a kind of existential salve, even though many of them may never again see the light of day. This show was a product of its times.

In the fall of 1964, the team was offered a production at the newly renovated Goodspeed Opera House in Connecticut, to open in June 1965. The deal was too good to pass up, the chance to open their summer season, take time to

100

revise and fix the show, and then open again at the end of the summer, in mid-August. The show then moved in November 1965 to the ANTA Theatre off Broadway, downtown near Washington Square Park in Greenwich Village, the perfect place for it, sharing more in common with radical, anti-establishment works like *Marat/Sade* and Wasaserman's own *One Flew Over the Cuckoo's Nest*, than with *Hello, Dolly!* or *The Sound of Music*. The ANTA had no fly space, no proscenium arch, no curtain, none of the trappings of traditional theatres. But the ANTA was officially categorized as a Broadway house because of its seating capacity, despite being some forty blocks from the rest of Broadway and only a few blocks from other off Broadway houses. So, as it would all its strange life, *Man of La Mancha* was born straddling the experimental world of off Broadway and the commercial world of Broadway.

Man of La Mancha was one of the first true "concept musicals," the kind of musical in which the overarching metaphor or statement is more important than the actual narrative, in which the method of storytelling is more important than the story. With brutal and erotically charged choreography by the legendary Jack Cole, the show starred Richard Kiley as Quixote and Joan Diener as Aldonza, and it won the New York Drama Critics Circle Award, the Outer Critics Circle Award, the Variety Drama Critics Award, the Saturday Review Award, and five Tony Awards, including best musical and best score. The show moved uptown in March 1968 to a regular Broadway house, the Martin Beck Theatre, then, oddly, moved in March 1971 to the off Broadway Eden Theatre, then again in May 1971 to the Mark Hellinger Theatre back *on* Broadway. It ran a total of 2,328 performances and was revived in 1972 (less than a year after the first production closed), and again with Kiley in 1977.

The world-famous French/Belgian songwriter and singer Jacques Brel saw the show in New York and fell in love with it. He brought it to Paris, playing the lead himself, opposite Diener. Luckily, a French cast album was made, preserving Brel's soulful interpretation. Productions of *La Mancha* have been mounted all over the world, and in September 1972 it even opened in the Soviet Union. The show was revived again in 1992 with Raul Julia and Sheena Easton, then again in 2003 with far less artistry, with the African American–actor Brian Stokes Mitchell as Quixote. Today, the show enjoys 300–400 productions each year.

In 1961, openly gay composer and clergyman Al Carmines had become the assistant minister and director of the arts program at Judson Memorial Church in downtown New York, near Washington Square Park (across the street from where *Hair*'s Jeannie would someday meet Frank Mills in front of the Waverly Theatre), a church in which much of the congregation was composed of theatre people and many were gay. Carmines opened the Judson Poets' Theater, dedicated to experimental theatre forms, especially those involving music, and he composed the scores for more than sixty shows there between 1961 and 1972. *New York* magazine writer Alan Rich later wrote, "The brand of musical theatre that Carmines has developed at Judson, abetted by a repertory company of bright, eager, variably talented, unpaid and enormously engaging young people, is the most captivatingly original development in music drama since Brecht-Weill."

Carmines' most successful show was the experimental musical *Promenade*, a show unlike anything New York had ever seen before. It started its life in 1965 as a one-act and later evolved into a full-length piece. With an absurdist script and lyrics by Maria Irene Fornes (playwright, pop artist, and onetime lover of writer Susan Sontag) and music by Carmines, *Promenade* had no plot—or rather, an absurdist plot organized by shuffling a stack of index cards. Fornes made three piles of cards, one pile of locations, one pile of character types, one pile of open-ing lines. She drew a card from each pile and then wrote until she ran out of steam; another card from each pile got her going again; and so the script was formed.

The central characters, two escaped prisoners named only "105" and "106," crash a bizarre party of rich people and from there the story unwinds in the strangest ways possible, darting frantically from the battlefield to the office of the Mayor and elsewhere. In fact, virtually no one in the show had real names, but were called Miss Cake, Miss I, Miss O, Miss U, you get the idea—a more absurdist version of Marc Blitzstein's label names. Fornes herself said, "It's a lot like movies from the 1930s, like Fred Astaire and Ginger Rogers. Everybody is lightweight, you know, you run, you cry, there's a meeting and then something happens and you go somewhere else." But Fornes and Carmines also addressed social issues in their show, not the least of which was the war in Vietnam.

After several years of tinkering, a full-length *Promenade* opened in June 1969 off Broadway at the new Promenade Theatre (renamed for the show). Clive Barnes of the *New York Times* wrote, "Presumably *Promenade* will be one of the more controversial musicals of the season—it will also presumably be one of the most successful. It is a joy from start to finish." He also called it "a giant step forward, backward, and around a blockhouse full of melody and moment, charm and charade. It is sweet and sauerbraten. It looks ahead to the past. It looks back in angered amusement. It zigs and zags and dances on its toe-tapping rhythms to make points that add up to a joy from start to finish." Stephen Bottoms wrote about Carmines' music in his book *Playing Underground*, "This eclecticism inevitably attracted critics who accused Carmines of having no orig-inal musical voice of his own, but it seems, with hindsight, that it was precisely this stylistic promiscuity that made his music so 'original.' Carmines blurring of musical boundaries, his ability to place the high modern and pop-culture on the same playful plane of consideration, made him one of the first 'postmodern' composers." The show won an Obie Award for best musical and ran for a year and 259 performances, its run cut short only by a badly chosen raise in ticket prices. It was revived in 1983 at the Theatre Off Park.

Sweet Charity, which opened on Broadway in January 1966, had begun life as two one-act musicals written by Bob Fosse and Elaine May. Early on, May's was discarded and Fosse's expanded into a full evening. Fosse co-wrote the new script under the pseudonym Bert Lewis. But Fosse wasn't a book writer so Neil Simon came in to doctor the script and Fosse took his name off it. Based on Federico Fellini's brilliant film *Nights of Cabiria* (though tamed down a bit), and with a terrific, jazzy, offbeat score by composer Cy Coleman and lyricist Dorothy Fields, *Sweet Charity* was fresh and fun though not all that groundbreaking. Still it did speak to current events, particularly one song, "The Rhythm of Life," which took wicked aim at the country's growing disenchantment with organized religion, its growing spiritual bankruptcy, and Americans' subsequent search for "alternative" spirituality.

The show confirmed Fosse as a true virtuoso auteur of modern musical theatre, and it confirmed Fosse's jerky, quirky style of choreography as a legitimate Broadway dance vocabulary. The show ran 608 performances and was nominated for eight Tonys, winning only one, for Fosse's choreography (*Man of La Mancha* swept the Tonys that year). A film version was made in 1969 but flopped at the box office, killed by its own idiosyncrasies, only now finally being reconsidered as a quirky masterpiece.

The burgeoning political activism in the United States when *Cabaret* hit the stage in 1966—and its increase by 1972 when the film version hit theatres— as well as director Hal Prince's desire to break through to a new kind of socially responsible musical theatre all conspired to make *Cabaret* another one of the most fascinating stage pieces of the 1960s and a show that speaks to our world in a new millennium more now than at any time since it first opened, as evidenced by the recent smash hit Broadway revival. Hal Prince has said, "It was only after we'd come by a reason for telling the story parallel to contemporary problems in our country, that the project interested me." The singer Sally Bowles represented the people who kept their eyes shut to changes and dangers in the world around them, and the novelist Clifford Bradshaw represented the new (perhaps naïve) breed of American activist who could no longer sit by and watch the government ignore the will of the people. Today, as activism at both ends of the political spectrum has experienced a renaissance in America, *Cabaret* as a cautionary morality play has tremendous resonance.

The show in its original form was a fascinating but flawed theatre piece. It was director Hal Prince's first experiment in making a concept musical, a form he would perfect later with projects like *Company, Follies, Pacific Overtures, Kiss of the Spider Woman*, and other musicals. Early in the process of creating *Cabaret*, Prince had gone to Russia to see theatre and had witnessed a provocative, confrontational, rule-busting production at the Taganka Theatre. It was everything Prince had been looking for. He later said, "The Taganka Theatre was traumatizing (in a good sense)." He would forever more gravitate toward theatre that challenged audiences, that intentionally made audiences uncomfortable, that made an audience confront their world in all its contradictions and ugliness. Fraulein Schneider's searing Act II showstopper, "What Would You Do?" was an aching cry of regret, an apology for choosing self-preservation. Sally's performance of the title song was innocuous, even cheerful on the surface while underneath she was deciding to have an abortion, veering closer and closer to nervous breakdown. This was a new kind of musical. Years later, Prince famously said in an interview, "Don't sell audiences short. They are open to the adventurous, the challenging, even the dangerous."

Cabaret opened in November 1966, starring Joel Grey, Bert Convy, Jill Haworth, Jack Gilford, and Kurt Weill's widow Lotte Lenya, with choreography by Ron Field. It ran 1,165 performances. Walter Kerr said in the *New York Times* that *Cabaret* "opens the door to a fresh notion of the bizarre, crackling, harsh and the beguiling uses that can be made of song and dance." The show went to London, with Judi Dench in the lead, and ran 336 performances, then another 59 in Vienna.

Other writers and directors further developed the concept musical in the 1970s and 80s with shows like *A Chorus Line*, *Chicago*, and *Nine*, but *Cabaret* paved the way. *Cabaret's* flaw lies in the fact that the concept musical was still in an embryo stage; Prince was traversing uncharted territory. The end product was groundbreaking and often shocking, but it was only half a concept musical. Believing that Broadway audiences in 1966 still needed a central romantic couple and a secondary couple (as in *Oklahoma!*, *Brigadoon*, *Pajama Game*, and others), Prince and his collaborators essentially created two shows, a realistic book show with traditional musical comedy songs, and a concept musical with songs that commented on the action and the central metaphor of the show. Critic Martin Gottfried wrote of the original, "*Cabaret* is two musicals, and one of them is enormously striking and magnificently executed." Composer John Kander loves to quote the review in *Variety*, which said, "It is unlikely there will be much of an audience for this sort of thing."

When Bob Fosse made the film version of *Cabaret* in 1972, he jettisoned all the traditional book songs, and the piece became a full-fledged concept musical. In 1987, when Prince revived the stage version, the show's creators revised the show again, giving Cliff back his homosexuality (from the show's source material), incorporating some improvements from the film version, trying things audiences had not been ready for in 1966. In 1993, British director Sam Mendes went even further with a production at London's Donmar Warehouse, trimming the show's fat, better focusing the show's central metaphor, and creating yet another version that better integrated the two separate styles Prince first created. In Mendes' version (London, 1993; Broadway, 1998), the entire show was placed in the Kit Kat Klub, on the club stage, and the dialogue scenes became "acts" in the club. This better integrated the two parts of the show and eliminated the wall between actors and audience, placing the audience on three sides of the stage, only a few feet from the action, rather than across an orchestra pit, *involving* them in the action.

Cabaret was based on several chapters from Christopher Isherwood's somewhat autobiographical novel *Goodbye to Berlin*, and it seems that new versions of this story have always appeared at times of crisis in America. The original novel appeared at the close of World War II; the nonmusical stage version debuted during the McCarthy era; the stage musical opened during the Vietnam era; and the movie musical opened in the midst of the Watergate era. Each of these times has also been a turning point in regard to the social standing of American women and gays. Each subsequent version of this story has been braver, edgier, more explicit, and only as the millennium turned could it be told completely truthfully. Only then could Cliff finally be fully gay, just as Christopher Isherwood—the real Cliff—was. Only then could the Kit Kat Klub be as sexual and as decadent as it really was. Only then, after musicals like *Assassins* and *Kiss of the Spider Woman*, were musical theatre audiences ready for the disturbing extremity that this story really demands.

Back in 1966, Americans were beginning to distrust their government with a level of disillusionment not seen since Herbert Hoover and the Great Depression. John F. Kennedy had been killed and with him his dream of a new kind of America. Lyndon Johnson was beginning to lie to the country about Vietnam, and the optimism of post–World War II America was fading quickly. The Beat writers and artists first expressed that disillusionment in the 1950s, and here in the middle 1960s, the hippies were about to take up the charge against what they considered an increasingly misguided establishment.

Cabaret tapped into the growing political anger in America in 1966, but another show attacked the issues head on. Critic and playwright Richard Schechner said of the 1966 experimental musical *Viet Rock* "the theme and scope, the variety and density of *Viet Rock* would have excited Brecht." In *The Village Voice*, Michael Smith wrote, "*Viet Rock*, vividly expressed, is a breakthrough . . . extraordinary on at least two counts. It is the first realized theatrical statement about the Vietnam war and a rare instance of theater confronting issues broader than individual psychology." The reviewer for *Variety* called it, "Wild . . . an acid indictment . . . ensemble acting effects that have to be seen to be believed. . . . *Viet Rock* has been brilliantly staged. These Open Theater types are contributing something new to the concept and technique of stagecraft." Al McConagha, of the *Minneapolis Tribune*, anticipated what the critics would later write about *Hair*, when he wrote, "*Viet Rock* is more important than what it means . . . it is an original and gutsy bit of theatre. It is a theatrical demonstration that ambushes an audience with an extraordinary evening of theater and it wins as an emotional gut shot at the tragedy of the times."

Viet Rock was a show partly written, partly group-devised through improvisation in rehearsal, a practice already widely used in the experimental theatre community. The famous director Gordon Craig argued that it was very likely that Shakespeare used the same method, that he lifted story ideas from other works and from English history, brought them to his company of actors and let them improvise scenes. Though there's no doubt as to the Bard's genius with words, it isn't impossible to believe the beautiful psychological complexity of his work came from the input of more than one mind.

While it's true that playwright Megan Terry was no Shakespeare, she achieved, to a lesser extent, many of the things that made Shakespeare's work special, painting on an epic canvas the great human events of birth, death, war, love, and loss. She used both low and high comedy, tragedy, satire, parody, music, dialogue and monologue, mime and poetry.

Called the Mother of American Feminist Drama, Terry's process was fascinating. Each show began as an idea, filtered through extensive improvisation by company members, then solidified into a text. But the text was hardly a finished product. Her plays continued to evolve as they were performed, sometimes *over*evolving, first achieving a kind of balance and artistry, then losing it as change continued. Like *Hair*, even once the script of *Viet Rock* was published in 1967, subsequent productions did not feel the necessity of sticking slavishly to the text. Each production was a source of rediscovery and reconstruction. Because of this creation process, the end result rarely had the kind of structure and logic to which mainstream theatre seemed shackled, for better or worse.

Instead of each scene following logically from the one before, the scenes in *Viet Rock* were connected in other ways, in what Richard Schechner called "prelogical ways." A scene could connect to the previous scene psychologically. It could go off on a tangent from the scene before. It could further explore or compress the previous scene. It could act as counterpoint or could stop the action dead to explore mood or relationship. The connection between two scenes might be nothing more than the free association that comes from improvisation. In fact, *Viet Rock* opens this way, with the actors coming onto the stage at the beginning and lying down. As a song is played, the actors become a human, primordial flower, newborn infants and their mothers, naked army inductees and doctors, and then those same inductees and their mothers.

These scenes or "action-blocs" (Terry's term) could in many cases be rearranged without damaging the show. This rearranging changed the show, changed its focus, but it didn't cause the show to crumble as it would have with most musicals. But it's important to note that those connections, those transformations from one moment to the next, are not random or accidental. They are the work of a playwright at the height of her power, knowing what to use and what to throw away, knowing how to weave a complex tapestry whose accumulated power is undeniable, working in a new form that may have been misunderstood but was no less legitimate than what was happening in the commercial theatre of Broadway.

Viet Rock aggressively confronted its audience with an angry antiwar message. The *New York Times* described part of the show like this:

> After the girls have made themselves into an outlined airplane and flown future heroes
> to the jungles where the napalm burns, they drop to their knees for more choral

unison: *"Citizens arrest! Make love, not war!" They get robot replies in return. If
they have battered out a rhythmic "Innocent people are being burned!" they get a
short, snappy, automated "Gee, we are sorry about that" back from the boys.*

*A boy crawling on his belly lifts his head for a split second to intone "I can't
wait till I get there and make a killing on the black market!" Three Vietnamese
women, moving their mouths in soundless spasms of anguish, are waved away
loftily by a lady-like voice: "Usher, please escort these ladies to the powder room.
I think they'd like to freshen up." Uniformed lads on a three-day spree in Saigon
accompany their dancing with fiercely inflected slogans: "Let's go gay with L.B.J.!
I got syphilis today because of L.B.J.!"*

The acting style rejected conventional naturalistic acting or dialogue. The text
rejected plot and linear structure. In a bit of comic artistic self-reference that
doubled as political comment, a politician in one scene declares "This administration, of which I am a part of, indulges in anything but realism."

The way Megan Terry and the Open Theatre created *Viet Rock* was a blue-
print for many who came after, involving the actors in shaping a work for performance, expanding the American musical comedy form to include rock music,
borrowing clichés of the mass media, and having the actors leave the performance space to interact with the audience. Jerry Ragni, one of the creators of *Hair*,
was a part of this ensemble and creation process, adding to the piece along with
the other actors, and he brought all these techniques with him to his next project. *Hair* used many of the devices and techniques of *Viet Rock* but did it better—
or perhaps more accurately, did it more accessibly and more commercially. *Viet
Rock* was a landmark theatre piece in many ways, but hidden away downtown
at Café LaMaMa, nobody knew about it. Uptown, on Broadway, everybody knew
about *Hair*, so *Hair* got all the credit.

Hair opened first at Joseph Papp's Public Theatre in October 1967 for a limited, eight-week run, under the direction of Gerald Freedman (an assistant to Jerome
Robbins throughout the 1950s). When its run ended, Papp and independent producer Michael Butler moved the show to the Cheetah, a New York disco. Papp then
pulled out, and after massive revisions (including thirteen new songs), new cast
members, a new director (Tom O'Horgan), a new choreographer (Julie Arenal; they
wanted the movement to look more spontaneous, less "choreographed"), and the
addition of designers Jules Fisher and Robin Wagner, Michael Butler moved the
show to Broadway, opening it in April 1968 at the Biltmore Theatre. Butler's
astrologer picked the opening date to ensure a successful run. The show ran for 1,742
performances on Broadway. During its long life, *Hair* acted as a launching pad for
the careers of Diane Keaton, Melba Moore, Donna Summer (in the German production), Tim Curry, Nell Carter, Peter Gallagher, Joe Mantegna, Ben Vereen, Cliff
DeYoung, Meat Loaf, and many other performers who went on to great success. Various revivals were attempted in the years following, either fully staged or in concert, but none of them succeeded, largely due to too much polish, too much vocal
training, too little understanding of the raw, visceral "happening" that *Hair* was.

Saturday Review said, "Director Tom O'Horgan is pushing the medium to new limits by moving away from the verbality of multisensual theater. Instead of finding conventional musical-comedy performers to impersonate hippies, he has encouraged a bunch of mainly hippie performers inventively to explore their own natures with song and dance." In the *Journal of Popular Culture*, Irving Buchen wrote, "*Hair* cannot be cut short as mere sensationalism; nudity there is, but it is selective, functional, and even discrete. It is not the new drama of assault or insult, although the audience is never immune from incursions into its midst. It is radical but not violent; eclectic but not chaotic; sexually free wheeling but not perverse." He called it "an authentic glimpse into a pre-verbal state—perhaps, into the origins of drama itself as chant and dance." When *Hair* opened, John J. O'Connor wrote in the *Wall Street Journal*, "No matter the reaction to the content . . . I suspect the form will be important to the history of the American musical."

And it was, paving the way for the nonlinear concept musicals that dominated musical theatre innovation in the 1970s: *Company*, *Follies*, *A Chorus Line*, and others. And yet, some Broadway establishment figures refused then and now to accept this radical departure. Even today, some people can't see past the appearance of chaos and randomness to the brilliant construction and sophisticated imagery underneath. (See the book *Let the Sun Shine In: The Genius of Hair* for a more detailed discussion of the show.) In the late 1960s, *Hair* was the revolution the artists of off Broadway and off off Broadway had been waiting for. Most surprising of all, it was an enormous hit. Director Tom O'Horgan said at the time that he saw *Hair* as a once-in-a-lifetime opportunity to create "a theatre form whose demeanor, language, clothing, dance, and even its name accurately reflect a social epoch in full explosion." *Hair* was a truly psychedelic musical, literally reproducing for its audience the sensation of tripping on LSD, perhaps one of the only examples ever on Broadway. Like *Viet Rock*, *Hair* was made up of a barrage of images, often very surrealistic, often overwhelming, coming at the audience fast and furious, not always following logically; but when taken together, those images formed a wonderful, unified, and ultimately comprehensible whole. At its best, the show really could cause the kind of euphoria and disorientation in its audience that one associates with psychedelic drugs.

And it can't be overemphasized how much the *look* of *Hair* changed Broadway. *Hair* did away with so many longstanding traditions and habits. Gone were brightly colored costumes with white piping, gone were costumes that looked like they were made for a musical, each girl in a different pastel shade of the same dress, gone were the grotesque fake eyelashes and bad wigs women had to wear on stage, gone was the heavily artificial makeup and ghoulish eyeliner, gone was the need to force every physical movement onto the beat whenever music was playing, gone was standing down-center facing the audience for every solo, gone was pretty much everything fake. On top of all the other new things, *Hair* *looked* like nothing Broadway had ever seen. It would take a few years for the new style to take hold, but it would, and soon, most musicals would be costumed the same way as nonmusicals.

Meanwhile, another, less obvious expression of the hippie movement had found its way to the stage. In 1966, two fledgling producers had approached song-writer Clark Gesner, who had written several character songs about the *Peanuts* comic strip. They wanted to create a full-length musical featuring Gesner's songs and using *Peanuts* creator Charles Schultz' original strips as dialogue scenes. In the spirit of the times, the show was to some extent group-created, shaped and molded in rehearsal. The show, dubbed *You're a Good Man, Charlie Brown,* directed by Joseph Hardy and choreographed by Patricia Birch, opened off Broadway in March 1967 at Theatre 80 at St. Mark's and became an instant hit.

It looked both backward to *Candide* and forward to *Cats.* Certainly Charlie Brown was second cousin to Candide, perpetually beaten up by the world but always still soldiering on. And just as *Cats* wasn't really about cats but more about the foibles of human beings, so too *Charlie Brown* was not really about kids but about the contradictions and inanities of adult society. The song "Little Known Facts" was an obvious metaphor (to those looking for such things) for the tortured logic of organized religion, at least from the counterculture's perspective. The show's finale, "Happiness," fully expressed the hippies' philosophy of enjoying the simplicity and beauty of the world around us, letting go of life's headaches and irritants, a full-throated declaration of love for the simple joys. As in the strip that gave it life, each character in the show was a personality type—the impassioned and oblivious artist Schroeder, the Zenlike philosopher (and fetishist) Linus, the pagan, pleasure-centric Snoopy, the controlling bitch Lucy, and the long-suffering, ordinary, hopelessly passive Common Man Charlie Brown. In fact, the whole show was a quirky but determined exaltation of the Common Man, utterly consistent with hippie philosophy. Though its characters were all stand-ins for adult personalities, their innocence and wide-eyed wonderment also hoped to teach their audience something about living more fully by the end of the show.

Schultz's comic strip was once described by fellow comic strip artist Garry Trudeau (*Doonesbury*) as "the first Beat strip." Edgy, unpredictable, way ahead of its time, the *Peanuts* strip had debuted in October 1950 and was regularly suffused with commentaries on literature, art, classical music, theology, medicine, psychiatry, sports, law, faith, and the still taboo themes of intolerance, depression, loneliness, cruelty, and despair. Trudeau said the strip "vibrated with 1950s alienation. Everything about it was different." And now that the Beat culture had evolved into the hippie culture, a new sensibility had become clear in this material.

The producers wisely left *You're a Good Man, Charlie Brown* off Broadway where it belonged, with its bare set and abstract cubes, rather than try to move it to Broadway to make more money. Richard P. Cooke wrote in the *Wall Street Journal,* "The characters live in a zone where childhood and adult wisdom and disillusionment meet." He called it "an unusually worthwhile evening based on what might have seemed an unlikely foundation for the stage." Walter Kerr wrote in the *New York Times*, "*Charlie Brown's* combo, the best in town, embraces a handful of absolutely real, utterly earnest, deeply philosophical, and slightly insane undersized people." It ran 1,597 performances and sent out several national tours. One company played Boston for a full year. The show was revived on Broadway in June 1971 but it only ran a month. It was revived again on Broadway in 1999, after a short tour, with new dialogue scenes from Schultz's strips, two new songs (and much reorchestration throughout) by Andrew Lippa, and the character of Patty now morphed into Sally. It lasted only about five months and 149 performances, but it was nominated for four Tonys and won two, for Roger Bart as Snoopy and Kristin Chenoweth as Sally. Perhaps it was never really meant for Broadway.

The next socially conscious musical opened in April 1967, but though it was an interesting attempt at addressing racism through the language of musical comedy, it only partially worked. With a book by Arthur Laurents, music by Jule Styne, and lyrics by Betty Comden and Adolph Green, *Hallelujah, Baby!* tried to follow the history of black civil rights in twentieth-century America, through the life of one (non-aging) woman, taking a page from *Love Life*. It was an important experiment but it was doomed from the start. Lena Horne was slated to star but dropped out early on. David Merrick was set to produce the show but left the project when Horne left. The show went through numerous producers, directors, and choreographers, and ended up with the young Leslie Uggams in the lead. It ran a respectable 293 performances and it won four Tonys, including one for best musical.

Hallelujah, Baby! closed in January 1968, just a few months before *Hair* transferred to Broadway. It's tempting to wonder if its politics and its structure would have been better received after *Hair* changed the rules on Broadway. That same year, another black show opened, *The Believers*, written by black authors Josephine Jackson and Joseph A. Walker, making *Hallelujah, Baby!* look antiquated by comparison. *The Believers* told the *whole* story of African Americans. The *New York Times* said, "*The Believers* has something to say about being a Negro in the United States that its predecessors (how quickly they have dated!) did not say. Instead of ending with a whimper of pain, or a cheerful (or threatening) plea for racial togetherness, *The Believers* ends with the crisp, jaunty rattle of an African drum."

Hallelujah, Baby! also happened to close the same month a new show called *Jacques Brel Is Alive and Well and Living in Paris* opened at the Village Gate. The musical theatre was now thriving and evolving at a fever pace and, more than almost any other piece written for the musical stage in the 1960s, *Jacques Brel Is Alive and Well and Living in Paris* utterly defied description. It was an evening of independent songs, yet it was more than a revue. It didn't have a plot or an immediately recognizable cast of characters, so it was not really a book musical.

It has been called the world's first libretto-less musical. In reality, it is a one-man concept musical with a cast of four. Two women and two men portray one character: the real life folk singer and poet, Jacques Brel. The words are Brel's, the opinions, insights, and razor wit are Brel's. The underlying, sometimes nearly hidden optimism is Brel's. In a sense, the show is more a character study than anything else, but is it a character study of Jacques Brel the man or of Western civilization at the end of the twentieth century? Eric Blau, one of the creators of the show (and one of the people who helped *Hair* along its way), said that Brel wrote about the way we live in a world we did not create.

Jacques Brel was born in Belgium in 1929 but moved to Paris as a young man to be a singer and songwriter. By the early 1960s, Brel had established a reputation as one of France's greatest writers and interpreters of modern songs. (In France, the writing of popular songs is much more respected than it is here in America, and serious poets and playwrights write pop lyrics.) Though Brel himself insisted his lyrics were not poetry, they had an intensity of images, uncommon rhythmic patterns, and a sophisticated structure that confirmed his stature as a major artist. In 1957, the first American recording of Brel's songs was released but with only moderate success. In 1961, singer Elly Stone had begun singing two of Brel's songs, "Ne me quitte pas" ("Don't Leave Me") and "La valse á mille temps" ("The Waltz in 1,000 Time"), in an off Broadway show called *O, Oysters!* Though the show did not run long, Stone continued to perform the Brel songs. In January 1968, Eric Blau and Mort Schuman opened an off Broadway musical using twenty-six of Brel's songs, and they called it *Jacques Brel Is Alive and Well and Living in Paris*, a parody of a then popular slogan about God meant to affirm that He was still with us. It gave the show an odd yet subtle sense of spirituality. The show ended up running for five years and 1,847 performances.

After its off Broadway run ended, the show enjoyed a limited engagement of four weeks on Broadway in 1972, and several Broadway producers asked for an extended run, but the show's producers refused. Broadway was not really the place for this show. It's been revived twice in New York since then, and has been produced around the world. A film version was released in 1975, which included an appearance by Brel himself singing his best-known song in France, "Ne me quitte pas" (a song not in the stage show). Since the show first opened, Brel's songs have been recorded by artists as diverse as David Bowie, Judy Collins, and Barry Manilow, and the show continues to be produced throughout the world. Brel died in 1978 at age 49 but they didn't change the title.

Back in 1968, Broadway was facing big changes. Originally a project for director-choreographer Bob Fosse and bookwriter Neil Simon (who had worked together on *Little Me* and *Sweet Charity*), *Promises, Promises* opened in December 1968 and turned out to be something special indeed, even with Robert Moore replacing Fosse as director (after several others demurred) and wunderkind Michael Bennett taking over choreographic duties. Moore had never directed a musical before and had only directed one play. With a score by pop composer Burt Bacharach and his lyricist Hal David, the show adapted Billy Wilder's dark, Oscar-winning film *The Apartment* for the musical stage.

Pop music rarely turned up on the Broadway stage before now (*Hair* had only just opened on Broadway) and this show had real pop songwriters creating sophisticated, surprising, thrilling—and completely integrated—theatre songs. (Bacharach and David had written one musical before this, the 1966 television musical *On the Flip Side*.) Bacharach's music utterly stunned Broadway. No one had ever written music like this for the stage before, constantly shifting rhythms, unusual harmonies and melodic intervals, dropping and adding beats, changing time signatures and key signatures seemingly at random, yet all in the vocabulary of 60s pop. Almost every song in this show broke half a dozen rules. But underneath it all was a brilliant, confident, sophisticated sense of structure and form, and an unerring sense of how to set a lyric on a melody, how to let a line soar, how to get out of the way and let an emotion ache.

Bacharach and David were already changing the face of pop music with songs like "Alfie," "This Guy's in Love with You," "The Look of Love," and other hits. Now they were doing the same to theatre music, clearing the way for the even bolder experiments of Stephen Sondheim in the 1970s. And the *Promises* orchestrator Jonathan Tunick (who would also later work with Sondheim) made extensive use of electronic instruments for the first time in a Broadway musical, and used backup vocals sung from the pit, also a first. Though microphones had been used on Broadway since the early 1940s, this was the first show to consciously create a "studio" sound with a trained sound designer, pop record producer Phil Ramone. David's lyrics were just as exciting and just as *right*, and did the heavy lifting required of modern theatre lyrics, intelligently and consistently advancing plot and character. Unlike other pop songwriters who have written for Broadway, Bacharach and David didn't seem to care if these songs would "cross over" to become pop hits; more than half the score couldn't work out of context. The show was also notable for its young conductor, Harold Wheeler, the first black conductor of a Broadway show that wasn't specifically a "black musical." Wheeler would go on to become one of the great Broadway orchestrators, working on *Don't Play Us Cheap!*, *The Wiz*, *Dreamgirls*, *Little Me*, *The Tap Dance Kid*, *The Life*, *Swing!*, *The Full Monty*, *Everything's Ducky*, and others.

The musical followed the film plot pretty faithfully in its story of a junior executive, Chuck Baxter, who lends his apartment out to higher-ups for their extramarital affairs. Unfortunately Chuck falls in love with the woman his boss is bringing to the apartment for a fling, who then tries to commit suicide in Chuck's bed on Christmas Eve. Neil Simon's script was just as surprising and innovative as Bacharach's music. One of the devices Simon used was breaking the fourth wall, allowing Chuck to step out of a naturalistic scene now and then to talk directly to the audience, to comment on the scene and even on the show's storytelling, all while the scene behind him froze. Chuck was the protagonist but he was also at times a puppet master, controlling, even distorting the action to feed his own fantasies, telling us the story the way *he* wanted it to happen, not the way it "really" happened. And yet Chuck never lied to us for long; he would confess his manipulation and let the show take control again. This was a show that was experimental and commercial at the same time, a show whose creators took gigantic risks over and over but who had the experience to keep it accessible to mainstream audiences.

Promises, Promises opened in December 1968 and ran an impressive 1,281 performances, followed by a fourteen-month national tour. It was nominated for seven Tonys and won only two, for best actor (Jerry Orbach) and best featured actress (Marian Mercer), losing the best musical award to *1776*. Still, the critics loved the show. Martin Gottfried wrote for *Women's Wear Daily*, "There are songs and more songs and more songs, one better than the other—tricky rhythm songs, funny songs (not just funny lyrics but funny *music*), fresh harmony songs, lovely little guitar songs. . . . *Promises, Promises* is easily the most satisfying and successful musical in a very long time."

One of the last musicals of the decade was also one of the least likely to succeed. History teacher turned pop songwriter Sherman Edwards had written the history musical *1776* in a time when old-fashioned patriotism was seen as quaint at best, when rock music was trying hard to take over Broadway, when nudity was everywhere. And here was a musical about the debate over American independence in 1776. What was Sherman thinking?

Well, since before 1961, he had been working on his pet project, spending enormous amounts of time researching in Philadelphia. Bookwriter Peter Stone had been approached as early as 1961 to help Edwards write the script but Edwards had resisted. Finally in late 1967, Stone sat down and heard Edwards play the score, and he loved it. He said about the opening song, "The minute I heard that, I knew I wanted to do it. Because in that song is the entire fabric and level of the show: You are involved with people whom we'd never dealt with before except as cardboard figures. This room had flies, it was hot, and these men were not perfect. There's more information about the Continental Congress in the opening song than I learned in all my years at school." Finally, America could see its Founding Fathers as activists, as radical as anything on America's streets in 1969.

During out-of-town tryouts, nearly half the show's twenty-three songs were cut. But like that first Congress, it kept battling against all odds and succeeded anyway. Historian Marc Kirkeby calls it "a one-of-a-kind work of sophistication without irony, corn without camp, and history (rearranged but largely accurate) without apology." In fact, the events and debates of the show are so historically accurate, Edwards included an appendix to the published script detailing exactly what was true and what wasn't. With direction by Peter Hunt and choreography by Onna White, the show won the 1969 Tony Award for best musical (over both *Hair* and *Promises, Promises*), ran on Broadway for three years and 1,217 performances, ran a successful two-year national tour, ran in London, and then was filmed by Peter Hunt and much of the original cast, including Howard da Silva, the original Franklin, who had suffered a heart attack early in the Broadway run and missed being on the Broadway cast album.

On the other end of the cultural spectrum, *Tommy*, the first of the great rock operas began life as a concept album in 1969 by the British rock group The Who. Composer Pete Townshend has said in interviews that calling his work a rock opera was a bit facetious on his part, but the piece does use the mechanics and structure of grand opera, though somewhat primitively, alongside the vocabulary of rock and roll. So what other label would be more appropriate? He said of his work, "It's a good story in itself, it's exciting, yet at the same time deep down below is a thread. If you're a seeker you get something from it. That was really what I was trying to aim at with *Tommy*, so that somebody who wasn't interested at all in spiritual matters would still be able to dig it." But it came at a time when rock-and-rollers *did* want something deeper. Rock and roll had changed.

More than any previous generation, the youth of the 1960s lived their lives to popular music. It was a philosophical expression and a communal experience more than just an escape or a soundtrack for social dancing. The questions teenagers were asking were bigger than who to take to the prom; now the questions were about God and war and politics and eternity. John Connick wrote in *Helix*, in 1967:

> You can't really communicate to the outside how a hundred thousand children of Muzak freaks, who in most cases never bother to study or even think about music, are involved in a single art form to the point where they virtually stake their entire sanity on it. Go to a house and someone hands you a joint in front of a record player and it's assumed that you are going to sit for a couple of hours, not talking, hardly moving, living to music.

It had been many decades since people had *listened* to music this intently. And the creators of rock music understood its paradoxical nature—at once, both commercial product and social commentary, both entertainment and catalyst for awareness and action. Because of the Vietnam War, popular music now had a self-awareness and an irony that was undeniable. It had an obligation to address not just teen angst and misfired romance, as in the 1950s, but also political issues and social injustices. It was a lot to ask of rock music. Some of the songs of the era rose to the challenge; some did not.

But *Tommy* tapped into all of this as it spun its tale of the "deaf, dumb, and blind kid" Tommy Walker, who as a child witnesses his father's murder and retreats inside himself. His mother and stepfather try everything—including LSD—to cure him but nothing works. Eventually Tommy confronts his demons and emerges from the darkness, is declared a messiah, and becomes an overhyped pseudoreligious figure, another trap from which he must escape. The story ends vaguely, as Tommy's followers abandon him and he faces the future alone. Packed with war, adultery, child molestation, abuse, drugs, religious hypocrisy, and empty celebrity, this was a story full of the rage and confusion of the sixties, one that confirmed the conclusions that the youth of America (and Britain, to a lesser extent) had come to—the only solution was to "drop out." The original album went double-platinum and spent forty-seven weeks on the Billboard charts, yielding several single hits, most notably "Pinball Wizard."

The Who toured for years doing concerts of the musical, while unauthorized stage versions went up all over the U.S. and the U.K. In 1975, Ken Russell made a bloated but gleefully psychedelic film version with Roger Daltry, Ann-Margret, Oliver Reed, Jack Nicholson, Elton John, and others. Then in 1991, after years of saying no, Townshend agreed to a fully mounted Broadway stage version to be directed and co-adapted by Des McAnuff. It opened in the summer of 1992 at the LaJolla Playhouse in California, then moved to Broadway in April 1993, where it ran 899 performances. This new stage version departed in major ways from the original album, watering down the story, sanitizing several incidents in the story, softening the ugliness that made the original so compelling. The child-molesting Uncle Ernie, the sadistic Cousin Kevin, and all overt references to drugs were removed or made palatable. In fact, Tommy even reconciled with his abusive relatives at the end of the new version. And rather than allowing the audience to fill in the gaps in the narrative, rather than allowing the audience to *participate* in the experience as they had with *Hair, March of the Falsettos, Follies, Assassins,* and other unconventional narratives, the new version spelled everything out for its audience.

Jon Pareles, rock critic for the *New York Times,* wrote, "Nearly everyone seems to like it. Everyone, that is, except people who cared about *Tommy* in the first place. Those sourpusses, with me among them, can hardly believe that the Broadway extravaganza had the chutzpah to bill itself as *The Who's Tommy.* The changes turn a blast of spiritual yearning, confusion, and rebellion into a pat on the head for nesters and couch potatoes. The musical seeks neither spiritual fulfillment nor political ferment; the revised goal is domestic comfort." He ended his review with, "Business as usual built upon a rock opera that once promised more."

As Broadway liked to do in the 1980s and early 1990s, it had made *Tommy* into a mainstream consumable product and lost everything that was special about it. The producers were mystified as to why the show didn't run longer, never suspecting that by emasculating Townshend's near-masterpiece, they betrayed the show's longtime fans. It was now a toothless, theme-park pop musical, no longer the gritty, cheeky rock opera Townshend had written, no longer the score that had made history in 1969.

7

In Comes Company
The 1970s

To a large extent, the 1970s marked the end of the Rodgers and Hammerstein revolution. It was the decade that gave permanent berth to both the concept musical and the rock musical, both explored during the sixties but now taking their rightful place, shows that rejected the sunny optimism of earlier decades and instead revealed the feelings of rage and loss that pervaded America in this era of Vietnam and Watergate.

The concept musical had been germinating since Marc Blitzstein's *Cradle Will Rock* in 1937, but it wasn't until *Company* in 1970 that the concept musical was poised to change everything. The rock musical had been born with *Expresso Bongo* in 1958, but it became a fixture on Broadway during the seventies, partly because the definition of *rock* was so pliable, so inclusive by then. A rock musical could be *Jesus Christ Superstar, Two Gentlemen of Verona, The Rocky Horror Show,* or *Grease,* none of which sounded anything like the others; and yet they all shared a disdain for authority and a taste for rebellion to which only the language of rock and roll could give full voice.

Also, for the first time since the 1920s, black musicals became commonplace on Broadway again, some admittedly put together by all-white creative teams, some just black casts in originally all-white shows, but there were more and more black musicals created mostly or entirely by black artists. And for the first time, a significant black audience for Broadway musicals was forming.

The 1970s also cemented the idea of the director-choreographer, the new breed of artist who had his hand in every aspect of a show, often including its original conception. Yes, Jerome Robbins had introduced this hyphenated job with *West Side Story,* and Bob Fosse had taken over with *Redhead* and *Sweet Charity.* Gower Champion had had three successes this way, *Carnival, Bye Bye Birdie,* and the phenomenon *Hello, Dolly!* But it wasn't until the seventies and beyond that it became commonplace, in the persons of Fosse (*Pippin, Chicago, Dancin', Big Deal*), Michael Bennett (*A Chorus Line, Ballroom, Dreamgirls*), and later on,

116

Gower Champion again (*42nd Street*) and Tommy Tune (*Best Little Whorehouse, Nine, Grand Hotel, The Will Rogers Follies*). Once upon a time, the power had belonged to the stars, then later to the writers, and now to the director-choreographer. The trend has waned a bit today, but a few hyphenates are still out there, including Tommy Tune and Graciela Daniele.

In terms of material, the avant-garde, experimental theatre of the 1960s was now finding commercial parallels on and off Broadway, and with it came nudity and four-letter words. But as the rules changed, some theatre artists had trouble navigating the new terrain. The failure rate for new shows rose exponentially, and the 1970–71 season had the fewest new musicals opening in Broadway history.

That was partly because the economics of Broadway had changed. Ticket prices were rising far more quickly than the cost of living, and prices were rising because production costs were rising, both on and off Broadway. In earlier decades, a run of 500 performances would qualify as a major hit. In the 1970s, a show would rarely break even with a run of that length because budgets had ballooned so much. *The Rothschilds* ran 507 performances and lost $650,000. Stephen Sondheim, James Goldman, and Hal Prince's *Follies* ran 521 performances and lost $700,000. Also during this time, off Broadway became more and more like Broadway, and less and less willing to take risks. So off off Broadway became the new off Broadway. All this caused a rampage of musical revivals on Broadway—safer investments with proven track records—a few of which were radically reconceived, most of which were bland, lesser re-creations of the originals.

But there were other problems too. The New York City theatre district was rife with garbage, porno houses, prostitutes, drug dealers, and thieves. Many people were afraid to go there. The producer of the musical *Don't Bother Me, I Can't Cope* even offered theatregoers free cab rides home after the show to make them feel more comfortable. There were several high-profile "cleanup" efforts undertaken, but little changed. For the first time in decades, new Broadway theatres were being built by optimistic producers and developers, but patrons were scared to visit them.

The other change during the seventies was the way regional theatre, off off Broadway, and off Broadway became the proving grounds for Broadway. With skyrocketing production costs, Broadway became more a showplace for shows developed elsewhere and less a place to create interesting new art. Almost half the plays and musicals produced on Broadway during the 1970s did not originate there. More than forty shows came to Broadway from off Broadway during that time, about twenty-five from off off Broadway. Another twenty percent of Broadway shows during that time originated in other countries and that trend would only increase during the 1980s.

But there were still quite a few quality shows birthed by the Great White Way during the seventies. The first Broadway musical of the decade—well, the first that didn't close after a few performances—was the musical adaptation of black actor-playwright Ossie Davis' hit play *Purlie Victorious*, opening in March 1970. Howard Taubman had written in the *New York Times* that the original play "unrelentingly forces you to feel how it is to inhabit a dark skin in a hostile, or at best, grudgingly benevolent world." The musical version, its title shortened to *Purlie*, had a book by committee—Davis, lyricist Peter Udell, and director Philip Rose—and music by Gary Geld. (Udell, Geld, and Rose would collaborate again in 1975 on *Shenandoah*.) There was nothing terribly groundbreaking about *Purlie*, but it was solid, socially conscious musical theatre.

Set "not too long ago," it told the half-comic, half-serious story of a southern preacher fighting a David-and-Goliath battle against an old rich white man who has kept the African Americans of southern Georgia in economic slavery even in the supposedly progressive 1960s. The show addressed serious issues and indulged in some pointed social satire, but along the way it offered plenty of comedy, an exceptionally strong score, a not too syrupy love story, and an incredible cast headed by Cleavon Little, Melba Moore, Novella Nelson, and Sherman Hemsley. The show ran 689 performances and became the first successful musical of the decade. Melba Moore's rendition of "I Got Love" became a big pop hit.

But the seventies *really* got rolling in April 1970 with Stephen Sondheim and George Furth's brilliant concept musical *Company*, the breakthrough of all breakthroughs. Though nothing like *Company* had ever been produced on Broadway before, the American musical *had* been evolving, and there was a clear path toward the convention-shattering *Company*. Playwright George Furth had initially written some unusually subtextual one-acts about marriage and showed them to his friend Stephen Sondheim, who brought them to director-producer Hal Prince. Prince suggested turning them into a musical and creating a central character, an unmarried man who stands outside these marriages looking in. The three began work on the new show, first called *Threes*, then changed to *Company*.

When *Company* opened, audiences were still not fully accustomed to concept musicals or to shows that dealt with the warts-and-all reality of love and marriage. John Lahr wrote in the *Village Voice*, "In *Company*, no one dreams, only survives." Despite the 60s, audiences still wanted shows about ideal love and happy endings. *Company* snubbed its nose at this shallow view of life. The show presented five married couples—Harry and Sarah, a study in gentle, collaborative self-deception; Susan and Peter, who are getting divorced, discarding legal marriage, the only way they can maintain a happy and committed relationship; David, a control freak, and Jenny, his submissive wife; Amy and Paul, who've been living together for years and are finally getting married; and Joanne and Larry, each married several times, who understand each other with a depth no one else could reach. Robert's observations of these couples revealed subtle details, tiny moments that spoke volumes, hidden artfully beneath the surface ordinariness and superficiality of modern life.

Only Harry and Sarah can understand each other's addictions. Only Paul understands Amy's fear of the symbolic intensity of legal marriage. Only Larry sees the scared, vulnerable woman Joanne keeps so perfectly hidden under emotional scar tissue and a mask of cool cynicism. These five couples have issues and dysfunction galore, but they love each other and they face life's difficulties *together*. These are the lessons and joys Robert must understand before he can decide whether or not to commit to someone himself. Each couple teaches Robert a different lesson about commitment. If some people thought the end of the show was ambiguous, they were right. Sondheim wrote four different climactic songs for the show, each a different decision for Robert; but even "Being Alive," the one that survived, doesn't completely resolve Robert's ambivalence. Rebelling against musical theatre's traditional oversimplification of the human condition, Sondheim, Prince, and Furth were determined to make a theatre piece about the real world. All we know by the end is that Robert has chosen a path; where it will lead him is anyone's guess. *Company*'s story did not end because nothing ends in real life; we always just keep going. Happy Endings are never really endings in real life and *Company* was about real life.

Not everyone loved *Company*, but everyone agreed it was something new and courageous; and even today, it remains remarkable in its form and ambition. Most of the songs in the show are commentary songs, often sung by characters not involved in the scene, addressing the audience directly. Only occasionally ("Barcelona," for example) does a song grow organically out of the scene as in traditional musicals. What audiences were seeing onstage was a collection of Robert's memories and impressions. The audience swam around inside Robert's head, privy to his thoughts about his friends and, therefore, about commitment, all happening in the seconds before he opens the door to his thirty-fifth birthday party. That concept was the rationale for the episodic, seemingly random nature of the scenes, as well as the fact that the audience saw everyone and everything through Robert's cynical eyes. As Robert slowly formed a more mature understanding of relationships, the characterizations of the married people got deeper and more complete; the more Robert understood them, the more fully they were portrayed in his mind and onstage. Since the show was about Robert's mental journey and transformation, it made sense that the audience took that journey with him. This was no ordinary musical and yet it was a hit.

The critics didn't all agree, but Walter Kerr wrote in the *Times*, "*Company* is brilliantly designed, beautifully staged, sizzlingly performed, inventively scored, and it gets right down to brass tacks and brass knuckles without a moment's hesitation, staring contemporary society straight in the eye before spitting in it." Martin Gottfried said, "*Company* is brutally unsentimental mostly because it is so grownup and frightfully honest."

Leading man Dean Jones left the show after four weeks of performances for personal reasons and was replaced by Larry Kert. The show was nominated for fourteen Tony Awards (a record not equaled until *The Producers*) and it won

119

seven, including best musical, best music, best lyrics, best book, best director, best producer, and best scenic design. The show also won the New York Drama Critics Circle Award. It ran 706 performances, then opened in London the following year with some of the original cast and ran 344 performances.

Jones returned to do a reunion concert of the show in 1993 in Los Angeles with all but one of the original cast, not just singing the score, but also recreating the original choreography. The show was revived off Broadway in 1978 for a limited run, then in 1980 at Playwrights Horizons, then off Broadway at the York Theatre in 1987, and then again on Broadway in 1995 produced by the Roundabout Theater. The 1995 production boasted an outstanding cast, but it was a pale shadow of *Company*, without its intelligence, without subtlety or nuance—and inexplicably adding back the deleted song "Marry Me a Little"— all this making people think the show was unrevivable. It's not. In 1996, a much smarter, much more interesting revival was produced by the Donmar Warehouse in London, directed by the then unknown Sam Mendes, later to work miracles on *Cabaret* and direct the film *American Beauty*. In 2001, *Company* was produced in Brazil, and then in 2002, it was part of the six-show Sondheim Celebration at the Kennedy Center in Washington, DC.

Company was every bit the revolution that *Show Boat* and *Oklahoma!* had been, and it changed the way we talked about Broadway musicals. They weren't "musical comedies" anymore, and the 1940s label "musical play" was passé. Now they were just "musicals." After nearly a century, the musical was finally officially its own art form, no longer just an adjective.

John-Michael Tebelak, who conceived and wrote the hit Biblical musical *Godspell*, one of the most successful musicals of the 1970s, spoke about his impetus for writing the show in an interview in *America* magazine in 1971. He had attended an Easter Vigil service but was disturbed by what he experienced: the congregation seemed bored and the priest seemed to be in a hurry to finish. Tebelak wanted to make the religious experience once again accessible to the masses.

Tebelak assembled a cast of college friends in 1970 to mount the first production of *Godspell* at Carnegie Tech School of Drama, with a script taken almost entirely from the Gospel of Matthew. Members of the cast set Episcopal hymn texts to their own original pop tunes. The show was a success and moved to Café LaMaMa, and then in May 1971 to the Cherry Lane Theatre off Broadway, where the producers decided they needed a full, unified score. Another Carnegie Tech grad, Stephen Schwartz, was shopping around his idea for a musical called *Pippin Pippin*, and was invited to write the new *Godspell* score (he kept one of the original songs, "By My Side," intact). Completed in five weeks, Schwartz's soft rock score with lyrics taken mainly from hymns, psalms, and other religious sources, was interpolated into the already-running off Broadway show. After a run of 2,118 performances, the show moved uptown to Broadway in June 1976, where it ran an additional 527 performances. *Godspell* ran in New York for six years, was made into a movie, was revived off Broadway in 1988 and in 2000, and still has road companies touring the world.

Godspell wasn't entirely new. Many of its devices were culled from the experimental theatre movement of the sixties. Just as *Jesus Christ Superstar* built on the experiments of *Tommy*, so too *Godspell* built on the experiments of *Hair* and other shows, creating a "happening" more than a conventional stage show. Off off Broadway playwright Robert Patrick's *Joyce Dynel* had already tread this territory in 1969 with its carnivalesque travesty on the life of Christ, with hippies reenacting episodes from the Bible under the leadership of a gay poet (played by Patrick), using comic songs, slapstick, acrobatics, and other tools of comedy and vaudeville. According to some reports, Tebelak openly admitted that he based *Godspell* on devices he had seen in Tom O'Horgan's production of Paul Foster's experimental theatre piece *Tom Paine* at LaMaMa.

Still, *Godspell* is the show that become a worldwide sensation, and it was something arguably special, not a revue or a variety show but a happening, a literal religious experience. Unfortunately, far too often over the years in local and regional productions and in tours, the spiritual side of the material has been ignored in favor of gags and cute choreography. These productions can still be entertaining, but they are rarely as moving as they should be. The Last Supper and the crucifixion are not powerful moments in these lesser productions because no emotional foundation has been created. Those familiar with Christianity know that they *should* be moved, but they aren't. For the show to succeed, the audience must be "converted" (in the broadest sense) along with the cast. Likewise, many productions add a resurrection (usually tied to the curtain call) that the show's creators never intended. Stephen Schwartz has written, "*Godspell* is not meant to have a resurrection. *Godspell* was never meant to be a musical version of the story of Jesus. It is rather the story of the formation of a community. By the end of the play we are supposed to feel that this community is going to thrive after Jesus is gone based on the lessons learned from his teachings."

Tebelak based the show's original concept on Harvey Cox's 1969 book *Feast of Fools*, which argued (as the hippies did) that for religion to once again reach the people, it had to reclaim its festivity. Much of organized religion had become so somber, so serious, that the joy had gone out of it. From this concept, Tebelak seized on the idea of using clowns to recapture that lost feeling of celebration and revelry. The cast of *Godspell* put on clown makeup and colorful costumes after being drawn together by Jesus. The cast as ordinary people becoming clowns illustrated a dramatic change, a very visible kind of conversion. This hybrid of clowns and flower children was a familiar image to audiences of the early 70s. It is not, however, to audiences today, so contemporary productions often look for a different basic concept in which to work, discarding the trappings of the hippie movement for more relevant images. Still, when done well, *Godspell* retains its power and is one of the most produced musicals in the world today.

The next new black musical—the first of many to include the word *Don't* in its title—was *Don't Bother Me, I Can't Cope*, which first opened at Vinnette Carroll's Urban Arts Corps Theatre, snuggled into a downtown loft space. It first played in several theatres around New York during the 1970–71 season, then went on a minitour to Washington, DC, Philadelphia, and Detroit, before returning to New York. *Don't Bother Me* was a decidedly less angry show than other black pieces, and one of its creators, Micki Grant, said in an interview, "I believe there is room for all kinds of theatre; it doesn't have to be one or the other. There's room for angry Black theatre and there's room for a show like ours, a show that has pride and dignity and music that is indigenous to our background. The show is *us*, and we hope we are communicating to everyone. We are not doing this show to be separate." The idea that there could be more than one philosophy of black theatre was the mark of the subgenre's maturity.

Vinnette Carroll, who conceived and directed *Don't Bother Me*, was a genuine visionary and the founder of the Urban Arts Corps, created in the late 1960s so that "a black actor could have a place to learn his art and not have to rely on just being black to get a job." Carroll also said "white producers won't pick up anything intellectual by us, no matter how good it is. They only want the singing and dancing. It's where the quick money is." *Don't Bother Me* was the group's first major success. It opened off Broadway in April 1972 at the Playhouse Theatre, running for 63 performances. Then it moved to the Edison Theatre on Broadway in June 1972 where it ran an additional 1,002 performances. The show won two Obie Awards, two Drama Desk awards, an Outer Critics Circle Award, an NAACP Image Award, and one Tony nomination.

In May 1970, something else quite unusual, quite extraordinary hit the stage, another unlikely but fascinating experiment. New York schoolteacher Stephen M. Joseph had put together a collection of poetry called *The Me Nobody Knows*, written by inner-city kids, mostly African American and Nuyorican (Puerto Rican New Yorkers) ages seven to eighteen. Herb Schapiro thought it should be a musical. Following in the nonlinear footsteps of *Hair*, he enlisted composer Gary William Friedman, lyricist Will Holt, director Robert Livingston, and choreographer Patricia Birch, and they made a musical out of the desperate longings, dreams, fears, joys, and barely intact innocence of real ghetto kids.

Far from being depressing, Clive Barnes reported in his *New York Times* review, "as I left, the audience was cheering, and it was not cheering gloom, but the victory of the human spirit over circumstances. For the slums these kids find themselves in may be squalid, but the kids are beautiful. And the show, assertive and passionate, reflects that beauty." The show opened off Broadway at the Orpheum Theatre in May 1970 and ran 208 performances, then moved to the Helen Hayes on Broadway in December 1970, and later the Longacre Theatre, for a total Broadway run of 370 performances.

Melvin Van Peebles, who was becoming a major force in black theatre, opened *Don't Play Us Cheap!*, based on a French novel, at San Francisco State

College in November 1970. It was such a success it moved to Broadway in May 1972. With Peebles' show *Ain't Supposed to Die a Natural Death* already playing Broadway by that time, he became one of the few writers ever to have two Broadway shows running at once. A black slice-of-life show, *Don't Play Us Cheap!* was set at a Saturday night party at Miss Maybell's "railroad flat," and takes the form of a raucous counterpart to Sondheim's *Company*, weaving together several character studies, and in the process providing a character study of an American culture that television and movies weren't yet showing us in 1971.

This was an honest, rowdy, deeply felt concept musical, the kind of show only Melvin Van Peebles was writing. *Variety* wrote, "Unlike *Ain't*, this new show does not seem to be infused with hate, and it offers what appears to be a racial attitude without foul language, deliberate squalor, or snarling ugliness. The points are made with humor rather than rage and they are probably more palatable and persuasive for general audiences." But, of course, Van Peebles wasn't all that concerned about "general audiences." With outstanding arrangements by Harold Wheeler, *Don't Play Us Cheap!* ran 164 performances and was nominated for two Tonys, including best book.

In 1971, Prince and Sondheim were back, this time with a show that explicitly presaged the death of old-fashioned musicals. *Follies* opened in April, with a book by James Goldman, a score by Sondheim, choreography by hotshot Michael Bennett, and direction by Prince and Bennett together. The show depicted a reunion of former *Follies* girls in their old theatre just before it gets torn down, and it focused on two of those girls and their husbands, all regretting roads not taken, all still living in the past, all surviving in carefully constructed illusions.

Beneath the surface, *Follies* was about the death of cutesy, escapist musicals and revues (like the wrongheaded revival of *No, No, Nanette* that was running at the time) and about the destruction and loss of the American dream in the Vietnam era. Just as *Godspell* had been informed by the innocence, joy, and love of the hippie culture, *Follies* was informed by the disillusionment and loss of America's innocence during Vietnam. Sondheim would return to the theme of a false American Dream in his later musicals, including *Merrily We Roll Along*, *Bounce*, and especially *Assassins*. As a young *Harvard Crimson* reviewer destined to be the senior critic for the *New York Times*, a college-age Frank Rich wrote about the show, "Its creators are in essence presenting their own funeral." The old-fashioned musical was now dead. Or was it? Would it ever be fully extinct? *Nanette* was still running. . . .

On a deeper, more personal thematic level, *Follies* was about illusion and delusion, and about both the necessity and danger of illusion; subtextually, it was about the lies America had told itself throughout the 1950s and 1960s, lies that were only now being exposed. Each of the four main characters lived in an illusion that he or she needed in order to survive but that was also dangerous. Over the course of the show, we saw each of those illusions dismantled. By the end of the evening, the party and the other guests have disappeared, the audience left wondering where they are, were they ever really there, or was it all a dream, a hallucination? Through the subtext, Prince and Sondheim were declaring that musical theatre would (or at least *should*) no longer participate in America's self-deception.

Sondheim's score mined the past, but more in tribute than in parody. Half his score paid loving homage to styles and times gone by, with songs like "Beautiful Girls" (in the style of Irving Berlin and Jerome Kern), "Rain on the Roof" (in the style of Vincent Youmans and Otto Harbach), "Ah, Paris" (in the style of Cole Porter's list songs), "Broadway Baby" (in the style of DeSylva, Brown, and Henderson), "Who's That Woman" (in the style of the Gershwins), "One More Kiss" (in the style of the operetta composers Friml and Lehar), "Loveland" (in the style of Kern and Harbach), "You're Gonna Love Tomorrow" (in the style of Burton Lane, the Gershwins, or maybe Rodgers and Hart), "Love Will See Us Through" (in the style of Harold Arlen and Yip Harburg), "Buddy's Blues" (an Al Jolson or Eddie Cantor number), "Losing My Mind" (a song Arlen or Kern might have written for Helen Morgan), "Lucy and Jessie" (in the style of Kurt Weill or Eubie Blake), and "Live, Laugh, Love" (in the style of Porter or maybe Noel Coward).

The other half of the score was pure, ambivalent, aching Sondheim, full of unexpected melodies, rich harmonies, ironic wordplay and more deeply felt emotion than the old-fashioned numbers could ever muster. As Sara Krulwich wrote in the *New York Times* in 2005, "A hallmark of Mr. Sondheim's greatest lyrics is this ability to express the inner lives of his characters with a precision and depth that transcends their capacity to express themselves, but still feels natural and profoundly truthful. The creation of such layered work is something most songwriters don't even consider. For Mr. Sondheim, the ultimate perfectionist, it has always been a necessity."

Follies aggressively pushed the concept musical forward, replacing traditional chronology with a stream-of-consciousness structure, but it also stalled the new genre, because it cost so much and lost so much. It was the second most expensive musical ever produced up to that point (after the flop *Coco*), costing $800,000. *Follies* ran 522 performances—not a failure artistically or historically, but certainly one financially. Douglas Watt of the *Daily News* called it "a pastiche so brilliant as to be breathtaking at times. Indeed, it struck me as unlikely that the tools and resources of the Broadway musical theatre had ever been used to more cunning effect than in this richly imaginative work."

In 1985, an all-star, two-night concert version was produced at Lincoln Center starring Mandy Patinkin, Barbara Cook, Lee Remick, George Hearn, Carol Burnett, Elaine Strich, Betty Comden and Adolph Green, and others. The show was revised, softened, and opened in 1987 in London, but didn't do well, some argued because it had been dumbed down. It was then revived on Broadway in 2001 to moderate success. Of the 2001 revival, Nancy Franklin wrote in the *New Yorker*, "It is possible to think *Follies* is a great show and yet not entirely love it; to think that it's invaluable and yet not feel embraced by it. You may walk out of the theatre feeling a little mixed up inside, as though you had just received the most unforgettable parting kiss of your life."

But of course that was the point.

The title referred to so many things: the *Ziegfeld Follies* certainly, but also the folly of escapism in entertainment, the folly of living in the past, and the symbol of the *Follies* as a kind of contrived American innocence that was never real to begin with and that was destroyed forever by the Vietnam War. *Follies* was both an old-fashioned revue in its pastiche numbers harkening back to the lavish Broadway confections of the 1920s, 30s, and 40s, and a fiercely modern American concept musical exploring a nonlinear idea through the use of many of the devices once the territory of *Hair* and other experimental pieces.

But if frothy old-fashioned musicals had been laid to rest by *Follies*, how could one explain the success of the *No, No, Nanette* revival or *42nd Street* a decade later or, for that matter, *Grease*? The phenomenon that was *Grease* began its long life in the summer of 1971 in a basement theatre in Chicago where an audience of a hundred sat on the floor on newspaper. The set consisted of backdrops painted on brown paper. At that time the show had far less music and far less plot, and no central characters. But it did have infectious songs like "Greased Lightning," "Beauty School Dropout," "Those Magic Changes," and "We Go Together." New York producers Ken Waissman and Maxine Fox saw the show and recognized its honesty and the appeal of its rough edges.

Once the producers decided to bring *Grease* to New York, they set about finding a production staff. One agent tried to sell them on hiring the bright young director-choreographer Michael Bennett, but they didn't think he was right for *Grease*. They were probably right. They asked Gerald Freedman to direct, since he had helmed the original off Broadway production of *Hair*, an equally raw, unpolished theatre piece, but he turned them down without even reading the script. They finally settled on Tom Moore and choreographer Patricia Birch who had created such interesting, *real* choreography for *The Me Nobody Knows*. The producers wanted everything about the show to feel rough, unpolished, unglamorized—*honest*—an idea the subsequent film and the 1994 revival did not understand.

Though *Grease* was largely brain candy, it very honestly captured a major turning point in American culture, that moment when The Teenager appeared out of thin air. Until the 1950s, children were children until they married and moved out. But suddenly, due to postwar prosperity and the invention of the suburbs, children didn't all have to work anymore. Teenagers had leisure time they had never had before. They had pocket money. Some even had cars. And for the first time in human history, teenagers were teaching teenagers about sex, with predictable amounts of (now comic) misinformation. And that's what *Grease* was about, a new era in the history of human sexuality. Nearly every song in *Grease* was about sex, and nearly every scene demonstrated these kids' ignorance about the topic. The show's lyrics were vulgar, there were jokes about condoms, Rizzo thinks she's pregnant, and Marty worries that Vince Fontaine may have slipped an aspirin into her coke at the dance in order to knock her out and rape her. This was a show about real stuff, trivial to us but life-and-death to these kids, and like *Hair*, it was a show that would fall apart in too slick a production.

After only three and half weeks of rehearsal (again, in an effort to keep it from looking too polished), *Grease* opened off Broadway at the Eden Theatre on Valentine's Day 1972. The reviews were negative to mixed. One hapless television reviewer said, "The worst thing I've ever seen opened tonight at the Eden Theatre." It ran 128 performances anyway. And then the show moved in June 1972 uptown to the Broadhurst Theatre. It was nominated for seven Tony Awards but won none. The 1978 film version starring John Travolta, Olivia Newton-John, and Stockard Channing became one of the most successful movie musicals of all time. In December 1979, *Grease* on stage broke the long-run record. The show made several moves during its Broadway run and finally closed April 13, 1980 after a total run of 3,388 performances. The original production paid back its investors four thousand percent. The show also ran for over two years in Mexico—under the title *Vaselina*—becoming the longest-running musical there.

Over its life, *Grease* gave starts to many now well-known actors, including John Travolta (who had begun as Doody in the first national tour), Richard Gere, Treat Williams, Patrick Swayze, Adrienne Barbeau, Barry Bostwick, Jeff Conaway, Greg Evigan, Marilu Henner, and Judy Kaye. A glitzy, neon-heavy revival of *Grease* opened in May 1994, painfully misdirected and misunderstood by Tommy Tune's protégé, director-choreographer Jeff Calhoun. But despite the lack of taste or honesty, it was apparently perfect for the theme park Broadway had become and it ran 1,503 performances. It was not, however, *Grease*.

In the seventies, no one would have expected to see yet *another* Broadway musical based on the Bible. And they certainly didn't expect it to be based on a pop/rock album about the last seven days in the life of Jesus Christ. After all, the youth movement of the sixties had been about spirituality but *also* about a rejection of institutionalized religion. Drug use was not just an escape for young people; they believed it was also a means to help disaffected youth find the spirituality they believed their parents had lost in the meaningless hypocrisy of organized religion. In 1967, Father James Kavanaugh had published his book *A Modern Priest Looks at His Outdated Church*. Looking at their parents and the rest of the "older generation," American youth saw evidence that mainstream religion had reduced religious experience, the act of living through faith, to nothing more than symbols and metaphors, subverting and short-circuiting the religious experience. They believed that mainstream religious traditions and rituals got in the way of true faith and the search for ultimate truths. And because more young Americans than ever before were attending college and while there, studying other world religions, they were finding that the Christian creation/Genesis story, the sacrifice/crucifixion and resurrection of Jesus Christ, the miracles performed by Jesus, and most of the rest of the central stories of Christianity had shown up in other world religions long before the birth of Christianity. Though this did not automatically discount all of Christianity for them, it did throw its claims of absolute and unique truth into question. As a result, many young adults began exploring the older Eastern religions.

Into this world came *Jesus Christ Superstar*, a musical not about divinity but about political activism, a story arguably focused more on Judas than on Jesus. In October 1969, Tim Rice and Andrew Lloyd Webber had recorded the title song as a single in London, and it had been released in May 1970, shooting to the top of the British pop music charts. In October 1970 they released the full-length album of their rock opera. It wasn't the first of its kind—*Tommy* gets that distinction—but it was certainly a landmark. By February, the single reached the top of the American charts.

The show opened on Broadway at the Mark Hellinger Theatre on October 12, 1971, under the flamboyant, extravagant, over-the-top direction of *Hair's* skipper, Tom O'Horgan, running 711 performances. It then opened at the Palace Theatre in London in August 1972 in a much scaled down version (as the authors had always wanted), and it became the longest-running musical in London. A film version was already in preparation and it was released in October 1973. Rice and Webber shot to international stardom. Since its creation, the show has been translated into eleven languages and played twenty-two countries, grossing well over a hundred million British pounds. The show was not just the first rock/pop opera on stage, but also the first to employ an iconic logo as an *über* marketing tool, forging a path for future pop operas like *Evita*, *Les Misérables*, *Miss Saigon*, *Phantom of the Opera*, *Sunset Boulevard*, and most famously, *Cats*.

Strangely, O'Horgan's outrageous sensory-assaulting Broadway production wasn't what had been originally intended. Producer Robert Stigwood had wanted to stage the piece more simply, perhaps using projections and television screens to underline Tim Rice's themes of celebrity and stardom. He first hired Frank Corsaro, a veteran theatre director who been working in opera. Corsaro seemed perfect for the project. But Corsaro was in a severe auto accident and was unable to do the show. O'Horgan replaced him, and no one involved—Stigwood, Rice, or Webber—was particularly happy with the way the show turned out. It started its run selling out every night, riding the popularity of the album, but the enthusiasm diminished quickly and the show never made it to its second birthday.

Clive Barnes wrote in the *New York Times*, "Once [O'Horgan] startled us with small things, now he startles us with big things. This time, the things got too big. For me, the real disappointment came not in the music, but in the conception. There is a coyness in its contemporaneity, a sneaky pleasure in the boldness of its anachronisms, a special undefined air of smugness in its daring." In

London, the show was staged more simply and more honestly by Jim Sharman, who would soon be helping to birth *The Rocky Horror Show*. It ran there for eight years.

Today many people don't like Lloyd Webber's work, but the composer of *Superstar* is a different Lloyd Webber from the one who wrote *Phantom of the Opera* and *Sunset Boulevard*. When he began his career, he wrote in the rock and roll idiom, a musical language he knew and loved. No one can deny that he can write a beautiful melody, but his musical vocabulary has always been limited. Consequently, he excelled in the relatively simple, repetitive language of rock and roll—*Joseph*, *Superstar*, and *Evita*, even *Cats*—but when he tried later to write in a more classical, more sophisticated style, his limitations showed through. What seems driving and primal in *Superstar* sounds merely repetitious in the classical European sound of *Phantom* or the pseudo-jazz style of *Sunset Boulevard*. His writing ability hasn't diminished, but when he changed styles his limits were thrown into sharper relief. Our expectations changed and he couldn't. Most critics believe that, unlike other theatre writers, Lloyd Webber has not grown as a composer over time. Luckily, we can still enjoy *Jesus Christ Superstar* and *Evita*, both set on the cynical, literate, and provocative lyrics of Tim Rice.

But rock and roll—*pure* rock and roll—doesn't usually make for very good theatre music. For much of the twentieth century, popular music and theatre music were the same. The musical theatre provided pop singers with hundreds of songs. But when rock took over the popular music scene, Broadway was slow to catch up. During the seventies, Broadway producers tried to use rock and roll to give theatre attendance a boost. Unfortunately, in the early 1970s, the people who were listening to rock were not the people who were buying theatre tickets. A few shows succeeded with mellower, hybrid "Broadway pop" music, like *Superstar*, *Pippin*, *The Wiz*, and *Godspell*, but pure rock just didn't work on stage. More pop/rock musicals made it in the eighties, once rock and roll fans were old enough to be ticket buyers—*Dreamgirls*, *Little Shop of Horrors*, *Song and Dance*, *Evita*, *Cats*, and others. Even later the pop/rock musicals that succeeded (*Les Misérables*, *Miss Saigon*, and *Blood Brothers*) employed a greatly altered kind of soft rock music.

The reason pure rock and pop music doesn't usually work in a stage musical is largely its intrinsically repetitive nature. Rock music uses far fewer chords than classical or theatre music does; in extreme cases, an entire song can use only four chords (and many pop songs in the 1950s did just that). The kind of musical development and invention necessary to hold an audience's attention over two hours is usually missing entirely. Likewise, rock lyrics are by their nature also highly repetitive. A typical pop song repeats its chorus many times, usually with the exact same lyric each time. Conversely, a theatre song has to convey a great deal of information about character, situation, subtext, foreshadowing, and plot. Because of its repetitiveness, a rock song just doesn't have the time and space to communicate that much information. Part of the appeal of rock and roll is its simplicity, our ability to sing along after hearing the first chorus; but theatre music that's too simplistic will put an audience to sleep. Rock is about the beat; theatre songs are about information.

When setting the story of Jesus' last seven days in *Superstar*, lyricist Tim Rice approached the story as history instead of scripture, Jesus as political activist instead of the Son of God. This approach was considered blasphemous by many people. Most of the show's critics believed that the story of Jesus should not be set to rock music, the music of rebellion. But Jesus was a major political and social rebel of his time; he fought against the establishment, the high priests, the Pharisees, the people with *power*. What better way to tell his story than with the contemporary sound of rebellion? Keeping the stories of Jesus and his views in antique forms takes the teeth out of his activism. There's no reason people should not celebrate their beliefs in the language and music of their lives. Today, *Superstar* doesn't seem so controversial because rock and roll is now the music of adults, and guitars are now allowed in Catholic masses. But imagine the uproar if the Catholic church began allowing rap music as part of the liturgy.

The greatest objection of all was that *Superstar* did not include the resurrection. Tim Rice told an interviewer that he did not believe Jesus was the Son of God, but for him, that made the story all the more amazing. Rice said in interviews that the action of *Jesus Christ Superstar* is fictional, a version of how it *might* have been. Because he treated the story as history, he took the facts he could establish and filled in the blanks himself. Several characters in the show are only sketchily drawn in the Bible stories—Mary Magdalene, Pilate, Caiaphas—but to bring them to life on stage (or on LP), Rice had to flesh them out, give them personalities, inner life, motivation, backstory. The Bible is event driven, but *Superstar* is character driven, focusing not on what happened, but on why. As with most musicals or plays based on famous historical events (*Evita*, *1776*, *Two by Two*), we already know the basics of the plot, so more time can be spent on subtext, on inner life, on what made these people act as they did. *Superstar* focuses on the doubt that all the characters experience—the apostles, Mary, the priests, Pilate, and especially Judas and Jesus—making these characters people we can relate to and understand. We are able to put ourselves in Jesus' place and understand the turmoil and terror he must have felt. Because of the approach Rice took, it doesn't really matter in the context of the show whether or not Jesus was the Son of God; his followers believed it, and that's all that matters. The issue of religion is all but absent from the show, a conscious choice on the part of its creators, but a contentious choice to make and one that many subsequent directors have consciously tried to subvert.

In October 1971, a new show opened on Broadway that in years past would have opened off Broadway or even off off Broadway, *Ain't Supposed to Die a Natural Death*, subtitled *Tunes from Blackness*. Its creator, Melvin Van Peebles, already had created what would later be seen as the first "Blaxploitation" film, *Sweet Sweetback's Baadasssss Song*—the first Hollywood film to target a black audience exclusively—and it was a monster commercial success. Van Peebles was now trying to do the same thing on Broadway. Far from the politics of *Hair* or the good-hearted comedy of *Purlie*, this show was a hard-edged look at the people who lived in the slums of Harlem—prostitutes, pimps, homeless people, corrupt cops, drag queens, and others. Historian Glenn Litton described the show this way: "A blind man gets up his courage to introduce himself to a girl but she's really a he in drag, two lesbians swap news, the one standing in the street while the other shouts down from the Women's House of Detention, a girl is raped by two policemen. These and similar episodes built to a unique number in musical theatre history: a confrontation between the all-black cast and its audiences. The song was 'Put a Curse on You' and it indicted everyone, especially the exploitative white, for the sufferings of those in the black ghetto. Van Peebles didn't stop there. He ended his show with a ghetto riot." The show was tried out at Sacramento State College before coming to New York.

Clive Barnes wrote in the *New York Times*, "Black is coming to Broadway these days, and I mean real black, not just someone singing 'Ol' Man River'." He went on, "It is by no means a comfortable evening and many Broadway theatergoers will not understand what it is saying." To keep ticket sales up, Van Peebles invited black celebrities like Bill Cosby and Ossie Davis to do guest appearances in the show. But the mainstream press didn't want to promote this show. Television shows that regularly hosted casts and writers of other Broadway shows would not invite Van Peebles on the air; NBC's *Today* show was the exception.

One of the ways most Broadway shows sold tickets was through "theatre parties" sponsored by social clubs and other organizations. But no one had ever gone after African American theatre parties until *Purlie*. Now *Ain't Supposed to Die a Natural Death* put forth new efforts in that direction and proved to Broadway that there was a black audience out there just waiting to be invited. Van Peebles also started holding postshow discussions to involve the audience more fully, something serious regional theatres did, but never a Broadway show. *Ain't Supposed to Die a Natural Death* ran 325 performances and earned seven Tony nominations. Though *Don't Play Us Cheap* and *Don't Bother Me, I Can't Cope* were both created before *Ain't Supposed to Die*, the other two didn't make it to Broadway until later.

In 1971, *Hair*'s composer Galt MacDermot opened a multiracial rock musical version of Shakespeare's *Two Gentlemen of Verona*, with lyrics by playwright John Guare and an adapted book by director Mel Shapiro. Building on many of the themes in *Hair*, MacDermot and his collaborators returned to linear storytelling, though not without putting their own distinguishing mark on Shakespeare's original. First playing at the New York Shakespeare Festival's Delacorte Theatre in Central Park, it opened on Broadway in December, where it ran 613 performances and received nine Tony nominations, winning two for best musical and best book. It also won the New York Drama Critics Circle Award. The show was revived by The Public Theatre in 2005.

Clive Barnes wrote of the Delacorte production in the *New York Times*, "The New York Shakespeare Festival Public Theater is currently doing Shakespeare a power of good and turning Central Park into a place of celebration with its new production of *Two Gentlemen of Verona*. It is *jeu d'espirit*, a bardic spree, a midsummer night's jest, a merriment of lovers, a gallimaufry of styles and a gas. It takes off." After its move uptown, Barnes wrote, "It has a surge of youth to it, at times an almost carnal intimation of sexuality, and a boisterous sense of love. It is precisely this that the new musical catches and makes its own. The musical also has a strange New York feel to it—in the music, a mixture of rock, lyricism and Caribbean patter, in Mr. Guare's spare, at times even abrasive lyrics, in the story itself of small-town kids and big-town love. It also has a very New York sense of irreverence. It is a graffito written across a classic play, but the graffito has an insolent sense of style, and the classic play can still be clearly glimpsed underneath."

This was the only one of the post-*Hair* projects to succeed. MacDermot went on to write two other shows in the next couple years, *Dude* (with *Hair* co-author Gerry Ragni), and *Via Galactica*. Both were huge flops and closed fast. MacDermot would never have another show on Broadway.

All these important shows—*Purlie, Company, Godspell, Don't Bother Me, I Can't Cope, The Me Nobody Knows, Don't Play Us Cheap!, Follies, Grease, Jesus Christ Superstar, Ain't Supposed to Die a Natural Death, Two Gentlemen of Verona,* and a number of others—had begun life in 1970 and 1971. The seventies were going to be an important period in the development of the musical theatre, giving lie to the belief that the so-called golden age had stopped in 1964.

The next big thing on Broadway was *Pippin*, a largely under-appreciated musical with a great deal more substance to it than many people realized. With music and lyrics by Stephen Schwartz and a book by Roger Hirson (greatly tampered with—some say completely rewritten—by Bob Fosse, though Hirson denies it), it opened on Broadway in October 1972. But the real star of the show was not the Leading Player, played by Ben Vereen, or Pippin, played by John Rubenstein. No, the real star was director-choreographer-bookwriter-dictator Bob Fosse.

After *Godspell* had opened, songwriter Stephen Schwartz had returned to looking for a producer for a show he had written in college called *Pippin, Pippin*. Stuart Ostrow agreed to produce it, but wanted a new script. By the time the new book was written by Roger Hirson, now called *The Adventures of Pippin*, an entirely new score had to be written as well. The show now told the story of a young man named Pippin going on a quest for fulfillment and self-awareness and the traveling troupe of *commedia dell'arte* players who play out his life for him, so that he can experiment with various life choices in relative safety. To stage the show, Ostrow hired Bob Fosse. But Fosse didn't like the show. He thought it was cute and sentimental, and Fosse had developed a reputation for dark, often disturbing musical theatre. He wanted to make *Pippin* into more his kind of show.

He created the character of Leading Player, a narrator, Devil, and Best Buddy, who accompanies Pippin on his quest, and who also controls the events as they are played out. In Fosse's version, Leading Player and his troupe wanted Pippin to perform their very special Grand Finale—setting himself on fire—and they made sure that Pippin failed at everything he tried, so that the finale would be his only remaining stab at greatness. The show became relentlessly dark and cynical.

It originally opened with the troupe of players arriving in a field with their wagon of props; Fosse's new opening set them on the stage the audience was watching—complete naturalism. The original happy ending became a compromise instead of a victory; instead of finding true happiness, Pippin finds he must settle for less than he really wants. Fosse turned the love song "With You" into an orgy. He remade the entire show as a parade of frightening, disturbing, often psychedelic episodes in which Pippin finds less and less satisfaction.

Stephen Schwartz, Roger Hirson, and John Rubenstein (who played Pippin) all disliked the rewrites and the style of the show as it was finally set. But it opened in October of 1972 and was generally regarded as something innovative and exciting. The reviews were mostly positive, declaring that though the score was less than stellar, Fosse's unusual conception and direction had made the show into an incredible piece of theatre. *Pippin* won five Tony Awards that year, including best director and best choreographer for Fosse, and best actor for Ben Vereen. Neither the show's script nor its score won Tonys. After the Broadway run, Schwartz had much of Fosse's material taken back out of the script and his and Hirson's work restored. It is this tamer, watered-down version which is now available for amateur productions. The 1981 videotaped production of the show that was released commercially, though it is only an imitation of the original without Fosse's involvement, does include much of Fosse's original material.

Because the show rejected a Happily-Ever-After in favor of a real-world ending of compromise and doubt, and because it was happening in real time and on a stage, *Pippin* was one of the most naturalistic musicals ever produced. Though the show-within-a-show was set in Charlemagne's France, it was *really* about the here and now; it was sprinkled with anachronisms in the costumes and dialogue, and made no pretense at being a period piece despite its characters' historical names. The show dealt with the coming of age, the rites of passage, the lack of role models and guideposts for young adults in disillusioned 1972 America, and with the hopelessness that had become more and more prevalent among young Americans. Because of its 1970s pop score and its subsequent, gentler licensed version, the show later gained a reputation for being merely cute and harmlessly naughty; but in its original form, the way Fosse envisioned it, the show was crazily surreal, fiercely disturbing, and arguably brilliant—including the underrated but highly sophisticated score.

Pippin ran 1,944 performances, its long run due in part to a new idea in advertising Broadway shows: television commercials. Fosse begged producer Stuart

Ostrow to let him film a thirty-second commercial for *Pippin* and Ostrow agreed to pay for it. So Fosse used Ben Vereen and two women (dubbed by the cast "the Manson Trio") dancing a soft shoe section from the song "Glory." No set, no spectacle, no singing, just a soft shoe and a voiceover. It wasn't what you'd expect to sell a musical like *Pippin* but it did; after all, *Pippin* was about style and attitude, minimalism more than eye candy. Ticket sales skyrocketed. Lots of shows followed suit and television became the biggest piece of the Broadway advertising budget. By the time it closed, *Pippin* had earned a net profit of more than $3.3 million.

The next musical to open in 1972 looked backward, but in an interesting way. *Hair* co-author Jim Rado wrote the music and the lyrics and, with his brother Ted, the book for a kind of sequel to *Hair*, the rock musical *Rainbow*, which opened off Broadway at the Orpheum Theatre in December. With a hefty score of forty-two songs, it picked up exactly where *Hair* left off, following Claude's after-death journey, although its central character was now the allegorically named Man who had been killed in Vietnam and found himself on the "other side," in Rainbow Land. The characters included a mother and father, Jesus Christ, Buddha, a wizard, a girl and her lesbian twin, a stripper, and the President and First Lady. Man went to Washington to confront the President about Vietnam and the President finally saw the horror and absurdity of the war, apologized to Man, and ended the war. Ironically, in the real world, U.S. bombing of Vietnam had stopped and peace talks had begun, but they had fallen apart, and on opening night of *Rainbow*, as the show's fictional President agreed to end the war, the real President resumed bombing.

Douglas Watt's review in the *Daily News* was mixed. He wrote, "High spirits and lively music can combine to produce a whale of a party, and, given the advantage of form, they can make for an entertaining evening of theater, too. But although *Rainbow*, which came to the Orpheum last night, is spirited and tuneful, it is also shapeless and, when all is said and done, mere child's play." Clive Barnes of the *New York Times* liked the show more. He wrote, "It is the first musical to derive from *Hair* that really seems to have the confidence of a new creation about it, largely derived from James Rado's sweet and fresh music and lyrics." Still, it had only a short run and never transferred to Broadway. Rado continues to revise it with hopes of another major production.

In 1973 director-producer Hal Prince resurrected *Candide*, the musical satire by Leonard Bernstein and a phalanx of other writers. It had flopped miserably in 1956 but had gotten relatively strong reviews, one calling it "a work of genius." Hal Prince put the show back together, this time with a new script by Hugh Wheeler and new songs by Bernstein and Stephen Sondheim. The new production played the Chelsea Theater, then moved to the Brooklyn Academy of Music in December for a limited run of 48 performances. The show was such a hit, it moved to the Broadway Theatre in March 1974.

Not only was material rewritten for this revival, but the entire show was turned on its head. The creative team went back to Voltaire's original 1759 novel for inspiration and found the humor the show had lacked in 1956. They cut a character, consciously put together a *very* young cast, added songs, added a narrator (who also played several characters) and completely transformed the physical look of the show. Prince gutted the Broadway Theatre and created an "environmental" production, in which the entire theatre became the environment of the story, the action happening all around and through the audience, on fourteen small stages, connected by bridges and ramps. The audience sat around and through the playing area on stools, so they could rotate as the action moved. The idea of environmental theatre was not new. It wasn't even new to Broadway because the flop *Dude* had tried it (in the same theatre). But this was the first time it had *worked* with a musical.

Clive Barnes wrote in the *New York Times*, "*Candide* is even sharper, funnier, wittier, and if possible, more musically elegant." Barnes went on to say about the 1956 production, "It was a show sunk by its book, and just as much, by the conventional approach. Hal Prince, the new director, has said to hell with the past. He has put the entire thing into a giant fun-house of an environmental theatre. Prince has, in the past, given Broadway innumerable gifts, but nothing so gaudy, glittering and endearing as this. It is one of those shows that take off like a rocket and never come down." This *Candide* enjoyed a run of 740 performances, winning four Tony Awards for Prince, Wheeler, and the costume and set designers. It was also given a special Tony Award, which led in 1977 to the establishment of a best revival Tony Award. The show also won a New York Drama Critics Circle Award.

Prince revived the show again in 1982 for the New York City Opera, with the full-sized chorus restored, some original music put back, and some new book scenes. But on a proscenium stage with opera singers rather than theatre actors, it just wasn't the same. Prince did it again in 1997 with a Broadway revival at the Gershwin Theatre, basically recreating his 1982 direction. It ran 103 performances.

The Rocky Horror Show, that great cult phenomenon with music and lyrics by Richard O'Brien and a script by O'Brien and (uncredited) by director Jim Sharman and the original cast, first hit the London stage in 1973. At its core *Rocky Horror* told a tale we've heard many times before, back even before Shakespeare, of braving a wilderness, of surviving lost innocence, of sexual awakening, about acceptance of difference, about birth and death, forgiveness and redemption, about the fall from grace of a transgressive god. And yet there was something special and relevant there, born as it was in the midst of London's alternative theatre movement and at the beginning of the punk rock era. Of its first production in London, Jack Tinker wrote in the *Daily Mail*, "Richard O'Brien's spangled piece of erotic fantasy is so funny, so fast, so sexy, and so unexpectedly well realised that one is in danger of merely applauding it without assessing it. That would be a pity. Because I believe Mr. O'Brien has something quite nifty to say."

Rocky Horror explored American sexual hang-ups, the excesses of the Sexual Revolution, and the sometimes cruel myth of the American Dream. It used as its vocabulary pop culture icons like Charles Atlas and muscle magazines, Frederick's of Hollywood, old sci-fi movies with scantily clad women, horror movies with barely sublimated sexual fantasies, glam rock with its blurring of gender lines—all icons that represented the history of Americans hiding sex behind other things. And perhaps it's *Rocky's* underlying condemnation of America's sexual puritanicalism and hypocrisy that keeps the show relevant today. *Rocky* satirizes sex in America by personifying in Brad and Janet the two responses American society had toward the sexual revolution of the 1960s and 70s, and the revolution itself personified by the gender-vague, pansexual Frank N. Furter. In the real world, half of America (Brad) responded to the Sexual Revolution by fighting even harder than before to stop the progression of sexual freedom, to demonize homosexuality, to condemn sexual independence in women, to blame all of America's ills on sex, to brand (or *re*brand) otherwise healthy expressions of sexuality as dirty and inappropriate. The other half of America (Janet) responded with an almost manic sexual celebration and a kind of aggressive experimentation that today may seem outrageous. Both reactions in the real world probably made the early stages of the AIDS pandemic worse than it should have been. And *Rocky Horror* rightly satirizes both reactions. Both sides went too far.

The Rocky Horror Show is about a time in America when our nation stood at a crossroads. Sexual oppression was ending (or at least, beginning to fade) and America had to decide how it would move forward. But neither the people who celebrated this new era or the people terrified by it acted responsibly; neither side caused AIDS, but both sides helped it spread. Of course, *Rocky Horror* is not about AIDS. It was written in 1973. But it is about sexual politics in America. And watching it today, we can see a moment in time when it wasn't yet too late, when the devastation of a generation of innocent men and women should not have been inevitable. We can love the music, laugh at the jokes, and sing along with "The Time Warp," but we should never forget that *Rocky Horror* is *about* something.

Because the show was created entirely by British artists, it has the advantage of objectivity in its exploration and satire of these mostly American phenomena. Also because it was created by Brits, we can see its cross-dressing elements not entirely as subversive transgressions but instead just one more example in a long tradition of cross-dressing, from boys playing girls in Shakespeare's original plays to men playing women in British pantomime to the later androgyny of British glam rockers like David Bowie, Elton John, Freddie Mercury, Bryan Ferry, Boy George, and others. The cross-dressing in *Rocky* was perhaps the *least* subversive element when it opened in London.

Many of the people involved with the first productions of *Rocky Horror* have said in later interviews that they believe the subsequent American productions in Los Angeles and New York and the film version lost much of what was important about the show, its grit, its rawness, its confrontational directness, its relationship with its audience—a relationship quite different from the one the film developed with its audience. The original *Rocky* confronted and challenged its audience. Like *Hair*, *Rocky* was born out of the alternative theatre experiments of the 1960s. When it was mainstreamed (to the extent that *Rocky Horror* can be mainstreamed), when it was made slick and expensive, when the sets got better, when the score was orchestrated, some believe the show lost its politics, its proto-punk look, its edge, its soul. One listen to the original London cast album from 1973 reveals a *very* different show from the one many of us know today. Those who know only the film may not really understand what *Rocky* was in an upstairs, sixty-seat theatre.

All this may explain why the original production in London got such positive reviews and all subsequent productions and the film have gotten such negative reviews. The material was not changed in any substantial way, but its presentation was changed greatly. Perhaps the reason *Rocky Horror* has not been embraced by the critical community since 1973 is that they haven't seen *Rocky* as it was meant to be.

The show's original three week run in London had been extended to five weeks, then it was transferred to an old movie theatre destined for demolition. After the cinema was demolished, it moved to the King's Road Theatre. It was named best musical of 1973 in the *London Evening Standard*'s annual poll of drama critics and ran 2,960 performances. Critic Irving Waddle wrote, "This is theatre made out of the rawest and crudest ingredients, and forming a charge strong enough to obliterate anything standing in its tracks." Michael Billington wrote in *The Guardian*, "It achieves the rare feat of being witty and erotic at the same time." The *New Statesman* wrote, "The intention of course is to celebrate such freaks of pop culture as Hammer films, Alice Cooper, and the sci-fi of Michael Moorcook; and the result has tremendous invention, energy, and glee, right up to the final paean to bisexuality." The show has since been translated into over a dozen languages and played more than twenty countries. According to some accounts, *Rocky Horror* created the punk movement in London. Its look was the look of a new London subculture that would change the look and sound of rock and roll forever.

After unprecedented success in London, the show was brought to the Roxy Theatre in Los Angeles, but it wasn't the same there—flashier, slicker, less sincere, less innocent—and it didn't do as well. The producers then took it to Broadway, and for whatever reasons—some thought it was the New York critics' resentment that the show had opened in L.A. first—the show was panned and was a dismal flop, running only forty-five performances. It received one Tony Award nomination for lighting design but lost.

Clive Barnes wrote in the *New York Times*, "It was unexpected, unpretentious, and the cinema itself [in the original London production], from the peeling walls to the grubby seats, provided it with the perfect ambiance. It now looks flashy, expensive, and over-produced. Why did not someone understand—before the Los Angeles paint job—that the entire point of *The Rocky Horror Show* in London was that it was tacky?" Once the show's creative staff lifted *Rocky* up out of the realm of low-budget, minimalist, fringe theatre, they betrayed the low budget B-movies that were *Rocky*'s source material, and many argued they also lost *Rocky*'s soul.

A film version of *Rocky Horror* was made and it too was a big flop . . . until enterprising movie theatres started running the film at midnight. Some say it first happened in Austin, Texas, others say it was at the Waverly Theatre in New York (immortalized in *Hair*'s song "Frank Mills"). Within a few months, a cult hit had been born. Stage and screen director Jim Sharman and designer Brian Thompson had consciously made the film more gothic, less punk than the stage version had been.

The show was revived in London in 1999 and on Broadway in 2000 in a soulless carbon copy of the film. Of the New York revival, Clive Barnes wrote in the *New York Post*, "It was then [in 1973] bizarre, sweet and oddly charming. Arriving on Broadway two years later in an ill-advised and pointless cabaret setting, it looked weird, preposterous and distinctly charmless, and went belly-up after 45 performances. The current over-produced Broadway offering, directed by Christopher Ashley, clearly believes that nothing succeeds like excess and has piled encrustation upon ornamentation." Production designer David Rockwell was praised for capturing the "contemporary zeitgeist" with his *Rocky Horror* design, but apparently no one noticed that *Rocky* isn't about 2000; it's about 1973.

Rocky Horror had finally added intelligence and insightful satire to "sex musicals" in 1973, and *Let My People Come: A Sexual Musical* took it even further. With music and lyrics by Earl Wilson Jr. and direction by Phil Oesterman, the show opened in January 1974 at the Village Gate, where it ran an impressive 1,327 performances. It then moved to Broadway in July 1976, where it played another 122 performances at the Morosco Theatre before closing. A national tour was sent out and a cast album recorded. Much more than just a revue and less than a linear book musical, sitting strangely in that netherworld with other shows like *Jacques Brel* and *Songs for a New World*, the score included songs like "Come in My Mouth," "The Cunnilingus Champion of Company C," "I'm Gay," "Fellatio 101," and of course, "Let My People Come."

The producers, knowing full well how edgy their show was, never announced an official opening and never invited the critics. Mel Gussow of the *New York Times* came anyway, hated it, and panned it (*he sure showed them!*), but its success just continued. The cast was nude through much of the show, and even stood at the exits nude afterward to say goodbye to the audience. During its off Broadway run, in an effort to close the show down, the New York State Liquor Authority tried to strip the Village Gate Theatre of its license to sell alcohol at intermission. The theatre fought back and won, but not without a huge legal bill.

Not only was the show full of nudity and all about sex, its title was just as provocative as its content. Based on Moses' famous declaration in the Bible to "Let my people go," this show asked for sexual freedom from the powers that be (the modern day Pharaohs?), and in the process angered lots of "decent" folk. Interestingly, after the original off Broadway opening, the composer-lyricist and choreographer both took their names off the show's credits in protest over changes.

In 1974, playwrights Doric Wilson, Billy Blackwell, Peter del Valle, and John McSpadden formed The Other Side of Silence (TOSOS), the first professional theatre company in America to deal openly and honestly with the gay experience. Composer Steve Sterner and playwright del Valle's musical *Lovers* opened the Basement Theater on Church Street in downtown Manhattan. A remarkably forward-thinking, surprisingly well written concept musical, *Lovers* was an unlikely and (probably) unintentional companion piece to *Company*, an in-depth look at contemporary relationships, but in this case, strictly gay male relationships. What was amazing for 1974 was the show's content, not the usual fare found in the gay theatre and literature of the time, but instead material that audiences would have expected from a "straight" musical. *Lovers* focused on long-term relationships among gay men in New York, exploring love and sex, the act of "coming out," anniversaries, arguments and apologies, and the difficult terrain of gay monogamy.

Like *Company*, *Lovers* didn't have a strong, central plot, but there was certainly a strong central concept and the characters—an older couple together twenty years (one of whom dies), a couple into leather and sadomasochism, and a couple who were both Broadway dancers—were consistent throughout the show. Unlike *Company*, *Lovers* was mostly upbeat, romantic, cheerful, and proud. Its full name was *Lovers: The Musical That Proves It's No Longer Sad to Be Gay.* This was a fun show, tuneful and witty, but also serious-minded underneath it all. It defiantly and aggressively flipped the bird at mainstream theatre, daring in 1974 to suggest that gay relationships are pretty much like straight relationships, that gay people can be happy and loving, and more than anything, that all gay men are not like the self-loathing, bitter, hateful creeps in the earlier Broadway play *The Boys in the Band*, the only other representation of gays many people had seen on stage. The script and lyrics were clever, truthful, and frequently quite daring. The music was well-constructed, clearly (sometimes *too* clearly) finding its roots in *Hello, Dolly!*, *Sweet Charity*, *Company*, *Promises, Promises*, and *Applause*. After its initial run, it moved to a successful off Broadway run.

TOSOS went into hibernation in 1979. When the company had begun there were no other full-time gay theater companies; when it suspended production, the Gay Theater Alliance listed a hundred and fifty gay companies around the world. Then in June 2001, Doric Wilson, Mark Finley, and Barry Childs revived the company, now TOSOS II, opening with *Look Again!*, a series of concert readings surveying pre-AIDS plays and musicals.

Another interesting seventies musical, *The Robber Bridegroom*, likewise defied conventions and expectations, though in other directions. It was like no other musical ever conceived, with a "caller" calling scene changes like square dances, with an ensemble watching the proceedings from around the stage and playing multiple roles (in a nod to *Hair*), and with a score that sounded like genuine bluegrass, traditional Broadway, and Sondheim all at once. The words and music did the kind of heavy lifting many musical theatre scores couldn't manage, clearly informed by the concept musicals that had gone before it but also doggedly determined to follow Sondheim and Hal Prince's primary dictum: form follows content. In adapting Eudora Welty's novelized folktale, composer Robert Waldman and lyricist-bookwriter Alfred Uhry set out to translate Welty's tale into musical theatre terms, not to write a musical merely "based" on source material. They found musical theatre equivalents for Welty's folksy storytelling style as well as musical vocabulary so utterly organic to the characters—whiny, moaning, dissonant strings for the malevolent stepmother Salome (that's *Suh-LOW-mee*), throbbing, rhythmic pulsations, and some of the most erotic lyrics on Broadway for the lustful lovers Jamie and Rosamund. Even all these years later, few Broadway scores can boast the bold eroticism of songs like "Rosamund's Dream," "Sleepy Man," or "Deeper in the Woods," a song so full of sexual imagery it's almost unbearable and also utterly delicious.

The show began life as the very first production of producer Stuart Ostrow's nonprofit Musical Theatre Lab, at the Theatre at St. Clement's in New York, an institution that would further refine the "workshop" process for creating musicals. This first production of *The Robber Bridegroom* starred Raul Julia as the gentleman robber Jamie Lockhart. Then producer-director John Houseman's group The Acting Company took the show to the Saratoga Performing Arts Center in upstate New York, now with newcomers Kevin Kline and Patti LuPone in the leads, both recent graduates of Julliard, of which Houseman had been one of the founders. Houseman then took it on to the Ravinia Festival in Chicago during the summer of 1975. The Acting Company opened the show in New York (as a one-act) in October 1975 for a limited run of fifteen performances off Broadway at the Harkness Theatre, in rotating repertory with *The Three Sisters*, *Edward II*, and *The Time of Your Life*. Kline and LuPone remained in the leads, with Gerald Freedman (*Hair*'s original director) at the helm. The production went on a very successful national tour for a year with the cast from the Harkness. While on tour, the producers decided the show was doing well enough with audiences that they should open it on Broadway. So while the tour was still running, they opened a new production on Broadway. Unfortunately, that meant no one who had created these roles would be able to play them in the Broadway production.

The show was retooled, with an expanded, reordered score, and two new leads, Barry Bostwick and Rhonda Cullet, but still under the direction of Gerald Freedman. This new, full-length version opened on Broadway at the Biltmore Theatre (*Hair*'s Broadway home) on October 9, 1976. Only one song from the earlier version, "The Real Mike Fink," was dropped, but several were added, including "Once Upon a Natchez Trace," "Two Heads," Rosamund's Dream," and "Where Oh Where." It lasted only four months and 145 performances, but it remains one of the theatre's most adult, most sophisticated—and most deliriously *fun*—musicals.

Even though Ostrow was a commercial producer (*The Apple Tree, 1776,* and *Pippin,* among others), his nonprofit Musical Theatre Lab continued to develop new works of the musical theatre, first at St. Clements Church, then at the Kennedy Center, then in the early 1980s at Harvard University, and currently at the University of Houston, where Ostrow now teaches. Over the years, the innovative program has shepherded and developed musicals including *Really Rosie,* Arthur Miller's *Up from Paradise, American Passion, Crosstown Bus, Doll,* and many, many others.

During the 1960s, Jerry Herman had made a name for himself as the composer of perky, upbeat musicals that seemed to run forever about strong quirky women. His first Broadway show, *Milk and Honey,* did well, but he really conquered Broadway with *Hello, Dolly!* and *Mame.* But it was with *Mack and Mabel* in October 1974 that Herman secured his place in history as an *important* composer, not just a popular one; this was the show that lifted him above the likes of Frank Wildhorn and Bob Merrill and placed him squarely among the likes of Stephen Sondheim and Jerome Kern.

Mack and Mabel told the mostly true story of the real-life romance between silent movie era director Mack Sennett (creator of the Keystone Kops) and his star Mabel Normand. It was a deeply emotional, deeply complex, wholly adult story matched by sophisticated, achingly beautiful music and smart, adult lyrics. This was the best thing Herman had ever written and the show was blessed with Robert Preston and a still relatively unknown Bernadette Peters as the leads. Preston's "I Won't Send Roses" and Peters' "Time Heals Everything" were shattering expressions of real love that made even the loveliest moments from *Dolly* and *Mame* seem like child's play. But though everyone thought *Company* had prepared audiences for this kind of clear-eyed, real-world story, *Mack and Mabel* lasted only 65 performances. Maybe it was because director Gower Champion tried to make it into another *Hello, Dolly!* Maybe, like *Cabaret,* the show tried too hard to hedge its bets with conventional elements to balance the edgy stuff. Maybe *Mack and Mabel* was brave but not quite brave enough. Maybe today's regional theatres would accept it more on its own terms. Maybe today's theatre artists would commit more fully to the show's dark intentions.

Whatever the reasons, the show flopped. The reviewers thought the book was not focused or smart enough, that the show was overproduced, and that the creative team tried way too hard to keep it from being the serious, sad, adult musical it was. But it remains Herman's best score and Herman's own favorite. Yet it seems the theatre community didn't like Jerry Herman of the Frothy Musicals attempting Serious Musical Theatre. The 1976 Tony Awards committee nominated the show itself, Robert Preston and Bernadette Peters, Gower Champion twice (once as director, once as choreographer), Michael Stewart's book, and Robin Wagner's sets—but no nomination was to be found for Herman's magnificent score.

Then, one of the musical theatre's greatest shows, a genuine legend, a true masterwork, opened off Broadway in April 1975. Its strange title, so nonspecific and enigmatic, so intentionally anonymous, was *A Chorus Line*. And though it had a precedent or two (like *The Me Nobody Knows*), *A Chorus Line* essentially created (or at least popularized) a new genre, documentary musicals, a kind of show that presents people's real lives in their own words (more or less), only somewhat edited and shaped, without forcing those lives into a conventional story line.

Its creation had started two years earlier. In the winter of 1973, Tony Stevens and Michon Peacock, who had just choreographed the flop *Rachael Lily Rosenbloom (And Don't You Ever Forget It)*, decided the only way they were going to get a quality project to work on was to create one themselves. They invited established choreographer and aspiring director Michael Bennett to help them. These three decided just to get a bunch of dancers together to talk about their lives and work, with the possibility of fashioning a theatre piece out of the discussion. One of the dancers there was Nicholas Dante, who wanted to be a writer. After the sessions, Bennett tapped Dante to write whatever script might emerge, and Dante and Bennett interviewed even more dancers. Bennett talked to producer Joe Papp at the New York Shakespeare Festival, who agreed to finance a workshop. Bennett asked Bob Avian to be his assistant, Marvin Hamlisch to write the music, and Ed Kleban to write the lyrics. Then Bennett made the dancers audition—to play themselves.

The first workshop began in August 1974. Bennett's plan was just to work and work until they had a finished show ready for the public—however long that took—and then open it. The first workshop lasted six weeks. On the last day, Bennett faked an injury to get material for a scene late in the show when Paul is injured. He got the raw emotion he wanted, but he also alienated some of his fellow dancers. Then Bennett hired James Kirkwood to co-write the script—without telling Dante first. In January 1975, they began a second workshop.

Bennett said of the dazzling finale he was planning, "It will be the end of chorus lines as we know them. The audience will be horrified at how the chorus line robs the dancers of their personality. We will do every kind of chorus line, and the audience will be appalled at the inhumanity of it. They won't be able to applaud. They'll be speechless." Of course it never worked that way. Audiences found the finale thrilling. But the dark underbelly was unmistakable for those who looked for it. After all the physical torture, the agony, the indignities and injustices, the relentless rejection, these dancers get what they've always wanted, only to find out they've become cogs in an assembly line, faceless, nameless cogs.

The decision was made to leave the dancers in rehearsal clothes—in some cases, the exact clothing they had worn to those first meetings—except for the gaudy, gold, spangled costumes of the finale. The set was to be a black empty stage, with a single tape line across the front, and at the back, there would be a line of three-sided, revolving columns (*periaktoids*), with mirrors on one side, black on one side, and a dazzling sunburst for the finale on the third side.

A Chorus Line opened off Broadway at Papp's Public Theatre in April 1975 and ran 101 performances. For the first four weeks the dancers performed at night and rehearsed during the day, trimming, adding, rewriting, restaging. During this time, Bennett brought in Neil Simon to doctor the script (he was nicknamed "Doc"), but without telling Dante or Kirkwood, and Simon added many of the one-liners in the show. One of the most interesting changes during this time was the title of Val's big number. Originally called "Tits and Ass," the creators all felt it was exactly what they wanted but it never got the laughs they expected. Then they realized they were giving the joke away in the program with the song's title. So they changed it to "Dance: Ten, Looks: Three," and it brought the house down every night after that.

Of the off Broadway production, *Variety* wrote, "The musical has just about everything. The basic idea is original, the story is engrossing, funny and frequently touching, and the characters are identifiable, colorful and unpretentiously gallant. There is spectacular dancing, enjoyable music, lively pace, brilliant scenery, costumes and lighting, plus a finale that brought the consistently responsive opening night audience to its feet, cheering." Bennett would never realize his dream of a disturbing finale. But the show was his now; it no longer belonged to the dancers. Their stories were no longer their own. Almost all the acclaim went to Bennett, not to the performers and not to the writers.

The show was groundbreaking in so many ways. There was so much music, more than most other shows at the time, such well crafted musical development, extensive underscoring, the use of leitmotifs, and fascinating, touching, searing, character-driven lyrics that sometimes didn't even rhyme. The show was full of subject matter that had rarely been articulated on a musical stage before, about divorce, plastic surgery, homosexuality, erections, cross-dressing, domestic violence, tortured childhoods, and so much more. The characters onstage represented such incredible diversity—the *real* America Broadway rarely saw—including two Latinos (Paul, Diana), one Asian (Connie), one Jew (Greg), one black man (Richie), and three gay men (Bobby, Greg, Paul—and maybe Zach). *A Chorus Line* put musical theatre on notice—from now on, musicals would show us America as it really was, not the shallow fantasies of *Annie Get Your Gun* or *The Pajama Game*.

This was also the real Broadway community. Musical theatre was no longer a whites-only art form. This was what America looked like, though sadly it still wasn't really what Broadway audiences looked like. And oddly, though the character Paul was based on Latino write Nicholas Dante, the role was first played by the Caucasian actor Sammy Williams, who won a Tony for it. Dante would later play the role on tour and on Broadway, and he was the first Latino to win a Pulitzer Prize for drama.

A *Chorus Line* underlined an important change that was taking place on Broadway. No producer could afford a huge chorus anymore. Those days were gone. From now on—and *Chicago* was going through this at the same time—the chorus would double speaking roles, and there would rarely again be the kind of large casts Broadway had once seen in every show. The *Village Voice* had written in its review, "A *Chorus Line* is, in effect, the last Broadway musical." *Follies* had sounded the death knell for the old-fashioned musical comedy, and now A *Chorus Line* did the same for the big, expensive musical spectacle.

For the moment.

A *Chorus Line* moved to the Shubert Theatre on Broadway in July 1975 and began previews. The official opening was set for September 28, but there was a musicians' strike, so it was pushed back to October 19. The show quickly became a monster hit. It was nominated for twelve Tony Awards, and won nine, including best musical, best book, best score, best director, and best choreography. It also won the Pulitzer Prize for drama, the New York Drama Critics Circle Award, six Drama Desk Awards, an Obie Award, and later on, the Los Angeles Drama Critics Circle Award, the London Evening Standard Award for best musical, and years later, a special Tony Award for being the longest-running Broadway musical. More than six hundred and seventy Broadway shows came and went while A *Chorus Line* ran in New York. It opened in London in 1976, then Vienna and Paris. In August 1987, A *Chorus Line* broke the 5,000 performance mark, the first Broadway musical to do that (though *The Fantasticks* off Broadway already had), but Bennett had died of complications from AIDS a month earlier. A *Chorus Line* finally closed in April 1990, having run 6,137 performances on Broadway. The show has made more than fifty million dollars in profits over the years. In 1985, a clumsy, poorly conceived movie version was released that betrayed the original in too many ways.

As with many things, money soured the experience of A *Chorus Line*. Bennett and Dante had taken a small portion of their writing royalties and, in a complicated formula, shared it with the dancers. But many of the performers whose lives had become the substance of the show—and whose actual images had become part of the ubiquitous *Chorus Line* logo—still felt cheated. And once the show had opened on Broadway, some performers were paid more than others, and of course that angered those who received less. The dancers got even angrier when they saw all the side profit being made from the cast album, from merchandise, and other products. And because of the enormous exertion and stamina the show required, some cast members turned to performance-enhancing drugs. Writer James Lipton (later of the television show *Inside the Actors Studio*) and composer Cy Coleman sued Bennett, claiming the idea for the show was theirs. An out-of-court settlement was reached.

But *A Chorus Line* will always truly belong to every dancer, every actor who has ever appeared in a musical anywhere, and also to everyone who has ever interviewed for a job, met a fiancée's parents, or gone on a first date. It's about life. In 1990, two members of the original cast, Thommie Walsh and Baayork Lee, teamed up with Robert Viagas to write *On The Line: The Creation of A Chorus Line*, to tell the story of the show from the perspective of the original cast.

Meanwhile, in November 1974, Bob Fosse assembled his cast for *Chicago*, and during the very first week of rehearsals he was rushed to the hospital for pains in his chest. He had had a mild heart attack and needed open heart surgery, which was not nearly as common then as it is now. The producers decided they'd have to postpone the show. Miraculously, they managed to keep the cast together until Fosse could go back to work.

Like Oliver Stone's film *Natural Born Killers*, *Chicago* took the form of that which it criticized. Based on a satirical play about two actual murder cases from the 1920s, *Chicago* was a scathing satire of how show business and the media make celebrities out of criminals—and thereby make crime attractive—and its story was told through a succession of vaudeville acts. Like much of Fosse's other, later work, *Chicago* was a show overflowing with raw sexuality, creating a world that was shocking, frightening, intentionally offensive. When *Chicago* opened in June 1975, there had not been a musical of such savage satire since Brecht and Weill's *Threepenny Opera*. Bob Fosse made theatre pieces about the decadence of our world, the lies and conceits and compromises, the deals with the devil we all make, and as in *Sweet Charity*, *Pippin*, and Fosse's film version of *Cabaret*, *Chicago* is a show that makes the audience uncomfortable. This was the third time Fosse would use the false glamour of show business, the lie at its core, as a metaphor for life. He did it first with the film of *Cabaret*, then with *Pippin*, and he'd push this idea to its furthest extreme with the autobiographical film *All That Jazz* in 1980. He attacked hypocrisy wherever he saw it, even in his own work. He knew that the world of *Chicago*, in which killers are made into stars, wasn't far at all from the real world.

The primary premise of *Chicago* is that the world of crooked lawyers and a public who craves violence is as frightening in its own way as the crimes themselves. Fosse, John Kander, and Fred Ebb created a show with an attitude that never softened. Unlike other musicals about show business, this one never tempers its cynicism with compassion. Like the works of German writer-director Bertolt Brecht, this show breaks the fourth wall and addresses the audience; indeed, because the entire show is written as a series of vaudeville acts, the audience actually becomes a part of the show, as they had been with *Cabaret*. In fact, the more we enjoy the show, the more we like Velma, Roxie, and the other "Merry Murderesses" in the Cook County Jail, the more we prove the show's point. We find decadence entertaining, seductive, tantalizing. The audience is actually a character in the piece. Like *Assassins* and *Sweeney Todd*, this show points the finger of blame at us, and we're having too much fun to notice.

The original nonmusical *Chicago* was written in 1926 by *Chicago Tribune* reporter Maurine Dallas Watkins, based on two actual 1924 murder cases. In 1942, a film version was made called *Roxie Hart* with Ginger Rogers in the title role. Sometime in the 1950s actress and dancer Gwen Verdon saw the movie on television and thought it would make a great musical. But Watkins, the playwright, would not release the rights to the play. It wasn't until Watkins died in 1969 that Verdon finally got the rights from the playwright's estate. Verdon convinced Fosse to do the show, and they brought it to the song writing team of Fred Ebb and John Kander, who Fosse had worked with on the film version of *Cabaret*. It was Ebb's idea to tell the story in the language of vaudeville, not only to establish period but also create the metaphor of show business as life, a metaphor Fosse had become obsessed with. With Verdon playing Roxie, they cast Chita Rivera as Velma Kelly, Jerry Orbach as Billy Flynn, and Barney Martin as Amos Hart.

Though Fosse's taste had always tended toward the dark side—Fred Ebb referred to him as the Prince of Darkness—it had now gotten darker. Before the open heart surgery, the darkness had been a kind of caricature; now it was real. Fosse had seen death and it had changed him. And it changed *Chicago*. For the song "Razzle Dazzle" Fosse staged couples simulating sex on the sides of the stage while the lawyer Billy Flynn sang about flimflamming the court and the public. In other words, we're getting screwed, Fosse told us. Eventually, he was convinced that was too dark and he restaged the song. Despite some out-of-town troubles the show came to New York in good shape, and it opened in 1975. It ran 898 performances, partly because during the run Liza Minnelli replaced an ailing Gwen Verdon for a while and boosted ticket sales. *Chicago* garnered eleven Tony nominations, but lost all of them to *A Chorus Line*. In 2003, Orbach was given a special award by the Drama League for appearing in more performances of American musicals than any other living actor, including *The Threepenny Opera*, *Carnival*, *The Fantasticks*, *Promises, Promises*, *Chicago*, and *42nd Street*.

Fosse's dancer girlfriend and sometime muse, Ann Reinking, stepped into *Chicago* late in its Broadway run, before going on in 1978 to wow Broadway in Fosse's "anti-musical" *Dancin'*. In 1992, Reinking choreographed *Chicago* for the Civic Light Opera of Long Beach with Juliet Prowse and Bebe Neuwirth. A few years later, the Encores! Series in New York asked Reinking and director-performer Walter Bobbie to stage a concert reading of *Chicago*. It was so well received that it was transferred in 1996, with only minor changes, into a Broadway house for a regular run. Reinking used Fosse's dance vocabulary for the choreography but took a different, much lighter approach to the material. The cast included Neuwirth, Reinking, James Naughton, and Joel Grey. But in this newer version, the show was taken out of its period context, some of the script cut, and much of Fosse's nastiness and brutal (but legitimate) cynicism was rejected in favor of a sunnier feel. The show suffered for it. It lost its teeth and much of its original impact, and now thousands of theatregoers think they've seen *Chicago* even though they haven't really. . . .

Chicago was redeemed in 2002 with a brilliant, utterly electrifying film version, directed and choreographed by Broadway veteran Rob Marshall with a screenplay by Bill Condon. It was nominated for a staggering thirteen Oscars, and won six, including best film. The film starred Renée Zellweger, Catherine Zeta-Jones, Richard Gere, Queen Latifah, John C. Reilly, Christine Baranski, Taye Diggs, Lucy Liu, with a cameo by the original Velma, Chita Rivera. Elvis Mitchell wrote in the *New York Times*, "It's rare to find a picture as exuberant, as shallow—and as exuberant about its shallowness—as the director Rob Marshall's film adaptation of the Broadway musical *Chicago*. It's the raw expenditure of energy and the canniness of the staging that should pull audiences in and keep them rooted."

In January 1976 Stephen Sondheim and Hal Prince shocked critics and audiences once again with their next project, *Pacific Overtures*, with a script by John Weidman, with uncredited help from Hugh Wheeler. (Weidman's father had written the scripts for the musicals *Fiorello!*, which won a Pulitzer, and *Tenderloin*.) Borrowing liberally from the devices of Japan's Kabuki theatre traditions (as well as Bunraku and Noh), including a Reciter as narrator, a *hanamichi* runway extending from the stage out through the audience, and the portrayal of all female roles by male actors (except in the final scene), *Pacific Overtures* told the historical tale of Commodore Perry's expedition to Japan in 1853 and the resulting encroachment upon Japan by the West. The show's title is an ironic quoting of a phrase Commodore Perry coined himself. Weidman had originally written the piece as a nonmusical play, and he and Sondheim now created one of the most ambitious pieces of musical theatre ever attempted until that point.

Following closely in the footsteps of Bertolt Brecht's Epic Theatre, *Pacific Overtures* used devices like direct address to the audience, commentary songs, Brecht's famous alienation effect, and historical panorama. Sondheim's music, though not fully, authentically Japanese music, was the most authentic Oriental sound Broadway had ever heard, even incorporating several Japanese instruments. It was certainly far more authentic than Richard Rodgers' scores for *The King and I* or *Flower Drum Song* had been.

While overtly political (like the team's *Assassins* would be years later), this musical successfully made the political issues personal through the characters of Kayama, a minor samurai who becomes happily Westernized, and Manjiro, a fisherman who has been to the West but now rebels against the Western intrusion by becoming a fiercely traditionalist samurai. In his book *Approaches to the American Musical*, Robert Lawson-Peebles called *Pacific Overtures* "Stephen Sondheim's acid contribution to the American bicentennial celebrations." Told from the Japanese point of view (as much as possible from a third-year Yale Law School student), Weidman's script indicted Western imperialism and expansionism.

One of the biggest challenges of the production was casting. The production team needed to find a cast of thirty-five Asian men. But at that time it was very difficult for Asians to get cast on Broadway (and it's only slightly better now), so few Asians even trained for the musical theatre and that made the potential actor pool for the show extremely limited. Much of the rehearsal time was therefore spent teaching the performers the basics of musical theatre performance, as well as working extra hard to teach them Sondheim's difficult, dissonant music. It was refreshing that the team wanted to cast Asians to tell this Asian story, rather than cast Caucasians as Asians, as Broadway had done for years, but it made the casting and rehearsal process frustrating. The Japanese musicians they hired also had a tough time adjusting to Western musical practices. In traditional Oriental music, exact pitches, harmonies, and rhythms are less important than in Western music.

The show ran 193 performances and won two Tonys for design. Clive Barnes at the *New York Times* wrote, "It tries to soar—sometimes it only floats, sometimes it actually sinks—but it tries to soar. And the music and lyrics are as pretty and as well-formed as a bonsai tree. *Pacific Overtures* is very, very different." Other reviews were similar. Walter Kerr wrote in the *Times*, "Normally, Prince and Sondheim know very well what they are about as they turn their restless talents to experimentation—and their restlessness is one of their greatest virtues—but a mishap has occurred here. They do seem firmly knowledgeable, and possessed of a possible idea, as they approach the visual appurtenances of *Pacific Overtures*. But what, really, do they have in mind? When are we seeing through Japanese eyes, when through our own? And what is the drift of what we see and hear, psychologically, socially, personally? We're emotionally baffled—if our emotions continue to function at all—throughout."

A much scaled down version of the show opened in March 1984 at the York Theatre Company, then moved in October 1984 to the Promenade Theatre off Broadway, running for 119 performances. The English National Opera opened the show at the London Coliseum in September 1987 for a limited run. The New National Theatre of Tokyo produced the show in October 2000, then brought it to the Kennedy Center in Washington, DC, in 2002, directed by Amon Miyamoto. In late 2004, a new production of the show, still directed by Miyamoto, opened on Broadway, the first musical ever on Broadway helmed by a Japanese director.

In October 1976, off Broadway played host to a fascinating new musical, *The Club*, by Eve Merriam, a renowned American feminist poet, playwright, director, and lecturer, working with music arranger Alexandra Ivanoff. Merriam had also written the 1971 satirical protest musical *Inner City*, based on her own book *The Inner City Mother Goose*. *The Club* was Tommy Tune's first directing assignment, originally written in 1973 during the height of the feminist movement and in the early days of the national debate over the Equal Rights Amendment. The show revolved around five men who frequent a gentlemen's social club in 1903, talking about cigars, the stock market, drinking, women, billiards, and their upcoming Spring Frolic.

So what was so fascinating? The tuxedoed, cigar-smoking gin sippers who spout off string after string of crude sexist quips were played by an entirely female cast (listed only by first initials and last names in the programs). Of course, women were beginning to wear suits already, particularly in business, so the cross-dressing of *The Club* was only a little removed from the real world of 1976. Some commentators had even suggested that men themselves were already in drag when they wore formal evening wear.

Using music hall songs from the late 1800s and early 1900s, Merriam took audiences into the jaunty atmosphere of a men's club circa 1903 and made them think twice about what's funny and what's not. Feminist commentator Erika Munk said, "The language isn't obscene but mild. Indeed, they're exactly the jokes which still live in spirit on TV, at a family reunion—that's what's *not* funny." Alisa Solomon wrote, "The all-women cast as the targets of such jokes aren't supposed to know about them—much less throw them back in the tellers' faces." Nancy Scott called the show's premise "a feminist boomerang." As the "men" on stage rehearse their cross-dressing Spring Frolic, we see pre–*Victor/Victoria* women playing men playing women.

Originally produced at the Lenox Art Center by the Music-Theatre Performing Group in the summer of 1976, *The Club* transferred that fall to New York's Circle in the Square Downtown where it ran an impressive 674 performances—right in the middle of International Women's Year. For the most part, male critics hated it and female critics found it thrilling, though there were exceptions. The *New York Post* called the show "a refracting lens for the condescension and bigotry that pervade those good old songs, and by implication, our culture." David McCaughna wrote a piece about the show in the *Toronto Star Sunday Magazine* called "(Fe)Male Schauvinist Pigs" and he called the show a "a musical Rorschach test." For those fighting for the Equal Rights Amendment (endorsed by thirty-three women's magazines), this show became a rallying cry for many women in America. One of the strangest results was the discomfort female audiences members felt when they discovered they were actually attracted to the men-women on stage. The show won an Obie Award, and Tommy Tune was nominated for a Drama Desk Award for best director.

A very different kind of musical opened next, every bit as subversive in its own gentle way, a show that would become one of the most popular musicals of all time, *Annie*, based on the classic *Little Orphan Annie* comic strip. It was a bit soft and gooey, sure, almost gleefully old-fashioned, but it was also street smart, political, satirical, and skillfully crafted, harkening back to shows like *Of Thee I Sing*, *The Cradle Will Rock*, and *Finian's Rainbow*. *Annie* was ostensibly about kids but it was *not* a kids' show; it was an adult musical that understood exactly America's mood at the time. It took potshots at Herbert Hoover but audiences knew it was talking about Nixon. It was set during the Great Depression, but audiences knew it was really about the 1970s. Unlike its later, vastly misguided film adaptation, *Annie* the stage musical was smart and fiery, not so much about an indefatigable orphan as it was about the indefatigable American Spirit, a story audiences were thirsty for. With a book by Thomas Meehan (who would later co-write *The Producers* and *Hairspray*), music by Charles Strouse, and lyrics by Martin Charnin, *Annie* was a first-class Broadway musical, one of those that everybody said would never make it, and it proved that audiences will always respond to good storytelling, especially when it taps into the cultural and political zeitgeist.

After a long development process, *Annie* finally came to New York and opened at the Alvin Theatre in April 1977, directed by Charnin and choreographed by Peter Gennaro. Martin Gottfried wrote in the *New York Post*, "Innovative? It's practically reactionary—a book show thoroughly, even brazenly conventional, from structure to style. Yet the damned things works." The show ended up running 2,377 performances. It won seven Tonys, including best musical, best book, and best score. It also won the New York Drama Critics Circle Award, seven Drama Desk Awards, and five Outer Critics Circle Awards. It ran in London for 1,485 performances, then went on to Mexico, Australia, Denmark, Spain, South Africa, Japan, and elsewhere.

A completely different view of America came next. *The Best Little Whorehouse in Texas* had a score by Carol Hall and a book by Larry L. King (based on his article in *Playboy*) and director Peter Masterson, and it surprised everyone, just as political and just as pointed in its social commentary as other serious 70s shows. Part of the reason *Best Little Whorehouse* worked so well as a musical— the reason it *had* to be a musical—is that it dealt with people whose emotions cannot be openly expressed. The heroine Miss Mona would never tell anyone the depth of her regret over the choices she's made or the profundity of loss she feels in closing the Chicken Ranch. But her song "The Bus from Amarillo" can get at that depth of emotion through its music. No speech could ever convey the diner owner Doatsey Mae's secret desires without feeling a bit silly, but when blended with the sweet, sad music of her song "Doatsey Mae," those most hidden feelings take on a level of legitimacy and dignity that are very moving. The crusty sheriff would never say out loud that he loves Mona, so the simple, gentle waltz of "Good Ol' Girl" does it for him, even though the lyric never once says "I love you."

Best Little Whorehouse told the true story of the high-profile closing down of a 130-year-old brothel outside the small town of LaGrange, Texas in 1973. But *Whorehouse* isn't really about sex any more than *Fiddler on the Roof* is about violins. At its most basic, *Whorehouse* was about how putting life on TV changes it, how it changes people, how the TV camera impacts that which it records. Parallel to those issues, the show was also about America's never ending parade of moral and sexual hypocrisy. The Chicken Ranch, the whorehouse of the show's title, had been around since 1844. Everybody knew it and nobody seemed to care. But put it on "the tee-vee" and suddenly it's a scandal, it's an outrage, and one denounced by politicians who had all frequented the place themselves.

Texan Larry L. King (no relation to the talk show host) had written an article for *Playboy* in April 1974 about the closing, called "The Best Little Whorehouse in Texas." Actor Peter Masterson saw the article in early 1976 while acting in *That Championship Season* on Broadway, and the way he tells it, "It hit me: *Goddamn, this is a musical!*" Masterson brought it to songwriter and fellow Texan Carol Hall. In spring 1976, Hall called King. But King didn't like the idea. He said, "Look, my ignorance of the subject is absolutely awesome. I've only seen three musicals in my life and didn't care for any of them. I saw a number of dramas, but I quit musicals after three. Not my cup of whiskey." He went on, "As a writer it irritates me when the story comes to a screeching halt so a bunch of bank clerks in candy-striped suits and carrying matching umbrellas can break into a silly tap dance while singing about the sidewalks of New York." Hall and Masterson promised King this would be a different kind of musical. So eventually King gave in, and the three formed a tight but often cantankerous threesome, none of whom had ever written a Broadway show before. In October 1976, they brought some friends together and did an informal reading of an early draft in Carol Hall's living room. In King's subsequent tell-all book *The Whorehouse Papers*, he writes about hearing the opening number for the first time and thinking, "*My God, that's beautiful! This fucking thing may work!*" That night, Masterson announced a workshop production at the Actors Studio in New York.

Despite problems and massive rewrites, the show went on. A representative from Universal Pictures saw a performance and immediately made an offer, not just for film rights but for stage rights as well. Universal wanted to produce it off Broadway, and maybe even on Broadway. In preparation for the off Broadway production, Tommy Tune was hired to re-choreograph the show and co-direct with Masterson. Again, rewrites continued and songs were added and cut. Yet so many problems persisted—most notably, they couldn't get the Act I ending to work—that the off Broadway opening had to be postponed twice.

And as the opening approached, three of the seven TV stations in New York City refused to use the show's title on the air, so commercials were created that never once mentioned the title. Some stations agreed that the word *whorehouse* could air as a graphic but it could not be spoken. At first, none of the New York papers would run ads with the title. Eventually, a couple independent papers relented, and eventually the other papers caved—except for the *New York Times*. It wasn't until ten days before the off Broadway opening that the *Times* finally accepted an ad with the show's title. Later on, when the show toured, newspapers across the country refused to print the title and so ads were run that sold tickets to "The Best Little Chicken Ranch in Texas," "The Best Little Bawdy House in Texas," "The Best Little Blank in Texas" (no kidding), and, most vague of all, "The Best Little House in Texas." And the furor continues today. As recently as 1997 a student production of *Whorehouse* at Wentworth Institute of Technology outside Boston was cancelled by faculty, who deemed the title "dangerous for students."

The show finally opened off Broadway at the Entermedia Theatre on April 17, 1978, where it ran 85 performances. Most of the critics loved it. Clive Barnes, in the *New York Post*, wrote, "Considering the subject matter, the show is beautifully clear-eyed and totally free of the gooey sentimentality you might have feared. It calls a spade a spade with a frankness that is exhilaratingly delicate." *Time* magazine said, "This is the best new musical of the season."

The show was a hit, and the producers moved it to the 46th Street Theatre on Broadway, a theatre just vacated, conveniently enough, by the flop musical *Working*, which had run only twenty-five performances. *Whorehouse* opened on June 19, 1979, where it stayed for 1,584 performances. *Women's Wear Daily* called the show "more fun than a beer-totin' hayride at a Mardi Gras," and said the whorehouse was "actually located in that vast desert between respectability and profanity." Edna Milton, the real-life model for the show's Miss Mona, was given two small, nonspeaking roles in the show, although she drove everyone involved crazy. And Marvin Zindler, the model for the crazed TV reporter Melvin P. Thorpe, was flown up to see the show, which he loved. The Broadway production received seven Tony Award nominations, for best musical, best book, best director, best choreographer, best featured actor (Henderson Forsythe as the Sheriff), and two best featured actress nominations (for Carlin Glynn as Mona and Joan Ellis as Shy). The show won two Tonys but the Tony telecast butchered (through bleeping) the performance of "The Aggie Song." *Sweeney Todd* won best musical. *Women's Wear Daily*, one of the top magazines of the clothing industry, credits *Whorehouse* for the western-wear trend that gripped America in the early 1980s.

A cheaply sentimentalized and sexed-up movie version was made in 1982 with Dolly Parton, Burt Reynolds, and Dom DeLuise, though Larry L. King had wanted Shirley MacLaine and Willie Nelson to play the leads. The movie watered down the content, rewrote the ending (even though it was a true story), added wildly inappropriate porn-fantasy costumes for the girls, and did only moderately well at the box office. The era of movie musicals was over and *Whorehouse* in its watered-down state had little that was fresh or exciting about it. All that had been taken out. A truly terrible stage sequel was attempted by most of the same creative team in 1994, called *The Best Little Whorehouse Goes Public*. It ran fifteen performances and Universal Studios lost about seven million dollars on it. The original *Whorehouse* was revived haphazardly in 2001 for a national tour starring Ann-Margret and Gary Sandy. Despite efforts to reproduce the original sets and choreography, it was missing all the bite and grit and heart of the original. As had happened with *Rocky Horror*, no one seemed to understand what made the original *Whorehouse* so special, and so no one could recapture that original magic.

Another political musical, this time with a much harder edge, opened in Los Angeles in July 1978 at the Mark Taper Forum. *Zoot Suit*, written and directed by Luiz Valdez, was a huge hit, breaking all attendance records. After twelve weeks at the Taper, it moved to the Aquarius Theatre in Hollywood (once occupied by *Hair*) where it played to more than half a million people during its year-long run. It was honored with a Los Angeles Drama Critics Circle Award. The founder of the Latino theatre company El Teatro Campesino, Valdez had begun work on the show in 1977, drawing from the infamous Zoot Suit Riots in Los Angeles, a massive street fight between sailors and Mexican American boys that escalated into more than a week of fighting in June 1943. Eventually, a small group of young Chicano men were put on trial and imprisoned at San Quentin on trumped up murder charges.

Zoot Suit was a musical docudrama, focusing on one of those men, Henry Reyna, and his activist lawyer, determined to reverse what many people saw as a blatantly racist verdict. In the tradition of *The Threepenny Opera, The Cradle Will Rock,* and other Brechtian theatre pieces, *Zoot Suit* pulled no punches, portraying complex Latino characters and culture honestly for the first time, making clear, strong political statements without apology. It harkened back to the fiercely political theatre of the 1930s.

Zoot Suit moved to New York and opened at the Winter Garden Theatre on Broadway in March 1979, the first Broadway show ever to be written by a Latino writer, but it played only forty-one performances, despite a Tony nomination for actor Edward James Olmos and despite its incredible success in Los Angeles. Latino audiences did not flock to see the show on Broadway and conventional wisdom said that white audiences found it too confrontational. One theory advanced for the lack of an audience for the show was that New York Latino culture was so markedly different from Los Angeles Chicano culture. Also, very little was done to market the show to the Latino community. A film version was made in 1982, and it was nominated for a Golden Globe for best picture. But this was not a conventional movie version of a stage musical that was reimagined for the screen, finding filmic equivalents for the show's stage devices. Instead, it was basically a filmed recording of the stage musical on a soundstage, not usually a formula for box office success, but a valuable historical record of the landmark stage version. Valdez later found a mainstream audience with his rock and roll biopic *La Bamba,* and some speculated that a bigger budget might have garnered *Zoot Suit* the same kind of acceptance. The *San Francisco Chronicle* called *Zoot Suit* "astonishing, a brilliantly executed blend of vibrant music and passion, myth and reality . . . a fabulous celebration!" The *Hollywood Reporter* called it "infectious, buoyant, offbeat, stylish, commanding and fresh as new paint."

Meanwhile, Tim Rice and Andrew Lloyd Webber, who had brought us *Joseph and the Amazing Technicolor Dreamcoat* and *Jesus Christ Superstar,* were working on their last show together, the political potboiler *Evita.* They had begun work in 1974 and had recorded a concept album with Julie Covington as Eva Peron, in 1976. It was becoming business as usual now for rock/pop operas to make a studio concept album first, and only afterward put the show on stage. This sometimes caused problems because the score was initially written to be heard and not to be seen (a problem from which Tim Rice's *Chess* would suffer later on). Director Hal Prince took the recording, really just disconnected moments in the story, and made it a three-dimensional, unified, coherent musical drama. In June 1978, the show opened in London at the Prince Edward Theatre, with Elaine Page in the lead. Larry Fuller choreographed, as he would for Prince on *Sweeney Todd*.

Evita told the highly fictionalized story of the infamous Eva Peron, from her roots in a small town in Argentina through her meteoric rise to first lady of Argentina as wife of Juan Peron. Though Eva was a real historical figure, Tim Rice's sung-through libretto took only the basic outline of her life and fashioned it into a fascinating, often thrilling soap opera, a Shakespearean tragedy of intrigue, deception, betrayal, greed, and power, a kind of monstrous Cinderella tale mixed with *Richard III*. As with *Superstar*, Rice and Lloyd Webber weren't interested in facts; they were interested in telling a compelling story, toying with social issues, and making great theatre. Rice also used real-life Argentine revolutionary Che Guevara as a kind of narrator and commentator, even allowing his two central characters to meet in Act II, something that never actually happened. Guevara represented the Argentine masses that Eva so skillfully hoodwinked and used for her own gain. Some critics complained that the show tampered too much with historical fact, but audiences didn't care.

With *Evita*, Rice was his usual smartass, acerbic, cynical self, and Lloyd Webber wrote the most mature score of his career—one he would sadly never equal. In *Superstar*, Lloyd Webber had sometimes reused musical ideas for dramatic purposes, but sometimes just at random. In his later scores, like *Cats* and *Phantom of the Opera*, his reuse of music would become increasingly random and nondramatic. But here, in *Evita*, he took care to follow the precepts of Wagner and Sondheim, only reusing musical material to make a connection, to develop character, to add subtle commentary on the action. *Evita* proved Lloyd Webber was capable of this kind of mature writing, and his later shows may just prove he doesn't always care. Interestingly, though the writers were British, most of the creative staff in London and in New York were Americans. Even with British material, Americans—particularly Hal Prince—still knew better than anyone else how to put on a musical. But the era of the Pop Opera was coming. . . .

Evita opened on Broadway at the Broadway Theatre in September 1979, with Patti LuPone in the lead and Mandy Patinkin as Che Guevara, then at the Shubert Theatre in Los Angeles in January 1980. *Evita* ran in London for 2,900 performances and in New York for 1,567 performances. Three national tours crisscrossed the United States for three and a half years. After years of speculation over who would star in the film—Barbra Streisand, Meryl Streep, John Travolta, and Elton John were all mentioned at one point—the vaguely anemic film version was released in 1996 with pop star Madonna as Eva and Anthony Banderas as Che. They restored one song from London, "The Lady's Got Potential." Madonna was roundly dismissed but Banderas surprised many with his smoldering performance and his strong pop/rock singing. Unfortunately, the film tried to soften Eva, and though that might have been a fair interpretation of history, it was a rotten choice for this musical. The musicalized Eva was a nasty ambitious bitch, whether or not the real Eva was. Director Alan Parker ended up with a so-so film of a terrific stage show.

Back on Broadway, Sondheim and Prince returned with another unlikely project in March 1979: *Sweeney Todd, The Demon Barber of Fleet Street*, one of only three musicals that Stephen Sondheim has initiated himself (the others are *Passion* and *Bounce*). Sondheim had seen a nonmusical stage version of *Sweeney* by Christopher Bond in London (at the same theatre where Joan Littlewood had once worked), while working on *Gypsy*, and he knew it should be a musical. Sondheim's goal was to tell this bloody British legend of murder, meat pies, and bloody revenge with a mix of edgy American musical theatre and the French *Grand Guignol* style.

Sondheim intended the show to be an intimate chamber musical with few sets. But Hal Prince went in another direction with it on Broadway—big and epic. And though it does work big, keeping it small is still the way it is the most effective, the most chilling, the most personal. After all, at the end of the show, the cast points to the audience and accuses them of being like Sweeney and Mrs. Lovett themselves, just as easily motivated by revenge and greed; and the closer the audience is to the characters and the murders, the scarier they become. This is not a show intended to leave an audience happy and safe in the knowledge that Good always triumphs over Evil. *Sweeney Todd* is meant to disturb. It is both social commentary and horror story, a musical *Twilight Zone* set in nineteenth-century England. Like any good horror movie, there is a great deal of musical underscoring and musical foreshadowing. The music in the show was almost continuous and filled with leitmotifs that identified important concepts and plot elements. The show even opened with a pipe organ, putting us in mind of films like *The Phantom of the Opera* and other horror classics.

Budgeted at $1.3 million and with 271 separate investors, *Sweeney Todd* ran 557 performances on Broadway with Len Carious and Angela Lansbury, then went on a national tour starring Lansbury and George Hearn, which was videotaped for commercial release at its last stop in Los Angeles. Unfortunately, despite its successful run on Broadway, the original production still lost $400,000—such were the economics of Broadway as the 1980s began. The show won eight Tonys, including best musical, best score, best book, and best director. It also won the New York Drama Critics Circle Award. Richard Eder wrote in the *New York Times*, "The musical and dramatic achievements of Stephen Sondheim's black and bloody *Sweeney Todd* are so numerous and so clamorous that they trample and jam each other in that invisible and finite doorway that connects a stage and its audience." He went on, "There is more of artistic energy, creative personality, and plain excitement in *Sweeney Todd* than in a dozen average musicals. Sondheim has composed an endlessly inventive, highly expressive score that works indivisibly from his brilliant and abrasive lyrics. It is a power-ful, coruscating instrument, this muscular partnership of words and music."

Sweeney Todd was revived in March 1989 by the York Theatre off off Broad-way and ran 24 performances in an extremely scaled down version. Sondheim had always said he wanted fog and streetlamps and actors jumping up behind the audience, scaring them to death. The original plan in 1979 had been to do *Sweeney* in the environmental theatre in which Hal Prince's *Candide* had played, with the action of the show played all over the theatre, in and around and throughout the audience. But the theatre couldn't be kept in that configuration until *Sweeney* was written, so that planned was scrapped. Now finally in 1989, *Sweeney* was becoming the chamber musical it was supposed to be. In Septem-ber 1989, it moved to Circle in the Square, where it ran 189 performances, star-ring Bob Gunton as Sweeney, Beth Fowler as Mrs. Lovett, and Jim Walton as Anthony. The production was nicknamed *Teeney Todd*. As the new century began, another revival surfaced in London, in which director John Doyle com-bined cast and band into a postmodern *Sweeney Todd* in which a small ensem-ble of actors played all the roles as well as all the musical instruments. This production opened on Broadway in 2005 starring Michael Cerveris and Patti LuPone.

On December 8, 1979, as the decade was running out, *Grease* became the longest running musical on Broadway with its 3,243rd performance, surpassing *Fiddler on the Roof*. Musical theatre purists were outraged that this silly 1950s confection had outrun the brilliant *Fiddler*, much the way the same people were outraged years later when *Cats* outran *A Chorus Line* to snag the number one slot. Finally, musical theatre lovers could claim with some legitimacy that the Golden Age of musical theatre might be ending . . . or at least pausing. . . .

8

Do You Hear the People Sing?
The 1980s

The 1980s brought with them some of the most mediocre musicals to hit Broadway in years, including forgettable mistakes like *Bring Back Birdie, Merlin, Doonesbury, The Tap Dance Kid, The Rink, Harrigan 'n Hart, Leader of the Pack, Grind, Big Deal, Raggedy Ann, Smile, Starlight Express, Teddy and Alice, Chess, Legs Diamond, Aspects of Love,* and others. Some of these were written by top-notch talent (like Kander and Ebb's *The Rink*), and some had strong material derailed by bad productions (like Tim Rice's *Chess*), but many of them were just bland.

It seemed to many that the musical was dead.

But not all the eighties shows were mistakes. In July 1980, Andrew Lloyd Webber was hosting his annual Sydmonton Festival where he tried out his new projects for invited guests. This time he was playing songs from a new project called *Cats* based on T. S. Eliot's 1939 book of children's poems, *Old Possum's Book of Practical Cats.* Under the leadership of director Trevor Nunn, the show soon went into rehearsal and opened in London in May 1981.

It was a character study really, virtually no plot, only a few relationships, just a bunch of cats, harkening back to the massively produced spectacles of the 20s and 30s. Yet Eliot's verses, though intended for kids, were remarkably insightful in their commentaries on human adult behavior, and Trevor Nunn and choreographer Gillian Lynne were very serious about communicating that deeper layer of meaning to an audience. They saw that these poems worked cross-generationally: kids could enjoy the show as pure fantasy, while adults could enjoy it as piquant social commentary. Many people were skeptical about Nunn of the Royal Shakespeare Company directing a musical. *What did he know from musicals?* But that was why he was perfect for this project. He approached *Cats* the same way he'd approach *Antigone* or *King Lear*, entirely through character. It was the only way the central conceit of *Cats* could work. The cast spent days of rehearsal on character work, improv, movement exercises. Everybody involved approached the show as if it were the most serious of dramas, the most deeply textured work imaginable. Though *Cats* clearly wasn't all that, the seriousness paid off. The cast—both in London and on Broadway—did a remarkable job of inhabiting these very feline bodies and very human personalities. And audiences responded, not just to the spectacle (including a stage full of oversized trash) but to the deep humanness of the proceedings. Eliot's widow had found a fragment of a poem that didn't make it into the book about Grizabella the Glamour Cat, and she became the emotional center of the show, the outcast who must be redeemed so that everyone might be redeemed, an unmistakable Christ figure. With her ultimate ascension to the Heavyside Layer, Lloyd Webber finally gave audiences the resurrection he and Tim Rice had denied them in *Jesus Christ Superstar*.

This was also Lloyd Webber's first real dance musical, and he wrote it specifically because England was in the midst of an incredible explosion of dance. For the first time, musical theatre performers in England were training to sing, act, *and* dance. For the first time, England had homegrown "triple threat" performers. It was the perfect time for a British dance musical.

The show moved to Broadway in October 1982 and the producers gutted the Winter Garden Theatre in order to recreate their semi-environmental set that stretched out into the audience and up into the balcony. That first Broadway cast included several performers who would go on to great stage careers, some already in their prime: Betty Buckley, Ken Page, Harry Groener, Terrance Mann, and others. The show went on to win seven Tony Awards, including best musical, best book, best score, best director, and two design awards. But the critics were strangely offended by the show. The *New Yorker* called it "a mighty spectacle about mighty little." Howard Kissel said the score was "remarkable largely for the shamelessness with which it seems to recycle other people's tunes." Lloyd Webber would suffer this criticism for his entire career.

But many of the critics missed the point. First and foremost, this was spectacle, the kind Billy Rose and Florenz Ziegfeld so expertly wrought earlier in the century. But second, this was about peeking into a secret fantasy world to perhaps understand ourselves and those around us a little better, no different from watching *Star Wars* or reading *Animal Farm*. Eliot was no slouch, having written some of the most celebrated and densest poetry in history, and his words and insights were at the center of all this. No, this wasn't Eliot's *The Wasteland*, but it *was* something of arguable substance. And though the evening didn't wear its intelligence or insights on its sleeve, those things were there. Lloyd Webber's music was not groundbreaking or entirely original, but it was clever, varied, and sometimes utterly beautiful. Not every composer is Sondheim, and perhaps when you're setting Eliot, you don't need to be. One could argue that Eliot's words coupled with Sondheim's music would be too dense for an audience to absorb on one hearing. Maybe Eliot needed a less sophisticated, less groundbreaking composer to give his poetry breathing room.

Still, Lloyd Webber was writing in his pop/rock vocabulary where he was most comfortable and usually at his best. He hadn't yet entered his pretentious pseudoclassical period, and his songs for *Cats* were often quite fun. His already established use of odd time signatures, of periodically dropping or adding beats (seemingly at random but sometimes for dramatic reasons), of "wrong" blues notes, of tunes that seem to be going one direction and suddenly end up elsewhere—all that was there. It had probably been done in a more sophisticated manner in *Superstar*, and even more so in *Evita*, but it was still here in *Cats*. And only a handful of composers could have written a song like "Memory," a melancholy ballad that occasionally slips out of time, sort of losing its place, ignoring the time signature for a phrase or two, beautifully and artfully dramatizing the wandering, crumbling mind of the cat Grizabella.

The downside of *Cats* and shows like it was the new mindset they brought with them to Broadway. In the era of the megamusical, producers wanted every audience throughout the entire run of a show to see the *exact* same performance, even if a show ran twenty years, rejecting the inherent spontaneity and unpredictability of live theatre for the consistency and frozen performances of film. For these shows, when a replacement actor joined a show, he or she was required to play it *exactly* as the person had before them, no variation, no exceptions. Actors in these shows became imitators, cogs in an already running machine, rather than creative artists. This change helped sap the creative energy of Broadway for a long while.

Cats closed on Broadway September 10, 2000, after 7,485 performances, having been seen by more than ten million people and grossing over three hundred fifty million dollars. It finally closed in London on May 11, 2002, after twenty-one years and 8,950 performances seen by over eight million people. It was now the longest-running show ever on Broadway. Was it a masterpiece? No. Was it a good musical, better than people gave it credit for being? Yes.

The second British Invasion had begun.

Way back in 1973, French lyricist Alain Boublil had been invited to the Broadway premiere of *Jesus Christ Superstar* and it changed his life. Already a big fan of musical theatre, here he saw a work that combined the conventions of grand opera, historical subject matter, and contemporary pop musical vocabulary. He decided instantly that he wanted to write in that form, and that same night, realized the French Revolution would be a perfect subject. In collaboration with several friends (including composer Claude-Michel Schönberg), the pop opera *La Revolution Française* was written, recorded, became a best selling album in France, and soon after was staged at the Palais des Sports, a sports arena in Paris, for a full season's run. Several years later, Boublil convinced Schönberg to make a pop opera of Victor Hugo's epic novel *Les Misérables*, which was *not* about the French Revolution as many reviewers declared, but instead centered on the famous student insurrection of 1832 in Paris, more than forty years after the French Revolution. In 1980, the French concept album of *Les Misérables* was recorded and sold 260,000 copies; that same year the show was staged at the Palais des Sports, and played to over 500,000 people in more than a thousand performances.

In the fall of 1981, a friend brought the recording to Cameron Mackintosh, British producer of *Godspell, Cats, Little Shop of Horrors*, and other successful musicals, the commercial genius who was responsible for turning the American musical into an international art form. Mackintosh immediately decided to produce *Les Miz* (as it was soon nicknamed), under the direction of Trevor Nunn and John Caird, both of the Royal Shakespeare Company. But he felt it needed to be restructured and further adapted as it was translated into English. Though French audiences knew the source novel intimately, British and American audiences did not. Also, French theatre is different from English-speaking theatre. Director John Caird said of the show, "It was clear from the start that the French version was not performable as it stood, as a mere English adaptation. The French musical version was basically a series of tableaux in the French tradition interlaced with large-scale pieces of symphonic music in order to prepare for set changes, so there were some great long interludes which none of us in London felt were useable."

Mackintosh hired poet James Fenton to do an English translation and adaptation. The first order of business was a prologue to provide the backstory French audiences hadn't needed. But before long, Mackintosh reluctantly fired Fenton. His work was taking far too long and was ending up far too poetic and grand for these characters. Still, his prologue and some of his other material has survived in the show. So Mackintosh then brought in poet and lyricist Herbert Kretzmer, who translated, adapted, and added new material to the show. He added numbers like Javert's "Stars," "Carousel," and others. He completely changed the placement and purpose of songs like Fantine's "La Misère," which became Eponine's "On My Own." The song "La Nuit" became "Lovely Ladies," completely changing its context and purpose.

Auditions and rehearsals began in July 1985. Mackintosh said in an interview, "We didn't want that traditional, slightly amateurish British aspect of musical theatre where brilliant classical actors let their hair down. We saw *Les Miz* as musical theatre with performers at the height of their powers combined with a classical theatre [the Royal Shakespeare Company] also at the height of its powers." The first preview in October 1985 ran almost four hours. By opening night at the Barbican Theatre, thirty minutes had been shaved off, and cuts would continue for some time. But the advance tickets sales for the show were very low, much lower than the Barbican was used to, and the producers were very nervous. To make matters worse, the show received generally scathing reviews in most of the London papers and Andrew Lloyd Webber made it publicly clear that he hated it. In the *Observer* the morning after opening night, the review's headline was "Victor Hugo on the Garbage Dump." Critic Michael Ratcliffe called the show "a witless and synthetic entertainment," and said that the creators had "emasculated Hugo's Olympian perspective and reduced it to the trivialising and tearful aesthetic of rock opera and the French hit parade of ten (fifteen?) years ago."

But within three days after opening, adoring audiences had spread the good word, ticket sales skyrocketed, and the show played to sold-out houses from then on. The day the bad reviews came out, the box office broke all previous sales records, selling five thousand tickets in the first three hours of the day. As the producers had hoped, the show then transferred to the Palace Theatre in London's West End in December 1986. That same month, the show opened for an American preview in Washington, DC, then moved to Broadway in March 1987. Before the show closed on Broadway in 2003 after 6,680 performances, forty-six professional companies had performed *Les Miz* in a total of twenty-three countries and 203 cities. There have also been thirty-one versions of the cast album released.

Les Miz was showered with awards wherever it went. In London, it won an Olivier Award (the British version of the Tony) for best actress (the American Patti LuPone as Fantine), and it won the London Critics Circle Award for best musical. In Washington, DC, it won three Helen Hayes Awards. In New York, it won eight Tony Awards, for best musical, best book, best score, best director(s), best featured actor (Michael Maguire), best featured actress (Frances Ruffelle, the original Eponine from London), best set design, and best lighting design. It also won the New York Drama Critics Circle Award, the Outer Critics Circle Award, five Drama Desk Awards, and the cast album won a Grammy Award. In Japan, it won the Artistic Festival Prize. In Australia, it won two Music Critics Circle Awards. And in Los Angeles, it won three Los Angeles Drama Critics Circle Awards.

In a completely different vein—and scale—composer William Finn had been working on three one-act musicals about a character named Marvin. In the first of the trilogy, *In Trousers*, Finn explored Marvin's crushes on teachers and other women, his blossoming neuroses, and his eventual realization that he was really in love with a man named Whizzer Brown, in the less than subtle song "Whizzer Going Down." *In Trousers* had opened in December 1978 and ran twenty-eight performances at Playwrights Horizons.

The second chapter in the trilogy—and the most interesting of the trio— *March of the Falsettos*, opened at Playwrights Horizons in April 1981, in their seventy-five seat theatre, with direction by James Lapine. It soon moved to their hundred-and-fifty-seat house, then in October moved to the Chelsea Westside Theatre for an open-ended run, eventually chalking up 268 performances. It won the Outer Critics Circle Award for best musical. Frank Rich wrote in the *New York Times*, "The songs are so fresh the show is only a few bars old before one feels the unmistakable, revivifying charge of pure talent." He went on, "Mr. Lapine's wildly resourceful staging has a zippy, slam-bang sense of confidence that has been lacking in most bigger musicals this season. And no wonder, *March of the Falsettos* is that rare musical that actually has something to be cocky about."

In this second installment, Marvin tries to force Whizzer, his wife Trina, and his prepubescent son Jason, into some kind of awkward hybrid family. When that doesn't work, Marvin leaves Trina for Whizzer, while Marvin's psychiatrist Mendel romances and marries Trina. At the end of *March of the Falsettos*, Marvin has lost Trina and Whizzer both, and in the last song, he tries to reconnect with Jason. Marvin finally realizes that he himself must grow up, must become more fully an adult, before he can be a real father to his son (a theme the show shares with *Mame*).

In the third chapter of the trilogy, *Falsettoland* (1990), Marvin, Trina, and Mendel plan Jason's bar mitzvah while Whizzer comes back into Marvin's life. But Marvin only gets a temporary Happily Ever After because Whizzer has AIDS and by the end of the show he has died. The third installment is interesting because when Finn wrote the first two pieces, AIDS didn't even exist, so Finn had no idea how Marvin's story would turn out.

March of the Falsettos and *Falsettoland* were presented on a double bill in October 1991 at the Hartford Stage in Connecticut, under the direction of Graciela Daniele. In 1992, Finn and Lapine officially combined *March of the Falsettos* and *Falsettoland* into a full-length musical called *Falsettos*. They did a fair amount of subtle rewriting, adding and cutting things, reassigning lines, altering music, even adding one full song, Trina's hilarious *tour de force*, "I'm Breaking Down." But once the full-length version was available, the one-acts were rarely produced, which is unfortunate because *March of the Falsettos* by itself is superior not only to its two siblings but also to the full-length *Falsettos*, with more raw attitude, more adult emotion and less easy sentiment. The full-length *Falsettos* opened at the John Golden Theatre on Broadway in April 1992 and ran 487 performances. It was nominated for seven Tony Awards, and won for best book and best score. It wouldn't be the last time a musical would win both best score and best book, but not best musical.

Another groundbreaking musical opened in 1981, the hit *Dreamgirls*, a monumental achievement in full integration of all the elements of musical theatre, but also yet another black musical created by white guys: composer Henry Krieger, lyricist and bookwriter Tom Eyen (of *The Dirtiest Show in Town*), director-choreographer Michael Bennett, and co-choreographer Michael Peters. The show had a long gestation period, including four separate workshops, and an extended tryout run in Boston before coming to New York. It opened on Broadway in December 1981, the most expensive Broadway musical to date, costing $3.5 million. The show's story followed the rise of a black girl group suspiciously like Diana Ross and the Supremes, who did not understand that they were making pop music history. In fact, the similarities were so numerous that the creators had to continually deny that their show was based on fact. Of course, no one believed them.

The score for *Dreamgirls* traced the history of black music from the sixties through to the present. It even included one rap song, long before rap had been noticed by the general public. The music itself explored the ongoing practice of white singers appropriating and sanitizing black musical styles, and more specifically, black songs—an ironic topic for white guys writing a black musical. The music also beautifully chronicled the background story of *Dreamgirls*, of the convulsive changes in American culture being wrought by the civil rights movement, and also of the cultural assimilation that was black artists' only ticket to commercial success. The music was so pervasive that very little dialogue was necessary. Borrowing vocabulary from the world of opera but staying within the stylistic confines of Motown, rock and roll, rhythm and blues, soul, and rap, the score made use of recitative, arias, extensive counterpoint, and extended musical scenes. The Act I finale, Effie's searing cry of rage, "And I'm Telling You I'm Not Going," sung by Jennifer Holliday, regularly brought audiences to their feet. There was so much music in the show that it couldn't fit on a single LP. It wasn't until the release of a two-CD live recording of a 2001 concert version that the entire score was preserved.

Bennett's direction fully incorporated cinematic effects on stage for the first time—close-ups, reverses, split screens, wipes, superimpositions, tracking shots, all without a screen in sight. And musical theatre staging would never be the same. Some efforts in this direction had already been attempted, in *Follies* and *A Chorus Line*, both of which Bennett worked on. The *Dreamgirls* set that allowed Bennett's experiments consisted of five lighting towers that glided, spun, and danced, changing the proportions of the stage, changing perspectives, changing the audience's focus. In every department, this show was a triumph.

Dreamgirls ran 1,544 performances. It received twelve Tony Award nominations, and won five of them, including best book, best choreography, and three acting Tonys. The cast album also won a Grammy. Surprisingly, the show got mixed reviews, though everyone raved about Jennifer Holliday. Frank Rich wrote in the *New York Times*, "When Broadway history is being made, you can feel it. What you feel is a seismic emotional jolt that sends the audience, as one, right out of its wits. While such moments are uncommonly rare these days, one popped up last night at the end of the first act of Michael Bennett's beautiful and heartbreaking new musical *Dreamgirls*." He went on to say, "*Dreamgirls* is the same kind of breakthrough for musical stagecraft that *Gypsy* was." But in the *Daily News*, Douglas Watt wrote, "*Dreamgirls* represents an inordinate expenditure of talent and money on a musical that resembles a series of rehearsal periods for some slick TV commercial."

The show did not go to London. It was revived on Broadway in 1987, with the national touring cast, and ran 177 performances. Michael Bennett died of complications from AIDS in July 1987, shortly after the revival opened, having won a total of eight Tony Awards. Tom Eyen also succumbed to the disease a few years later in 1991. Finally in December 2006, a film version was released.

Songwriter Maury Yeston had begun to write the stage musical *Nine* in 1973, nearly a decade before it opened on Broadway in May 1982. Yeston (who would go on to write the score for *Titanic* and half the score for *Grand Hotel*) was obsessed with Federico Fellini's crazily autobiographical film 8½, about the midlife crisis of a famous Italian film auteur. In fact, Fellini gave his film its title as a joke: his lead character was so blocked artistically that his story didn't even get a real title (its original title was *La Bella Confusione*), just a number. Fellini had already directed seven full-length films and one short, and he had co-directed two films, so this was number eight-and-a-half.

Because the musical was no longer Fellini's work, the new title *Nine* referred to the age to which the central character Guido wishes he could return. Yeston began writing songs for a stage version of the film, working with Mario Fratti, who adapted the original Italian screenplay into English. In 1979, a workshop was done with lyricist-director Howard Ashman (*Little Shop of Horrors*) at the helm. Several new songs were created and the show's ending was discovered. This surrealistic, stream-of-consciousness musical presented on stage the extended nervous breakdown of film director Guido Contini, played by Broadway veteran Raul Julia. Guido has contracted to write and direct a new film, but he can't come up with a story. After recent box office failures, he is drifting, hiding from his producer at a Venetian spa, examining his past through the flawed relationships with the many women who have come in and out of his life. The action moves in and out of Guido's imagination and fantasies, as his women, past and present, swirl around him, and he plummets inexorably toward a breakdown.

In the fall of 1981, Yeston teamed up with director-choreographer Tommy Tune, co-choreographer Thommie Walsh (already immortalized as a character in *A Chorus Line*), and playwright Arthur Kopit. At that point, several characters had to be cut, including a male producer, his daughter, a critic, and others. The decision was made to cast the show entirely with women around the one male character, the antihero Guido. Later on, four boys were added to the cast for a flashback. It was then that the overture was written, to be performed vocally by an "orchestra" of women, all the women in Guido's life, past and present. Tune staged the show more minimally than any Broadway musical in a very long time, finding at last that inimitable style that marks a Tommy Tune musical. With the entire cast clad in black and a set made entirely of white tile to suggest the spa, the show looked like no other. Tune's production moved dreamlike in and out of scenes, in and out of songs, in and out of chronological order and conventional storytelling, creating an impressionist musical that challenged audiences and musical theatre traditions.

The show won five Tony Awards out of ten nominations. The wins included best musical, best featured actress (Liliane Montevecchi), best director, best score, and best costumes. Frank Rich wrote in the *New York Times*, "In this, his most ambitious show, Mr. Tune provides the strongest evidence yet that he is one of or theater's most inventive directors—a man who could create rainbows in a desert. Mr. Yeston, a newcomer to Broadway, has an imagination that, at its

163

best, is almost Mr. Tune's match. His score, giddily orchestrated by Jonathan Tunick, is a literate mixture of showbiz and operatic musical genres that contains some of the season's most novel and beautiful songs. Together, Mr. Yeston and Mr. Tune give *Nine* more than a few sequences that are at once hallucinatory and entertaining—dreams that play like showstoppers." He went on to say, "There's so much rich icing on *Nine* that anyone who cares about the progress of the Broadway musical will have to see it."

Nine ran 732 performances. Productions were mounted in several other countries. A concert version was presented at London's Festival Hall in 1992, with Liliane Montevecchi and Jonathan Price, and then a full production was mounted at London's Donmar Warehouse in 1996. A successful Broadway revival was mounted in 2003 with film star Antonio Banderas in the lead, alongside theatre stars Chita Rivera, Jane Krakowski, and others. That production won Tonys for best revival and best featured actress (Krakowski).

Alan Menken and Howard Ashman's musical *Little Shop of Horrors*, based on Roger Corman's gleefully low-budget 1960 film, opened off off Broadway at the WPA Theatre in May 1982. It quickly moved off Broadway to the Orpheum Theatre in July 1982, where it ran 2,209 performances. Innocent, goofy, and campy on its surface, *Little Shop* also dealt with many serious themes, vigilantism, pop culture and the American Dream, poverty in America, and more. It traded in the kind of deep emotional sincerity amidst broad surface comedy that would inspire later shows like *Bat Boy*.

Audrey's emotional ballad "Somewhere That's Green" walked the tightrope between comedy and aching emotion, asking quite forthrightly if the American Dream really even exists. Can the hero Seymour, a guy with horribly humble beginnings, really rise to fame and fortune? Is it only possible by abandoning morality, in this case by literally murdering his way to the top? The show's plot, based loosely on Goethe's *Faust*, was a strong but still comic indictment of America, of celebrity, of television, of the Rose Bowl, of *Life* magazine, of Americans' distrust of doctors, and of rampant spousal abuse in America. The tuneful and sophisticated score inspired by early sixties doo-wop was matched by intelligent, thoughtful, emotional, and thoroughly literate lyrics, full of acrobatic interior rhymes and arcane literary references.

Charles Isherwood wrote about the somewhat anemic, less sincere 2003 Broadway revival of *Little Shop* in *Variety*, "This show pioneered the kind of tongue-in-cheek approach to musical theater that has since set up shop all over the Great White Way. From its source in celluloid (and no classic!) to its self-mockingly ditzy book and lyrics (by the late Howard Ashman) to its rhythmic score that looked sideways to the world of the pop charts rather than back to Broadway history, *Little Shop* was a harbinger of bigger things to come. Traces of its influence can be found in shows as disparate as *Urinetown* and *Mamma Mia!*, while its most successful spawn would be that big-haired behemoth just across 52nd Street, *Hairspray*." He went on, "It's certainly true that musicals hatched from the spores of this unassuming little show have, in a sense, eaten Broadway, which is increasingly hostile to species of musical theater that seek to do anything other than show audiences a goofy good time. It's only fair that the mother of them all should get a bite of the action at last."

An excellent film version was made in 1986 by Frank Oz, with the original stage Audrey, Ellen Greene, alongside Rick Moranis and Vincent Gardenia, with cameos by Steve Martin, John Candy, James Belushi, Christopher Guest, and Bill Murray. But though the tragic stage ending was filmed, test audiences didn't like it and it was reshot with a new, happier ending, much to the annoyance of fans of the stage show. The first release of the DVD contained the original ending as bonus material, but producer David Geffen was furious and had all copies recalled. The DVD was rereleased without the original ending included, so the first release has now become a collector's item.

Stephen Sondheim and James Lapine's *Sunday in the Park with George* began its life in late 1982 as a not-yet-musical called *Seurat*. By May 1983 the creators had a mostly complete first draft of the script and just five songs. It opened for a limited twenty-five-performance run at Playwrights Horizons in July 1983, sitting precariously on the edge between traditional plot-driven musicals and the concept musicals developed mostly by Sondheim and director Hal Prince. Just as there seemed to be two Richard Rodgers, the jazzy composer partnered with Larry Hart and the romantic composer who wrote with Oscar Hammerstein, so too there were now two Stephen Sondheims, the brassy, aggressive songwriter who had partnered with Hal Prince and now the more minimalist, more emotionally naked composer writing with Jim Lapine. Like earlier concept musicals, *Sunday* explored an idea more than told a story, and yet it did still tell a story. The difference is that the exposition and conflicts are established in the 1880s but the resolution comes a hundred years later to a protagonist who is a different man and yet the same.

The central action of the story centered on George Seurat (in French it's "Georges" but in the play it's just "George"), the famous impressionist painter. Yet the story that bookwriter James Lapine fashioned was almost entirely fictional. *Sunday* explored the eternal battle between Seurat's work and his life with his mistress Dot. She loves George for his artistic passion and talent, and yet it's his art that keeps them apart. At the end of the first act, Dot leaves for America with another man, leaving George to finish his famous painting, *Un dimanche après-midi à l'Ile de la grande jatte* ("A Sunday afternoon on the island of La Grande Jatte"). In Act II, Seurat's great-grandson, a light sculptor also named George, is in the midst of a personal and artistic crisis of his own, facing the same issues as his ancestor. By the end of the show Dot returns, and she and George (the twentieth-century George) reunite. Their musical argument from Act I (in 1886), "We Do Not Belong Together," returns at the end of Act II (in 1984) as the inspiring "Move On." Despite the odd premise and the confusing time line, the show thrilled audiences, many of whom were moved to tears by the enormity and density of emotion expressed onstage.

Lapine and Sondheim had discussed at great length the idea of turning Georges Seurat's famous painting into a musical. But they couldn't initially figure out how to approach it. A visual artist himself, Lapine kept wondering why no one in the painting was looking at anyone else. He also noticed that the central character was missing: the painter. Those two observations were enough to start the two men writing a speculative tale about the events leading up to the creation of this painting. But it's about more than just why the people in the painting aren't looking at each other; it's more specifically about why the woman in front is placed so prominently. Sondheim and Lapine's answer was that she was Seurat's mistress, Dot, and the show became about George's struggle—and the struggle of all serious artists—to reconcile his obsessive passion for his art with his often ignored personal life.

This is a musical with great relevance to our modern world. Though on its surface the show is about an artist trying to find his voice and reconcile his life with his art, it's about much more. As with any great work of theatre, the more particular it gets, the more universal it becomes. This is a story about our epidemic inability to sustain relationships, as evidenced by a fifty percent divorce rate in America and skyrocketing domestic violence. This is a story about juggling a career with a relationship, an issue that speaks strongly to women at the beginning of the twenty-first century. It's about art and commerce, an issue that has become a political firestorm as Congress works to eliminate funding for the arts, as corporate arts funding dwindles, as computers make it cheaper to replace musicians and other artists with software.

Sunday in the Park with George does on stage what Seurat's painting does on canvas—catches people in the midst of living their lives, but in a formal, decidedly unnaturalistic style. The musical just sits back and watches people come and go, being lazy or combative, happy or otherwise, and because we only get snippets of most of these characters' lives, we don't get resolutions to their many problems. Like the hundreds of people we each encounter every day without really knowing them, many of the characters in the show just pass through this park; but in this case they are frozen for all time, caught not all at one moment but at many moments all at once.

Sunday in the Park opened on Broadway in May 1984 and ran 604 performances. Sondheim didn't provide the two most important songs, the show's emotional payoffs, "Lesson No. 8" and "Children and Art" until just before opening. Frank Rich wrote in the *New York Times*, "In his paintings of a century ago, Georges Seurat demanded that the world look at art in a shocking new way. In *Sunday in the Park with George*, their new show about Seurat, the songwriter Stephen Sondheim and the playwright-director James Lapine demand that an audience radically change its whole way of looking at the Broadway musical." He went on, "Mr. Sondheim and Mr. Lapine have created an audacious, haunting and, in its own intensely personal way, touching work. Even when it fails—as it does on occasion—*Sunday in the Park* is setting the stage for even more

166

sustained theatrical innovations yet to come. If anything, the show owes more to the off Broadway avant-garde than it does to past groundbreaking musicals, Mr. Sondheim's included. . . . In creating a work about a pioneer of modernist art, Mr. Lapine and Mr. Sondheim have made a contemplative modernist musical that, true to form, is as much about itself and its creators as it is about the universe beyond."

But Sondheim lost the 1984 Tony for best score to Jerry Herman for *La Cage aux Folles*. And Lapine lost the Tony for best book to Harvey Fierstein, also for *La Cage*. *Sunday* ended up losing several Tonys to *La Cage*, including best actor, best director, and best musical. Jerry Herman's acceptance speech proved to be a bit controversial. He said, "This award forever shatters a myth about the musical theatre. There's been a rumor around for a couple of years that the simple, hummable show tune was no longer welcome on Broadway. Well, it's alive and well at the Palace!" Theatre people speculated for months about whether or not that was meant to be a slam against Sondheim and *Sunday*. Herman swore it was not. *Sunday* did, however, win the Pulitzer Prize for drama that year. Just as Andrew Lloyd Webber was often considered the anti-Sondheim, Jerry Herman was too. Where Sondheim was always groundbreaking and complex, Herman was often happily conventional and old-fashioned. Strangely enough, Herman's *La Cage aux Folles* was both as conventional as it could be and also a little bit groundbreaking.

But Herman hadn't been the producers' first choice to write the score. Originally, the show was to have been called *The Queen of Basin Street*, set in New Orleans, with a score by Maury Yeston, a book by Jay Presson Allen (who had written the *Cabaret* screenplay), direction by Mike Nichols, and choreography by Tommy Tune. Instead, the producers scrapped it all and started over. Now the show had a score by Herman, a book by Harvey Fierstein (who'd just had a big hit with the play *Torch Song Trilogy*), direction by Arthur Laurents, and choreography by Scott Salmon. Opening on Broadway in August 1983 and running for a whopping 1,763 performances, it was built like the most standard and old-fashioned of musicals, up to and including its charming, tuneful, but nothing-new score, picking up right where Herman had left off with *Hello, Dolly!* and *Mame*, almost as if he had forgotten his experiments with *Dear World* and *Mack and Mabel*. With a lovely, old-fashioned script by Harvey Fierstein, lovely, old-fashioned designs, and lovely, old-fashioned direction by Arthur Laurents, *La Cage* was definitely your parents' kind of musical.

Except.

The central characters are a middle-aged gay French couple, Georges and Albin, who run a drag club in St. Tropez, and the plot centers on their son's engagement to the daughter of a right wing "family values" zealot. The son selfishly asks Albin (the "woman" of the couple, in a throwback to earlier stereotypes) to disappear for the Big Dinner with the future in-laws, to be replaced by the son's biological mother. When the biological mother doesn't show, Albin appears in drag and, since it's a musical comedy, charms them all. *La Cage* was slyly subversive in placing a gay couple at the center of an old-fashioned, 1960s-style musical comedy, but it was also both timid and a bit self-loathing in keeping that couple as sexless, stereotyped, and as nonthreatening as possible. Gay-themed plays went back as far as the 1930s. Gay musicals went back to the late 1960s and early 1970s. Why be so timid and dishonest in 1983? Partly because Broadway musicals were getting more and more expensive and going to the theatre was becoming a special event, not a regular choice for a night of entertainment. Theatregoers were no longer *theatregoers*. Broadway was becoming the place where tourists went for a Big Night Out, not a place where artists went to take risks. Foreign tourists who didn't speak English were becoming an ever bigger chunk of the Broadway audience.

Sure, there were some artists still doing important work on Broadway, but the Great White Way was no longer the place to find much innovation or rule busting. *La Cage* was relatively safe, just like Broadway. It pointed backward, not forward, but that's how Broadway worked for the moment. Remember, this was a Broadway where the sweet and harmless *La Cage aux Folles* could win the Tony Award for best musical over the stunning masterpiece that was *Sunday in the Park with George*.

The Gospel at Colonus, a fascinating mix of Christianity and Greek tragedy, first opened in November 1983 at the Brooklyn Academy of Music's Next Wave Festival, for a limited run of thirty performances. Its life continued with subsequent engagements in Houston, Washington, DC, Philadelphia, Los Angeles, Atlanta, Minneapolis, Cleveland, Chicago, San Francisco, and Seattle. It toured to Spoleto, Italy, to the Barcelona Festival in Spain, and to France. The show then opened on Broadway in March 1988 at the Lunt-Fontanne Theatre, where it ran only 61 performances. The work was adapted and directed by acclaimed writer and director Lee Breuer, with music composed, arranged, and directed by Bob Telson.

The Gospel at Colonus is an oratorio set at a black Pentecostal service, in which the Greek myth of Oedipus, replacing Bible story, is sung, acted, and preached by the characters of the play-within-a-play, addressing the audience directly in a range of rhetorical styles, sometime with two actors playing one character, one the speaking voice, the other the singing voice. The show won many awards, including an Obie for outstanding musical, a Los Angeles Drama Circle Critics Circle Award, and an award from the National Institute for Music Theater. It was nominated for a Pulitzer Prize, a Tony Award for best book, and a Grammy for best recorded theatre score. It was taped at the American Music Theatre Festival in Philadelphia for the PBS Great Performances series, for which it was nominated for an Emmy.

Sadly, Broadway still wasn't doing too well. Only one new hit Broadway musical opened in the 1984–85 season, an unlikely musicalization of *Huckleberry Finn* called *Big River*, with a book by William Hauptman and a score by

168

pop-country songwriter Roger Miller. The show had started its life a bit wobbly in 1984 at the American Repertory Theatre in Cambridge, Massachusetts, on the Harvard University campus, then moved to the La Jolla Playhouse in California, in the process undergoing major changes; the creators jettisoned the show's original sepia-toned production design and fiddled with the material itself. But the show that opened on Broadway in April 1985 was a genuine hit. It took Mark Twain's classic novel and turned it into a serious, adult musical full of political and social commentary, never shying away from the more gruesome, more unsettling moments in the novel. The $2.5 million show ran 1,005 performances and won seven Tony Awards (in an admittedly fallow field), including best musical, best book, best score, and best director (Des McAnuff). But the season was so artistically barren that they eliminated the category of best choreographer at the 1985 Tonys because there was no one worth nominating. They also eliminated the categories of best actor and actress in a musical. And the New York Drama Critics Circle decided not to give a best musical award that season or the next.

In August 1985, the New York Shakespeare Festival presented another odd new musical at their outdoor Delacorte Theatre in Central Park, *The Mystery of Edwin Drood*, a strange hybrid show, a return to old-fashioned musical comedy conventions, but with a sly postmodern layer of comic irony.

Drood is a musical about musicals, and oddly enough, one of the few fully naturalistic musicals, because the very act of singing is motivated. Composer-lyricist-bookwriter-orchestrator Rupert Holmes offers up a comic goldmine as a framing device: the audience is at the Music Hall Royale in London, and the music hall's regular cast of British rowdies are about to present their adaptation of Charles Dickens' unfinished novel *The Mystery of Edwin Drood*. This device allows the show to freely admit to all the artifice, posturing, and shoehorning that traditional musical comedy generally asks us to politely ignore. Older musical comedies frequently gave us a leading actor inexplicably strolling downcenter in the middle of a scene in order to belt out the title song, but here the same practice is funny and wry because here, the framing device justifies it and simultaneously admits the idiocy of it. Likewise, the periodic shoehorning of irrelevant numbers into a musical comedy plot is taken to an extreme, as the whole cast of *Drood* stops the action to step out of the scene and perform the troupe's signature number, "Off to the Races." We accept all this from *Drood* even though we would no longer accept the same conventions in a 1920s musical comedy. And that's funny too.

The score offers one beautiful surprise after another, from the rowdy opener, "There You Are" (written for the Broadway transfer)—significantly written in the second person, placing the *audience* at the center of the show, rather than the *actors*—to the chillingly beautiful melancholy of "Moonfall," the comic mania of "A Man Could Go Quite Mad" (one of the musical theatre's great character songs), the charmingly shy "Never the Luck," and the manic patter number, "Both Sides of the Coin," among other gems. Holmes, who also composed many hit pop songs, knows how to repeatedly surprise us without losing us. His songs are both sophisticated and accessible, both ironic and deeply emotional.

So why not present the tale in a more straightforward manner? Partly because the gloomy, melodramatic, and slowly paced Dickens is hard to musicalize—the story is not as grand and epic a tale as *Les Miz*, and yet not as ambiguous and ironic as a Sondheim show. But the more practical reason is that the central gimmick of Holmes' version is that the audience itself fleshes out the plot elements that Dickens left undone when he died. In order for the audience to vote on the necessary questions of plot resolution, the show needs a textual justification for the actors to go out into the audience and record the vote. The framing device of the music hall accomplishes this with great humor, great energy, and a never ending source of cheerfully cheap gags to boot. Long before interactivity had become such a widespread and ever growing phenomenon in popular culture, *Edwin Drood* became the first genuinely interactive Broadway musical, unable to end without the participation of the audience and thus, literally a different show every single night. The show moved to Broadway in December 1985 and ran 608 performances. It was nominated for nine Tony Awards and won five of them, for best musical, best actor (George Rose as the Chairman), best director (Wilfred Leach), best book, and best score. It also won five New York Drama Desk Awards and the Outer Critics Circle Award for best musical.

In an unprecedented move, the producers changed the show's name to *Drood!* (what is it about musicals and exclamation points?) in late 1986, in an attempt to boost ticket sales, though why they thought a title change would help remains a mystery. The title was later restored. The show was rewritten in 1987 for London, dropping "A Man Could Go Quite Mad"; its delicate balance upset, the show flopped. The song was later restored.

One of Andrew Lloyd Webber's greatest commercial successes, *Phantom of the Opera*, opened in London in October 1986. Like *Cats*, its phenomenal success sadly eclipsed Lloyd Webber's much stronger earlier work *Evita*, and came close to eclipsing *Jesus Christ Superstar* as well.

In the summer of 1985, Lloyd Webber performed the first act of *Phantom* at his annual Sydmonton Festival, with lyrics by Richard Stilgoe, who had written the lyrics for Lloyd Webber's bland kiddie musical *Starlight Express*. In the spring of 1985, Lloyd Webber released *Phantom*'s title song—a bizarre disco anthem in the middle of an otherwise pseudoclassical score—and it rose to number seven on the British pop charts. But Lloyd Webber was now feeling Stilgoe wasn't up to the task of finishing the lyrics. An invitation to co-write the lyrics went to Lloyd Webber's former partner Tim Rice, but Rice was hard at work on *Chess*. Lloyd Webber finally settled on the unknown, twenty-five-year-old Charles Hart. The only problem Hart and Stilgoe had was that Lloyd Webber would write the music in finished form, then hand it off to the lyricists. As a result, too many of the show's lyrics ended up going on longer than they needed to, in order to accommodate the already finished music. Rather than collaborating with his lyricists, Lloyd Webber expected them to conform their work to his. Period. It made for some of the most banal, nonspecific lyrics ever heard on the professional stage. And once again, Harold Prince came in, reconceived the entire piece for the stage, connected all the dots, and made it into theatre.

After *Cats*, it seemed to some that Lloyd Webber chose bad lyricists on purpose. Frank Rich of the *New York Times* said in a television interview, "Throughout his career, he's really been held hostage by his lyricists. If a composer is working with unsophisticated lyrics, he's in trouble." When he worked with Rice, Lloyd Webber wrote more sophisticated music. In *Phantom*, his use of music is mostly random, a tune reused here or there merely for the sake of reusing it, rather than for dramatic development. A reused melody still may be pretty but it's no longer emotionally satisfying. And no surfeit of swelling strings can compensate for that.

The $8.5 million show was well received in London and moved to Broadway in January 1988 with a sixteen million dollar advance. Despite lukewarm reviews, it won seven Tony Awards. In reviewing the show on Broadway, Frank Rich wrote in the *New York Times*, "*The Phantom of the Opera* is as much a victory of stagecraft over musical kitsch as it is a triumph of merchandising *über alles*. Mr. Lloyd Webber has again written a score so generic that most of the songs could be reordered and redistributed among the characters (indeed among other Lloyd Webber musicals) without altering the show's story or meaning." Certainly not something that could be said about the shows of Stephen Sondheim (with whom Lloyd Webber shares a birthday), who happened to be preparing a show of his own.

Phantom is the highest-grossing stage show (or movie, for that matter) of the twentieth century, bringing in $3.2 billion, having been staged in ninety-one cities in fifteen countries and seen by eighty million people. The original cast album sold more than twenty-five million copies. The hopelessly misdirected, badly cast, but beautifully designed eighty-million-dollar film version was released in 2004. And in January 2006, *Phantom of the Opera*, the last of the megamusicals still running in New York, became the longest running musical in Broadway history, passing *Cats*.

While *Phantom* was running in New York, Frank Rich was interviewed by British television about Lloyd Webber's work. "Clearly, Andrew Lloyd Webber has a huge talent for anticipating public taste," Rich said. "But it's not a cynical one. He's not pandering to the public as a Hollywood executive might. He hasn't found a formula and stuck to it. Otherwise, he'd be doing the fifteenth Biblical musical by now. Instead, he's picked incredibly varied topics, from the Bible to trains to cats to a single woman's odyssey in New York to a horror tale such as *Phantom of the Opera*. The question raised by his career, however, is whether his music and the format of his music varies as much as the subjects of his shows. Stephen Sondheim, the foremost American composer of musicals, also picks eclectic subject matter, but there's no confusing the score of *Sweeney Todd* with the score of *A Little Night Music*. In the case of Lloyd Webber, you could possibly confuse the shows because there is an artistic sameness."

But then again, could the same be said of Cole Porter or, to a slightly lesser extent, Jerry Herman? Despite his successes, Lloyd Webber has also had a string of flops, including *Aspects of Love, Sunset Boulevard, By Jeeves,* and two shows that couldn't even make it to New York, *Whistle Down the Wind* and *The Beautiful Game*. Though Lloyd Webber's earlier, rock-oriented work has had a lasting effect on the art form, the rest of his shows probably won't.

The Next Big Thing on Broadway during the eighties was Sondheim's. And once again, Sondheim proved that he offered stimulation, both intellectual and emotional, while Lloyd Webber was now only offering *simulation*, the imitation of emotion.

Into the Woods was one of Stephen Sondheim's few commercial hits. It was given readings in 1985 and 1986 in New York, then opened at the Old Globe Theatre in San Diego in the fall of 1986, in a form fairly different from what ended up on Broadway. Songs were cut and added, the plot was reworked, characters were cut, and the character of the witch was completely rethought. It opened on Broadway in November 1987 and ran 764 performances.

The show was a "crossover" musical for Sondheim, both artistic and commercial, combining the innocence of fairy tales, magic, and the mystery of the woods with the adult concepts of morality, sexuality, the consequences of actions, responsibility to the community, and the complexities of parent-child relationships. This is a different fairy tale world than we're used to, one in which wicked stepsisters aren't ugly and beautiful people can be bad, in which tough questions don't have easy answers. James Lapine's book and Sondheim's score provide a weird mix of escapism and hard-edged reality that still manages to succeed in creating a unified world. The show's book tells the intricate story while Sondheim's score provides the themes and lessons.

The show starts with the familiar phrase, "Once upon a time . . ." then hits the audience with a loud jarring vamp, to wake us up and tell us this will be no ordinary children's story, that *Into the Woods* is a fairy tale with balls. During the first act the main characters all make wishes, and each gets his or her wish by the first act finale. Like *The Fantasticks*, the first act gives us a simple, traditional Happily Ever After; then the second act examines what happens *after* the Happily Ever After. The show essentially gives us what we want in Act I, then snatches it back from us in Act II, just like other Sondheim shows.

Throughout history, literature has treated the woods as a dark place free of society's rules but also its protections, where people find their true selves and learn important lessons before returning to the safety of the civilized world. *Into the Woods* acknowledges that in the real world, love is not ideal, princes are not perfect, choices are not easy, human relations aren't simple, and every action has a repercussion. Even after these people all get what they wished for, they want more. After the ball is over, Cinderella is bored. After Jack steals the gold from the giant, he goes back to steal more. After the Baker and his Wife get their child, they find they want a bigger house. After the Prince marries Cinderella, he still fools around with the Baker's Wife. When Cinderella confronts him, he tells her that he thought marrying her was all he ever wanted, but he found that he still wanted more. He says, "I was raised to be charming, not sincere." The condition of never being satisfied has serious ramifications in this very adult fairy tale world. The story is consciously chaotic. The Baker and his Wife, the only two characters not taken from traditional fairy tales, were created to tie together all the stories, and also to wreak havoc in the other stories. Each character's actions now have implications for everyone else. The added complications of these new combinations create new dramatic situations and tensions.

The music for the show is both very simple and very sophisticated. Sondheim wrote short, jaunty melodies that sound very much like children's songs. Many of the songs in the first act are brief and self-contained, while the songs in Act II are longer and often interconnected. The lyrics have a great many rhymes and alliterations, which help make them sound even more like children's songs. Of course, because the lyrics are Sondheim's, there is important character and thematic development underneath the alliteration and multiple rhymes. When the Tony Awards came around this time, Sondheim experienced some déja vu. After losing so many *Sunday in the Park* Tonys to *La Cage*, this time *Phantom of the Opera* beat out *Woods* for the best musical Tony. Curiously, though, *Woods* won the Tonys for best score and best book. There was much speculation about how the best musical could not have the best score and book, but it would happen again. . . .

Into the Woods opened in London in September 1990, with one new song, "Our Little World," for the Witch and Rapunzel, partly based musically on "No More," making an important connection between the two sets of parents and children. The show would go on to become a staple of school and community theatres across America, and a film version was developed and penned by Lowell Ganz and Baabaloo Mandel, to be directed by Penny Marshall, with help from Jim Henson's Creature Shop. Sondheim even wrote some new songs. But the film was never made. A tepid revival hit Broadway in 2002 and flopped, and in 2004 a Japanese production was mounted at Japan's National Theatre.

The fiercely political South African protest musical *Sarafina!* opened off Broadway at Lincoln Center in October 1987. First produced at the often controversial Market Theatre in Johannesburg, South Africa, the show was conceived, written, and directed by Mbongeni Ngema, with songs by Ngema and Hugh Masekela, in the midst of South Africa's vigorous, growing political theatre scene. Director Ngema had auditioned seven hundred kids for his show, and selected about thirty, who then lived with him in his house for the three months it took to mount the show. But these weren't actors, so Ngema had to teach them basic stage skills, diction, the discipline of stage acting, and his mantra, "Think, focus, believe. Don't just do it. Believe." In a stroke of conceptual genius, Ngema costumed the band as the ever present government soldiers keeping an eye on activist students, and these band members sometimes stepped into the scenes, using their musical instruments as guns, both avoiding the use of realistic weapons (though the substitutions became even more disturbing) and also underlining the metaphor of music as a political weapon.

Sarafina!—its cast, band, and creators—came to New York from South Africa with their fact-based, agitprop musical about school children in Soweto who stand up against government apartheid. The musical followed proudly in the footsteps of *The Cradle Will Rock* and *Hair*. The opening of the subsequent film version provided the story's historical context: in 1976 the South African government declared a State of Emergency, and the army marched against and slaughtered schoolchildren who were protesting government oppression. For the next thirteen years, schoolchildren waged a campaign of resistance. Approximately 700 students were killed, over 10,000 were arrested, many more tortured and assaulted. *Sarafina!* is the story of one young girl caught up in the struggle for freedom in South Africa just before the release of Nelson Mandela and the end of apartheid.

Director Ngema told his young cast that though the government of South Africa had an embassy in the United States, the *people* of South Africa did not. Therefore, the company of *Sarafina!* had to be the ambassadors for their people, to show Americans the truth about life and death in South Africa. But *Sarafina!* was intensely subversive in a way many Americans did not understand. The South African government had demanded that all blacks speak and write only in the white-created language of Afrikaans, but the blacks knew that they could never tell the world the truth and never be educated outside their country if they did not learn English. So the students refused to learn Afrikaans, and their refusal led to the riots of 1976 and great bloodshed. Merely by performing *Sarafina!* in English, Ngema and his company were breaking the law.

Despite the show's often joyous, triumphant spirit, it did not shy away from the terrifying violence of that time and place, and one scene late in the show dramatized the students being mowed down by police with machine guns. This was a show, like those in the 30s, the 60s, and the 70s that had a political agenda and felt no need to hide it. No one could walk out of the theatre without feeling some amount of outrage over South Africa's sins. But Ngema had to warn his young cast to be careful about what they said to the American press. One wrong comment and they could be arrested upon their return home. After 81 performances off Broadway, the show transferred to Broadway where it ran another 597 performances. The show received five Tony nominations including best musical, best score, and best direction, but won none of them. In 1988 a documentary film was made about the show called *Voices of Sarafina!*, produced by Lincoln Center, including lots of performance footage. In 1992, a full-fledged film adaptation debuted, with Whoopi Goldberg as the students' favorite schoolteacher.

The last of the great megamusicals, *Miss Saigon* opened in London in September 1989. The show was loosely based on *Madame Butterfly* but transplanted to the Vietnam War, with music by Claude-Michel Schönberg, lyrics by Alain Boublil, and English lyrics and "additional material" by Richard Maltby Jr. Much of the *Les Miz* team was reunited by producer Cameron Mackintosh, except this time Mackintosh hired director Nicholas Hytner and choreographer Bob Avian. But magic didn't spark quite as brightly this time. Reviewers noticed uncomfortable similarities to *Chess, Cats, Grease, Sweet Charity, Les Miz,* and other shows, and reviews were generally mixed to negative. Still, despite its inferiority to its older sibling, it would still run in London for ten years, finally closing in October 1999, after 4,263 performances.

When the time came to bring the show to Broadway, Mackintosh faced some problems. He wanted his two London leads, Jonathan Pryce and Lea Salonga, to come to New York and open the U.S. production. But in August 1990, Actors' Equity officially refused to allow the Caucasian Pryce to play the role of the Amerasian character the Engineer on Broadway. The union demanded that Asian actors be given the chance to play the Asian characters in the show. But Mackintosh wanted Pryce and he threatened to cancel the $10.9 million Broadway production and return the show's $25 million advance sales. Equity backed down.

But *Miss Saigon* also had trouble finding a Broadway house big enough to hold the show as it was designed in London. *Les Miz* had to move theatres to make room. *Miss Saigon* took the idea of megamusicals to an extreme; its sets included an almost-life-sized helicopter that landed on stage, a twenty-foot-tall, eight-hundred-pound statue of Ho Chi Minh, and a Cadillac that appeared onstage in the last number. The show became the first musical to charge a hundred dollars for its mezzanine seats. For many theatre artists, *Miss Saigon* represented all that was wrong with the musical theatre—foreign product, (perceived) racism, overproduced spectacle, and skyrocketing costs and ticket prices. The show finally opened in April 1991, and ran 4,092 performances, closing in December 2000. Three of the leads, Pryce, Salonga, and Hinton Battle, won Tony Awards, but though the show had gotten eight other nominations, it didn't win any of them. It did win four Drama Desk Awards and three Outer Critics Circle Awards. The national tour employed thirty-seven trucks to haul the sets from city to city. The Fox Theatre in St. Louis literally had to knock out the back wall of the theatre and expand its stage to make room for the *Miss Saigon* touring production.

Miss Saigon's biggest troubles lay in its often awkward English lyrics by Maltby and in its split personality. Half the show—the half featuring the Engineer—was a latter-day *Cabaret*, all vulgar, nasty, biting social satire. The other half—the half featuring the lovers Chris and Kim—was overblown romantic melodrama. Never did either half take prominence in the show and never did the show figure out which it wanted to be. Constantly jerking the audience back and forth between these two disparate worlds, the show would never be as satisfying as *Les Misérables*. Strangely, because of the beautiful music, the show worked far better as a cast album than as a theatre piece. Still, like Mackintosh's other shows, *Miss Saigon* was a serious money maker. Nineteen *Miss Saigon* companies have opened in seventeen countries and ninety-eight cities, playing in nine different languages. There have been eleven different cast recordings.

The late 1980s were becoming a time of issues in Broadway musicals. In 1989, Tommy Tune tackled oppression of the working class in Weimar Germany in his overwhelmingly sensory—but surprisingly low tech—*Grand Hotel*, which opened on Broadway in November and became a modest hit. But it almost didn't make it to the stage, and its story is a good lesson about how musicals operate. Based on Vicki Baum's 1929 novel, *Menschen im Hotel* (*People in the Hotel*), as well as her 1930 Broadway play, *Grand Hotel*, and the resulting all-star MGM film in 1932, the musical version was first produced by the Los Angeles Civic Light opera. Called *At the Grand* in 1958, it had a score by Robert Wright and George Forrest (the *Kismet* team), and a book by Luther Davis. The action was transplanted from 1928 Berlin to 1958 Rome. Characters' jobs and personalities were changed, some characters were cut, two comic gangsters seemingly right out of *Kiss Me, Kate* were added. The show played Los Angeles and San Francisco, but never went further. The creators revisited the show in 1988, changing the locale, period, style, characters, and songs, and renamed it *The Grand* for another production.

Director-choreographer Tommy Tune saw this production and decided he wanted to mount the show for Broadway. But he wanted to do it differently. He found a passage in Vicki Baum's autobiography in which she said that her ideal movie version would be "an expressionistic, almost abstract hotel, a constantly moving maelstrom of faces, bodies, backgrounds, phones, bells, beds, objects." Tune loved that.

He assembled a cast and began a six-week workshop with veteran music director Wally Harper in the lobby of the old Diplomat Hotel near Times Square. He also began tinkering with the show's script. He said to the actors, "I want a collage. Let's make this like pointillism." He asked them to improvise, to overlap lines, to embellish, to borrow from each other. He wanted the action—and the music—never to stop. He searched for the darker moments in the show and brought them forward. He placed the entire cast in chairs ringing the stage, observing every scene they weren't in, to constantly remind the audience of the artificiality of the theatre, a device borrowed from Bertolt Brecht. He said to his cast "Think of our show as if we are in 1928 with Brecht and the Berliner Ensemble."

After the first two weeks of performances in Boston, Tune decided the creative team could not fix the problems that needed fixing, so he called in veteran bookwriter Peter Stone (*1776*, *Woman of the Year*, *My One and Only*) to come to Boston as "play doctor." Composer Maury Yeston (*Nine*, *Titanic*) was asked by Tune to come in and write some new songs as well. The problem seemed to be that Tune was directing a very old-fashioned 1958 musical in a very modern concept-musical style, and it just wasn't working. Tune had been making some changes himself, but he needed new writers. Yeston wrote several new songs and extended musical sequences to better fit the style Tune was trying to create and the minimalist set Tony Walton had designed. Tune also figured out the most important lesson—if the source material is strong (as the novel was), *don't screw around with it!* The earlier version of the show had tinkered with it far too much. Tune was circling back toward the novel.

There were two lines from the famous novel that had informed everything Tune was up to—"The music never stops at the Grand Hotel" and "Life goes on at the Grand Hotel." Scenes and songs rarely played in their entirety, almost always interrupted, interpolated, interwoven. This was a show about perpetual motion. The plot focused on five stories: Otto Kringelein, the Jewish bookkeeper who is dying and has come to spend his last days at the Grand Hotel; Flaemmchen, the unmarried but pregnant typist who is prepared to sell her body to get to Hollywood; Baron von Gaigern, a penniless nobleman turned cat burglar; Elizaveta Grushinskaya, an aging ballerina who must face the end of her career; and Herr Preysing, a morally weak businessman whose mistakes are about to bring his entire world crumbling down around him. These stories intertwined, danced, and moved in and out of each other, as the show looked at love, death, sex, money, power, the false glitter of America, and the early rumblings of Nazism in Germany. The show took place in Berlin in 1928 and it unfolded in the shadow of what everyone knew would be coming to Germany in a few short years.

After the Boston run, Tune went to his producers and asked for time and money to retool the show. The producers agreed. So the show came back to New York and went back into rehearsal, which was highly unusual. They began intercutting scenes, cutting back and forth cinematically. They fattened the role of the doctor who narrates the show and gives the audience important information, and they brought back and emphasized the doctor's morphine addiction. They deepened the love story. They changed the focus of the show's end from tragic to more hopeful. They wrote an entirely new, extended musical opening in which all the main characters were introduced. Only five songs remained from the original *At the Grand* by this point. Maury Yeston had added seven new songs and had rewritten lyrics to a dozen more.

The show ran for an unusually long preview period, then opened on Broadway and ran for two years and 1,018 performances. It earned an impressive twelve Tony nominations and won six, for best director, choreographer, scenic, lighting, and costume design, and for Michael Jeter (Kringelein) as best featured actor. The show also won five Drama Desk Awards, the Outer Critics Circle Award, and many others. Frank Rich wrote in the *New York Times*, "Tommy Tune may have the most extravagant imagination in the musical theater right now, and there isn't a moment or a square inch of stage space, that escapes its reach in *Grand Hotel*. *Grand Hotel* will fascinate those who are interested in the theater, especially the musical theater." Most of the critics agreed.

After its opening, musical theatre historian Ethan Mordden wrote in a *New York Times* feature story, "There is so much to take in that it spins past one even as it dazzles. Perhaps it is a two-visit musical, like *Cabaret*, *Pacific Overtures*, or *Dreamgirls*—shows which, because of compositional sophistication or textured staging, must be *absorbed* to be appreciated. That's art as it should be."

Significantly, the dance world was also very excited about *Grand Hotel*, not just in the way dance permeated the show, but also in the deeply integrated way it shared the duties of storytelling. Tune was honored with numerous dance awards for his work on *Grand Hotel*. And the *New York Times* even sent its dance critic Jennifer Dunning to review the show. This was the kind of theatre dance that Balanchine had first explored, that Agnes DeMille had developed, and that Jerome Robbins and Bob Fosse had raised to an art form. Tommy Tune was picking back up a major thread of musical theatre history that had been largely ignored during the 1980s. Interestingly, this was also the season Broadway saw *Jerome Robbins' Broadway*, a stunning revue of Robbins' musical theatre choreography, lovingly recreated by the best dancers in the business.

But that was the past. What did the future hold?

9

Songs for a New World
The 1990s

The last decade of the century brought with it a real dilemma regarding American musicals. Why were all the most imaginative, most insightful, most daring new productions of classic American musicals being staged by foreign directors? The 1990s saw British director Sam Mendes' amazing, eye-opening work on both Sondheim's *Company* and Kander and Ebb's *Cabaret*; British director Nicholas Hytner's brilliantly revisionist staging of *Carousel*; Australian director Christopher Renshaw's smart and sexy new *King and I*; and British director Trevor Nunn's revelatory new *Oklahoma!* Why weren't Americans doing work like this?

True, American directors were also doing revivals and "revisals" (awkwardly revised and rewritten revivals) of great American musicals, but Des McAnuff's Broadway revival of *How to Succeed in Business Without Really Trying* lost all the show's bite and half its humor; and despite its commercial success, Walter Bobbie's *Chicago* abandoned the show's central metaphor, its ironic period setting, its brutal social satire, and the dangerous sexuality that had made the original so brilliant. It became nothing more than an unexceptional dance concert in black leather. And let's not even get into the messes that were the Broadway revivals of *Company*, *Once Upon a Mattress*, *The Sound of Music*, *Grease*, or *Damn Yankees*. Perhaps the answer is that American directors were just too close to these shows, had seen them too many times, knew them too well, and were too used to seeing them done in shallow, mediocre productions. Perhaps only foreign directors were able not only to see these shows fresh but also maintain a healthy respect for the art form that too many commercial directors in America seemed to have lost. The only worthwhile revival during this period that was directed by an American was Hal Prince's excellent *Show Boat*, which originated in Canada.

On the other hand, the chokehold the British had over the commercial musical theatre all through the 1980s, with *Cats*, *Phantom of the Opera*, *Les Misérables* (yes, created by Frenchmen but produced by Brits), *Joseph and the*

179

Technicolor Dreamcoat, Song and Dance, Me and My Girl, Aspects of Love, Starlight Express, and others, was finally lessening. In fact, by mid-decade, Americans would decisively take back their indigenous art form with some of the most adventurous new work the musical theatre had seen since the sixties and seventies. By the middle of the decade, the American musical theatre would be healthier than ever, more audacious, more daring than it had been in many years. The millennium would end with some real hope for the future of the art form, though not necessarily limited geographically to New York and Broadway.

Still, the future wasn't entirely rosy. The 1993–94 season signaled what would later be called the Disneyfication of Broadway. The opening of Disney's artless live-action *Beauty and the Beast* in April 1994 set off lots of complaints that Broadway was turning into Disneyland. In the *New York Times*, David Richards wrote, "It's long been known as the Fabulous Invalid and the Great White Way, but we may have to start calling it Six Flags Over Broadway. . . . While there has always been a raffish, thrill-seeking side to theatergoing, the distinction between Broadway and a theme park grew decidedly narrower during the 1993–94 season." But this was also the decade that would return American musical theatre to its gutsy, provocative, muscular roots, with shows like *Bat Boy, Hedwig and the Angry Inch, A New Brain, The Ballad of Little Mikey, Songs for a New World, Floyd Collins Avenue X, Violet, Dream True,* and others, none of which ever made it to Broadway. Maybe the Great White Way *was* becoming a theme park, but it didn't matter that much to the art form; the most exciting new musicals were rarely on Broadway anymore.

In 1990, a new name emerged in musical theatre that would split musical-lovers for years to come: composer Frank Wildhorn, a far less talented Lloyd Webber clone. He would go on to write several gutless, paint-by-number pop musicals during the nineties, all of which contained nice enough songs and none of which were any good as storytelling. Wildhorn's muse Linda Eder would take center stage in some of these shows, proving she had a dynamite, rafter-shaking voice reminiscent of Barbra Streisand, but like Wildhorn, her talents didn't impress as much in the context of a book musical. Wildhorn declared more than once that he would bring pop music back to Broadway. Instead, all he brought was mediocrity.

The first of the Wildhorn shows began its public life in 1990. *Jekyll & Hyde,* based on the classic Robert Louis Stevenson story, with lyrics by Leslie Bricusse (pronounced BRICK-us) was first released as a concept album featuring Linda Eder and Colm Wilkinson (star of *Les Miz*). Bricusse had written several musicals in an earlier partnership with Anthony Newley, including *Stop the World—I Want to Get Off* and *The Roar of the Greasepaint, The Smell of the Crowd,* as well as musical films like *Doctor Dolittle* and, with Henry Mancini, *Victor/Victoria.*

Theatre fans were excited to hear this preview of a new musical from a new voice, but the songs succeeded as pop anthems far more than as theatre songs. They were well crafted songs, some of them, many of them tuneful, even exciting in some cases, with predictable modulations for final verses; but the lyrics were largely generic and vague, having only a tenuous connection to the story, rarely advancing character or plot, almost never genuinely dramatic, never deeply emotional, not specific or compelling in the way theatre songs must be. A swell of the orchestra or a canny change of key could not replace good storytelling. Wildhorn would have the same problems with all his subsequent theatre scores. He could write a great, belty pageant number, but he didn't know how to tell a story.

Jekyll & Hyde had its first performances at the Alley Theatre in Houston, the first full-scale musical that theatre had done, with Eder as Lucy and Chuck Wagner (from *Into the Woods*) as Jekyll/Hyde. Already altered greatly since that first album, the creators would continue to rewrite the show for most of the 1990s. In 1992, the show was workshopped in New York with Terrence Mann in the lead(s), and most everyone agreed it was not stageworthy. In 1994, a new, expanded, two-disc concept album was recorded, this time with Eder and Anthony Warlow, timed to kick off two more productions and a national tour. In 1995, the show was produced by the Alley Theatre again, and then at Seattle's 5th Avenue Musical Theatre Company. Then came a thirty-four-city American tour, starring Eder and Robert Cuccioli. And they kept rewriting. Unfortunately, one of the new problems with the show was its derivative staging, one moment from *Cabaret*, then *Sweet Charity*, a little *Pippin* here, a little *Sweeney Todd* there, then a touch of *Evita*. The director was fired and replaced.

Eventually, after years of rewrites—and surprisingly, with a passionate, expanding fan base derived from the recordings and the tour—*Jekyll & Hyde* opened on Broadway in April 1997. By now some songs from the show had become beauty pageant and ice show standards. Still tinkering with the show, five songs were dropped for the second national tour. But the lyrics were still banal and the score was still a collection of power ballads instead of a theatre score. In the 1920s, that would have been enough. It no longer was.

Still, the show ran on Broadway until January 2001 on the popularity of those same power ballads and lots of repeat business, racking up an impressive 1,543 performances, thanks in part to the show's rabid fans, the self-dubbed Jekkies, who saw the show over and over, in some cases hundreds of times, creating online discussion groups and role-playing games based on the show. Steve Oxman wrote in *Variety* that the show was "overwhelmed by a muddy story adaptation, uninspired staging, transparent lyrics and a forgettable, old-fashioned score. Lacking a point of view, or even accessible characters, the show is perpetually cold. Director David Warren may be trying to bring out the gothic quality of Stevenson's story, but even when scenes of suspense or emotional confrontation are set up, the production squanders the opportunities." He went on, "When Hyde goes on a killing spree in a musical montage beginning the second act, the number becomes bizarrely comic, since Hyde is more absurd than threatening and his victims have already been portrayed as emblems of inhuman bureaucracy. In a tale of good and evil, there's a problem when murders elicit a giggle."

It was, quite famously, not nominated for a best musical Tony Award in a season with virtually no competition. It was nominated for only three Tonys, two for design, one for Cuccioli, and won none of them. Just before closing, the show was videotaped for commercial release and pay-per-view television, with TV star David Hasselhoff in the lead. If there was any doubt before, *Jekyll & Hyde* proved that bad reviews could no longer kill a Broadway show, and that touring before Broadway was a good marketing strategy. The show would have a long foreign life, going on to play cities all over the world, in Germany, Sweden, Japan, Spain, Belgium, Hungary, Australia, and elsewhere.

And Wildhorn would be back soon, with *The Scarlet Pimpernel*, which would gain the title of the biggest money loser in the history of Broadway; as well as the almost spectacularly awful *Civil War*, which would run only sixty-one performances. While it lasted, Wildhorn did what few before him had done—he had three shows running on Broadway at once. Andrew Lloyd Webber had done it twice. Stephen Sondheim had done it once. And now Frank Wildhorn had too.

In April 1990, *A Chorus Line* finally closed, after 6,137 performances and almost fifteen years, by far the longest-running Broadway musical. Unfortunately, director-choreographer-conceiver Michael Bennett wasn't there to share in the glory. Many saw the closing as a sign that the musical was dead as well, although pundits had been seeing those death signs for decades. Most of the original cast was in the audience that night and at the show's end producer Joe Papp came onstage to introduce both the final cast and the original cast. One of *A Chorus Line*'s greatest legacies was that for fifteen years its profits funded Papp's New York Shakespeare Festival, the nonprofit theatre that first produced the show downtown. Up through 1990, the show had grossed more than $280 million. At the time, few people expected *Cats* to last the seven years more it needed to beat *A Chorus Line*. But it would.

Also in April 1990, director-producer Hal Prince was at the State University of New York at Purchase, working on a new show called *Kiss of the Spider Woman*, with a score by John Kander and Fred Ebb, and a book by Terrence McNally, based on Manuel Puig's famous novel about political prisoners in Argentina who learn to use imagination and storytelling as their only means of survival. The show focused on two cellmates, Molina, a gay window dresser jailed for his homosexuality, and Valentin, a fierce, passionate revolutionary and political prisoner. When the torture gets too horrific, when the walls feel like they're closing in, Molina—and later Valentin as well—escape into a movie musical fantasy world, where the glamorous femme fatale Aurora seduces handsome young men before killing them.

The show was the first offering by a new organization Prince had begun called New Musicals, a musical theatre lab safely located far away from the harsh lights of Broadway at the State University of New York at Purchase, where artists could work without the usual pressures of critics and "industry" people—"pressures that encumber the spirit with which you do your work," Prince said in a *New York Times* interview. Prince saw that Broadway was no longer the focal point for exciting new musical theatre. "In the future there are going to be shows that have played all over the world and have never played on Broadway," he said. In fact, it had already begun.

The first season of New Musicals was slated to develop four new shows, *Spider Woman*, *The Secret Garden*, *My Favorite Year*, and *Fanny Hackabout Jones*. Unfortunately, only *Spider Woman* would be produced before New Musicals shuttered. Prince had asked the New York press not to come to SUNY-Purchase, to allow these new shows to be developed without reviews. But the critics came anyway. British critic Sheridan Morley was the first to review the show for the *International Herald-Tribune*—he says he didn't know about the critical embargo—and once his review appeared, other critics descended upon Purchase like locusts, most of them publishing mixed or negative reviews of a musical that was admittedly not ready to be reviewed. Visually, the show kept leaping back and forth from the drab prison cell to MGM-style technicolored fantasy sequences full of pretty chorus girls. The fantasy sequences undermined and trivialized the realistic scenes, sapping the show's considerable potential strength. Its split personality didn't work and neither did much of the material. But the creators had had no time to figure that out. The work could no longer be done the way Prince had hoped, and so the New Musicals project—and the show—ended prematurely. Three of the four shows planned would end up on Broadway anyway, but the loss of New Musicals was very disappointing to those who cared about the American musical theatre.

But *Spider Woman* wasn't finished. Kander, Ebb, and McNally continued to work on the show, adding seven new songs and cutting eight, completely rethinking the physical look of the show, and completely rethinking the structure of the story and the interplay between the blending of the real world and fantasy. The show was remounted by theatre impresario Garth Drabinsky and his company Livent at Toronto's St. Lawrence Centre, in June 1992, with a new cast that featured Chita Rivera, Brent Carver, and Anthony Crivello. In this production the fantasy sequences happened entirely within the prison set, more effectively and dramatically mixing the real and fantasy worlds, never letting the audience forget the horrors the political prisoners face, never letting Molina and Valentin fully "escape," even during the most "escapist" numbers.

That same production then moved to London in October 1992 where it won the London Evening Standard Drama Award and an Olivier Award, both for best musical. Drabinsky noted that this was "the first musical in years with an American creative constituency to open in Toronto and London ahead of New York, and it will therefore reach Broadway in 1993 as an established hit, rather than as the risky endeavour it appeared when it was first considered there back in 1990." *Kiss of the Spider Woman* finally opened in New York at the Broadhurst Theatre in May 1993, where it ran three years and 906 performances. The show won seven Tony Awards, including best musical and best score. The show was choreographed by Rob Marshall, who would soon become one of the top choreographers on Broadway and who would helm the amazing film version of Kander and Ebb's *Chicago* a decade later.

Newsday called the revised version "the only new show with a wild heart and a fresh eye, the only one that budges the form in a seriously extravagant theatrical direction, the only one with a book that's stylish, the only one with an accessible gotta-dance score that isn't exclusively content to sound like music we've heard before." New York's *Daily News* said that it "transforms what might be cruel melodrama into something provocative, disquieting, and operatically haunting."

Kiss of the Spider Woman was significant for putting Latino characters front and center in a Broadway musical. *Zoot Suit* had done it first, but *Spider Woman* did it more commercially. *Spider Woman* also was one of the few Broadway musicals to acknowledge the existence of Latin America, much less take its politics seriously. Producer Garth Drabinksy said in an interview, "I have to believe that a work will have an importance in terms of the statement it's making, and without preaching, *Spider Woman* satisfies that criterion." Interestingly, the role of Latino political activist Valentin would be taken over during the run by Brian Mitchell (later Brian *Stokes* Mitchell, the future star of *Ragtime* and other shows), and Vanessa Williams would step in as Aurora, both African Americans. Tickets sales had dropped to about seventy percent of capacity when the producers hired Williams in late June 1994, and by August the show was back to standing room only. In a rare move, the producers took the cast back into the studio to make a second cast album, this one with Williams, Mitchell, and Howard McGillin, the new Molina.

Once on This Island was a kind of story-theatre musical with music by Stephen Flaherty, book and lyrics by Lynn Ahrens, and direction and choreography by the former Fosse dancer from Argentina, Graciela Daniele. The show enjoyed a four-week workshop in the fall of 1989, then opened in May 1990 for a three-week run at the 146-seat Playwrights Horizons, a theatre incubator that would also generate other musicals in this decade, including Sondheim's *Assassins*. After its run at Playwrights Horizons, *Once on This Island* moved to Broadway in October. Based on the novel *My Love, My Love* by Trinidad-born Rosa Guy, the show told the fable-like story of the island girl Ti Moune who rescues the rich, young, light-skinned black man Daniel after a car accident. She falls in love with him but he is the son of a rich land owner and cannot marry beneath his station. Instead of the darker-skinned Ti Moune, he marries his longtime fiancée, a light-skinned woman, injecting the issue of internal racism into the story. Ti Moune tries to drown herself in sorrow, but the Gods prevent this and instead turn her into a tree guarding the gate to Daniel's home. We find out that someday Daniel's son will fall in love with another peasant girl under this tree and they will marry, giving the show a kind of cosmic happy ending. Flaherty and Ahrens hit pay dirt with *Once on This Island*. They would go on later to write the masterpiece *Ragtime*, also choreographed by Daniele.

Once on This Island celebrated traditional, bare-bones, human storytelling in its decidedly low-tech approach. Its simple unit set was painted in bright primary colors, looking more like a child's shoebox theatre than a Broadway musical. Its actors were not just characters, but also sets, props, special effects, sound effects, and commentators, an approach owing much to earlier shows like *The Robber Bridegroom* and *Hair*. This radical rejection of the massive spectacles of the 1980s would inform many of the most exciting musicals of the nineties, including *Floyd Collins*, *Songs for a New World*, *Rent*, and *Violet*.

Of the production at Playwrights Horizons, Frank Rich wrote in the *New York Times*, "In *Once on This Island*, the stage has found its own sugar- and cartoon-free answer to *The Little Mermaid*. A ninety-minute Caribbean fairy tale told in rousing song and dance, this show is a joyous marriage of the slick and the folkloric, of the hard-nosed sophistication of Broadway musical theater and the indigenous culture of a tropical isle." He went on, "*Once on This Island* has the integrity of genuine fairy tales, in that it doesn't lead to a saccharine ending but to a catharsis, a transcendent acceptance of the dust-to-dust continuity of life and death." The show ran 469 performances on Broadway. It received eight Tony nominations but won none of them. But some in the black community balked at this "black" musical, since it was (once again) written by white folks and, some said, didn't fare very well in terms of Caribbean authenticity.

Many people were even more offended by the idea of a musical about presidential assassination when *Assassins* opened in December 1990 at Playwrights Horizons, especially because it came in the midst of the first Gulf War. Composer Stephen Sondheim and bookwriter John Weidman were surprised by this reaction. Certainly, they argued, if *Assassins* were a play without music, no one would think twice about its unusual content. Simply because it was a musical, some people thought the show trivialized its subject. Contrary to what those people believed, an art form can't be trivial in and of itself; only the ways in which people use that art form can be.

The American musical theatre has proven time and again that serious subjects and stories can be treated as powerfully with music as without; many argue that music adds *more* power. But the creators of *Assassins* took an unconventional—and controversial—approach to their subject, seeing the history of assassination in our country as a distinctly American tradition, savage though it may be. Instead of portraying the assassins as aberrations on the fringe of society, Sondheim and John Weidman saw them as the walking wounded, victims of our society's high expectations and false promises, disciples of a darkly alternative American Dream. Unlike the Sondheim musicals written with James Lapine, *Assassins* was a visceral, in-your-face, outrageous theatre piece, exhilarating and terrifying at the same time. From the moment the audience heard "Hail to the Chief" in waltz time—the wrong meter—they knew things were amiss. This was not the comfortable, relatively safe picture of America they were used to seeing in old-fashioned musicals; this was an America in which we might well lose our way. But this was also the *real* America, a country won with guns, a culture suffused with violence, a population often lied to.

The book and score of *Assassins* were among the most interesting in all of musical theatre. The show was a kind of neovaudevillian collection of both songs and dialogue scenes that were connected thematically, though they did not tell a conventional linear story. Like the Sondheim musicals *Company* and *Follies*, this was a character study, and before the show was over, audiences realized that the assassins weren't the only characters being examined; the show was also looking at the character of our country, a country in which a too-hyped American Dream and easy access to guns have provided a handful of neurotics with both the motive and means to kill a president. It is also a country in which we want everything explained in ten-second sound bites. The Balladeer wants a neat and simple motive for John Wilkes Booth's act of violence—bad reviews, sibling rivalry. But from the very beginning, *Assassins* declared that there are no easy answers. Booth *believed* in his cause, *believed* that the country he loved so deeply was being torn apart, *believed* that Lincoln was the cause. *Assassins* took Booth, Czolgosz and the others seriously, rather than dismissing them as loonies (with one or two exceptions), and in the process gave us a rare glimpse inside history that offered real insight instead of just smug superiority.

As usual, Sondheim's score held as much drama and subtext as the script. His music grounded the scenes in each time period; with two exceptions, the entire score was written in traditional American song forms appropriate to each assassin's period. For Sondheim, those forms included not only folksongs and cakewalks but also John Philip Sousa marches, barbershop quartets, show tunes, even 1970s pop ballads.

Unfortunately, all this complexity and nuance was lost in the original production at Playwrights Horizons under the heavy-handed direction of Jerry Zaks, who would soon triumph with a high-energy revival of *Guys and Dolls* on Broadway. Though he was a strong director, Zaks was more wrong for this project than just about any other director working in New York. A master of musical comedy with a delightful sense of whimsy and Cohan-esque pacing, he was ill equipped to shepherd this dark, moody concept musical. As a result of this—and perhaps also because of the hyper-patriotic mood of the country during the first Gulf War—*Assassins* didn't make it to Broadway. It was later produced in London with a new song, "Something Just Broke," that many Sondheim fans rejected as not organic to the rest of the show. *Assassins* was to have been revived on Broadway in the fall of 2001 by the Roundabout Theatre Company, but then came the terrorist attacks of September 2001 and the nervous producers put the production on permanent hold. Some fans believed that the attacks made a production of *Assassins* even more important than it had been before, that America needed to *understand* violence like this. The show finally opened on Broadway in 2004, to high praise and five Tony Awards, but the show was tinkered with and the production team made some unnecessary mistakes.

Once a project of Hal Prince's New Musicals, a new musical adaptation of the classic novel *The Secret Garden* opened on Broadway in April 1991. The show itself was not particularly remarkable, though it was very good. What was remarkable was the creative staff. For the first time in a long time (well, since the feminist musicals of the 1970s), almost the entire creative staff was female. The show had a book and lyrics by playwright Marsha Norman, music by Lucy Simon (sister of pop songwriter Carly Simon), and direction by Susan Schulman. The dance arrangements were by Jeanine Tesori, who would go on to write the scores for *Violet, Thoroughly Modern Millie,* and *Caroline or Change.* The sets were designed by Heidi Landesman, costumes by Theoni V. Aldredge, and lighting by Tharon Musser. The *New Yorker* called the creators "very much the daughters of Sondheim." *The Secret Garden* ran a healthy 706 performances and won three Tonys. And it has had a long life in regional and community theatres.

Something completely different followed a year later. *Jelly's Last Jam* opened on Broadway in April 1992, with a book and direction by the brilliant alternative director George C. Wolfe, music by Jelly Roll Morton (who claimed to have invented jazz) and Luther Henderson, and lyrics by Susan Birkenhead. Based on Morton's life, the show starred Gregory Hines, Savion Glover, and several other black performers who would go on to successful Broadway careers, including Keith David, Stanley Wayne Mathis, Ann Duquesnay, and Tonya Pinkins. The show's choreography was by Hope Clark and Hines. The *New York Times* called it "musical theatre at its American best. Anyone who cares about the future of the American musical will want to see and welcome *Jelly's Last Jam.*" Equal parts confessional and exorcism, Wolfe's show was a surrealistic survey of the complicated, decadent, often demeaning life of the great jazz innovator, all from the vantage point of a purgatory-like jazz club called The Jungle Inn, presided over by the God-like, pseudo-Dickensian Chimney Man. Morton reviews his life and all its contradictions and humiliations, though not always voluntarily. By the end he is redeemed in some way, perhaps by *Jelly's Last Jam* itself and its honest examination of his life and career, finally giving him proper credit for his contributions to American music.

The show ran 569 performances on Broadway. Frank Rich wrote in the *New York Times*, "As for Mr. Wolfe, a visionary talent who is making his Broadway debut, he has given *Jelly's Last Jam* ambitions beyond the imagination of most Broadway musicals, many of the street's current hits included. The show is not merely an impressionistic biography of the man who helped ignite the twentieth-century jazz revolution, but it is also a sophisticated attempt to tell the story of the birth of jazz in general and, through that story, the edgy drama of being black in the tumultuous modern America that percolated to jazz's beat. And that's not all: *Jelly's Last Jam,* a show in part about what it means to be African American,

187

is itself an attempt to remake the Broadway musical in a mythic, African American image."

That same month, in April 1992, another black musical debuted at Chicago's Steppenwolf Theatre, Tug Yougrau's *The Song of Jacob Zulu*, about the apartheid era in South Africa. It had a score by vocal group Ladysmith Black Mambazo and it was directed by Eric Simonson who would later work on Paul Simon's *The Capeman*, a similar musical about bigotry and injustice. Some people called *Jacob Zulu* a play; some called it a musical. Later in New York, it was nominated for a Tony for best play, but many reference sources say it was nominated for best musical. It centered on the true story of a nineteen-year-old African boy who had set off a bomb in a shopping center in South Africa at Christmas time 1985, killing five people and injuring more than fifty. *The Song of Jacob Zulu* examined the forces of apartheid that led to this unspeakable tragedy, how an otherwise respectable, "good" young man, the son of a minister, could commit such an act of violence.

In 1987, Yougrau had returned to his native South Africa to research the story of the real-life Andrew Zondo, the inspiration for the fictional Jacob Zulu. He wrote, "There emerged a story of great power, a tragedy like that of the Bible or the Greeks." Zondo had come from Natal, the same area that was home to the members of Ladysmith Black Mambazo. So Yougrau decided he had to use Mambazo in his piece, singing both traditional pieces and new songs written for the show. He wrote, "I decided to fictionalize the story to have the central figure stand for the whole generation of young black South Africans who have been sacrificed to history, who are unschooled and potentially explosive." In 1990 he submitted an outline to the Steppenwolf's New Plays Project. In 1991, Yougrau met with Mambazo's manager and founder Joseph Shabalala, and discovered to his amazement that Andrew Zondo had been Shabalala's cousin! At Christmastime 1991, one of Mambazo's founders was murdered in South Africa. But work continued. Yougrau used actual trial transcripts, lifted a character from *Oedipus Rex*, and led the company in improvisations. In the spring of 1992, the show opened in Chicago. The *Chicago Tribune* said, "This powerful work indicts South African apartheid via a complex plunge into the mindset of modern evil." It then opened on Broadway in the spring of 1993. The show was nominated for six Tony Awards. Shabalala and Ladysmith Black Mambazo were also honored with the prestigious Drama Desk Award for best original score.

Another look at young people would soon follow, the megahit *Rent*. In 1996, shortly before his death at age thirty-five, up-and-coming composer Jonathan Larson wrote:

> In these dangerous times, where it seems the world is ripping apart at the seams, we can all learn how to survive from those who stare death squarely in the face every day and [we] should reach out to each other and bond as a community, rather than hide from the terrors of life at the end of the millennium.

These words, discovered on his computer by his family after he died, serve as a fitting tribute to his only Broadway musical, *Rent*. (An earlier work of his, *Tick, Tick ... Boom!*, would be produced off Broadway after his death.)

Larson, a hardworking, long-suffering, not-yet-recognized composer-lyricist-bookwriter had been working for seven years on the cheerfully transgressive *Rent*, a 1980s rock/pop riff on Henri Murger's hilarious and tragic nineteenth-century French novel *Scenes de la vie de Bohème*, and to a much lesser extent on the famous Puccini opera *La Bohème*, also based on Murger's novel. (Most sources say *Rent* is based on the opera, but the musical has far more in common with the novel.) Larson's version of the story was set in modern-day New York City's East Village, and it focused on a group of artist friends trying to find themselves and find connections in a hostile world. Murger's poet Rudolph became Roger the HIV-positive songwriter. Marcel the painter became Mark the filmmaker. Gustave Colline became Tom Collins (both philosophers) and Alexander Schaunard became Angel Dumott Schunard (both musicians). Musette the singer became Maureen the performance artist. Monsieur Benoit the landlord became Benny the roommate turned landlord. And in Larson's greatest departure, Mimi the elegant gold digger became Mimi the S&M dancer.

When *Rent* opened, everybody made a big deal out of its connection to the opera *La Bohème*, ignoring the source novel. But while *La Bohème* the opera romanticizes death (which was very trendy in 1896 when it premiered), *Rent* celebrates life with all its might. While *Bohème* is tragic, *Rent* is joyous. While *Bohème*'s bohemian world is romantic and poetic, the world of *Rent* is tough, gritty, angry, and *real*. While *Bohème* has the lilting "Musette's Waltz," *Rent* has the cynical, sensual "Tango Maureen." While *Bohème* observes the bohemians from a distance, *Rent* is written *by* a bohemian, someone who had trouble paying the rent, whose friends were dying of AIDS, and it fully inhabits that world.

Rent has been so many things to so many people. It was a show about personal loss but it became a show about the *art form*'s loss of a brilliant new voice in Jonathan Larson. It was the first musical in decades that younger audiences really identified with, that spoke in their voice, that voiced their concerns, that tackled their issues. It breathed new commercial life into the Broadway musical, possibly signaling the beginning of the end of the great divide between pop music and theatre music which had existed since the advent of rock and roll in the 1950s. Even the title means different things to different people. It represents the financial burden young people feel as they graduate college full of knowledge but absent any marketable job skills, thrown into a real world where high ideals don't pay the rent. But the title also highlights the temporary nature of these characters' lives, the month-to-month living without permanence or promises. The characters Collins and Angel sing to each other in the song "I'll Cover You" that though love can't be bought, at least it can be rented. In other words, their happiness won't be forever—both of them have AIDS—but it's theirs for a while.

And the word *rent* also means torn, Larson's favorite meaning of the word. Certainly these characters are torn between conflicting desires, between comfort and idealism, between love and dignity, between anger and pain, between the fear of intimacy and the fear of being alone. *Rent* can mean shredded in grief or rage. It means split apart when it describes communities, families, or other relationships. And it also means torn open by painful feelings, something nearly every character in the show feels at some point. All the complexity of that simple, four-letter word parallels the construction of this fascinating musical.

Larson's lifelong goal was to combine the Broadway tradition with contemporary pop music, a very difficult task at which many before him had failed. In June 1993, New York Theatre Workshop did a reading of *Rent*. The show was a mess but showed real promise. Another reading was done in 1994, this time with guidance from director Michael Greif (rhymes with *life*). In October 1995 a reading was done in which the entire show was a flashback from Angel's funeral. In December 1995 Larson finished another revision that returned to the earlier structure. He wrote a one-sentence summary of the show: "*Rent* is about a community celebrating life, in the face of death and AIDS, at the turn of the century." After seven years of workshops and rewrites, the show was scheduled to open in previews off Broadway at New York Theatre Workshop on January 25, 1996.

But Larson had been feeling ill. He'd been to two hospitals; one diagnosed him with food poisoning, the other with the flu. The night before the first preview, after a great final dress rehearsal, Larson went home, put a pot of water on the stove for tea, collapsed, and died of an aortic aneurysm. Both hospitals were wrong and both probably could have saved his life. Though the comparison was missed at the time, Larson's death eerily paralleled director-choreographer Gower Champion's death just a few hours before opening *his* last show, *42nd Street*.

After Larson's death, as previews began, the artistic team found themselves trying to figure out what Larson would have changed and what he would have kept working on. They went through his notes to see what he still had been unhappy with and did their best to make decisions they thought he would have made. His one-sentence summary helped guide them through the difficult process of finishing a show without its author—and all while mourning the death of their friend. After two weeks of previews in early 1996, the show opened to rave reviews and standing ovations. Four months later it moved to Broadway and became the biggest thing to hit the Great White Way since *Phantom of the Opera*. Larson received a posthumous Pulitzer Prize for his work. He had frequently told his friends that he knew he was the future of musical theatre and he just might have been if he'd had the chance.

Rent opened on Broadway at the Nederlander Theatre on April 29, 1996, almost exactly a century after the premiere of Puccini's *La Bohème*, to both mixed and rave reviews. The *New York Times* called it an "exhilarating, landmark rock opera," and said it "shimmers with hope for the future of the American musical."

Most other critics agreed. On opening night, the performance began with Anthony Rapp, who played Mark, dedicating the show to the memory of Jonathan Larson. *Rent* was nominated for ten Tony Awards and won four, including best musical, best score, and best book. It won six Drama Desk Awards, three Obie Awards, the New York Drama Critics Circle Award for best musical, an Outer Critics Circle Award, and a Drama League Award.

As had happened with *Hair* twenty-eight years before, *Rent* had mined the work of the alternative theatre community and discovered a gold mine. In 1992, Larson had written of his show, "*Rent* exalts Otherness, glorifying artists and counterculture as necessary to a healthy civilization." Larson and, later, many commentators called the show a *Hair* for the nineties and indeed it shares much with the 1967 landmark rock musical. Daphne Rubin-Vega, who originated the role of Mimi, said, "We didn't want to go to Broadway to become Broadway stars; we went to kick the motherfuckin' doors of Broadway open, because it's old-school and stodgy. We were invited there and that was cool."

The show became a cultural phenomenon. The cast soon found themselves in the *New York Times*, *Newsweek*, *Vanity Fair*, *Rolling Stone*, and *Harper's Bazaar*. They appeared on *The Late Show with David Letterman*, *The Charlie Rose Show*, and *The Tonight Show*, and sang "Seasons of Love" at the 1996 Democratic National Convention. Frank Rich, now a *New York Times* political columnist, having retired as senior theatre critic, wrote in a *Times* op-ed piece, "At so divisive a time in our country's culture, *Rent* shows signs of revealing a large, untapped appetite for something better." Both the classical music reviewer and the pop music reviewer for the *Times* weighed in on *Rent*, neither raving but both finding much to admire.

Because the producers were as new to Broadway as the cast was, they did things very differently. They set aside the first two rows at each performance as $20 seats so that the people the show was written for could afford to see it. These special tickets went on sale at 6:00 P.M. each night and the line usually formed by noon on weekdays and often twenty-four hours in advance on weekends. *Rent* fans—called Rent Heads—would bring tents, food, and music to pass the time while they waited. Some had seen the show dozens of times. In July 1997 the line was replaced with a lottery system. The actors loved having the $20 seats in front; they said the first two rows were always the most lively, the most passionate, and the most appreciative.

Unfortunately, *Rent* blew out the voices of its cast, mostly young performers without the experience or skills to care for their voices during a long run. In August 1997, *New York Times* critic Mel Gussow wrote an article about cast replacements in *Rent* at a single performance. "Inserted in that program were no fewer than eight separate small slips of paper naming new actors playing roles that evening." At another performance, Gussow noted, *nine* of the regular actors were out. In fact, *Rent*'s musical challenges, and the rock and roll style of performance, meant that dozens of actors were hurting themselves vocally performing the show, getting severe vocal fatigue, getting nodes on their vocal chords, or just getting sick from the exertion of the doing the show eight times a week. Some commentators suggested that *Rent* might just ruin a whole generation of young Broadway musical actors.

At the same time that *Rent* was being developed, one of the most innovative, most shocking, most brilliant new musicals in years was being born. John Cameron Mitchell and Stephen Trask's rock musical *Hedwig and the Angry Inch* began its life in 1994 at a drag club in Manhattan called Squeeze Box. Mitchell and Trask had met not long before and talked about working on a piece together. Trask was a gay songwriter and front man for the band Cheater. Mitchell was a gay actor, a veteran of shows like *The Secret Garden, Big River, Six Degrees of Separation,* and others. Mitchell told Trask he wanted to create a theatre piece that used a real rock band playing real rock music. Trask was interested, so they started throwing around ideas.

At first, talk centered on an autobiographical character Mitchell had been working on, Tommy Speck, the son of a general. But Trask was more fascinated by a character named Hedwig, an east German transsexual living in a Midwestern trailer park; eventually the two characters would intersect. As the two writers began work, Mitchell bought Trask a copy of Plato's *Symposium,* showed him the central story explaining the origins of gay, lesbian, and straight love, and asked him to write a song based on that story. Trask came back with the moving, defiant, fairy tale–like "The Origin of Love."

In January 1994, Hedwig made her first appearance at Squeeze Box, where Trask was the music director and Cheater was the house band. The club was unique in the drag world because the performers did not lip synch; they actually sang. And Hedwig was unique because she was quickly becoming a fully formed, fully emotional, fully human character with backstory, not just a drag creation with a funny name. Mitchell would bring Hedwig back every six months or so, to develop the material and to try out new songs. Mitchell and Trask had created their own Broadway musical workshop, in the tradition of Michael Bennett. And since the show was conceived as a concert at which Hedwig tells her life story, no traditional set was necessary, just a stage for the band and Hedwig.

Soon, Peter Askin came on board as director. He said in an interview, "It was a mess, but it was a wonderful mess," the same thing people had said about *Rent.* A ragtag group of producers planned to mount a first full production, on the tiny budget of $29,000. By now, Hedwig's story had a clear through-line. She began life as Hansel, a boy in East Berlin before the Berlin Wall came down. An American soldier meets Hansel and they fall in love, but for the soldier to bring him back to America as his wife, Hansel has to go through a physical exam. So the soldier takes him to a back alley surgeon for a sex change operation, but it's horribly botched, leaving Hansel with just a stub of a penis—*an angry inch.* Back in America, the soldier soon abandons Hansel—now Hedwig—and she is left in a trailer park in Kansas. There she meets Tommy Speck, the general's son, they fall in love, and Hedwig transforms him into the rock star Tommy Gnosis (a word meaning special mystical or spiritual knowledge). But Tommy also abandons Hedwig, and she is left playing small tacky venues as Tommy plays major stadiums. Now, with her band The Angry Inch and her eastern bloc husband Yitzak (played by a woman), Hedwig tells us her story in the context of a confessional concert.

Hedwig and the Angry Inch was unusual in so many ways, not the least being that the entire show, every note of music, is fully naturalistic: Hedwig sings because she's performing a concert. It was also unusual because it used glam rock, a little punk, some guitar rock, some piano power ballads. Trask said, "Most rock musicals are just silly because they're made by people who don't know anything about rock music." That was not the case here. Trask could write in any style and he knew the various rock idioms intimately.

Hedwig and the Angry Inch first opened off off Broadway at the Westbeth Theatre Center in February 1997. But they wanted a special space for the show, not a typical theatre. Mitchell heard about an old hotel down by the river that might have a theatre. He visited the Hotel Riverview in Manhattan's meat packing district where the Titanic's surviving crew had been taken, and he found it had an old, rarely used ballroom. It was there that the new *Hedwig* family decided to set up housekeeping. The show opened at the newly christened Jane Street Theatre on Valentine's Day 1998. But the show didn't catch on right away. "People weren't coming. It was really slow," Mitchell said. "It was too rock and roll for some of the uptown theatre people. It was too rock and roll for maybe the gay audience. And it was too 'theatre' for the rock audience." But the show picked up steam.

It ran 857 performances and won the Obie Award and the Outer Critics Circle Award for best off Broadway musical. The *New York Times* said, "*Hedwig and the Angry Inch* brings theatre alive with the pounding sounds of rock and the funny sad voicing of a painful past. It is also an adult, thought-provoking musical about the quest for individuality." *Time* magazine called the show "a poignant meditation on loneliness, gender confusion, and the Platonic notion that sex is the effort to reconnect two halves of one ideal being." Mitchell was succeeded in the lead by Michael Cerveris (of *Tommy* and *Titanic*, who also took it to London), Kevin Cahoon, Donovan Leitch, Ally Sheedy, Asa Somers, and Matt McGrath. A rabid fan base rose up around the show, self-dubbed Hed Heads. David Bowie and Madonna came to see it. New Line Cinema bought the screen rights and released it in July 2001, starring and directed by Mitchell, in the midst of the movie musical rebirth. The film won the Audience Award and the Directing Award at the Sundance Film Festival.

In 1994, Stephen Sondheim's most personal, most emotional, most searing musical yet, *Passion*, opened on Broadway with music and lyrics by Sondheim and a book and direction by James Lapine. Based on a 1981 Italian-French film, based in turn on an 1869 autobiographical Italian novel, it contained many of the elements Sondheim seems to look for in a project and everything his fans expect from his musicals: deeply complicated, profound emotions, a central character who is an outsider, a love that seems impossible. This intermission-less roller coaster of a musical, which rarely even stopped for applause, told the story of the handsome military officer Giorgio who is having an affair with a married woman, Clara, and also being stalked by an obsessive, dying divorcée, Fosca, whose ex-husband was a fake count who swindled and abandoned her.

Passion was unlike most other musicals, clearly an alternative work that belonged *off* Broadway, not on, playing with notions of time and space and portraying emotions more extreme, more raw than anyone had seen onstage in a long time. The show's central themes, that beauty is power, that emotional longing is deadly, are as true today as they were in 1863 Italy, yet it's hardly the message with which a musical theatre audience expects to leave the theatre, even today. *Passion* did not suggest that love is the answer to all our woes, as many musicals do; it suggested instead that love will destroy your life.

Some of the theatregoers who saw the original Broadway production of *Passion* were confused by it. It was a love story, of course, but a very different kind of love story, a reverse beauty and the beast tale, one about unwanted love in a world consumed by physical beauty, one that began with a Happily Ever After and then deconstructed that myth. People didn't know what Sondheim and Lapine wanted them to think about the obsessive, demanding, selfish Fosca, a kind of emotional terrorist. Should they feel sorry for her, laugh at her, root for her? In all their shows together, Sondheim and Lapine refuse to tell audiences what to think. They present people and situations that aren't black and white, and leave audiences to draw their own conclusions. But though audiences may accept that from straight plays, it still confuses them when a musical is presented that way.

David Richards in the *New York Times* called the show, "an unalloyed love story, one that wants to penetrate the heart's deepest mysteries." Theatre scholar Robert Brustein believed the reason audiences were confused was that *Passion* was not really a musical and didn't really belong on Broadway; he thought it was an opera. Sondheim himself has said that Fosca is not really a musical theatre character; she's an operatic character living in a musical, a character of supernatural emotion and extreme tragedy. After all, how often does someone really die of love in a musical?

Passion ran an only moderately successful 240 performances. Despite audiences' indifference to the show, it won several Tonys, including best musical, best actress (Donna Murphy as Fosca), best book, and best score. We can only speculate whether it might have lasted longer and been more accepted off Broadway, where audiences were still a bit more adventurous. Then again, James Lapine's direction was surprisingly cold and controlled for a work of such passion. Surely this was a show that should seem to spin out of control. And though Donna Murphy as Fosca was thrilling, Jere Shea as Giorgio was as stiff and bland a leading man as Broadway had seen in a while. Later productions fared better and the material was reconsidered by its critics.

Different questions about love and sex were asked in *The Ballad of Little Mikey*, which first opened in Los Angeles in January 1994, with book, music, and lyrics by Mark Savage. Gay literature and theatre had undergone a profound change sometime in the early 1990s. Before that time, most gay stories were about how hard it is to be gay, about how hard it is to come out of the closet, about facing rejection and discrimination, about trying to find love in a world that hates homosexuality. But at some point in the last decade of the millennium, things changed for gay Americans and gay artists. Suddenly being gay wasn't so outrageous. Suddenly there were gay characters all over mainstream television. Suddenly kids were coming out of the closet in high school, and some gay kids were never even *in* the closet. There were suddenly gay high school proms, gay high school students forming gay student clubs, gay celebrities and politicians—even Republicans—coming out of the closet publicly in record numbers.

Gay literature and theatre turned a corner. Instead of stories about dealing with the pain of being an outcast (as in *The Boys in the Band* and *La Cage aux Folles*), gay stories were now being written about finding love, building relationships, dealing with family, work, friendships. Though the main characters were gay, the stories were about gay people facing the same problems, obstacles, and dramas straight people face.

The Ballad of Little Mikey embodied this change within its own structure. As the show opens, Mikey, a man in his thirties, has been offered a high-paying, mainstream job, but to take it he will have to give up the gay-oriented nonprofit law project he runs and the other political projects he's involved in. As he prepares to do this, he looks back over his life and the path he's taken to get to where he is. The show divides its time between the present and flashbacks set in 1979 and 1980. The scenes in the past seem on the surface to conform to the older kind of gay literature, in which the topic is the difficulties gay people face, while the scenes in the present are about relationships and other issues—*not* about being gay. *The Ballad of Little Mikey* never made it to New York but has been produced all over America, reaching more audiences and enjoying more success than it ever would have in New York.

Another kind of groundbreaker opened for a limited run in New York at Playwrights Horizons in February 1994, the a cappella doo-wop musical *Avenue X*, with music by Ray Leslee and book and lyrics by John Jiler. It ran only forty-eight performances and never transferred to Broadway or off Broadway, but it has had a long, active life at regional theatres throughout the United States. Set in 1963, the show tells the story of antagonism between the Italian and African American residents of a Brooklyn neighborhood. On one side of the street is South Bensonhurst, a neighborhood of Italian Americans; on the other side are newly built housing projects occupied by African Americans. This enforced integration makes for intense hatred, terrifying violence always bubbling just under the surface. *Avenue X* is the gritty but uplifting story of two young men, Pasquale and Milton—a kind of platonic Romeo and Juliet—from opposite sides of the street who come together to sing doo-wop. In them, we see not only the explosive racial situation in the early 1960s, but also the kind of effort that would eventually lead to the civil rights movement. Though the story itself is fictional, its milieu is real.

This was not a conventional musical. The songs in *Avenue X* are nearly all diegetic; the actual act of singing is part of the fabric of the story, not just a language used to tell the story (as with most musicals), so the normal rules don't apply. The characters are aware of their music (as in *Pippin*, *Chicago*, *Hedwig*, and parts of *Cabaret*) and that changes monumentally how the music works. Just as a character in a play might physically turn away to avoid a painful moment, just as another character might run away from embarrassment, the characters in *Avenue X* take shelter and hide in the simplicity of their love songs. Armed only with their religion and their music, they are not equipped in the world of 1963 Brooklyn to deal with the complex demons of racial hatred. Some would argue, we're *still* not equipped.

So the score is written the only way it could be, in the form of seemingly simplistic love songs. These characters are not articulate people. They are not well educated. They don't really understand the issues they're facing. We get a glimpse in this show of the very beginning of people starting to question issues of race, of a few people seeing clearly for the first time what prejudice is about and why it's destructive. But, as the show makes so clear, it's only the beginning; these people don't yet understand these issues and they certainly don't know the answers. For these characters to articulate in their songs the kind of self-knowledge, social insight, and sophisticated worldview normal musical theatre characters might have, for them to offer commentary or explore more deeply their issues, would be a betrayal of who they are as characters. And it would be dishonest theatre. Pasquale and Milton can't tell us what they need and what they're about the way Tevye or Dolly Levi or Henry Higgins can, because *they don't know.* All they know they want is love and friendship.

Yet despite the unusual way the show's songs function, they do advance plot. They are the mechanism by which these characters try to avoid the impossible issues that have been thrust upon them. Their repeated escape into these songs, the *way* they use their music tells us a great deal about who they are, how they've been raised, what's important to them, and from what they're escaping. *Avenue X* shows us how these characters sometimes try to make sense of this new emerging world, how they sometimes run from that world, how they try to connect to one another, all through the intellectually inadequate but life-sustaining language of their music. But—and here's the central point of the show—ultimately, the simple language and emotion of their music is not enough to overcome the complexity of racial hatred. The greatest achievement of the show is in *not* giving these people too much self-knowledge and in *not* creating some fairy tale, irrelevant, happy ending. These people do not have the tools to deal with their world and so, in the end, they do a lousy job of beating down Evil. They still have a lot of learning to do.

This story sits on the cusp of two Americas. The first is the simple, straightforward, "white" America where the majority agreed on questions of morality and the minority was invisible, in which songs were trivial. The other is a new America in which blacks and whites had to live together, had to face each other, and learn to make a world (and music) that had room in it for everyone, something we're still working at, which is why the show has such resonance for us today and why its audiences routinely leap to standing ovations. The characters in *Avenue X* still dwell in the old, simple America in which their simple music was created, but their neighborhood has been thrust into the new America, where the old rules and the old simplicities no longer apply. In Act II, the music turns dissonant and complex in Winston's song "Africa." And at the end of the show, Milton and Pasquale are trying desperately to break through to a new kind of music, one that actually addresses the issues of their lives. But they're only beginning and they don't have time enough to finish the job. They must leave the work to others, and as we all know, that work will be done later in the 1960s. *Avenue X* isn't just a good show—it's smart, subtle, powerful, and artfully unconventional theatre, perhaps too subtle and too artful for Broadway.

Another smart, powerful musical, called *Violet*, was developed at the O'Neill Theater Center during the 1994 National Theatre Conference. It had music by Jeanine Tesori and book and lyrics by Brian Crawley, based on a short story, "The Ugliest Pilgrim," by Doris Betts. Lincoln Center had an option to produce the show but displayed uncharacteristic indifference to the piece and let their option expire. So the show opened at Playwrights Horizons instead in March 1997 for a limited run. Telling its tale through gospel, blues, and country music, all retuned to accomplish what only theatre music can, *Violet* focused on a young woman in 1964, horribly but accidentally disfigured by her father as a child. With a big scar across her face, she goes on a bus ride from North Carolina to Oklahoma to see a faith healer. Along the way she becomes romantically involved with a black soldier, and she ends up healing her own soul instead. But the show wasn't about where she's heading; it was about her journey. On a minimalist set and with Violet's horrible scar visible only in the audience's imagination, the show charted a profound and thrilling emotional journey, inescapably mixed up with the beginning of the most turbulent decade in American history, Vietnam, race issues, and other challenges.

Most of the critics loved it and the show won the New York Drama Critics Circle Award for best musical, and it has had a continuing life in regional theatres across America. But some criticized it for being too inaccessible. Tesori responded in *American Theatre*, "When you begin to write, more often than not you write in a complicated way. I'm still learning to be simpler, which happens as your craft gets stronger." She would go on to write new songs for a stage adaptation of *Thoroughly Modern Millie*, forcing herself to write in a simpler, more direct way, though with far less artistry and power.

Another unusual musical, called *Songs for a New World*, opened at the WPA Theatre in New York in 1995 for a limited twenty-eight-performance run. It started as a collection of already written songs by Jason Robert Brown, but by the time it was finished and expanded, it was one of the most artfully built, tightly constructed concept musicals in years. Brown has estimated that in its first draft, eighty percent of the score was songs from other projects, but by opening night, that had dropped to about forty percent.

One of the characters in *Songs for a New World* says "I don't want to philosophize. I just want to tell a story." And that line describes *Songs for a New World* perfectly; in fact, the show tells a whole collection of stories. It's not a book musical—there is no overarching plot and no consistent characters throughout the evening—but it is not a revue either. In its construction, it owes much to *Jacques Brel Is Alive and Well and Living in Paris* and the theatre experiments of the 1960s. It's a collection of independent scene-songs but it's also more than that. In a 1998 review in St. Louis' *Riverfront Times*, Mike Isaacson wrote, "*Songs for a New World* is that very rare beast: an abstract musical. There is no specific location other than the natural ambiguity of the human heart and mind." And yet it has a very strong sense of unity about it. Even though some of these songs were actually written for other projects over the span of several years, this show feels like it was planned as a unified whole from the beginning.

It accomplishes this mainly because every song in the show is essentially about the same thing: those moments in life when everything seems perfect and then suddenly disaster strikes, in the form of the loss of a job, an unexpected pregnancy, the death of a loved one, the end of a marriage, imprisonment, even thoughts of suicide. But it's even more about *surviving* those moments. It's about the way we regroup and figure out how to survive in a new set of circumstances—a new world—even against seemingly overwhelming odds. These are songs about that new world, a world in which the definitions of family, distance, money, technology, the very nature of human contact are changing every day, a world in which the rules *don't* apply as often as they *do*, a world in which the solutions our parents found don't work for us, in which today's answers probably won't apply tomorrow. For someone who has lost a job or lost a spouse, our everyday world becomes just as frightening, just as dangerous, just as uncharted as the New World once was to the Spanish Jews in 1492.

Composer-lyricist Jason Robert Brown came to New York City at age twenty, determined to write Broadway musicals. Because he had no contacts or connections, he decided to mount a cabaret show of songs he had written for various past projects. He had the good fortune to run into Daisy Prince, daughter of the legendary Broadway director-producer Hal Prince, at a piano bar where Brown was working. Out of the blue, Brown asked Daisy Prince to direct this show he was putting together, having no idea if she had ever directed anything before in her life. She agreed immediately. They worked on the material for three years but still had no opening number and no clear idea what the show was about. As they discarded existing songs, Brown wrote new ones. Finally it hit him. In his own words, "It's about one moment. It's about hitting the wall and having to make a choice, or take a stand, or turn around and go back."

They did a workshop of the show in Toronto, then brought it to the WPA Theatre in New York in fall 1995. Gannett Newspapers wrote, "Fear not for the future of the American musical theatre as long as talents like Jason Robert Brown keep coming." The score, as sophisticated as Sondheim, yet bursting with pop, rock, rhythm and blues, and jazz, was recorded in 1996 and released commercially. Since then, there have been more than a hundred productions of the show in America and in the U.K. Brown has become one of the strongest new musical theatre writers of this generation, going on to write exciting scores for shows like *Parade* and *The Last Five Years*. He has also kept busy as a music and vocal arranger on shows like *A New Brain*, *The Petrified Prince*, *john & jen*, and *New York Rock*.

1995 was also the year Randy Newman, successful pop songwriter and film composer, tried his hand at musical theatre. He had been developing his idea for nearly fifteen years, often throwing one or two songs from the developing work in his concerts. The concept album for his new musical *Faust*, an updating of Goethe's famous 1808 play, hit the market in 1995 at the same time the show's first production was staged at the La Jolla Playhouse in San Diego. But this was definitely not an old-fashioned musical. And it wasn't a show built around an existing pop catalogue, like the later jukebox-musicals *Mamma Mia*, *Movin' Out*, or *All Shook Up*. As should have been expected from the author of the satirical bigot-bashing song "Short People," Newman was at his cynical, nihilistic best with *Faust*, moving the story to the present and transforming the title character into an unlikable slacker college kid. Newman said of his title character, "Goethe's [Faust] is the wisest man on earth—he wants answers to everything. My guy's a freshman at Notre Dame who wants girls and money and puerile, baby stuff. The kind of stuff I'd want. He's consistently unfeeling and self-absorbed. I love him." Newman also focused far more than Goethe did on the relationship, such as it is, between God and Lucifer.

Of course, this wasn't the first time the Faust story had been musicalized. *Cabin in the Sky*, *Damn Yankees*, and *Little Shop of Horrors* certainly had tread that territory as well, but less faithfully. Newman went right to the source: Goethe's play. He said, "I just felt, as others have thought before me—hundreds of others—that it would make a great musical. And there's something so wise about it that it made me want to try to destroy it, in a way, and have all its wisdom frustrated by the nature of *real* human beings. I mean, the original Faust wanted knowledge. This kid is as far from that as you can be."

Newman's version of the classic story opened in a flashback. All the way back to 4004 B.C. We meet a God quite unlike the usual depiction of the

Almighty, here a smarmy, self-important, creepy-charming, not-quite-omniscient, postmodern, egomaniacal, control-freak God. When James Taylor recorded the role of God for the concept album, Newman told him, "This is like a Bing Crosby or Arnold Palmer kind of golf-playing white guy, a little bit full of himself. Like one of Van Johnson's roles." Who else but Randy Newman would reimagine God that way?

The show begins at a party up in heaven. God is tooting his own horn about his many accomplishments when a drunken Lucifer speaks up and says what no one else will say, essentially "Who cares?" He also theorizes that none of them actually exist and are only figments of the collective imagination of existentially terrified humans. Lucifer is banished from heaven and its great parties forever. Flash forward to the present. Now in charge of hell, Lucifer ("Lucky" to his friends) is just a hardworking stiff who can't catch a break. He's doing alright, but he'd like to be back up in heaven where they now have golf and roller coasters. So he visits God and proposes a bet. They'll pick a human, and if Lucifer can corrupt him, he gets back into heaven. They decide on Henry Faust, a schizophrenic slacker at Notre Dame University. Of course, Faust signs Lucifer's deal without even reading it (he never reads anything unless it's assigned). But God sends Cupid (a *pagan* god, Lucifer bitterly points out to Him) to make Faust fall in love with the good-hearted Margaret. But love doesn't reform the slacker. Instead, Faust kills Margaret's brother, poisons her mother, gets her pregnant, and then leaves her. Margaret drowns her baby and gets sentenced to death. Somehow, Faust does finally see the error of his ways and asks for forgiveness. That's enough for God, and Lucifer loses the bet. So Lucifer heads for Vegas. Blackout.

The score included some of the best music and lyrics Newman had ever written, from up-tempo gospel numbers to rhythm and blues to pure rock and roll to some achingly beautiful ballads, including "Sandman," a lullaby Margaret sings to her dead baby (originally written for the musical television series *Cop Rock*). The concept album featured James Taylor as God, Newman as Lucifer, Don Henley as Faust, Linda Ronstadt as Margaret, Bonnie Raitt (daughter of Broadway legend John Raitt), and Elton John. *Time* magazine called the show "bilious, outrageous, and full of flinty, funny challenge . . . his lyrics are like tasers, crackling out jolts to anyone who gets too close."

In October 1995, it opened a six-week run at California's La Jolla Playhouse, with hopes of a Broadway run. It was first directed by James Lapine, but Lapine wanted to turn it into something more serious, less flippant, and Newman didn't want that. So Michael Greif (who was still working on the evolving *Rent*) came aboard. Greif said in an *American Theatre* interview, "There are a number of father-son relationships in the play. I think that's where the play's soul is—how we all view youth. Either we're ridiculously absorbed by and indulgent of youth, or we're very close-minded and defensive and scared of the new."

But that *wasn't* what the show was about.

With a revised book by Newman and David Mamet, the assembled cast included David Garrison, Daphne Rubin-Vega, and Sherie René Scott. The show was then produced at the Goodman Theatre in Chicago in 1996. *Time* named it one of the Top Ten Theatrical Events of the Year. The *Chicago Tribune* said, "Randy Newman's *Faust* is not yet the Broadway musical it appears destined to be, and even as it is, it suffers from some excruciating moments of bad taste and bad judgment. But taken for what it is, right now and right here in its tryout time at the Goodman Theatre, it is an often giddily enjoyable show, filled with Newman's melodic songs, spiced with laugh-out-loud good humor, enlivened by marvelously crafty performances and gleaming with bright, professional polish." The *New York Times* said, "The score remains a shimmering, multifaceted gem, and it has been wonderfully orchestrated and sung in the Goodman production. But in this flashy, expensive-looking staging by Michael Greif, the hot, young director of *Rent*, Newman's original, subversive charms barely peep through."

The show was generally not all that well received and never made it to New York. It was dumbed down, sanitized, made palatable. The song "Feels Like Home," originally a deceitful love song sung by Martha to cynically seduce and then dump Lucifer, to distract him from his task, was reassigned in the stage version as a sincere love song between Faust and his girlfriend Margaret. Other choices like this followed. It was also foolishly overproduced, clearly none of the production staff trusting the material to stand on its own without special effects, stage smoke, and lots of money. And it was too long, running nearly three hours in La Jolla.

Newman says, "The director wanted [Faust] to be likable so you cared what happened to him. I loved him just the way he was. I've had three kids who've been 17, 18, 19 years old, and you don't like dealing with it when you're a parent, but there's this obduracy and completely stubborn lack of affect that I kind of admire. I *like* his arc being a flat line." Greif thought Faust was the show's central character, but Newman's sympathies and interest were clearly with the Devil, so the script and production were at war. Just as Paul Simon would learn later with *The Capeman*, Newman discovered an amazing resistance to breaking established rules of making musicals. And it's too bad. How can an art form advance if its rules can never be broken? Newman said later, "I thought it was the best thing I'd ever done. I *loved* the theatre. All that bullshit about it getting in your blood is true."

Chris Willman wrote in the liner notes for the cast album reissue, "You can't keep the greatest musical comedy of the last quarter-century down—even if the parallel ascendancy of *Sunset Boulevard* and *The Scarlet Pimpernel* is proof positive that there *is* a personal Satan." As the *Village Voice* said, "Broadway needs Randy Newman far more than Randy Newman needs Broadway."

Still, Broadway was doing better at the time than it had in quite a while, even without Newman. In November 1995, the experimental musical *Bring in 'da Noise, Bring in 'da Funk,* opened at Joseph Papp's Public Theatre off Broadway, directed by George C. Wolfe and choreographed by—and starring—Savion Glover, with music by Daryl Waters, Zane Mark, and Ann Duquesnay, and lyrics by Reg E. Gaines. It ran eighty-five performances at the Public, then in April 1996 moved to the Ambassador Theatre on Broadway. The show told the history of African Americans from the slave ships to the present day, almost entirely through tap dance. There was also some singing, there was some speaking, there were sets, there was a dramatic through-line, there was even a central metaphorical character—'da Beat. But no one was sure if this was really a musical or not, since it wasn't built like a normal musical. Then again, neither were *Hair, A Chorus Line, Follies, Songs for a New World,* or other alternative pieces. And like those other shows, this was created by artists at the very peak of their powers.

Combining hip-hop culture and tap, *Noise/Funk* (as it came to be called) was documentary, narrative, song and dance, history lesson, and quite literally, living history—the first hip-hop musical. Unlike most shows, every element was developed simultaneously, the songs, dance, structure, staging, music, and design. And because of this unusual process, and the unusual artists involved, the piece had a rare kind of unity that raised it to the level of great art. Many have called Glover a true genius (he was only twenty-two when *Noise/Funk* opened), and this show seemed to be proof of that. He had hit stardom at twelve, replacing the lead in *The Tap Dance Kid* on Broadway. From there it was *Black and Blue* in Paris, then *Jelly's Last Jam,* and other credits. The show—and Glover—asked an interesting question: can tap dance convey complex emotions, characters, and stories, the way ballet and jazz dance can? And can Glover's distinctive, heavy, "funk" style of tap bring a new generation to this art form? Glover said in several interviews that it was his intention to transform the art form of tap into something less like light entertainment and more deep personal expression.

The *New York Times* said, "*Noise/Funk* gives us what we crave every time we walk into a theater: beauty, pleasure, surprise and that vision of mastery that makes art worthwhile." The show won the Outer Critics Circle Award for choreography, the Drama League Award for Distinguished Achievement in Musical Theatre, two Drama Desk Awards including one for choreography, and four Tony Awards, for choreography (Glover), director (Wolfe), featured actress (Ann Duquesnay), and lighting design (Jules Fisher and Peggy Eisenhauer). It ran 1,123 performances on Broadway.

At the 1996 Oscar ceremonies, producer Quincy Jones made a bold statement when he eulogized the recently deceased Gene Kelly. Jones showed Kelly's legendary "Singin' in the Rain" number but in front of the screen, Savion Glover performed a tribute to and expansion of the number. This juxtaposition accomplished two things. First, it acknowledged, maybe for the first time to many people, that Kelly's tap dancing came from a wholly African American tradition. Second, it boldly drew a line from the very white tap traditions of Kelly to the more visceral, more urban black tap tradition that Glover was carrying on. It was a fascinating and thrilling time in musical theatre history.

And there was more on the way. Raucous comedy; moments of great tenderness; muscular, powerful American music; family, faith, and metaphysics—it was all there in *Floyd Collins*, one of the most impressive first efforts in the history of musical theatre, which opened in March 1996 at Playwrights Horizons, a venue fast becoming the musical theatre's best friend. With this show, composer-lyricist Adam Guettel (rhymes with *kettle*) established himself as the most likely candidate to lead the next generation into the musical theatre terrain that Stephen Sondheim had explored for the last fifty years. His collaborator Tina Landau, bookwriter, co-lyricist, and director, came from the experimental theatre community and brought with her a bold, fresh perspective. *Floyd Collins* was a musical full of complexity and sophistication fully worthy of Sondheim, shot through with the emotional force a story like this demands. Though it was about media exploitation, greed, glory, and prejudice, at its core it was even more about family, faith, and God. It was one of those musicals, along with *West Side Story*, *Company*, and *Ragtime*, that could have been written only by Americans. There was a brashness, a wide-openness, and a muscularity in *Floyd Collins* that is uniquely American.

A reading of the show was first done in Guettel's living room in 1992. After rewrites and further development, the show was then mounted in a full production at the American Music Theater Festival in Philadelphia in 1994, in a more operatic version. After fairly major revisions, *Floyd Collins* opened again March 3, 1996 off Broadway at Playwrights Horizons in New York. A cast album was released that created more interest in the show, and it was produced at several regional theatres in San Diego, Chicago, and St. Louis in 1999.

As many of the reviewers could see, *Floyd Collins* was one of the most interesting, most risk-taking, most emotional shows written in the 1990s, a show as unconventional in its storytelling and in its musical language as it is in its subject. Stephen Sondheim said during a visit to St. Louis in 1999 that he considered *Floyd Collins* the best musical written in the past twenty-five years. But other critics (including some at the *New York Times* and the *Village Voice*) missed a great deal about *Floyd Collins*, trying to force it into one or another existing category rather than allowing it to exist outside convention, creating its own unique category of musical theatre.

Other reviewers saw the promise of genius that lay behind this unique and special show. Ben Brantley in the *New York Times* said, "Tina Landau and Adam Guettel's ambitious, tuneful lesson in American history radiates good faith, moral seriousness, and artistic discipline." *Newsday* called it "one of the three or four truly great musical theatre scores of the decade." The *Daily News* said, "The score by Adam Guettel is an impressive blend of American vernacular and the ambitious harmonic style of post-Sondheim musicals." Judith Newmark said in the *St. Louis Post Dispatch*, "Unlike many works by young authors—musical or not, theatrical or not—*Floyd Collins* is not about its creator. It is not about his generation. It offers perspective instead of self-indulgence, imagination instead of ego." The show won the Lucille Lortel Award for best musical in 1996, an Obie Award for music, and a Drama Desk Award for sound design.

In response to criticism that *Floyd Collins* was inaccessible (a charge regularly leveled against Sondheim) Adam Guettel said in an *American Theatre* interview, "I would make the distinction between writing about what people care about, and writing about something that can be distilled into a marketable handle or sound bite and sold to any number of demographic groups. It's difficult to distill the story of *Floyd Collins* into a charismatic sentence. I've also encountered a lot of resistance to the perceived complexities of my work. I really don't mind. For me, it's about creating a convincing world—and when there are crunchy harmonies, I generally have arrived at them for dramatic reasons."

Fascinating, risky, groundbreaking musicals were still being written and produced. But not on Broadway. So in March 1996, a group of Broadway theatre owners, producers, and unions hired a consulting firm to explore the creation of a new foundation to finance new plays and musicals, a "theatre trust," to make loans and grants to producers to get new shows up. The city of New York provided half the money for the $100,000 study. In September, the mayor created a new Theatre Advisory Council. None of these efforts seemed to change the fact that Broadway had become a tourist attraction, no longer a national American theatre as it once was. Broadway just wasn't the place to go if theatre artists wanted to take risks, to break through to something new. Providing money for producing new shows solved only one of many problems Broadway was facing. The bigger problem was that the cost of producing a new show was so high, and a show had to run so long in order to break even, that innovation on Broadway was either impossible or accidental. Earlier in the century, when a show that ran a hundred performances was considered a hit, when a mediocre show could still run six months and maybe break even, when production costs were reasonable, when ticket prices were affordable, Broadway could take chances. Not anymore.

In late 1996, producer Cameron Mackintosh decided the Broadway production of *Les Misérables*, in its ninth year of performances, was looking tired. So in an unprecedented move, Mackintosh fired half of the thirty-eight actors in the show and went into a five-week *re*-rehearsal period. During this down time, the national tour was called in, to replace the current cast and keep the Broadway production open. The creative staff and new cast sat in a circle and read portions of the original novel out loud, hoping to reconnect with their source material. The show reopened in March 1997, exactly ten years after its first opening. All the leads were replaced except for Christopher Innvar (who had played the title role in *Floyd Collins*) as Javert. One actor, who had been playing Eponine, was reassigned to the role of Cosette. Peter Marks of the *New York Times* wrote about this move, "*Les Misérables* unveiled its refurbished Broadway production last night, and like a faded fresco lovingly restored, many of the original colors have returned. With some intelligent recasting decisions, a sumptuous costume makeover, and an infusion of vocal energy, the show has recovered from its near-death experience last fall."

Then, in early December 2000, Mackintosh overhauled the show again, this time the material. The show had been running three hours and twelve minutes, but because it ran longer than three hours, it incurred $23,000 a week in overtime costs (totaling about sixteen million dollars since the show's opening). The producers said that getting the show under three hours would keep it profitable and keep it running. It was either that or close it. So fourteen minutes were cut, usually small sections of songs. Interestingly, the touring production was left alone. The shortened show would continue to run on Broadway until May 2003.

The 1997–98 season was a tentative watershed for women musical theatre artists. Four new musicals with female lyricists opened, including *The Triumph of Love, High Society* (both with lyrics by Susan Birkenhead), *The Scarlet Pimpernel* (Nan Knighton), and *Ragtime* (Lynn Ahrens). And in addition to that, there was director Julie Taymor's megahit *The Lion King*, with a book co-written by Irene Mecchi. This wasn't an entirely new phenomenon. Women had been writing for musical theatre since its beginnings, and these contemporary women were definitely standing on the shoulders of Anne Caldwell, Dorothy Fields, Betty Comden, Carolyn Leigh, Joan Littlewood, Mary Rodgers, Elizabeth Swados, Gretchen Cryer, Nancy Ford, Micki Grant, Carol Hall, Lucy Simon, Marsha Norman, and others. Despite current artists like Ahrens, Tina Landau, Jeanine Tesori, and others, women are still in a wildly disproportionate minority, and having four women represented in one season was a big deal. A big deal that has not been repeated.

Halloween 1997 brought the world the brilliant absurdist rock musical *Bat Boy*, by Keythe Farley, Brian Flemming, and Laurence O'Keefe. It was clearly something new, something very special, and strangely enough considering its subject matter, something deeply moving. The show invited its audience back to the roots of theatre, back to Grotwoski's "poor theatre," a kind of theatre that's about the storytelling not the budget, where imagination is more important than money or technology, where the audience not only forgives cheap props but even embraces them. Musical theatre lovers thought the success of the aggressively low-tech *Rent* would teach Broadway a big lesson about what really matters, but it seems that it didn't. Now musical lovers were all hoping *Bat Boy* would do the job.

To be fair, *Bat Boy* was not about tweaking the conventions of Broadway musicals. Its authors did not set out to write a musical making fun of Broadway musicals. No, they wrote a show about a boy trying to find his place in the world, about the search for love and acceptance. But *Bat Boy* succeeds on more than one level. And while it tells its beautiful, touching, wacky story, it also laughs hard at the conventions of traditional musical comedy. The big Act I production number, "Show You a Thing or Two," recalls other time-telescoping

205

sequences like the "Poor Professor Higgins"/"Rain in Spain" scene in *My Fair Lady* or the prologue in *West Side Story*. *Bat Boy*'s "Children, Children" was originally meant to laugh at any play or movie that anthropomorphizes wild animals into cuddly humanlike creatures, but today it's hard not to see it more specifically as a comment on the artsy pretensions of the stage version of *The Lion King* (a show that didn't yet exist when *Bat Boy* was created), which not only makes animals human but also projects onto them some kind of *faux* primitivism. *Bat Boy* laughs at big cast shows like *Les Misérables* and *Phantom of the Opera* by making so very obvious the practice of actors playing multiple parts, in this case, switching gender and switching wigs in full view of the audience. *Bat Boy* laughs at big, unmotivated dance numbers by giving us a sudden, old-fashioned, song-and-dance number ("Show You a Thing or Two") in the middle of a gothic thriller. It laughs at the oh-so-serious, tragic-poetic musicals like *Phantom of the Opera*, *Jekyll & Hyde*, and *Jane Eyre*, that try so hard to be dark and important, that fall flat most often because of banal, uninspired lyrics that are only sometimes obscured by lush orchestrations and big sets.

Bat Boy's creators did not all come from the musical theatre world, and all these commentaries may not have been consciously intended by them; still, by rejecting some of the more ridiculous conventions of contemporary commercial theatre (musical and non-), by insisting on a theatre of imagination instead of high-tech machines, by using imaginative techniques from the world of improv and experimental theatre, *Bat Boy* did indeed comment on other musicals. By its very existence and its success, *Bat Boy* argued by implication that many musicals had gone too far, had gotten too high-tech, had lost the simplicity and joy of storytelling. *Bat Boy* had a small cast, a small budget, no special effects, yet it didn't suffer for all that—it ended up being *more* fun, *more* transporting, *more* magical, *more* emotional, because it returned to the roots of storytelling and relied on its audience to *participate* in the magic. Edgar, the bat boy, tried to teach the people of his town about tolerance and acceptance, while *Bat Boy* the musical tried to teach its audiences about what *really* matters in the theatre.

But make no mistake—*Bat Boy* was not a joke. Through the haze of its incessant lunacy, it was also an intelligent, insightful piece of social satire that tackled a handful of major contemporary American issues, including prejudice, bioengineering, bioethics, and the self-serving hypocrisy that poisons many of America's mainstream religions.

It all started with the satirical supermarket tabloid, the *Weekly World News*, which in 1992 began following every twist and turn in the bizarre life of a poor half-bat/half-boy who was found in a rural West Virginia cave. The *News* described him this way: "Discovered in a cave in Hope Falls, West Virginia, this half-bat has escaped from captivity and is currently at large. He can be identified by large, pointy ears and oversized eyes that make him profoundly sensitive to sound and light. The creature has reportedly attacked at least three people with his razor-sharp fangs and should be considered extremely dangerous." In

2001, the *Washington Post* published a tribute article to the *Weekly World News*, writing, "Funnier than *Saturday Night Live*, deeper than Leno or Letterman, smarter than *Mad*, more outrageous than *The Onion*, *Weekly World News* just might be America's best purveyor of social satire. The fact that it's disguised as a sleazy tabloid just makes it that much more delicious."

The show's genesis came in November 1996 in the lobby of the Actors' Gang Theater in Los Angeles. Keythe Farley, Gang member and director, and Brian Flemming, a screenwriter and film director, were working the concession stand during intermission for the musical *Euphoria*, when in wandered Larry O'Keefe, the composer-lyricist and music director of *Euphoria*. Farley and Flemming told O'Keefe they liked his music and lyrics and asked if O'Keefe would be interested in a project of theirs, based on a character named Bat Boy. They showed O'Keefe a cover of the *Weekly World News* featuring the bat boy's picture, a baby with huge fangs, bulging eyes, and pointy ears. They were determined to tell this poor creature's story—*from the beginning*. O'Keefe was shocked. "That's the ugliest thing I've ever seen in my life," he said. "I'll do it."

On Halloween 1997, *Bat Boy* made its world premiere at the Actors' Gang, Los Angeles' premier repertory theatre company, which created original works and reinterpreted classics through the prism of "The Style," a performance method derived from commedia dell'arte, from the work of the Theatre du Soleil in Paris, from vaudeville, and from political agitprop theatre. The Style is artificial and presentational, yet insists on deep truthfulness and high emotional stakes. All the authors agree today that The Style was instrumental in both the writing and the execution of *Bat Boy: The Musical*.

Director and co-author Keythe Farley developed what Flemming likes to call the "take-it-so-seriously-it's-funny-but-it-also-hurts" style of *Bat Boy*. Both Deven May (as Edgar) and Kaitlin Hopkins (as Meredith, his adopted mother) were in this first production, and together with Farley they found the extremely sincere approach that this very unusual musical demanded. Farley's mantra throughout the development process was "The Height of Expression, The Depth of Sincerity," a style of broad but truthful acting that the cast took to heart and that guided them throughout the L.A. and New York productions. Flemming says of his partner, "Keythe's major contribution to *Bat Boy* has gone largely unmentioned, but it was great and permanent."

Julio Martinez wrote in *Variety*, "The clever scenario, though outrageous, always contains an aura of intriguing plausibility. And to his credit, Farley creates a supercharged mix of heightened realism, surrealism, and fantasy that is always engrossing. The work is magnificently served by the emotion-charged, thoroughly realistic performance of May, who catapults himself body and soul into the seared psyche of this child who possesses the mind of a genius but the uncontrollable, blood-craving appetite of a beast."

Throughout 1999 and 2000, the show went through staged readings at the Directors' Company in New York, now with director Scott Schwartz (son of composer Stephen Schwartz) at the helm. The pace of the work was stepped up, aiming toward a 2001 New York opening. *Bat Boy: The Musical* opened at the Union Square Theatre in New York in March 2001, where it was a big hit. The *New York Times* said of the show, "It's remarkable what intelligent wit can accomplish . . . the show is a jaggedly imaginative mix of skewering humor and energetic glee." *Backstage* said, "Rarely do we see a piece of theatre that is at once so smart, silly, self-aware, and easy to enjoy as *Bat Boy*." But it suffered the same fate as many other New York shows after the terrorist attacks on September 11, and it closed that December. It's tempting to guess how long the show would have run if not for the attacks and whether it would have moved uptown to Broadway like *Urinetown* did. In a post–9/11 world, the hatred and discrimination leveled against Edgar took on a whole new dimension: anyone in America with a Middle Eastern background was now a potential victim of abuse, harassment, even imprisonment, based only on their appearance, their ethnicity, their clothing. The metaphor that was *Bat Boy* now held a power wholly unanticipated by its creators, but that power would not be felt in New York. Instead it began a vigorous life in regional theatres across America.

Also in 1997, Disney opened its most ambitious, most successful live stage show yet, *The Lion King*. Unlike *Beauty and the Beast*, it was not a straight stage adaptation/imitation of the animated feature. And unlike Disney's *King David* and *Aida*, it was not just another by-the-book pop opera. This time, Disney hired Julie Taymor, a designer-director who had helmed ambitious alternative projects like *Juan Darien: A Carnival Mass*. With a whopping twenty-million-dollar budget, Taymor designed the most surprising, interesting costumes and masks, based on theatre traditions and religious rituals from around the world. And Richard Husdon sets and stage effects were every bit the equal of Taymor's costumes and masks.

Vincent Canby in the *New York Times* described the opening moments this way: "The show's first spectacular sequence expands the mind for all that follows. As if called forth by tribal drums, the theater becomes alive with familiar creatures of dreamlike beauty, ostentatiously unreal and absolutely authentic in spite of the actor-handlers we see manipulating them. Virtually life-size elephants and a rhino, seemingly woven of rattan, lumber serenely down the aisles of the New Amsterdam, avoiding the feet of patrons they don't appear to see. Giraffes, their long necks bobbing ever so slightly, pick their way across the stage with an elegant diffidence that, you suddenly realize, is the way giraffes have always walked. Gazelles leap into view. A lone cheetah appears. Eventually the entire animal kingdom assembles, called together by Mufasa, the benevolent lion king, to acknowledge his son and heir."

Hans Zimmer came on board to write additional music and the South African musician Lebo Morake—known as "Lebo M"—signed on to arrange the stunningly beautiful African choral music, much of it based on his Disney album *Rhythm of the Pridelands* and his incidental music for the film. The show made its world premiere at the Orpheum Theatre in Minneapolis in July 1997, then moved to Broadway in November. Visually and vocally, *The Lion King* was one of the most spectacular, thrilling, and surprisingly low tech shows Broadway had seen in years. But the news wasn't all good. Elton John and Tim Rice's songs from the animated film were serviceable at best and embarrassing at worst, and the new songs they wrote for the stage production were just terrible. Nothing in the score revealed character or moved the plot forward, though the new material by Hans Zimmer, mostly scene changes and background singing, did establish time and place quite artfully.

The script was a mess of clichés and awkward dialogue. On top of that, the acting—from a clearly talented cast—was as mediocre as Broadway had seen in a long time. Characters and relationships simply were not a priority in this production.

But there was something hidden in the show. As Taymor pointed out in interviews, it was really two shows seen by two audiences. White audiences saw it as a primal fable; black audiences saw it as a story about race, about the roots of humanity in Africa, about Great Truths as expressed by African culture. White children in the audience saw wonderful, imaginative animals; black children at long last saw a king in a mainstream story who was *black*—even though the show was written entirely by white people. But it seemed as if Taymor had too many brilliant ideas for the physical production but no idea how to work with actors. Audiences were definitely entertained, for *The Lion King* was great spectacle, but it was rarely great storytelling. It was once again Broadway as theme park—really good theme park—but as more and more Broadway audiences were tourists and foreigners, that seemed to be a trend.

The reviews were mostly positive. But though Ben Brantley had many compliments for the show in the first of the *New York Times* reviews, he also had reservations. He wrote, "Although many of the actors have charm and freshness, they are hampered to some extent by the masks and puppet effigies that turn them into animals. You will gasp again and again at the inventive visual majesty of this show, realized through the masks and puppets of Ms. Taymor and Michael Curry, scenic design by Richard Hudson, and Donald Holder's wonderful elemental lighting. But you may be harder pressed to muster the feelings of suspense and poignancy that the film, for all its preachiness, really did evoke." He went on to say, "Garth Fagan's choreography is, for the most part, on the clumsy side. A romantic ballet in which the grown Simba and his lioness girlfriend discover their attraction while other pairs of lovers float in the air above them still seems like a concept waiting to be worked out. And the rendering of the show's best-known number, 'Hakuna Matata,' a paean to the easy life, surprisingly lacks effervescence."

The Lion King was nominated for eight Tonys and won six, including best musical, best director, best costumes, best sets, best lighting, and best choreography. No acting awards. But its commercial success was so overwhelming,

Disney actually considered opening a second production on Broadway to handle the demand for tickets. It never happened, though. The show opened in London in 1999.

Just a couple months after *The Lion King* came to Broadway, something utterly different opened next, a show so opposite *The Lion King* it was hard to believe both were Broadway successes. *Ragtime* was truly the next Great American Musical, comfortably taking its place among other masterpieces like *Show Boat, Carousel, West Side Story, Hair,* and *Company,* those rare musicals that are enduring and timeless, musicals that address important themes that continue to spark societal debate, that are uniquely American at their core, created by Americans with American settings and with something to say about the American consciousness, the American way of life, and American mythology. The ten-million-dollar musical opened on Broadway in January 1998, after several years of workshops and tryouts in Toronto and Los Angeles, under the direction of Frank Galati and with seamless choreography by Graciela Daniele.

The show opened at the Ford Center for the Performing Arts, a brand-new Broadway house (and the first to sell its naming rights to a corporation). It was a new era on Broadway. Producer Garth Drabinksy had hired the songwriting team through a contest of sorts, in which ten teams were asked to submit four songs each for the prospective musical. Composer Stephen Flaherty and lyricist Lynn Ahrens, the team behind *Once on This Island* and *My Favorite Year,* won the commission.

Ragtime, based on the epic novel by E. L. Doctorow, was muscular, expansive, emotional, and could only have been written by Americans. It embodied everything that the American musical has come to represent while it addresses the great social issues of the twentieth century, issues that we still struggle with a hundred years later—racism, immigration, social violence, political activism, poverty, and women's rights. The story centered on Coalhouse Walker Jr., a young black musician fighting against injustice in an America that hasn't caught up with him. His name and his story came from a nineteenth-century German novel *Michael Koalhaus.* Coalhouse is a murderer and a terrorist, yet he is the hero of a musical.

Written within the luxury of a three-year development process, including several workshops, a concept album, and two major, lengthy, pre-Broadway engagements in Toronto and Los Angeles—and with *über* producer Drabinsky and his company Livent at the helm—*Ragtime* was a musical in which every word, every note counted, in which music was not just a medium but also a serious dramatic device, in which not only did content dictate form, but form actually *became* content. It was inspiring, heart-wrenching, and overwhelming in all the best ways. And it was a textbook example of how to structure a serious musical score. Each act was constructed of one long dramatic arc instead of several smaller arcs, like most musicals. The scenes flowed seamlessly, cinematically, one into the next, the book, music, and lyrics so perfectly in synch, so perfectly in the same voice, that it almost seemed as if one mind wrote book, music, and lyrics. The proof of its greatness was that after many of its leads left the show, it still delivered, still held the power it had on opening night. No one could ever inhabit those characters like the show's original cast—Brian Stokes Mitchell, Audra McDonald, Marin Mazzie, Peter Friedman, Mark Jacoby, Steven Sutcliffe, Judy Kaye, and the rest—but even without them, the show was still dazzling, still thrilling.

Ragtime is a genuine masterpiece, an epic full of big, soul-stirring anthems, and that's what its detractors criticized most and its supporters loved most. It tells a big story of big ideas, big themes, and big emotions. It needs anthems to tell its story. Its language is formal, full of symbolism, grand in its intent and ambition. It's about big journeys, interior and exterior, both of the characters and of our country. Like Sondheim's *Follies*, it is about enormous changes in our individual and collective lives. And like *Sweeney Todd*, it's also the story of a man driven mad by grief, for whom revenge is the only choice.

Charles Isherwood wrote in *Variety*, "Magnificent in scope and munificent in spirit, the new musical *Ragtime* achieves the surprising feat—rare in any medium—of living up to its own million-dollar hype. This most thematically ambitious of all American musicals, set at the turn of the century, reverberates with ideas—about racism and social justice, the struggles of immigrants and the painful price paid by some for the American dreams of others—that remain hauntingly apt as we look forward to the next century." He went on to say, "Indeed, the sheer size of the show and the spectacle of its stagecraft make its determined attention to the hearts of all its characters surprising. That these artists, working at the top of their form, have managed to tell a story of this immensity without losing sight of its humanity is not a small magic trick; Houdini himself would be breathless with admiration." John Lahr wrote in the *New Yorker* about the show's final moments, "The living and the dead—the winners and losers in the American sweepstakes—sing the same song of hope. In this terrific final stage picture, America's blessings and its barbarity coexist. It is on this democratic vision of cohesion—both social and spiritual—that great societies and great Broadway hits are built."

Ragtime was a triumph in every way, but its producer Garth Drabinsky and Livent, got into legal troubles. The company taking over Livent drastically cut the *Ragtime* advertising budget, and soon ticket sales dried up. The show closed prematurely in January 2000, after 861 performances. Interestingly, at the Tony Awards, *Ragtime* won best book and best score but *The Lion King* won best musical. There was outrage in some places from serious musical theatre aficionados, but others realized that the best musical Tony did not always go to the best musical *per se*, but to the best *production* of a musical, and with that in mind, even those who preferred *Ragtime* could see how *The Lion King* might win. *Ragtime* also won Tonys for featured actress (Audra MacDonald) and orchestrations.

Legendary pop songwriter Paul Simon stormed Broadway in 1998 with *The Capeman*, a show with music by Simon and book and lyrics by Simon and Nobel

Prize–winning West Indian poet Derek Walcott. Unfortunately for Simon, it was the same month as *Ragtime* and just two months after *The Lion King*. Also unfortunately for Simon, it seemed nearly everyone in the theatre community was hoping he'd fail. The show told the tragic true story of Salvador Agron, a sixteen-year-old, cape-wearing Latino kid who stabbed two other youths in 1959 New York City. Agron was tried and sentenced to death until Governor Rockefeller commuted his sentence to life in prison. Finally released after twenty years, he became a model citizen. Significantly, the show never judged Agron, despite his crimes, following in the footsteps of Sondheim and Weidman's *Assassins*.

Walcott said in an interview in *In Theater* magazine, "I became interested in his moral stance and the idea that he was a result of his background: the prejudice, the pressures, the contempt. This child was supposed to be American, but in a way, he became a second-rate citizen." The show was about predestination, remorse, forgiveness, salvation. And it was very controversial. Some people in New York still remembered the "Capeman" murders. Families of the victims protested the show. Friends of Agron argued with how he was portrayed. But as Simon later said in a television interview, "Artists are supposed to raise questions. We're *supposed* to." It didn't help his position in the theatre community when he said in a January 1998 *Vogue* interview, "I really couldn't care less what the theater community, or whatever it is that they call themselves, thinks about this work. Because, quite frankly, I didn't write it for Broadway. I wrote it for me."

While it had its flaws, *The Capeman* was more often than not utterly thrilling, transcendent theatre, with an amazing, sensory-confounding production design, with dark, troubled, emotional music and lyrics, and with the perfect cast: Ruben Blades as narrator and the adult Agron, Latino pop star Marc Anthony as the young Agron, and Ednita Nazario as Agron's mother.

Simon had been working on songs for the show since 1989 and he began working with Walcott in 1993. Walcott said, "I thought it would be extremely challenging for Broadway. I always associate Broadway with an upbeat kind of formula. Even when something is supposed to be daring, it's normally safe in its daring." In 1997 Simon made a new album, his first in seven years, on which he sang most of the *Capeman* songs, with occasional help from Blades, Anthony, and Nazario. His plan was to give the cast and band this recording and tell them to imitate it. Broadway veterans were shocked: *That's not how you make a musical!* So Simon went to some of those veterans and asked their advice. They told him to stop working on the recording, get a director, and do a workshop. He was offended by the implication that they didn't think he knew what he was doing. He ignored their advice.

Eventually, Simon hired avant-garde modern dance choreographer Mark Morris to choreograph the show. As director, Simon first hired Argentine-born Susana Tubert, then fired her and hired Eric Simonson, who had directed *The*

Song of Jacob Zulu. A workshop was done in late 1996, but soon the team decided to fire Simonson too. Then, Morris *and* Wolcott directed for a while. Then they decided to let Morris do both jobs. After the workshop, twenty-two of the forty-five actors in the cast were fired, including Broadway veteran Priscilla Lopez. Meanwhile, the end of 1997 was spent giving interviews, trying to ignore the naysayers, and put up what was becoming an eleven-million-dollar Broadway musical.

A month before the opening, Morris was replaced (well, "assisted," but Morris was no longer at rehearsals) by veteran director Jerry Zaks. The creators felt the show needed That Broadway Touch, and so in came Zaks to do what he could in the little time left. Directors Mike Nichols and Nicholas Hytner had both turned the gig down. Under Zaks, several songs were cut or changed, and the running time was cut from almost three hours to a little over two and a half. All this cost another half million dollars. But nothing about this piece could be mainstreamed, and Zaks was the wrong guy for this material, just as he had been for *Assassins*. Crowley had designed brilliant, evocative, disorienting sets. The nearly entirely Puerto Rican cast believed in the show. And Paul Simon was a notorious control freak.

After an unprecedented *fifty-nine previews* during which work continued, *The Capeman* opened in January 1998 and ran only sixty-eight performances. The critics savaged the show. In the *New York Times*, Ben Brantley wrote, "It's like watching a mortally wounded animal. You're only sorry that it has to suffer and that there's nothing you can do about it." And yet, of the score he said, "Intricately weaving Latin American rhythms and inflections with the doo-wop harmonies in vogue in the 1950s, these songs have a contemplative, sensuous elegance all their own and remain a pleasure to listen to." Greg Evans suggested how to save the show in *Variety*: "Scrap the irredeemable book, make peace with the static nature of the show, and dispense with any foolhardy attempt to flesh out one-note characters or raise the barely-a-footnote real-life tale to the stature of social significance."

In reality, it was an interesting, compelling piece of musical theatre. But it was also as different from the Broadway norm as possible, which made its success an impossibility on the Broadway of 1998, which was also hosting *Jekyll & Hyde*, *The Scarlet Pimpernel*, *The Sound of Music*, *High Society*, *The Wizard of Oz*, *Footloose*, and *An Evening with Jerry Herman*. Simon, Walcott, Morris, Crowley, and the others were trying to tell stories in a new way, more fragmented, more dreamlike, less linear. They were trying to use music in a new way, more authentic, more purely ethnic. They were trying to expand the limits of scenic art, more abstract, more sculptural, less interested in literally representing time and place. They were trying to work in another cultural language, no longer content to see a minority culture strictly in terms of the dominant culture, to let these New York Puerto Ricans speak in their own voice and music. (Still, several Latino political groups protested what they called a perpetuation of stereotypes.) The show's creators were trying to see what else was possible, trying to break through to a new theatrical language. Did every experiment in the show work? No. Did most of them? Yes. And the standing ovations every night seemed to indicate that audiences loved this work. But when Broadway gangs up on you, your chances are slim. *The Capeman* ran a couple months and gave up. An announced national tour was converted to a concert tour, and then canceled altogether. The cast album was recorded but never released. It's tempting to wonder how it would have fared if it had started life at a more daring regional theatre and enjoyed a little success before braving the waters of Broadway.

Musical theatre was still moving forward despite Broadway, still breaking new ground, still challenging the status quo. But as the century drew to a close, it seemed that simple expressions of joy had become underappreciated in American theatre. Perhaps they were underappreciated in America. Joy was a cliché. Joy was a cop-out. It seemed that smartass, steel-jawed determination was far more acceptable than joy. Part of the reason joy had gone out of the theatre is that the earliest, silliest Broadway musicals and plays in the first part of the twentieth century had traded *only* in joy and happiness. In reaction to that (or perhaps, *over*reaction), the American musical theatre had steered in the last few decades more and more toward death, despair, and destruction, either societal or personal.

And then *A New Brain* opened at Lincoln Center in June 1998 with music and lyrics by William Finn, the quirkiest writer in the musical theatre. Few people probably noticed that the show's vocal arrangements were by Jason Robert Brown, composer of *Songs for a New World*, but it was hard not to hear Brown's musical voice in the show's jazz-pop company numbers. *A New Brain* marked Lincoln Center's renewed commitment to new musicals, a kind of celebration of the reinvigoration of American musical theatre at the turn of the new millennium. Soon Lincoln Center would also shepherd two other new musicals, Jason Robert Brown and Alfred Uhry's *Parade*, and Michael John LaChiusa's *Marie Christine*.

Really, *A New Brain* was pretty dark stuff, too. After all, the main character was in a coma with a deadly brain disorder for much of the show. But like a few other musicals of the past decade—*Songs for a New World, Floyd Collins, Rent, Bat Boy*—*A New Brain* took that despair and those images of death and turned the sophisticated angst of modern musical theatre on its ear. How many writers or composers would—or could—write a musical comedy about brain surgery, a musical that takes a surreal, circuitous path through unlikely subjects like sailing, genetics, homelessness, and children's television? Probably only William Finn.

It had been only three days after winning the Tony Award for his Broadway musical *Falsettos* in 1992 that Finn was diagnosed with an inoperable brain tumor. It wasn't a brain tumor, it turned out, but it was a congenital condition called an arterial venous malformation (AVM), just as deadly. It also wasn't inoperable, it turned out; the doctors did operate on Finn's brain and he came out of it good as new. It was upon his return home that he began writing songs about the experience—his still wobbly walking made it easier just to stay at the piano. In one interview, Finn said, "When I came out of the hospital, I couldn't sit at the piano without writing a decent song. At the piano, there was just all this gratitude that I was alive and this life spewing out of me—the piano was singing—and I was just there to write it down."

It started out as a song cycle, but soon it had turned into a full-length musical about a theatre composer, Gordon Schwinn, trapped in a job writing songs for an insipid kiddie TV show. He ends up in the hospital awaiting surgery, sure that he's dying. Though some of the events in the show were fictionalized, the most bizarre moments were the truest ones. Finn really did have occasional conversations with an outspoken homeless woman near his home. Finn's mother really did throw out all his favorite books while he was in the hospital. And he really did try to write a song while he was in the hospital, although in real life it was for a Wendy Wasserstein play, not a kiddie TV show called *Mr. Bungee's Lily Pad*.

Despite its subject matter, though, *A New Brain* managed to be one of the most life-affirming, most heartfelt musicals written in the last decades of the twentieth century, maybe a show only someone who actually faced death could have written, a companion piece, in many ways, to *Rent*. "The truths I learned I couldn't have learned any other way," Finn said in a *USA Today* interview. "That you're put here to do certain things, and you can't waste your time not doing it. You have to greet each day with enormous gratitude and hope and happiness." Then he added, "I know I sound like a new-age moron." But *A New Brain* wasn't only about brain surgery any more than *Fiddler on the Roof* was about that fiddler. Just as *Fiddler* was about the broader, more universal theme of tradition, *A New Brain* was about the more universal journey Gordon takes toward understanding that the world is how we perceive it and how we leave it. The world is neither good nor bad, gentle nor hostile; it just *is*, Finn was telling us.

Yet *A New Brain* did not ignore the darker side of its subject matter. After twenty years of the AIDS pandemic, with shootings in America's schools continuing unchecked, the homeless woman's admonition that we live in perilous times rang especially true for American audiences. Gay audiences saw Gordon's brain troubles as a metaphor for AIDS (especially since Gordon was gay) and though that wasn't intended by Finn, the comparison was understandable. Gordon goes through life-changing experiences and comes out on the other side realizing that all the things he thought were important just aren't, that "security" isn't worth the stifling of happiness, that happiness doesn't come from money or things, that we pass up everything that's beautiful in life every day, never taking time to notice or appreciate it all. It was a change that composer William Finn had gone through himself. It's rare that we get to see such personal work from an author both before and after a life-changing experience, but with Finn we could, looking back at the *Falsettos* trilogy in comparison with *A New Brain*, and it was exhilarating. There were still shadows of the old Finn in *New Brain*, in the nasty, frog-suited TV show host Mr. Bungee, in Gordon's manic mother, in songs like "And They're Off," but something was definitely different now.

The message of the show, that an artist cannot create until he learns to focus on what really matters in life and learns to let go of the soul-killing trivia of everyday life, grows out of the accumulation of (sometimes oddly illustrated) wisdom Gordon finds in his dreams and hallucinations. Each lesson he learns contributes to that greater understanding. But make no mistake, he's only *started* down that path when the show ends (like the end of *Company*). Whether or not he stays on that path, whether or not he finds and holds on to real happiness is left unanswered—just as in real life. This is no old-fashioned musical comedy; this is an adult, modern work of theatre that acknowledges the messiness and chaos—and pure joy—of real life.

The Asian musical *Heading East* was first created for California's Sesquicentennial Celebration, and it opened at the East West Players in Los Angeles in 1998, going on to tour the state of California. The show told the tale of one Asian family's humorous and dramatic experiences in California from 1848 to the present, a capsule not only of California history but also of the history of immigration in America. This one family's history, standing in for all our families, includes collisions with the California Gold Rush, the building of the transcontinental railroad, the 1906 San Francisco earthquake, the Depression, the internment of Japanese Americans during World War II, the communist witch hunts, the Korean and Vietnam wars, all the way up to the present. As in *Hallelujah, Baby!* and *Love Life*, its characters did not age as they moved through history's Great Events. Its score was not Asian in its sound but more a modern musical theatre score. This was the immigrant experience seen from the perspective of modern-day, assimilated Asian Americans. The show received mixed reviews. The premiere cast recording of *Heading East* was released in 1999, and the show was included as part of the National Alliance for Musical Theatre's 1999 Festival of New Musicals. *Heading East* was also the recipient of the 2001 Richard Rodgers Development Award for new musicals

Established in 1965, East West Players has been called "the nation's preeminent Asian American theater troupe" by the *New York Times* for their award-winning productions blending Eastern and Western movement, costumes, language, and music. The company has premiered over a hundred plays and musicals about the Asian Pacific American experience and has also held more than a thousand readings and workshops. By their estimates, their audiences are fifty-six percent Asian and forty-four percent non-Asian. In addition to many non-musical plays, the company has also produced *Little Shop of Horrors*, *A Funny Thing Happened on the Way to the Forum*, *Follies*, *Cabaret*, *Merrily We Roll Along*, *Sweeney Todd*, *Into the Woods*, *Company*, *The Fantasticks*, *A Chorus Line*, *The Threepenny Opera*, *Pacific Overtures*, *Godspell*, and *Passion*, all with predominantly

Asian casts. When they produced *Sweeney Todd*, Stephen Sondheim even wrote some new lyrics for them.

In March 1999, a decidedly different kind of musical opened off Broadway, *Dream True: My Life with Vernon Dexter*, with book and lyrics by Tina Landau (one of the creators of *Floyd Collins*) and music and additional lyrics by Ricky Ian Gordon. The show told the story of two boys with a connection so strong they can communicate through their dreams, even after decades of separation. The two friends, Peter and Vernon grow up in Wyoming in 1945, but Peter's mother sends him to New Haven to live with his psychiatrist uncle who can give him more opportunities. Peter doesn't like the change but he stays connected to Vernon through their dreams. As adults, they meet again by chance in New York in the 1960s, but now Vernon is gay and wants more than their long-held spiritual relationship. He wants a physical relationship as well. When Peter refuses, the two are separated—physically—again. The show did not receive great reviews, but it did tread some new ground and it allowed two of the musical theatre's more formidable artists to continue expanding their boundaries and their art form.

One of the most interesting trends in musical theatre at the end of the millennium was the explosion of classic Broadway musicals in Japan. In February 1998, *American Theatre* published an article on this phenomenon called "Annie Get Your Shogun." After the Second World War, the U.S. had taken possession of the Japanese theatre that housed the Takarazuka, a women's musical theatre company. Almost like a scene out of *Pacific Overtures*, the Americans renamed the theatre the Ernie Pyle Theatre, after the American war correspondent, and began producing musical revues for U.S. soldiers. One Japanese producer explained, "American soldiers introduced pop music, and the younger generation became accustomed to it. That served as the foundation for the Western musical being accepted in Japan." In 1963, the Japanese built the Imperial Theatre specifically in response to the huge crowds that flocked to the first Broadway musical to come to Japan, *My Fair Lady*. It was followed by *Hello, Dolly!* with Mary Martin, *The Sound of Music*, *West Side Story*, and others. Composer Harold Rome was commissioned by a Japanese producer to write a musical version of *Gone with the Wind* in 1970 (retitled *Scarlett* at first), which did well in Japan, moderately well in London (397 performances), not very well in Los Angeles, and never made it to Broadway.

During the 1970s, Japan saw *Applause*, *Jesus Christ Superstar*, and others. During the 1980s, Japan saw English-language tours of *The Wiz*, *A Chorus Line*, *42nd Street*, and others. This trend continued throughout the 1990s, with the producing organization Toho presenting about thirty musicals a year, now done almost entirely in Japanese, including productions of *She Loves Me*, *La Cage aux Folles*, *Man of La Mancha*, *The Sound of Music*, *The King and I*, *Irene*, and of course, *Les Misérables*. Other musicals in Japan included *The Fantasticks*, *Evita*, *Phantom of the Opera*, *Beauty and the Beast*, and *Cats*. In fact, *Cats* ran more than 3,500 performances.

The Shiki Theatrical Company today has an extensive training program specifically for musical theatre performers, with the goal of producing Japanese-language musicals of the same quality as their Broadway counterparts. Actor Koshiroh Matsumoto compared musical theatre and traditional Japanese Kabuki theatre: "Both are highly artificial. In each case, you have to transcend an audience's surprise, even displeasure, when an actor behaves in a way that seems unbelievable, such as suddenly starting to sing. Even the world *kabuki*, he adds, is a combination of Japanese words for *song, dance,* and *actor.*

The biggest Broadway hit of 2001 first opened in New York in the summer of 1999, both ending *and* beginning the millennium in a way that sent the musical theatre skidding off its tracks. In a good way. The show was called *Urinetown.* Its cast of newcomers was anchored by veteran John Cullum as the villain, capping off a career that had started with the last Lerner and Loewe show, *Camelot,* and also included Tonys for *Shenandoah* and *On the Twentieth Century.* Cullum connected the past to the future, standing astride the gap between old-fashioned, classic musical theatre and this new brand of smartass, postmodern musical theatre.

Cardiff Giant, a theatre company in Chicago, had been known for its outrageous, irreverent social satire, some scripted, some improvised. Two members of the (now defunct) group, Greg Kotis and Mark Hollmann, began working in 1995 on what would become *Urinetown.* Kotis was also a member of the alternative theatre group the Neo-Futurists, who specialized in evenings of brilliant one- and two-minute plays. During a trip to Europe with the Neo-Futurists, the nearly broke Kotis discovered to his dismay that most public toilets in Europe are pay-to-use. And the idea for *Urinetown* was born—a musical about a city in the not too distant future where toilets are *all* "pay-to-pee" and private toilets are outlawed, where all toilets are controlled by a large, malevolent, monopolizing corporation, the Urine Good Company. Not only was it an outrageous idea—especially for a musical—but it was at the same time sociologically interesting, touching on issues of overpopulation, dwindling natural resources, and the like. Amidst all the lunacy was a serious response to the theories of Thomas Robert Malthus and his *Essay on the Principles of Population* (1798), which examines the tendency of human beings to outstrip their resources and checks in the form of poverty, disease, and starvation to keep societies from moving beyond their means of subsistence. Pretty heady stuff for a silly musical about peeing.

Kotis approached his friend Mark Hollmann, who immediately returned with a finished song, "It's a Privilege to Pee." They continued working, feeling quite certain their creation was unproducible. By the end of 1997, a first draft of the script was finished. By June 1998, the first draft of the score was done as well. They put an ad in *Backstage* for actors to make a demo recording without pay. With demo in hand, they sent their script and recording to dozens of theatres and agents. With this show, they had decided to raise lots of questions and never answer them. They decided to subvert every convention of musicals, defiantly refusing to give any potential audience even a drop of what they craved. And yet, in certain ways, they were utterly true to conventional musical theatre, particularly in their show's structure—right out of the Rodgers and Hammerstein model. But no one would produce *Urinetown*. The authors received over a hundred rejection letters. And then the New York International Fringe Festival accepted them. They spent the spring and summer of 1999 rehearsing, rewriting, polishing, finding solutions. And so from a converted garage with no air conditioning on Stanton Street in lower Manhattan, *Urinetown* was born.

The score ranged from direct homages to *Threepenny Opera* to traditional ballads to hymns to gospel to Bach to the B-52s. In his preface to the published script, composer Hollmann lays out his rule for the show—a joke is funnier if you don't smile while you're telling it. In other words, an evening of obvious parody and gags would get boring; the work had to stand up as organic, carefully constructed theatre, no matter how outrageous the content.

A producing group called the Araca Group saw the show and decided it was worth developing. They brought in a new director, John Rando, and had an open casting call for a reading of the show. Only Spencer Kayden, as Little Sally, would stay with the show from the Fringe Festival all the way to Broadway. After a very brief rehearsal period, the reading was presented at New Dramatists in January 2000. From that reading, Dodger Theatricals, one of the strongest producing groups in New York, entered the picture, and they opened it off Broadway at the American Theatre of Actors in May 2001. The *New York Times* raved. The show received eleven Drama Desk nominations and two Obie nominations—and the Dodgers were taking it to Broadway. It was scheduled to open at the Henry Miller Theatre on Broadway on September 13, 2001.

But then came the terrorist attacks on New York on September 11, and all of Broadway shut down. Some shows never opened again. Eventually, the Henry Miller reopened, and *Urinetown* set its new opening for September 20. Business was tough for a while, but the show kept plugging, and by the spring, it had received ten Tony nominations, winning for best score, best book, and best director, but curiously, *again*, not best musical.

Urinetown was at its core a very funny and smart takeoff on the theatrical conventions of socialist 1930s theater like *The Threepenny Opera*, a sendup of musical theater in which Bertolt Brecht and Kurt Weill meet postmodern irony with a vengeance. The official slogan on the show's T-shirts was "An appalling idea, fully realized." Actor Daniel Marcus, who played Officer Barrel, said in an interview, "I call it a love letter to the American musical in the form of a grenade."

In fact, *Urinetown* was a double satire, laughing at the silly, happy conventions of old-fashioned musical comedy, but also laughing at shows like *Threepenny*, which reject those conventions and perhaps go too far the other way. It was the Ultimate Self-Referential Postmodern Musical, following in the footsteps of *Attempting the Absurd* and *Bat Boy*. Like those shows, *Urinetown* asks questions about what we expect from musicals, whether or not "issue musicals" are satisfying as entertainment, why certain stories or topics are musicalized, whether or not serious musicals are *too* serious. Each time Officer Lockstock and Little Sally talk about what musicals shouldn't do, they're actually addressing conventions certain musicals *have* done without success. And of course they're also breaking the rules by explicitly discussing the musical they're in, acknowledging that they are characters in a musical, as *Attempting the Absurd* had done. Yet *Urinetown* still succeeds as a "serious" musical because ultimately it addresses serious issues.

Bruce Weber in the *New York Times* said, "There simply is no show I've seen that gives such a sense that the creators and performers are always on the same page of an elaborate, high-spirited joke, that they are the proud members of a cabal that knows what it takes to make the world a better place and that they are thrilled to share what they know." He also called the show "a sensational piece of performance art, one that acknowledges theater tradition and pushes it forward as well." Of course, a few alarmists declared that *Urinetown* signaled the demise of the American musical theatre. They were clearly wrong, as the following years would prove.

Both *Urinetown* and Mel Brooks' stage adaptation of *The Producers* became hits but *Urinetown* was smarter, more insightful, and ultimately would exert more influence on the future of the art form. As the millennium approached, *Urinetown* was poised to become the *Show Boat* or *Company* of a new age of musical theatre, the new model that would replace the Rodgers and Hammerstein model, while *The Producers* was more like *High Button Shoes* with Tourette's syndrome.

10

An Era Exploding, a Century Spinning
The New Millennium

As the turn of another century greeted the musical theatre, the art form was turning as well. In January 2000, New Dramatists in New York sponsored a public debate called "Great Theatre Debates: The American Musical Has Entered a New Golden Age." But those arguing against this premise kept talking only about Broadway, stubbornly refusing to acknowledge that Broadway and musical theatre had not been strictly synonymous for decades, that the most exciting new work happens *away* from Broadway because an average big-budget Broadway musical can now cost ten to fourteen million dollars or *more*. Due in large part to the extinction of the single producer, the "impresario," now replaced by great, gangly committees of producers—and in some cases, giant corporations as producers—it was harder than ever to find a Broadway show with a unique, singular, artistic voice, and therefore the most adventurous work no longer appeared on Broadway.

In contrast, as the new century began many musical theatre artists across America and in Europe came to believe that after nearly sixty years of the Rodgers and Hammerstein model, it was time to move forward and explore new models and new paths. So, while working within the musical theatre genre, these artists began to explore and experiment with audience expectations; the relationship between actor and audience; the uses of physical space; the uses of music; the distortion or rejection of traditional linear storytelling, plot, and structure; and the role of the audience. Many new musicals strayed from, or in some cases utterly rejected, the Rodgers and Hammerstein model, but different shows and artists were rejecting different parts of that model.

Some artists had rejected the structural model, creating abstract musicals like *Songs for a New World* and *Bring in 'da Noise, Bring in 'da Funk*; or the surrealistic, hallucinogenic *A New Brain* and *Bright Lights, Big City*; or the chronologically unusual *The Last Five Years*. Some artists had rejected traditional models of content and themes with shows like *Rent, Urinetown, The Capeman, Naked*

221

Boys Singing, Bat Boy, Reefer Madness, The Wild Party, and *Hedwig and the Angry Inch.* Some rejected traditional notions of naturalism and the fourth wall with shows like *Hedwig, Capeman, Bat Boy,* and *Floyd Collins.* Some rejected traditional notions of what a song is, with shows like *Floyd Collins, Violet,* and *The Light in the Piazza.* Many of these shows brought a new kind of honesty to the art form, so baldly admitting their artifice, experimenting with self-referential humor, acknowledging and even directly addressing the audience, and portraying complex, *real* emotions that *real* people experience in the *real* world. Musical theatre was no longer primarily a fantasy world.

But some critics complained that these shows rejected traditional musical theatre without offering anything new in its place. While that may be true, that also may be alright. Maybe the old models have to be torn down, deconstructed, laughed at, before new models can be put in place. And some people were arguing that the new models were already in place.

But despite all the new blood and radical new approaches to musical theatre, the old guard were as pessimistic as they could be. Musical theatre was becoming a new animal and they didn't like it. Playwright Albert Innaurato wrote in 2000 in the *New York Times Magazine,* "Let's stop pretending that there's any life left in the once-transcendent American musical or any way to revive its bloated corpse given the immense costs, corporate greed, and reactionary old guard that now stifle all theatrical creativity." Critic Charles Isherwood wrote in *Variety,* "The world may survive the advent of the stage version of *Saturday Night Fever,* of course, but the future of musical theatre in the wake of this show's almost assured success may be irrevocably altered."

Well, *Saturday Night Fever* flopped and everyone promptly forgot about it, right along with *Urban Cowboy: The Musical* and other abominations. Second, these guys were talking about Big Broadway Musicals, not musical theatre. Unfortunately, they believed they were talking about the art form as a whole. It is true that many of the musicals on Broadway at the turn of the last century were either shallow revivals or shallower adaptations of movies, including *Footloose: The Musical, Thoroughly Modern Millie, Debbie Does Dallas: The Musical,* and too many more. Mainstream Broadway was returning to the 1950s in form and content, fully (re)invested in the old scene-song-scene-song structure and safe, shallow stories reaffirming middle-class, middle-American values. Shows like *Millie, The Full Monty, Dirty Rotten Scoundrels,* and *Wicked* were well-crafted, no question, but as bland as the models on which they had built: *Damn Yankees, The Pajama Game, A Tree Grows in Brooklyn, Plain and Fancy, Bells Are Ringing,* and *Flower Drum Song.* Sharing The Street with these new shows were shallow revivals of shows that deserved better, including *The Music Man, Man of La Mancha, Chicago, Jesus Christ Superstar,* and *Little Shop of Horrors.*

But maybe we were finally learning that Broadway is no longer the place to go to see the adventurous, the genuinely new, the inspiring, the surprising. And if we're very lucky, maybe Hollywood will take up some of the slack. Certainly

Moulin Rouge, Hedwig, Chicago, and *Rent* have proved that movie musicals can still work and, more than that, can still sell tickets. There are as many people in Hollywood as there ever were that can sing and dance as well as act. Maybe these films will bring back the movie musical and we'll see some risk taking there that we can no longer see much of on Broadway, since technology is making it easier and easier to produce independent films.

Obie Award–winning composer Polly Pen (*Goblin Market*) said in the *Village Voice*, "Part of [the despair] comes from people who have some sort of odd rules about what a musical is. What they're usually talking about is they're seeing something that has just changed, and they don't happen to like that change." In fact, in 1997, three-time Tony-winning performer Audra McDonald had recorded an album, *Way Back to Paradise*, containing only songs from new musicals by composers like Ricky Ian Gordon, Michael John LaChiusa, Adam Guettel, Jason Robert Brown, and Jenny Giering. Every year, the National Alliance for Musical Theatre produces a Festival of New Musicals. And then there's the National Music Theatre Conference, where *Violet* and *Avenue X* both premiered. The art form is as healthy as ever.

The *Village Voice* quoted Richard Rodgers in a January 2000 article on musical theatre: "One night a show opens and suddenly there's a whole new concept. But it isn't the result of a trend; it's because one, two, or three or more people sat down and sweated over an idea that somehow clicked and broke loose. It can be about anything and take off in any direction, and when it works, there's your present and your future."

It seems appropriate to requote here something from earlier in the book, from composer Jerry Bock in 1962: "Shortly it will happen. The American musical will shed its present polished state and become an untidy, adventurous something else. Shortly it will exchange its current neatness and professional grooming for a less manicured appearance, for a more peculiar profile. It will swell beyond or shrink from the finesse that regulates it now. It will poke around. It will hunt for. It will wander and wonder. It will try and trip. But at least it will be moving again, off the treadmill, out of the safety zone, crossing not at the green, but in between." It happened in the early 1960s. But it also happened in the 1970s, and again in the middle and late 1990s. And it will happen again every so often.

The year 2000 brought with it something that had never happened before in the history of the musical theatre. It began with the opening of *The Wild Party*, a new musical based on the famous jazz age poem about lust, death, jealousy, and addiction, with book, music, and lyrics by Andrew Lippa and direction by Gabriel Barre. The show was given readings in August 1996 and November 1997, and a full workshop in May 1999. It opened off Broadway at the Longacre Theatre in February 2000 but ran only fifty-four performances.

Then in April 2000, another show called *The Wild Party* opened, based on the same source, this one with a score by Michael John LaChiusa and a book by

LaChiusa and George C. Wolfe, the show's director. This *Wild Party* had its first reading in 1998 and a workshop in February 1999. It opened *on* Broadway at the Virginia Theatre, and ran just barely longer than the off Broadway *Wild Party*, sixty-eight performances.

The two shows told the same story but in ways so starkly different that it was nearly impossible to compare the two. Lippa's score mined far more accessibly the flavor of 1920s jazz, while LaChiusa's score was the kind of unconventional, sometimes atonal sound that kept most of his other shows from finding an audience.

Lippa's *Wild Party* won three Lucille Lortel Awards, the Drama Desk Award for outstanding music, and two Obie Awards. The LaChiusa *Wild Party* was nominated for seven Tony Awards, winning none of them. Of Lippa's version, Ben Brantley wrote in the *New York Times*, "This production's strong suit is summoning the anxious restlessness behind the hellbent hedonism of the days of Prohibition." The *New York Daily News* called it "sizzling, vital, and groundbreaking."

Of LaChiusa's version, Brantley said of the cast, "Even singing the jauntier examples of Mr. LaChiusa's vaudeville and jazz pastiches (with Stravinsky hovering in the background, natch), they tend to be as whiny and over-stimulated as a party of two-year-olds with no videos to watch," and he called the show "a cause for sorrowful head-shaking." John Lahr wrote in the *New Yorker*, "The enormous energy that comes across the footlights feels more like theatrical hyperventilation than revelation."

In April 2001, Mel Brooks' *The Producers* took Broadway by storm, breaking box office records and getting nearly universal rave reviews. The production under the direction of Susan Stroman was outstanding, though it was originally to be directed by her husband Mike Ockrent, who had helmed *Me and My Girl* and *Crazy for You*. But Ockrent died of leukemia in 1999, midway through the show's development. Brooks begged Stroman to take over direction as well as choreographing, and though it was sometimes painful, she agreed. Under Stroman's direction, the show's five leads (Nathan Lane, Matthew Broderick, Gary Beach, Roger Bart, and Brad Oscar) gave some of the most outrageous, most wickedly gleeful, most over-the-top performances many people had ever seen, giving the impression that the show itself might well be a perfect musical comedy. But it also left some observers wondering if the show would succeed as crazily without those five original leads. As it turns out, it wouldn't. The leads were better than the show.

Strangely enough, *The Producers* was pretty conventional in most ways—well made, but conventional. Sure, it told a lot of outrageous jokes, reveling perhaps too much in being politically incorrect, but that was nothing really new in 2001, after the *South Park* movie, *Urinetown*, *Bat Boy*, and other shows. And sure, Brooks and co-writer Thomas Meehan did actually improve a bit on the plot of the outstanding original film. But the book was standard musical comedy, the jokes and sight gags standard Brooks, and the songs, also by Brooks, were unfortunately second-tier show tunes. *The Producers* didn't look back, re-imagine, or take any big steps forward. It's true that its physical production referenced other shows (or was it more like theft?), the pigeon puppets referencing *The Lion King*, the valentine-inspired set for Little Old Ladyland mirroring the "Loveland" set from *Follies*, the dancer puppets in "Springtime for Hitler" based on the same idea in *Best Little Whorehouse*, the overhead mirror in "Springtime for Hitler" referencing both *Cabaret* and *A Chorus Line*. In July 2001, *Time* magazine published a story titled "Better Than the Producers." In it, Richard Zoglin wrote, "*The Producers* is a lot of very good things, but adventurous and groundbreaking are not among them." Instead Zoglin offers three other shows as better musicals—Jonathan Larson's *Tick, Tick . . . Boom!*, *Urinetown*, and Jason Robert Brown's *The Last Five Years*.

The Producers was well crafted but very much business as usual. Saying *fuck* on a Broadway stage just isn't that outrageous anymore. And simply being overt and aggressive about homophobic and sexist jokes doesn't necessarily diffuse them. Perhaps what will keep it running is that *The Producers* allows mainstream audiences to feel edgy and adventurous without having to engage any edgy or adventurous work. *Monty Python's Spamalot* would do the same a few years later and with equally uninspiring results, despite another excellent cast. But perhaps the thing *The Producers* will most be remembered for is driving ticket prices ever higher, creating "Broadway Inner Circle" tickets, the best seats in the house every night for $480 each!

Meanwhile, Jason Robert Brown's chronologically rebellious, two-character musical *The Last Five Years* opened at the Northlight Theatre, near Chicago, in May 2001. The show chronicled a five-year relationship, from first meeting to breakup. But it avoided the landmines of this overly familiar territory by telling the story in two directions. Jamie, young up-and-coming novelist (and autobiographical stand-in for Brown), tells us his story in conventional chronological order, while Cathy, an only occasionally successful actor, moves through the same story backward. Jamie starts at their first date; Cathy starts at their breakup. They only overlap at their wedding when the two stories meet for one moment of happiness. The result is a fascinating look at the way every relationship is seen from two different, usually competing perspectives. As with Sondheim's *Merrily We Roll Along*, even the happy songs aren't *really* happy because we know what's coming. Not only did Brown prove his endless talent as a composer and lyricist, he also demonstrated in this show an ever deepening understanding of the maddening complexity of human relations.

The show was supposed to open at Lincoln Center, but they backed out, spooked by threatened lawsuits by Brown's ex-wife who thought the show cut too close to reality. Finally, *The Last Five Years* opened anyway, off Broadway, in March 2002. *Time* magazine included it in its list of "10 Best of 2001," and it received the Drama Desk Awards for best music and best lyrics. *Newsday* said,

"Brown is terrific at writing about love without the cornball, a quality he makes both poignant and ironic here by having Cathy's songs start at the end of the marriage, while Jamie begins at the smitten beginning. . . . Their last five years may have been painful, but they make us feel much better about the future of musical theatre."

Then everything changed. On September 11, 2001, America was attacked by terrorists who flew commercial airliners into the World Trade Center towers in New York and into the Pentagon in Washington, DC. Another plane was heading toward the White House but was forced to crash in a field in Pennsylvania by heroic passengers who knew what was coming. Immediately following the attacks that morning, America shut down. All planes were grounded. Government offices closed. The New York Stock Exchange closed. All Broadway shows were canceled for that day, a Tuesday, and the two usual performances the following day. Broadway reopened on Thursday, September 13, but had lost an estimated $1.5 million dollars on those two days off. Several off Broadway theatres located in the vicinity of the World Trade Center had to stay closed for a while until the city declared the area safe again.

For months afterward, the economy struggled. And few industries were hit harder than the New York theatre. Tourism in New York evaporated overnight. Even after New York theatres reopened, many shows closed that would otherwise have run for months or years more. Some shows reduced the number of performances per week. Some off Broadway shows cut their ticket prices in half. *Urinetown* postponed its Broadway transfer. *Reefer Madness* postponed its first preview. *Bat Boy* had been hoping to transfer to Broadway, but there was no hope of that now; instead it posted a closing notice for December. *The Rocky Horror Show*, *Kiss Me Kate*, and other shows also closed. For the first time in its long run, *Les Misérables* began operating at a loss after September 11, and it would do so until producer Cameron Mackintosh finally pulled the plug in May 2003. The Roundabout Theatre canceled their announced all-star Broadway production of Stephen Sondheim's *Assassins*. Broadway touring companies also experienced devastating drops in sales.

Just ten days after the terrorist attacks, the *New York Times'* Bruce Weber went to see *Urinetown* again, this time on Broadway. And in his review, he couldn't help but see the show now in the context of the "new world" of terrorist attacks. He wrote, "It now seems to have been created with inadvertent prescience. It tells a story, after all, that presents innocent people victimized by conscienceless evil, kills off characters by having them thrown from a skyscraper, debates the appropriateness of murderous vengeance, illustrates the rage of those who suffer in poverty and perceive cruelty in capitalism, and in the end decries the presumption and wastefulness of people who don't recognize that they are privileged." He went on, "The result of all this is that watching *Urinetown* right now is simply the most gripping and galvanizing theater experience in town, equal parts visceral entertainment jolt and lingering provocation."

And isn't that what theatre at its best *should* be?

Life and theatre went on. In October 2001, Deaf West Theatre in Los Angeles mounted the Tony-winning 1985 Broadway musical *Big River*, but this time with a cast of both hearing and nonhearing actors, using sign language as part of the experience, sometimes using two actors—one hearing, one deaf—to portray one character. Deaf West had already done one musical before, *Oliver* in 2000, as well as several well-known plays, but *Big River* is what got the world to sit up and take notice, to realize finally that there's no reason deaf people can't take their place in the world of musical theatre.

The production was picked up by the Mark Taper Forum in Los Angeles in November 2002, and then the Roundabout Theatre in New York got interested and this new "deaf" *Big River* opened in New York in July 2003 for a limited run. The production was directed by Tommy Tune's one-time protégé Jeff Calhoun. Ed Waterstreet, Deaf West's founder, said in an *American Theatre* interview, "Growing up, I imagined some way to use all the dynamics of the theatre. Could we feel equal with hearing people and also get greater impact for both? Could we make something new and better for both?" Deaf West does not use closed captioning or interpreters on the side of the stage. They use what Waterstreet calls a "third language," a mix of sign language and unusual voicing techniques. Gordon Davidson, artistic director of the Mark Taper Forum, said, "It's magic. Our audiences loved *Big River* because it's good storytelling. People lost track of who's deaf and who's hearing. Without our hiding it, that just became invisible." With so many people looking for new life to breathe into musical theatre and into America's soul, maybe Deaf West had found it—allowing a whole new community of people not only to enjoy musical theatre but also to transform it along the way. While running in Los Angeles, the production won six Theatre L.A. Ovation Awards, five Los Angeles Drama Critics' Circle Awards, and five Back Stage West Garland Awards. After the Broadway run, two identical productions went on national tours.

In June 2002, London saw something new on its musical stage—the Indian musical *Bombay Dreams*. Award-winning Indian filmmaker Shekhar Kapur had talked to Andrew Lloyd Webber in the late 1990s about directing a screen version of *Phantom of the Opera*, but a different project emerged instead—a pop musical about the thriving film industry in India, affectionately known as Bollywood. Kapur said in an interview, "I spoke to Andrew about a film I wanted to do called *Bombay Dreams*, and that's where the whole idea came from. He immediately saw it as a good basis for a stage show instead. He'd just seen a Channel 4 documentary about Bollywood films and started to see a few of the films, too, because he was really impressed with their musical numbers. So I got a lot of CDs and DVDs to show him, and as he started to pick each song, I noticed that they came from the same composer. That composer was a very good friend of mine, AR Rahman, so I introduced them to each other."

The resulting show, with music by Rahman (composer of more than fifty film scores), lyrics by Don Black (*Song and Dance*), and a book by Meera Syal, was not at all groundbreaking, more a retread of pop musicals past, drawn in broad, melodramatic strokes, more interested in style than substance. But it was also a landmark in that it took the Indian culture seriously in a stage musical. Rahman said in *Playbill*, "We wanted the audience to be singing the songs when they went out of the theatre. We wanted to introduce the culture of India, the melodic structure of Indian *ragas*. They can have a peculiar sadness that goes with the slums and lifestyles of the people in Bombay, where the rich and poorest coexist. And when you hear the melody, it sticks with you." The show told the story of Akaash, a young slum dweller, who dreams of becoming a huge movie star in Bombay. He meets the beautiful Priya, the daughter of one of Bollywood's greatest film directors, and his career begins. John Peter wrote in London's *Sunday Times*, "*Bombay Dreams* is a terrific show: a big silky, sensual show, lush and lavish and extravagantly colourful." But other critics disagreed. The critic at the weekday *Times* criticized the musical for its "trite lyrics," "cardboard characters," "dialogue that would test the patience of Mother Teresa" and "the lamest ending in West End history."

Still, the show was a big popular success, recouping its $7.6 million investment in only fourteen months, and it was nominated for a 2003 Olivier Award for best musical. It opened on Broadway in April 2004 and closed the following January, not even coming close to recouping its fourteen-million-dollar investment, but then went out on tour anyway.

In August 2002, a fresh new musical comedy opened on Broadway, a stage musicalization of the classic film *Hairspray* which had been written and directed by John Waters (who readily admits his own love affair with Theatre of the Absurd). The stage musical had a book by Mark O'Donnell and Thomas Meehan, a score by veteran composer Marc Shaiman and lyricist Scott Wittman, direction by Jack O'Brien, and choreography by Jerry Mitchell, all working as one to create a wacky but heartfelt mix of old-fashioned and contemporary Broadway comedy, a strong retro-pop score, often outrageous humor, lots of dancing, and also a socially conscious message about race relations and various brands of prejudice. Composer Marc Shaiman had just hit it big co-writing the score for the *South Park* movie musical, and Shaiman's husband Scott Wittman co-wrote the lyrics, full of early rock and roll energy and fabulously quirky references to the Great Musical Comedies, including an unmistakable quotation of the last line of "Rose's Turn" from *Gypsy*. In its own innocent, tacky-charming way, *Hairspray* declared that ordinary people are the ones who change history, that move the world forward, not statesmen and soldiers, that sometimes good intentions really are enough.

Like the film, the stage musical focused on Tracy Turnblad, a "full-figured" teenager in Baltimore, who just wants to dance on *The Corny Collins Show* (a delicious low-rent copy of *American Bandstand*). But it's 1962 and "colored music" is becoming more and more popular, leaving some of the parents in Baltimore positively aghast. In fact, once a month Corny has Negro Day, co-hosted by

Motormouth Maybelle the gospel singer. But Tracy and Motormouth think the show should be integrated *every* day and they plot to make that happen.

The story is based loosely on Waters' life growing up in Baltimore, and *The Corny Collins Show* is based on the real-life *Buddy Deane Show* that ran on Baltimore TV from 1957 to 1964. Waters wrote in a piece for the *New York Times*, "The subtle shades of discrimination in my hometown were something the Broadway crew had to understand. As a child in Baltimore County, I used to lie in bed at night and hear 'colored people' walking to the tiny 'Negro community' near our house, singing a cappella the beautiful 'race music' that so scared our white parents. By junior high, every cool white kid I knew listened to all-black radio but very few had black friends. At white record hops, black singers could lip-sync their rhythm-and-blues hits but never dance with whites or with each other. You could really get shunned by whites and blacks for mixing the races socially. I even got beat up outside an art school in Baltimore for bringing a black girl as my date. And black cops would really hassle our racially mixed crowd, stopping our car for no reason and growling 'This isn't Greenwich Village, you know.' I knew."

In its construction, its plotting, and its innocence, *Hairspray* the musical is like any other musical—*of the 1950s!* But its content is slyly subversive, laughing at the blind racism in America's past, but also pointing out quite vividly that we haven't come as far as we should have, and that there's lots of work still to be done. The show also points out the absurdity of racist white folks listening to black music. *Hairspray* gleefully condemns prejudice against African Americans, against fat people, even against transgendered people, against anybody whom society brands as "different" (like John Waters?). Waters wrote in the *Times*, "The real reason I'm praying that *Hairspray* succeeds is that if it's a hit, there will be high school productions, and finally the fat girl and the drag queen will get the starring parts."

The show opened in August 2002 and is still running as this book goes to press. It was nominated for thirteen Tony Awards, and won eight, including best musical, best score, best book, best director (Jack O'Brien), best actress (Marissa Janet Winokur as Tracy), best actor (Harvey Fierstein as her mother Edna), best featured actor (Dick Latessa as the father), and best costumes (William Ivey Long). In fact, it was a very gay Tony broadcast that year—it was hosted by Hugh Jackman, about to open *The Boy from Oz* playing gay songwriter Peter Allen; the gay baseball play *Take Me Out* (with full frontal nudity) won best play; gay playwright and actor Harvey Fierstein won the best actor in a musical award; and when Shaiman and Wittman won for best score, Shaiman said to Wittman, defiantly into the microphone, "We're not allowed to get married in this world, but I'd like to declare in front of all these people, I love you and I'd like to live with you the rest of my life." Out of eight million viewers, only seventy-eight people complained to CBS. The world was changing.

Ben Brantley in the *New York Times* had some mild reservations about the show, but he wrote, "Like *The Producers*, *Hairspray* succeeds in recreating the pleasures of the old-fashioned musical comedy without seeming old-fashioned. Think of it, if you insist on such nomenclature, as a post-postmodern musical. It's a work that incorporated elements of arch satire, kitsch and camp—all those elements that ruled pop culture for the past several decades—but without the long customary edges of jadedness and condescension." Lots of comparisons were made with *The Producers* (Thomas Meehan co-wrote both scripts), and many critics thought *Hairspray* didn't quite measure up in laughs or inventiveness; but arguably, *Hairspray* is a more mature show because it has a point of view. Maybe *The Producers* delivered more belly laughs, but it was essentially a one-joke show, a show that really didn't have anything to say, and most of its laughs played to its audiences' nastier inclinations.

Hairspray never shared that smartass wink with its audience; *Hairspray* genuinely believed what it was saying. It was as good-intentioned and sincere as its leading lady without being sticky sweet, its big, generous heart reminding many people of the recent, more modestly scaled *Bat Boy*. Brantley ended his review by saying, "For *Hairspray* is, above all, Nice. This may be regarded as faint praise in New York, capital of Type A personalities. But Nice, in this instance, doesn't mean bland. Think of it spelled out in neon, perhaps in letters of purple and fuchsia. That's the kind of Nice that *Hairspray* is selling. And it feels awfully good to pretend, for as long as the cast keeps singing, that the world really is that way."

2003 also brought with it a shimmering new surprise that fully embodied the musical theatre's new life. As John Lahr wrote in the *New Yorker*, "Once upon a time in the early sixties, the composer Mary Rodgers suggested to her gloomy father, the composer Richard Rodgers, that he adapt for Broadway Elizabeth Spencer's novella *The Light in the Piazza*; the great man demurred. Four decades later, however, Mary Rodgers's son, the gifted composer and lyricist Adam Guettel, took up the challenge."

Adam Guettel, who had thrilled musical theatre lovers with his masterpiece *Floyd Collins* and his song cycle *Saturn Returns*, began working on *The Light in the Piazza* in 1999, inspired by the idea of writing a love story, consciously rejecting the new trend of self-referential, self-mocking, postmodern musicals. "The goal," he said at the time, "is to make the audience feel like they're in love or desperately want to be in love. . . . I want people to feel that feeling for those two hours." After abortive collaborations with playwrights Alfred Uhry and Arthur Laurents and after trying to write the script himself, Guettel finally joined forces with playwright and director Craig Lucas in 2001. Guettel and Lucas worked on *The Light in the Piazza* at the Sundance Playwrights Retreat in Wyoming. Seattle's Intiman Theatre helped develop *The Light in the Piazza* in a workshop in New York City in February of 2003 and entered into an agreement with the Goodman Theatre to co-produce the musical. The show premiered at the Intiman in the summer of 2003 and audiences quickly fell under its spell. After a run at the Goodman, it opened in New York and was nominated for a whopping eleven Tonys, winning six, including best score.

As it ran at the Goodman, critic John Lahr wrote, "Guettel's music and lyrics take nothing from the razzle-dazzle bargain basement of feeling; they represent, instead, a genuine expanse of spirit. Rather than selling a cheap-and-cheerful redemption, the show offers only the prospect of repair. *The Light in the Piazza* doesn't just want to make theatregoers feel good; it wants to make them feel deeply. This it does, and that is why, despite the show's quality, I suspect that the swamis of the rialto will pass on bringing it to Broadway. Still, Guettel's kind of talent cannot be denied. He shouldn't change for Broadway; Broadway, if it is to survive as a creative theatrical force, should change for him." Lincoln Center Theatre did bring the show to Broadway, but Lahr was right. The keepers of Broadway's flame had to make a decision as the new millennium got underway: was Broadway to become merely a tourist's theme park or was it to return to its roots as the artistic center of the musical theatre universe?

On a much sassier note, *Avenue Q* opened off Broadway in March 2003, then moved uptown. With music and lyrics by Robert Lopez and Jeff Marx and a book by Jeff Whitty, this intelligent musical comedy told the story of a charmingly dysfunctional outer-borough New York neighborhood whose twenty-something residents (including TV child star Gary Coleman, played by a woman) deal with everyday challenges like getting a job, finding an apartment, facing their own prejudices, and discovering that ever elusive purpose in life.

The unusual aspect of the show was that it was performed both with human actors and large puppets—one named Lucy T. Slut—that looked suspiciously like the residents of *Sesame Street*. It was in a very real sense a children's TV show for adults, live on stage. With songs like "Everyone's a Little Bit Racist," "If You Were Gay," "The Internet Is for Porn," and "It Sucks to Be Me," this was definitely an adult musical. In fact the message of "Everyone's a Little Bit Racist," that people don't always recognize their own racism, brought to mind Oscar Hammerstein's unintentionally racist lyrics and dialogue over the years and also the more recent flak over the unconsciously racist lyric in the opening number in Disney's *Aladdin*. Whitty said in an *American Theatre* interview, "We met with an older composer who told us we had to justify why we have puppets in the show. But anyone who was a kid from 1969 on grew up with puppets interacting with humans. For us, it's the most natural thing in the world." After the move uptown to Broadway, some commentators wondered aloud if *Avenue Q* could have done so if *The Lion King* hadn't come first and opened Broadway's collective mind to the idea of puppets in a Broadway musical.

Ben Brantley, in the *New York Times*, said, "*Avenue Q*, which opened last night at the Vineyard Theater, does indeed take its stylistic cues from *Sesame Street*, from its cheery urban streetscape to its singing puppets of assorted colors and dispositions. But don't be deceived. This canny toy chest of a show, a co-production of the Vineyard and the New Group, is the first mainstream musical since *Rent* to coo with such seductive directness to theatregoers on the fair side of forty in their own language." He went on to say, "For such demi-adults, irony is less a mind-set than a loosely worn style. *Avenue Q* may apply the coaxing, learning-is-fun attitude of children's educational television to the R-rated situations of post-collegiate life in the big city. But theatregoers who grew up from the late 1960s onward will instantly grasp the show's wistful and affectionate sincerity as well as its thorny humor."

Peter Marks wrote in the *Washington Post*, "*Avenue Q* is an encouraging event for the American musical. Just as shows of the past exploited the popular forms and musical styles of their day—from the operettas of the 1920s to the rock operas of the 1970s—this one adapts the format and sound of a genre with which millions of potential ticket-buyers (in this case, the boomer and Gen-X populations) are intimately familiar. From the instant *Avenue Q* begins, with a sunny theme song blaring from a pair of TVs, and the lights coming up on the charmingly shabby brownstones of Anna Louizos' urban set, we know exactly what street in Public Television Land the writers have in mind."

During its off Broadway run, the show won the 2003 Lucille Lortel Award for outstanding musical and outstanding sound design, and five Drama Desk nominations including best musical, best music, best lyrics, best book, and best actress in a musical (Stephanie D'Abruzzo). It was also nominated for the Outer Critics Circle Award for outstanding off Broadway musical. On Broadway, it won Tonys for best musical, best book, and best score. Unfortunately, due to a deal with a Las Vegas producer, the rights for the show were tied up for years, preventing any other theatre companies or artists from exploring and performing the show, a real shame for both audiences and the show itself—especially as the Las Vegas production closed quickly.

The 2002–2003 Broadway season broke new box office records, but largely because of higher ticket prices. Attendance actually *decreased* by about half a million people. Meanwhile, all hell was breaking loose on Broadway. Anticipating a musicians strike in March 2003, almost every musical on Broadway was rehearsing with a "virtual orchestra," an electronic synthesizing system that somewhat realistically reproduced the sound of a live orchestra. There were two systems, Sinfonia and OrchExtra, both developed by Realtime Music Solutions. The computerized music would be supervised during performances by a nonunion conductor and a "tapper" who would hit a single computer key to keep time. In response to the news, the decision to strike became even more likely. What most of the public didn't know was that Broadway was already using this technology for some shows to "enhance" the sound of a live orchestra.

The strike happened on March 7. Eighteen of the twenty-six shows on Broadway were closed, and neither side was prepared to make concessions. After four days without Broadway musicals, New York City Mayor Michael Bloomberg had had enough. He summoned representatives of the producers and the musicians union to the mayor's mansion, and a deal was hammered out. Broadway reopened. But the whole drama made musicians around the country nervous. If the technology was now available, how much longer would live orchestras be around? With production costs rising faster and faster, how long would it be before computers would be playing that famous overture from *Gypsy*?

The most unlikely hit of Broadway's 2004–2005 season was the genre-busting ensemble musical *The 25th Annual Putnam County Spelling Bee* (usually just nicknamed *Spelling Bee*). In 2002, a group of actors under the direction of Rebecca Feldman had created an audience-participation improv show called *C-R-E-P-U-S-C-U-L-E*, about a bunch of preteen brainiacs at a spelling bee. One of the actors was a nanny for playwright Wendy Wasserstein, who came to see it and loved it; she thought it should be a musical and suggested the actors contact composer William Finn, who was teaching musical theatre composition at New York University and who might be able to suggest a hot young song-writer. Instead, when Finn saw the show, he decided *he* wanted to write the score and he brought director James Lapine along for the ride.

The show changed greatly as it developed, and when it was ready for an audi-ence, Finn called his buddy Julianne Boyd, artistic director of Barrington Stage Company. In January 2004, a workshop of *Spelling Bee* was staged at Barrington, with a new script by Rachel Sheinkin, based on the improv show, that was fol-lowed by a full production there in summer 2004. The critics and audiences loved it, so the show moved on, this time to off Broadway's Second Stage, opening there in January 2005 for a sold-out run. It transferred to Circle in the Square for a Broadway run in May, and was nominated for six Tony Awards, winning two for best book and best actor (Dan Folger).

In the *New York Times*, Charles Isherwood wrote, "It's the more private but enduring triumphs—the connection finally made with a member of the oppo-site sex, the discovery of previously unknown pockets of self-esteem—that are really being celebrated in *Spelling Bee*. . . . William Finn's score sounds plumper and more rewarding than it did off Broadway. If it occasionally suggests a Sat-urday morning television cartoon set to music by Stephen Sondheim, that's not inappropriate. And Mr. Finn's more wistful songs provide a nice sprinkling of sugar to complement the sass in Rachel Sheinkin's zinger-filled book. Ms. Sheinkin sets off a new comic firecracker every time a contestant furrows a brow and asks to hear a word used in a sentence, in accordance with the rigid bee rules: 'Sally's mother told her it was her cystitis that made her special'."

Spelling Bee is a fascinating character study, utterly ignoring conventional narrative structure, spinning off into wild, funny, touching fantasies and inter-ruptions between the ever present pressure of the uniquely American spelling bee, giving us deep insights not only into the lives and personalities of the com-petitors, but also into the American need to compete, to be the best, to excel beyond those around us. It all adds up to a character study of America, just as *Assas-sins* and *Ragtime* did before it, asking us why spelling bees even exist, why every-thing in our culture *must* be a competition. Like *You're a Good Man, Charlie Brown*, *Spelling Bee* puts adults on stage playing children, but making it clear that the show isn't *really* about children; it's about *us*, every one of us. And Finn's score, even more offbeat, more expressionistic, more skillfully fragmented than his earlier work, also carried the show into new musical territory. But *Spelling Bee* worried many Broadway traditionalists who feared that the old-fashioned, Rodgers and Hammerstein model would soon disappear entirely from the Great White Way. And maybe it will.

In October 2004, another fascinating experiment in musical theatre had opened at the La Jolla Playhouse in California, the thrilling *Jersey Boys*, with a book by Marshall Brickman and Rick Elice, music by Bob Gaudio, lyrics by Bob Crewe, direction by Des McAnuff, and pitch-perfect choreography by Sergio Trujillo. This was the story of the 1960s pop group The Four Seasons, using their music to tell their story. It was a "catalog musical," like *Mamma Mia!* and others, building the story around a group's preexisting songs. But this was the first genuinely *mature* catalog musical, and it seemed to many that this relatively new form was finally finding its voice as a legitimate genre of musical theatre. Here the book did not contort itself to accommodate the songs; instead the book and music entwined around each so organically it seemed as if these songs had been written for this show.

More than any other catalog musical we had yet seen, this script boasted insightful, complex, sophisticated, deeply emotional writing. And the music in the show almost never stopped, more than thirty songs used in so many different, interesting ways, reminding us of the best of the Sondheim shows. The songs were sometimes just musical fragments, sometimes background music, sometimes moments of fantasy or memory, sometimes ironic Brechtian commentary. We saw "performances" of songs in clubs or concerts, but we also saw songs being written, rehearsed, and recorded. But what was most remarkable about the show was its very conception. This time, the *music* was telling the story of the *music!* Very few other musicals that have come before were this truly and entirely about the life force and emotion and power of music and its effect on people, its ability to reflect, to mourn, to celebrate, to illuminate. (*Avenue X* comes to mind. *The Sound of Music* doesn't.)

The show was an authentic home run and it opened on Broadway in November 2005 to cheering audiences and great reviews. All the critics raved about John Lloyd Young, an overnight Broadway star thanks to this show, in the role of Frankie Valli. But significantly, many of the critics were surprised by the excellence of the script. Clive Barnes' review in the *New York Post* was headlined, "Too Good to Be True," and he wrote, "It's a Broadway commonplace that the most important thing about a musical is the book—but no one goes out singing the book, so it's a commonplace often forgotten. Then comes a show like *Jersey Boys*, with a book that's as tight and absorbing as an Arthur Miller play. . . . It's a show still dynamically alive in music while, as a drama, it catches the very texture, almost the actual smell, of its time." Linda Winer of *Newsday* wrote, "Unlike the dim-bulb shows that use made-up stories as excuses to plug in hits by Elvis or the Beach Boys, this one is a straightforward biography of the group that defined a slick, street sound. Unlike the recent John Lennon bio, *Jersey Boys* doesn't get artsy with the material or overly selective about history. Nor is this a sanitized, glitz-revue in the tainted tradition of the long-running *Smokey Joe's Cafe*." *Jersey Boys* was nominated for eight Tony Awards and won four, including best musical, best book, and best direction. It was nominated for seven Drama Desk Awards and won two.

At the beginning of the twenty-first century, musical theatre as an art form is more vigorous and energized than ever, but Broadway is caught in a time warp of shallow, commercial safety, while big-money producers wait for the Next Big Thing. Historian Ethan Mordden has written of the current situation, "The artistry is that of a graffito artist, and the attitude that of a Kinko's clerk. And that's the new pop fun on Broadway." Others in the industry think he far overstates the doom and gloom, just as many before him have done.

The economic fallout from the terrorist attacks on September 11, 2001 continues, making us wait longer than we would have otherwise, just as the Great Depression did after *Show Boat*. But what will the next big thing be? And can we reasonably expect Broadway producers to recognize it when it appears? Will it be more intelligent, intimate work like *The Last Five Years* or *Bat Boy*? More artistically adventurous work like *The Light in the Piazza*? More nihilistic, postmodern stuff like *Urinetown*? Or more bland but safe shows like *Dirty Rotten Scoundrels*? There seem to be a lot of writers creating musicals that make fun of musicals these days. But the true artists right now—Adam Guettel, Larry O'Keefe, Jason Robert Brown, Jeanine Tesori, and others—are all working in different directions so anything could happen. Musical theatre really is changing. The Rodgers and Hammerstein revolution that began in 1943 is over now, and the more adventurous musical theatre artists are looking for new paradigms.

The pop opera has pretty much run out of steam, as evidenced by the closing of *Les Misérables* in May 2003, after 6,680 performances, leaving only *Phantom of the Opera* as the last dying breath of the British Invasion of the 1980s. One might think that that death will signal a return to character- and idea-driven musical theatre, rather than set- and orchestration-driven theatre, but that may not be true quite yet. After *Rent* opened, everyone thought it would start a revolution, with virtually no set, relatively pure pop music back on stage, a show all about pure storytelling and no spectacle. But very few shows followed that lead (although *Bat Boy* and *Urinetown* did), which is a surprise considering *Rent's* incredible success.

In 2005, Norman Lebrecht wrote about the new postmodern musicals in his online column, "The music in each of these shows amplifies this element of separation, licensing us to stand apart from what we are seeing and enter a third dimension where each of us can individually decide whether to take the plot literally or sardonically, whether to take offense or simply collapse in giggles. This degree of Ironic Detachment is the very making of the postmodern hit musical.

Ironic Detachment would be unattainable in a Tom Stoppard play because I.D. requires musical inflexion; it is impossible in opera and ballet, which are stiffened by tradition against self-mockery. Its application is unique to the musical comedy, an ephemeral entertainment which has found new relevance through its philosophical engagement with 21st century concepts of irony and alienation." But didn't *Of Thee I Sing, Guys and Dolls*, and other classics also traffic in Ironic Detachment?

Many new musicals are asking many new questions, as artists find their way in this new world. Must scenes in a musical follow in a "logical" sequence? Can a musical tell a story out of chronological order? Does it have to tell a linear story at all? Do scenes have to end with songs the way the Rodgers and Hammerstein model did? Do lyrics always have to rhyme? Must a show provide a clear resolution or answer at the end of the evening, or can it end by asking more questions? And further, what can we learn about communicating stories, issues, and concepts from television and movies, music videos, talk radio, modern dance, performance art, improvisation, and of course, cyberspace? How can we follow the lead of developing technology by making musical theatre truly interactive? Or conversely, can we shed all the trappings of technology and go back to the basics of the empty stage? Did *Hair* teach us some important lessons that we ignored? Is *Hair* still just as revolutionary and convention shattering as it was in 1967, for the simple reason that we didn't learn its lessons and carry its experiments forward?

Of course, just as with any big successes, the new musicals that are moving musical theatre in a new direction, shows like *Bat Boy* and *Urinetown*, are the victims of indiscriminate copycats. Lesser, new "shock musicals" have been popping up in New York, with titles like *Menopause: The Musical, Boobs! The Musical, Debbie Does Dallas*, and others.

Another new development in musical theatre began in 2003 as Broadway musicals began to launch open-ended runs in Las Vegas casinos. *Mamma Mia!* opened there in February 2003, followed by the Queen musical *We Will Rock You* in August 2004, then *Avenue Q* in late 2005, and a thirty-five-million-dollar *Phantom of the Opera* in 2006. Unfortunately, most of these shows are being condensed to ninety minutes, so Vegas audiences are getting *Reader's Digest* versions. Meanwhile, the profits are enticing, with far lower stagehand salaries and other costs, ten performances a week instead of Broadway's eight, and therefore a much higher potential for profit, a sweet deal indeed.

But with Vegas producers tying up rights for extended periods, sometimes as long as fifteen years, it hurts regional touring houses and regional theatres producing local shows. The theatres around the country that house Broadway touring companies will now have a smaller menu of shows to choose from—and predictably, the most commercial of those shows are the ones most likely to be tied up in Las Vegas. Likewise, the regional theatres that produce their own shows will no longer be able to get production rights to these musicals, again limiting the variety of shows with that all-important "straight from Broadway" label. It will be interesting to see how this experiment turns out and how it affects other theatres around the country. Perhaps it will necessitate the development of more original work in regional theatres.

On the brighter side, in the fall of 2004, the New York Musical Theatre Festival was created "to celebrate the art form and bring together the wide array of artists, writers, producers, theatre companies, and audience members who have contributed to the city's thriving musical theatre scene." Running for a full month in venues throughout Manhattan, the festival included full productions of new musicals, readings, screenings of film musicals, and much more. The festival was created by Musical Theatre Works, the York Theatre Company, the National Alliance for Musical Theatre, Amas Musical Theatre, the Genesius Guild, BMI, ASCAP, and the National Music Theater Network, among other organizations.

And away from Broadway, in New York's alternative spaces and also in theatres across America, hip-hop musical theatre is finally taking hold. These are musicals that use some of the conventions of American musical theatre but the vocabulary and style of hip-hop. To some, hip-hop and musical theatre seem as mutually exclusive as musical theatre and rock and roll once seemed, but as we know from history, the rules of musical theatre are made to be broken. So what *is* a hip-hop musical? Well, like concept musicals, a hip-hop musical is different things to different people. But at its core, it uses some or all of the elements of hip-hop culture: rap, break dancing, graffiti, and DJing.

As just one example of many, two Jewish Canadians, Eli Batalion and Jerome Saibil, created the wildly successful *Job: The HipHop Musical*, updating the Biblical story, with God and the Devil transmogrified into the record label president J. Hoover (Jehovah) and vice president Lou Saphire (Lucifer). Saibil said in an interview, "The whole thing is done through hip-hop. It's sixty minutes of nonstop rapping over fresh beats. So it's a musical, but it's a hip-hop musical; and it's a musical, but it's also a Biblical tale." It opened in Canada, then moved down into the U.S. The *Vancouver Sun* called it "so fresh and inventive that this truly marks the dawn of a new era in musical theatre." Batalion and Saibil followed it up with an equally successful sequel, *Job II: The Demon of the Eternal Recurrence.*

And, as mentioned earlier, Rodgers and Hart's classic 1938 musical comedy *The Boys from Syracuse* was transformed in 2003, bridging the leap from old-fashioned musical comedy to new millennium hip-hop theatre. A hip-hop version of the show appeared at the London Fringe Festival in 2003 called *Da Boyz*. In December 2005, the New York Theatre Workshop opened a new hip-hop musical called *The Seven*, written by Will Power, based on a Greek tragedy by Aeschylus, with choreography by the famed modern dance choreographer Bill T. Jones. Once again, so many people are trying so many things that anything could happen. . . .

So what is the future of musical theatre? Some of the "experts" will tell you it's dying or dead, merely because it's not what it used to be. But the world has changed so much since George M. Cohan, even since Rodgers and Hammerstein, how could anyone expect a living art form to remain stagnant when the world is changing around it? It seems musical theatre is such a part of America's culture and history—even today—that it will probably never die. Though movies and television can provide something close to the experience of seeing a nonmusical drama or comedy, those forms cannot approximate the energy and magic of a live stage musical, so though nonmusicals are doing less and less well commercially on Broadway and on tour, musicals are doing better than ever. We need what only musicals can provide, their brashness, their unique ability to mix reality and unreality, and most important, their music, their emotional muscle. The same extreme emotionalism that made musicals less "cool" in the cynical 1980s and 90s makes them cool once again, even essential, in the new world of post–9/11 America, a time when public emotion is once again legitimate, even expected, and equally, in a world in which once again humans are asking many big unanswered questions about right and wrong, morality and immorality, who we are and how we are connected.

Today, we need music to tell our most important stories because words quite often *lie* in our culture, and the more skillful the lies become, the harder it is to recognize them. But music can't lie; you always know what it's saying, even without words.

If music has charms to soothe the savage breast—*and it does*—then aren't these times in which we need, more than ever, to keep the music playing as we explore our individual and collective lives, as we tell our national story, as we tease out the complexities of being alive?

Index

Aarons, Alex, 21
Abbott, George, 38–39, 43, 45
Absolute Beginners, 76
Acting Company, The, 139
Action-blocs, 106
Actors' Equity, 40, 94, 175
Actors Studio (New York, NY), 150
Adams, Lee, 92–93
"Adelaide's Lament," 61
Adler, Richard, 91
Adrian, 86
Adventures of Pippin, The, 131
Aeschylus, 237
"Africa," 197
African Americans
    audiences, beginning of the end of segregated, 20
    black musicals (*see* Black musicals)
    laws against interracial marriage, striking down of, 91
    public schools, outlawing of segregated public schools, 52
    racism (*see* Racism)
    ragtime musicals and, 13
    seeing *The Lion King* as story of race, 209
"After the Ball," 28
"Aggie Song, The," 151
Agron, Salvador, 211–12
"Ah, Paris," 124
Ahrens, Lynn, 9, 184–85, 205, 210

Aida, 208
AIDS, 135
Ain't Supposed to Die a Natural Death: Tunes from Blackness, 123, 129–30, 131
Aladdin, 231
Alda, Robert, 62
Aldredge, Theoni V., 187
Aleichem, Sholom, 96
"Alfie," 112
"Alice Blue Gown," 16
"All Dressed Up (Spic and Spanish)," 43
Allegro, 57, 73
Allen, Jay Presson, 167
Allen, Peter, 229
Allen, Woody, 3, 77
All Shook Up, 199
All That Jazz, 144
"All Through the Night," 37
Altman, Robert, 3
Alton, Robert, 35, 45
"America," 69–70, 71
America (magazine), 120
American Bandstand, 228
American Beauty, 120
American Civil Liberties Union (ACLU), 70
American Idea, The, 10–11
American Music Theatre Festival (Philadelphia, PA), 168, 203
American Passion, 140
American Theatre, 1–2
    Adam Guettel interview, 204
    Ed Waterstreet interview, 227

Flower Drum Song review, 75
Japan, article on classic Broadway musicals in, 217
Jeanine Tesori interview, 197–98
Jeff Whitty interview, 231
Michael Greif interview, 200
Molly Smith interview, 3
Amherst Regional High School (MA), 70
"An American in Paris," 35
Anderson, Jonathan, 68
Anderson, Maxwell, 58–59
"And I'm Telling You I'm Not Going," 162
Andrews, Julie, 67
"And They're Off," 216
An Evening with Jerry Herman, 213
Animal Farm, 157
Anna and the King of Siam, 63
Annie, 7, 148–49
Annie du Far-West, 55
Annie Get Your Gun, 5, 44, 55, 142
"Annie Get Your Shogun," 217
Ann-Margret, 115, 151
Anthony, Marc, 212
Antigone, 156
Anyone Can Whistle, 83, 94–95, 96
Anything Goes, 35–37, 70
    about New Yorkers, 50

239

Anything Goes (*continued*)
  leading men in, 11
  on *Musical Comedy Time*, 60
  politics in, 5
  revisions, 37, 61
  revivals, 37, 44
"Anything Goes," 37
Apartment, The, 111–12
"Apology to a Cow," 1
Applause, 17, 138, 217
Apple Tree, The, 140
Approaches to the American Musical, 146
Araca Group, 219
Archibald, William, 54
Archy poems, 68
Arenal, Julie, 107
Arlen, Harold, 23, 124
Arnaz, Desi, 43
Aronson, Boris, 46
Around the World in Eighty Days, 57
Artaud, Antonin, 88
Artistic freedom, Broadway versus Hollywood, 37–38
Arts in Festival Prize (Japan), 160
Ashley, Christopher, 137
Ashman, Howard, 163, 164
Ashton, Frank, 79
Asian Americans
  casting Asians as Asians, problems with, 146–47
  upset by *Flower Drum Song,* 74–75
Askin, Peter, 193
Aspects of Love, 156, 172, 179–80
Assassins, 185–87, 212, 213
  audience allowed to participate, 115
  as brave show, 94
  as Brechtian, 29
  cancellation of all-star production after 9/11 attacks, 226
  The Cradle Will Rock as model for, 39–41
  as missing from golden age of musical theatre, 98
  musical styles to anchor scenes in time periods, use of, 25
  at Playwrights Horizons, 184

as pointing blame at audience, 144
as political, 5, 123, 146
as preparing audiences for extremity, 105
Astaire, Adele, 20, 21
Astaire, Fred, 20, 21, 38, 56
Atkinson, Brooks
  Anything Goes review, 38
  on *The Fantasticks,* 83
  on George M. Cohan, 10
  Love Life review, 57
  The Nervous Set review, 79
  West Side Story review, 71
Atlas, Charles, 135
Attempting the Absurd, 219, 220
At the Grand, 176, 177
Auden, W. H., 100
Audience Awards (Sundance Film Festival), 193
Avenue Q, 2, 4, 231–32, 236
Avenue X, 7–8, 180, 195–97
  as interesting theatre, 2
  National Music Theatre Conference, premiered at, 223
  power of music, as being about, 234
Avian, Bob, 141, 175

"Babalú," 43
Babes in Arms, 47, 50–51
Babes in Toyland, 12, 60
Babette, 12
Bacall, Lauren, 17
Bach, Johann S., 219
Bacharach, Burt, 111–12
Backstage, 208, 218
Back Stage West Garland Awards, 227
Bailey, Pearl, 17, 52, 93–94
Baker, Kenny, 60
Baker, Word, 82
Balanchine, George, 38, 46, 178
Baldwin, James, 52
Ballad of Little Mikey, The, 7–8, 180, 195
"Ballad of the Sad Young Men, The," 78
Ballet, integrated into Rogers and Hart story, 38

Ballet Russe, 38
Ballroom, 116–17
Bancroft, Anne, 84
Banderas, Antonio, 153, 164
Band Wagon, The, 41, 60
Baranski, Christine, 146
Barbeau, Adrienne, 126
"Barcelona," 119
Barnes, Clive, 102, 130
  Ain't Supposed to Die a Natural Death: Tunes from Blackness review, 130
  The Best Little Whorehouse in Texas review, 151
  Candide review, 134
  Jersey Boys review, 234
  Jesus Christ Superstar review, 127
  The Me Nobody Knows review, 122
  Pacific Overtures review, 147
  Rainbow review, 133
  on *The Rocky Horror Show,* 136–37
  Two Gentlemen of Verona review, 131
Barnes, Howard, 52
Barre, Gabriel, 223
Bart, Lionel, 81
Bart, Roger, 110, 224
Bartholomae, Philip, 14
Batalion, Eli, 237
Bat Boy: The Musical, 1, 2, 4, 180, 205–208, 214, 219, 224, 230, 235
  community in, 54
  copycats, as victim of, 236
  Little Shop of Horrors as inspiration for, 164
  9/11 attacks and, 208, 226
  traditional models, rejection of, 221–22
Battle, Hinton, 175
Baum, L. Frank, 12
Baum, Vicki, 176
Beach, Gary, 224
Beautiful Game, The, 172
"Beautiful Girls," 124
Beauty and the Beast, 180, 208, 217
"Beauty School Dropout," 125

Beckett, Samuel, 61
"Before the Parade Passes By," 92–93
Beggar's Opera, The, 28–29
"Being Alive," 119
Belafonte, Harry, 52
Believers, The, 110
Bells Are Ringing, 222
Belushi, James, 165
Bennett, Michael, 125, 182, 192
  Ballroom and, 116–17
  A Chorus Line and, 116–17, 141–43, 162
  Dreamgirls and, 116–17, 161, 162
  Follies and, 123, 162
  Promises, Promises and, 111
Benny, Jack, 93
Bentley, Eric, 30
Bergersen, Baldwin, 54
Berlin, Irving, 124
  Annie Get Your Gun and, 55
  patriotism and, 14–15
  revues as training ground, 18
  song style mastered by, 35
  Watch Your Step and, 13
Bernstein, Leonard, 23, 67, 78
  Candide and, 67, 68, 133
  The Cradle Will Rock and, 41
  on musical theatre, 5
  West Side Story and, 68, 69–71
Best Little Whorehouse Goes Public, The, 151
Best Little Whorehouse in Texas, The, 116–17, 149–51, 225
"Best Little Whorehouse in Texas, The," 150
"Better Than the Producers," 225
Betts, Doris, 197
"Bewitched," 45
B-52s, 219
Big Deal, 116–17, 156
Bigley, Isabel, 62
Big River, 168–69, 193, 227
Bilbo, Theodore, 56
Billboard Top 40 album charts, 71

Billington, Michael, 136
Birch, Patricia, 109, 122, 125
Birkenhead, Susan, 187, 205
Bizet, Georges, 51, 52
Black, Don, 227–28
Black, Jack, 73
Black and Blue, 202
Black Crook, The, 6
Blackface, 27
Black musicals
  Ain't Supposed to Die a Natural Death: Tunes from Blackness, 129–30
  The Believers, 110
  Brown Buddies, 32
  Cabin in the Sky, 46
  Carib Song, 54–55
  Carmen Jones, 51–52
  as commonplace in 1970s, 116
  Dahomey as first to play major theatre, 12
  Don't Bother Me, I Can't Cope, 121
  early all-black musicals, response to, 13
  Hallelujah, Baby!, 110
  Hello, Dolly!, 93, 94
  Jelly's Last Jam, 187–88
  Kwamina, 91
  Shuffle Along, 20
  The Song of Jacob Zulu, 188
Black Musical Theatre, 93–94
Blackwell, Billy, 138
Blades, Ruben, 212
Blaine, Vivian, 62, 63
Blake, Eubie, 19, 124
Blau, Eric, 110
Blaxploitation films, 129–30
Blitzstein, Marc, 30, 36, 102
  The Cradle Will Rock and, 39–41, 116
  Pins and Needles and, 42
  The Threepenny Opera and, 66
Blood Brothers, 128
"Blood Pressure," 61
Bloomberg, Michael, 232–33
"Blow, Gabriel, Blow," 35
Blyden, Larry, 74
"Boar's Tooth, A," 58

Bobbie, Walter, 145, 179
Bock, Jerry, 85–86, 96, 97, 223
Bolger, Ray, 38–39
Bollywood, 227–28
Bolton, Guy, 14, 15, 36, 37
Bombay Dreams, 227–28
Bond, Christopher, 154
Bon Voyage, 36
Boobs! The Musical, 236
Booth, John Wilkes, 186
Boston (dance), 19
Boston Post, 37
Bostwick, Barry, 126, 139
"Both Sides of the Coin," 169
Bottoms, Stephen, 102
Boublil, Alain, 158–59, 175
Bounce, 2, 123, 154
Bowie, David, 111, 135
Boyd, Julianne, 233
Boy from Oz, The, 229
Boy George, 135
Boys from Syracuse, The, 42–43, 50–51, 237
Boys in the Band, The, 138, 195
Bracken, Eddie, 68, 69
Bradley, Ian, 2
Brantley, Ben, 75
  Avenue Q review, 231–32
  The Capeman review, 213
  Floyd Collins review, 203
  Hairspray review, 229–30
  The Lion King review, 209
  The Wild Party review, 224
Brecht, Bertolt, 29, 144, 152, 176, 219
  Epic Theatre, 146
Brel, Jacques, 101, 111
Brennan, Eileen, 92
Brickman, Marshall, 234
Bricusse, Leslie, 180
Brigadoon, 7, 44, 54, 87, 104
Bright Lights, Big City, 2, 221
Bring Back Birdie, 156
Bring in 'da Noise, Bring in 'da Funk, 2, 201–202, 221
"Broadway Baby," 124
Broadway Musicals, 1
Broderick, Matthew, 224
Brook, Peter, 95, 96
Brook, The, 6

Brooks, Mel, 68–69, 220, 224–25
Brown, Jason Robert, 223, 235
  The Last Five Years and, 199, 225–26
  A New Brain and, 214
  shows involved with, list of, 199
  Songs for a New World and, 198–99
Brown, Lew, 124
Brown Buddies, 32
Bruce, Lenny, 77
Bruce, Thomas, 83
Brustein, Robert, 194
Brynner, Yul, 17, 63, 65
Buchen, Irving, 108
Buckley, Betty, 157
"Buddie Beware," 37
Buddy Deane Show, 229
"Buddy's Blues," 124
Bunraku theatre, 146
Burnett, Carol, 124
Burns, George, 93
Burrows, Abe, 60, 61, 88, 89
Burton, Richard, 67, 86
"Bus from Amarillo, The," 149
Butler, Michael, 107
Bye Bye Birdie, 76, 77, 116
Bygraves, Max, 81
By Jeeves, 172
"By My Side," 120

Cabaret, 7–8, 103–105, 120, 167, 179, 216
  audience becoming part of show in, 144
  aware of music, characters as being, 196
  as concept musical, 103
  conventional elements and edgy material, balance of, 140
  The Cradle Will Rock as model for, 39–41
  The Fantasticks as paving the way for, 83
  as making audience uncomfortable, 144
  as missing from golden age of musical theatre, 98
  as new kind of ultradark theatre, 75

parts of *Miss Saigon* as latter-day, 175
pieces of, in *Jekyll & Hyde*, 181
as political, 5
The Producers as referencing, 225
sex drives explored in, 50
as two-visit musical, 178
Cabin in the Sky, 46, 199
Caesar, Irving, 21
Cahoon, Kevin, 193
Caird, John, 159
Caldwell, Anne, 205
Calhoun, Jeff, 126, 227
Call Me Madam, 17, 62
Calloway, Cab, 17, 93–94
Camelot, 5, 67, 86–88, 218
Canby, Vincent, 69, 208
Candide, 67–68, 109, 133–34, 155
Candy, John, 165
"Can't Help Lovin' Dat Man," 27
Cantor, Eddie, 50, 124
Capalbo, Carmen, 66
Capeman, The, 188, 201, 211–14, 221–22
Capone, Al, 61
Carib Song, 54–55
Cariou, Len, 154
Carmen Jones, 51–52
Carmines, Al, 101–102
Carnival, 116, 145
Caroline or Change, 2, 187
Carousel, 48, 52–54, 57, 72, 179
  community groups performing, problems with, 7
  community in, 53–54
  complexity of real love in, 65
  foreign director, 64
  as frequently revived, 44
  as a Great American Musical, 210
  killing of hero, 78
  longing for shows like, 2
  looking at with fresh eyes, 99
  reality in, 53–54
  revisionist staging of production in 1990s, 73
  revival, 53

Sondheim on, 49
  staged as nonmusical, 52
"Carousel," 159
"Carousel Waltz," 53
Carradine, John, 69
Carreras, José, 70
Carroll, Diahann, 52, 90, 91
Carroll, Vinnette, 122
Carter, Nell, 107
Carver, Brent, 183
Castle, Irene, 13
Castle, Vernon, 13
Catalog musicals, 234
Cats, 7–8, 69, 128, 156–58, 159
  as commercial success, 170, 171
  developed in Great Britain, 86, 156
  iconic logo as marketing tool, 127
  in Japan, 217
  longevity, 84, 155, 158, 182
  as part of British chokehold of musical theatre in 1980s, 179–80
  reuse of music, 153
  similarities to *Miss Saigon*, 175
  similarities to *You're a Good Man, Charlie Brown*, 109
Cervantes, Miguel de, 99, 100
Cerveris, Michael, 155, 193
"Chain Store Daisy," 42
Champion, Gower, 190
  Bye Bye Birdie and, 116
  Carnival and, 116
  42nd Street and, 116–17
  Hello, Dolly! and, 91, 92, 93, 94, 116
  Mack and Mabel and, 140, 141
Channing, Carol, 68–69, 92, 93, 94
Channing, Stockard, 126
Chapman, John, 62, 68, 69, 89
Charisse, Cyd, 62
Charleston (dance), 19
Charlie Rose Show, The, 191
Charnin, Martin, 149
Chase, David, 75
Chayevsky, Paddy, 100

242

Cheater, 192
Chenoweth, Kristin, 110
Chess, 153, 156, 170, 175
Chicago, 36, 116–17,
    144–46
  acting in, 4
  aware of music, charac-
    ters as being, 196
  Bert Williams as inspira-
    tion for, 12
  as Brechtian, 29
  chorus doubling speaking
    roles, 143
  community groups
    performing, problems
    with, 7
  as concept musical, 104
  The Cradle Will Rock as
    model for, 39–41
  film version, 184
  as making audience
    uncomfortable, 144
  revivals, 179, 222
  as vaudeville, 57
Chicago Tribune, 145, 188,
    201
Chicken Ranch, The (La
    Grange, TX), 149
"Children, Children," 206
"Children and Art," 166
Childs, Barry, 138
China, dilemma of retain-
    ing culture and modern-
    izing, 63
Chocolate Soldier, The, 60
Chorus Line, A, 116–17,
    141–44, 155, 162, 163,
    202
  community groups
    performing, problems
    with, 7
  as concept musical, 104
  in Japan, 217
  longevity, 182
  as missing from golden
    age of musical theatre,
    98
  as nonlinear concept
    musical, 108
  The Producers as referenc-
    ing, 225
Cinderella legends, 16
City of Angels, 68
Civil War, 182
Clark, Hope, 187
Clark, Petula, 56

Clorindy, 6
Club, The, 147–48
Cobb, Lee J., 100
Cohan, George M., 60, 73
  as influence on Hammer-
    stein II, 26
  in invention of musical
    comedy, 10–12, 15
  musicals as genuinely
    new, 6
  New York setting of most
    shows, 50
  style of, 9, 14, 38
  talk-singing by, 67
Cole, Bob, 13
Cole, Jack, 101
Coleman, Cy, 103, 143
Coleman, Gary, 231
Coleman, Robert, 24, 57
Coleman, Shepard, 93
Collins, Judy, 111
Colvan, Zeke, 23
Comden, Betty, 110, 124,
    205
"Come and Be My Butter-
    fly," 92
Comedy of Errors, The, 42–43
"Come in My Mouth," 137
Commedia dell'arte, 82
Communism, 39, 40
Company, 1, 118–20, 131,
    179, 203, 216
  acting in, 4
  as Brechtian, 29
  called depressing by some
    critics, 57
  central plot, lack of, 138
  as character study, 186
  community in, 54
  as concept musical, 103,
    108, 116, 118
  dissonant, electrifying
    music in, 94–95
  The Fantasticks as paving
    the way for, 83
  as a Great American
    Musical, 210
  Lovers as having roots in,
    138
  as missing from golden
    age of musical theatre,
    98
  as nonlinear concept
    musical, 108
  as proof that audiences
    like what's good, 28

realism and, 3, 118–19
real-world story, 140
revival, 179
  as revolutionary, 119, 120
Complete Review, 96
Conaway, Jeff, 126
Concept musicals, 101,
    116
Condon, Bill, 146
Connick, John, 114
Contact, 50
Convy, Bert, 104
Cook, Barbara, 124
Cooke, Richard P., 109–10
Coppola, Francis Ford, 56
Cop Rock, 200
Corman, Roger, 164
Corsaro, Frank, 127
Cosby, Bill, 130
Covington, Julie, 152
Coward, Noel, 124
Cox, Harvey, 121
Cradle Will Rock, The, 1, 11,
    39–41
  acting in, 4
  as concept musical, 116
  as fact-based, 173
  ironic detachment in, 61
  as not escapist, 44
  reality in, 152
  as street smart, 148
Craig, Gordon, 105
Crawford, Michael, 94
Crawley, Brian, 197
Crazy for You, 70, 224
Creamer, Henry, 31
C-R-E-P-U-S-C-U-L-E, 233
Crewe, Bob, 234
Crivello, Anthony, 183
Crosby, Bing, 37, 200
Crosstown Bus, 140
Crouch, Stanley, 29
Crouse, Russel, 36
Crouse, Timothy, 37
Crowley, Bob, 213
Cryer, Gretchen, 205
Cuccioli, Robert, 181,
    182
Cue, 83–84
Cullet, Rhonda, 139
Cullum, John, 218
"Cunnilingus Champion of
    Company C, The," 137
Curry, Michael, 209
Curry, Tim, 107
Czolgosz, Leon, 186

Da Boyz, 43, 237
D'Abruzzo, Stephanie, 232
Da Costa, Morton, 73
Daffy Dill, 16
Daily Mail, 134
Daily Mirror, 24, 57
Daily News
    Candide review, 68
    Dreamgirls review, 162
    Floyd Collins review, 203
    Follies review, 124
    Guys and Dolls review, 62
    How to Succeed in Business Without Really Trying review, 89
    Kiss of the Spider Woman review, 184
    The Nervous Set review, 79
    Rainbow review, 133
    shinbone alley review, 69
    The Wild Party review, 224
Daltry, Roger, 30, 115
Daly, Tyne, 80
Damn Yankees, 44, 179, 199, 222
Dance
    emphasis on, 19
    as language, 49–50
"Dance: Ten, Looks: Three," 142
Dancin', 116–17, 145
Dandridge, Dorothy, 52
Daniele, Graciela, 117, 161, 184–85, 210
Dante, Nicholas, 141, 142–43
Darion, Joe, 68–69, 99, 100
da Silva, Howard, 42, 114
David, Hal, 111–12
David, Keith, 187
Davidson, Gordon, 227
Davis, Luther, 176
Davis, Ossie, 118, 130
Davis, Sammy Jr., 30
Day Well Spent, A, 91, 92
Dear World, 167
Death of a Salesman, 80
Debbie Does Dallas: The Musical, 222, 236
"Deeper in the Woods," 139
Deep Harlem, 31
DeHaven, Gloria, 60
De Koven, Reginald, 16
de Mille, Agnes, 48, 49–50, 52, 84, 178

Dench, Judi, 104
Desert Song, The, 17
Destry Rides Again, 78
DeSylva, B. G., 124
Dewhurst, Colleen, 100
DeYoung, Cliff, 107
Dickens, Charles, 168, 169, 170
Die 3groschenoper, 29–30
Diener, Joan, 101
Diggs, Taye, 146
Diller, Phyllis, 77, 93
Dillinger, John, 36
Dillingham, Charles, 13
Directing Awards (Sundance Film Festival), 193
Director-choreographer, 116–17
Dirtiest Show in Town, The, 161
Dirty Rotten Scoundrels, 222, 235
Disneyfication of Broadway, 180
Disney Studios, 12, 208, 210, 231
"Dixie," 11
"Doatsey Mae," 149
Doctorow, E. L., 210
Dodge, Jerry, 92
"Doing the Reactionary," 42
Doll, 140
Don Quixote, 99
Don't Bother Me, I Can't Cope, 117, 121, 130, 131
"Don't Leave Me," 111
Don't Play Us Cheap!, 112, 122–23, 130, 131
Doonesbury, 109, 156
Doyle, Arthur Conan, 68
Doyle, John, 155
Dr. Dolittle, 180
Drabinsky, Garth, 28, 183, 184, 210, 211
Drake, Alfred, 42
Drama Desk Awards, 122, 143
    Annie, 149
    Avenue Q, 232
    Bring in 'da Noise, Bring in 'da Funk, 202
    The Club, 148
    Floyd Collins, 204
    Grand Hotel, 177

Jersey Boys, 235
    The Last Five Years, 225
    Les Misérables, 160
    Miss Saigon, 175
    Rent, 191
    The Song of Jacob Zulu, 188
    Urinetown, 219
    The Wild Party, 224
Drama League Awards, 145, 191, 202
Dramatic Mirror, 15
Dramatic News, 13
Dramatists Toolkit, The, 53
Dreamgirls, 112, 128, 161–62
    based on *Supremes*, 76
    Harold Wheeler and, 116
    as two-visit musical, 178
Dream True: My Life with Vernon Dexter, 180, 217
Drood!, 170
Druten, John van, 63–64
Dude, 131, 134
Duke, Vernon, 46
Duncan, Todd, 46, 58, 59
Dunham, Katherine, 46, 54–55
Dunn, Mignon, 68
Dunne, Irene, 27, 63
Dunning, Jennifer, 178
Dunnock, Mildred, 82
Dupont Show of the Month, 100
Duquesnay, Ann, 187, 202

Easton, Sheena, 101
East Side Story, 69
East West Players (Los Angeles, CA), 216–17
"Easy to Love," 37
Ebb, Fred
    Cabaret and, 179
    Chicago and, 144, 145, 184
    Kiss of the Spider Woman and, 182, 183
    The Rink and, 156
    sociological insights in work of, 9
Eder, Linda, 180, 181
Eder, Richard, 154–55
Edward II, 139
Edwards, Sherman, 113
Eichmann, Adolph, 97
8½, 163

*Einen Jux Will er Sich
    Machen*, 91
Eisenhauer, Peggy, 202
"Elegance," 92–93
Elice, Rick, 234
Eliot, T. S., 156, 157
Ellis, Joan, 151
El Teatro Campesino, 152
Emmy Awards, 51
Emotionalism, 1–2
Encores! Series, 46, 145
English National Opera,
    147
Environmental theatre, 134
"Epiphany," 1
Espresso Bongo, 75–77, 116
"Espresso Party," 76
*Essay on the Principles of
    Population*, 218
Euphoria, 207
Evangeline, 6
Evans, Greg, 213
"Everyone's a Little Bit
    Racist," 231
Everything's Ducky, 112
Evigan, Greg, 126
Evita, 128, 129, 152–54
    as commercial success,
        170
    community in, 54
    iconic logo as marketing
        tool, 127
    in Japan, 217
    odd time signatures, use
        of, 158
    pieces of, in *Jekyll &
        Hyde*, 181
Eyen, Tom, 161, 162

Fagan, Garth, 209
Falsettoland, 161
Falsettos, 161, 214, 215–16
Fanny Hackabout Jones, 183
Fantasticks, The, 81–84,
    145, 172, 216
    as beat musical, 62–63,
        68
    in Japan, 217
    longevity, 143
Farley, Keythe, 4, 205, 207
"Fascinating Rhythm," 21
Faust, 88, 164, 199–201
Feast of Fools, 121
Federal Theatre Project,
    39–41
"Feels Like Home, 201

Feldman, Rebecca, 233
"Fellatio 101," 137
Fellini, Federico, 103, 163
"(Fe)Male Schauvinst Pigs,"
    148
Fenton, James, 159
Ferber, Edna, 23
Ferry, Bryan, 135
Festival of New Musicals
    (National Alliance of
    Musical Theatres), 216,
    223
Feuer, Cy, 62, 89
Fiddler on the Roof, 17, 70,
    85, 96–98
    about tradition, 149, 215
    in golden age of musical
        theatre, 98
    longevity, 155
Field, Ron, 104
Fields, Dorothy, 103, 205
Fields, Herbert, 23, 74
Fields, Joseph, 74
"Fie on Goodness," 87
Fierstein, Harvey, 167, 229
Fifty Miles from Boston,
    10–11
Finalletos, 34
*Fings Ain't Wot They Used
    T'Be*, 75, 80–81
Finian's Rainbow, 55–56,
    81–82, 148
    as frequently revived, 44
    leading men in, 11
    as political, 5
    revival, 56
Finley, Mark, 138
Finn, William, 160–61,
    214–16, 233–34
Fiorello!, 78, 85, 146
Firmat, Gustavao Péres, 43
Fisher, Jules, 107, 202
Fitzgerald, F. Scott, 35–36
Flaherty, Stephen, 184–85,
    210
Flanagan, Hallie, 39, 41
Flemming, Brian, 205, 207
Flicker, Theodore, 77
Flower Drum Song, 58, 68,
    74, 146, 222
Floyd Collins, 180, 203–204,
    230
    emotion in, 1, 214
    as interesting theatre, 2
    spectacles of the 1980s,
        rejection of, 185

traditional models, rejec-
        tion of, 222
Flying High, 60
"Fo' Dolla," 58
Folger, Dan, 233
Follies, 117, 123–25, 143,
    162, 202, 216
    about changes in people's
        lives, 211
    audience allowed to par-
        ticipate, 115
    as Brechtian, 29
    as character study, 186
    as concept musical,
        103
    as important show, 131
    as missing from golden
        age of musical theatre,
        98
    as nonlinear concept
        musical, 108
    The Producers as referenc-
        ing, 225
Fontanne, Lynn, 57
Footloose: The Musical, 213,
    222
Ford, Nancy, 205
Fornes, Maria Irene, 102
Forrest, George, 176
Forsythe, Henderson, 151
*Forty-Five Minutes from
    Broadway*, 10–11
42nd Street, 116–17, 125,
    145, 190, 217
Fosse, Bob, 84, 178
    All That Jazz and, 144
    Big Deal and, 116–17
    Cabaret and, 104
    Chicago and, 116–17,
        144–45
    conceptual work, criti-
        cism of, 2
    Dancin' and, 116–17,
        145
    *How to Succeed in Busi-
        ness Without Really Try-
        ing* and, 89
    Little Me and, 111
    Pal Joey and, 45–46
    Pippin and, 116–17,
        131–33
    Promises, Promises and,
        111
    Redhead and, 116
    Sweet Charity and,
        102–103, 111, 116

Foster, Paul, 121
"Four Little Angels of
    Peace," 42
Four Seasons, The, 234
1491, 72
Fowler, Beth, 155
Fox, Maxine, 125
Foxtrot, 19
Frankenstein, 27
Franklin, Nancy, 124–25
"Frank Mills," 137
Fratti, Mario, 163
Frazee, Harry, 21, 22
Freedley, Vinton, 21, 36
Freedman, Gerald, 107,
    125, 139
Friedman, Gary William, 122
Friedman, Peter, 211
Friml, Rudolph, 124
Fuller, Larry, 153
Full Monty, The, 112, 222
"Fun Life," 79
Funny Girl, 79, 94
*Funny Thing Happened on
    the Way to the Forum,
    A*, 94, 216
Furth, George, 3, 118–19

Gabriel, Gilbert, 33
Gaines, Reg E., 202
Galati, Frank, 210
Gallagher, Peter, 46, 107
Ganz, Lowell, 173
Gardella, Tess, 25
Gardenia, Vincent, 165
Gardner, Rita, 83
Garrison, David, 201
Gaudio, Bob, 234
Gaxton, William, 34, 35, 36
Gay, John, 28–29
Gay Divorce, 35
Gay Theater Alliance, 138
Geffen, David, 165
Geld, Gary, 118
Gennaro, Peter, 71, 149
Gentlemen Prefer Blondes, 5
George M, 11
George Washington Jr., 10–11
George White's Scandals, 18
Gere, Richard, 126, 146
Germany
    in invention of musical
        theatre, 6
    Threepenny Opera in,
        29–30
    in World War I, 14–15

Gershwin, George, 23,
    32–35, 124
Girl Crazy and, 33, 35
Lady, Be Good and,
    20–21
Let 'Em Eat Cake and, 35
New York setting of
    shows, 50
patriotism and, 14–15
political musicals, 32
Porgy and Bess and, 46
revues as training ground,
    18
Strike Up the Band and,
    32, 34
Of Thee I Sing and, 33–35
Gershwin, Ira, 32–35, 124
artistic freedom in New
    York, 37–38
Girl Crazy and, 33, 35
invented words to make
    rhymes, 25–26
Lady, Be Good and, 20
Lady in the Dark and, 23,
    47
Let 'Em Eat Cake and, 35
New York setting of
    shows, 50
patriotism and, 14–15
political musicals, 32
Porgy and Bess and, 46
Pulitzer Prize–winner, 33
revues as training ground,
    18
Strike Up the Band and,
    32, 34
Of Thee I Sing and, 33–35
word mangling and
    rhyme twisting by, 56
Gesamtkunstwerk, 4
Gesner, Clark, 109
"Getting to Know You," 64
Geva, Tamara, 38
Giering, Jenny, 223
Gigi, 87
Gilbert, Willie, 88
Gilbert, W. S., 32, 34
Gilford, Jack, 60, 104
Ginsberg, Allen, 77, 79
Girl Crazy, 33, 35, 50
Girl Happy, 43
"Girl I Left Behind, The,"
    11
"Girl That I Marry, The," 5
"Give It Back to the Indi-
    ans," 43

"Give My Regards to Broad-
    way," 10–11
Glass Menagerie, The, 80
Gleason, Jackie, 22–23, 60
"Glory," 132
Glover, Savion, 187,
    202–203
Glynn, Carlin, 151
Goblin Market, 223
Godspell, 120–21, 123, 131,
    159, 216
    built on experiments of
        Hair, 121
    hybrid "Broadway pop"
        music, as being, 128
Goethe, Johann von, 164,
    199–200
Goldberg, Whoopi, 174
Golden Age of musical the-
    atre, debate over, 18, 98
Golden Boy, 91
Golden Globe Awards, 152
Goldman, James, 117, 123
Gone with the Wind, 217
Goodbye to Berlin, 104–105
Good Morning, Dearie, 16
"Goodnight My Someone,"
    73
"Good Ol' Girl," 149
Gordon, Ricky Ian, 217,
    223
Gospel at Colonus, The, 168
Gottfried, Martin, 1, 104,
    113, 119, 149
Goulet, Robert, 84, 86
Governor's Son, The, 10
Grable, Betty, 93
Grammy Awards, 89, 160,
    162
Grand, The, 176
Grand Guignol style, 154
Grand Hotel, 116–17,
    162–63, 176
Grant, Cary, 67
Grant, Micki, 122, 205
Grease, 116, 125–26, 155
    as important show, 131
    longevity, 98
    revival, 179
    similarities to *Miss
        Saigon*, 175
"Greased Lightning," 125
Great American Musical
    (first), 23–24, 28
Great Britain
    American musicals as

overshadowing British musicals, 4–5
in invention of musical theatre, 6
Great Depression, 32, 34, 148
Show Boat, effect of the Great Depression on, 26, 31
Works Progress Administration (WPA) during the, 39
WW II as rescuing economy from the, 44
"Great Theatre Debates: The American Musical Has Entered a New Golden Age," 221
Greeks, classical
characters talking to audience, 10
music used in theatre by, 5
Green, Adolph, 110, 124
Greene, Ellen, 165
Greene, Schuyler, 14
Green Grow the Lilacs, 47
Greenwich Village Follies, The, 18
Greif, Michael, 190, 200, 201
Grey, Joel, 17, 104, 145
Grimes, Tammy, 69
Grind, 156
Groener, Harry, 157
Grotwoski, Jerzy, 205
Grove Dictionary of Music and Musicians, 7
Guardian, The, 136
Guare, John, 130, 131
Guest, Christopher, 165
Guettel, Adam, 23, 223, 235
Floyd Collins and, 203–204, 230
The Light in the Piazza and, 230–31
Saturn Returns and, 230
Guevara, Che, 153
Guinan, Texas, 36
Gulf War, 185, 186
Gunton, Bob, 155
Gussow, Mel, 137, 191–92
Guthrie, Tyrone, 67, 68
Guthrie, Woody, 56

Guy, Rosa, 184
Guys and Dolls, 60–63, 80, 89
as classic musical, 61
as frequently revived, 44
as integrated musical, 61–62
ironic detachment of, 236
leading men in, 11
politics in, 5
revival, 63, 196
Guzmán, Josie de, 71–72
Gypsy, 78, 79–80, 94, 154, 162, 228

"Hail, Hail, The Gang's All Here," 34
"Hail to the Chief," 185
Hair, 1, 82, 107–109, 111, 112, 152, 202
audience allowed to participate, 115
authors, 133
born out of alternative theatre, 136
as changing the rules, 108, 110, 125
community in, 54
as concept musical, 108, 122, 125
The Cradle Will Rock as model for, 39–41
directors, 107–108, 127, 139
as fact-based, 173
Godspell as building on, 121
as a Great American Musical, 210
lessons from, 236
lost best-musical Tony award to *Promises, Promises,* 113
low-tech approach borrowed by *Once on This Island,* 115
mining of alternative theatre community, 191
as missing from golden age of musical theatre, 98
as new kind of ultradark theatre, 75
as nonlinear, 122
nudity, 96, 108

as political, 5, 130
productions not sticking to text, 106
Two Gentlemen of Verona as building on themes from, 130
Hairspray, 2, 149, 228–29
influenced by *Little Shop of Horrors,* 164
as political, 5
"Hakuna Matata," 209
Hall, Adelaide, 32
Hall, Carol, 149, 150, 205
Hall, Juanita, 74
Hallelujah, Baby!, 110, 216
Hamlisch, Marvin, 141
Hammerstein, Oscar, I, 13
Hammerstein, Oscar, II, 46, 49, 51, 73, 221–22
Allegro and, 57, 73
Annie Get Your Gun and, 55
Carmen Jones and, 51–52
Carousel and, 52–54, 57, 65, 73
death of, 89–90
emotion in productions, 9
Fiddler on the Roof in style of Rodgers and Hammerstein, 97, 98
Flower Drum Song and, 73–75
imitations, 55
The King and I and, 46, 63–66
lyrics, style of, 25–26
Me and Juliet and, 73
musical theatre as art form of, 6
Oklahoma! and, 11, 47–49, 51, 52, 57, 65, 73
Pipe Dream and, 73
revolution, end of, 83
rule breaking by, 23, 53–54
Show Boat and, 24–26, 27
South Pacific and, 46, 57–58, 65, 73
teaming with Richard Rodgers, 44, 47–48, 165
unintentional racist lyrics, 231
Urinetown as fitting Rodgers and Hammerstein model, 218

Hammond, John, 52
Haney, Carol, 74
"Happiness," 109
"Happy Birthday," 5
Harbach, Otto, 21, 124
Harburg, E. Y., 55, 56, 124
Hard to Get, 36
Hardwick, Elizabeth, 96
Hardy, Joseph, 109
Hardy, Oliver, 12
Harlem Renaissance, 20
Harnick, Sheldon, 96, 97
Harper, Wally, 176
Harper's Bazaar, 191
Harrigan 'n Hart, 156
Harris, Richard, 30
Harrison, Rex, 63, 67
Hart, Charles, 170–71
Hart, Larry, 14, 49, 124, 165
    artistic freedom in New York, 37–38
    The Boys from Syracuse and, 42–43, 237
    The Comedy of Errors and, 42–43
    death of, 51
    declined to work on *Oklahoma!*, 47
    Hollywood, disenchantment with, 37–38
    leaving of, by Richard Rodgers, 44
    Love Me Tonight and, 50
    New York setting of shows, 50
    Pal Joey and, 44–45, 46
    patriotism and, 14–15
    Peggy-Ann and, 23
    revues as training ground, 18
    Too Many Girls and, 43
    word mangling and rhyme twisting by, 25–26, 56
    On Your Toes and, 38–39
Hart, Moss, 23, 47, 86
Hart, Teddy, 43
Hasselhoff, David, 182
Hauptmann, Elizabeth, 29
Hauptmann, William, 168–69
Have a Heart, 15–16
Haworth, Jill, 104
Hayworth, Rita, 46
Heading East, 216

Hearing-impaired people, productions for, 227
Hearn, George, 124, 154
Hedwig and the Angry Inch, 1, 2, 180, 192–93
    aware of music, characters as being, 196
    as missing from golden age of musical theatre, 98
    as proving that movie musicals can work, 222–23
    traditional model of content and themes, rejection of, 221–22
    traditional model of naturalism and fourth wall, rejection of, 222
Helburn, Theresa, 47
Helen Hayes Awards, 160
Helix, 114
Hellman, Lillian, 67, 68
Hello, Dolly!, 7–8, 91–94, 116, 140, 167
    community groups performing, 7
    in Japan, 217
    Lovers as having roots in, 138
"Hello, Dolly," 92
Hemingway, Ernest, 35–36
Hemsley, Sherman, 118
Henderson, Luther, 187
Henderson, Ray, 124
Heneker, David, 75–76, 76
Henley, Don, 200
Henner, Marilu, 126
Hepburn, Audrey, 67
Herald-Tribune, 31, 69, 80, 83
Herbert, Victor, 12–13
Here's Love, 72
Herman, Jerry, 172
    Hello, Dolly! and, 92–93, 140
    in *Hello, Dolly!*, 91
    La Cage aux Folles and, 167
    Mack and Mabel and, 140–41
    Mame and, 140
    Milk and Honey and, 92, 140
High Society, 205, 213
Highway to Glory, 100

Hines, Gregory, 187
Hip-hop, musical theatre and, 237
Hirson, Roger, 131, 132
His Lady Friends, 21
Hit the Deck, 60
Holder, Donald, 209
Holliday, Jennifer, 162
Hollmann, Mark, 218–19
Holloway, Stanley, 67
Hollywood Reporter, The, 152
Holm, Hanya, 57
Holmes, Rupert, 169–70
Holt, Will, 122
Homosexuality, and the theatre, 195
Honeymooners, The, 10–11
Hoover, Herbert (president, U.S.), 34–35, 105, 148
Hopkins, Kaitlin, 207
Horizon, 94
Horne, Lena, 110
Hot Mikado, The, 51
"Hot Time in the Old Town Tonight," 28
Houseman, John, 39, 40, 42, 139
"How Are Things in Glocca Mora," 56
"How Glory Goes," 1
How to Succeed in Business Without Really Trying, 88–89, 179
Huckleberry Finn, 168–69
Hudson, Richard, 208, 209
Hughes, Langston, 20
Hugo, Victor, 158, 159–60
Hunt, Peter, 113–14
Hunter, Mary, 54–55
Hwang, David Henry, 74–75
Hytner, Nicholas, 53, 175, 179, 213

I, Don Quixote, 100
I Can Get It for You Wholesale, 42
Iconic logo as marketing tool, 127
"Idyll of Miss Sarah Brown, The," 61
"If I Loved You," 53
"If You Were Gay," 231
"I Get a Kick Out of You," 35, 37

"I Got Love," 118
"I'll Cover You," 189
I'll Say She Is!, 20
I Love My Wife, 68, 90
Image Awards (NAACP), 122
"I'm Breaking Down," 161
"I'm Gay," 137
"I'm Just Wild About Harry," 19–20
"Impossible Dream, The," 99
Impresario, extinction of, 221
In Dahomey, 12
India, Bollywood, 227–28
Ingram, Rex, 46
Innaurato, Albert, 10, 222
Inner City, 147
Inner City Mother Goose, The, 147
Innovation, great rule of, 26
Innvar, Christopher, 204
Inside the Actors Studio, 143
Integrated musicals, 61–62
International Herald Tribune, 183
International Ladies Garment Workers Union (ILGWU), 42
International Women's Year, 148
"Internet Is for Porn, The," 231
In Theater, 212
Into the Woods, 49, 172–73, 181, 216
In Town, 6
In Trousers, 160
Irene, 16, 42, 217
Irma La Douce, 76
Ironic Detachment, 235–36
Isaacson, Mike, 198
Isherwood, Charles, 164–65, 211, 222, 233
Isherwood, Christopher, 104–105
"It Depends on What You Pay," 84
It Happened in Nordland, 12
"It Only Takes a Moment," 92
"It's a Privilege to Pee," 218
"It's Better with a Union Man," 42
"It's Getting Dark on Old Broadway," 20

"It's Not Cricket to Picket," 42
"It Sucks to Be Me," 231
"It Takes a Woman," 93
Ivanoff, Alexandra, 147
"I've Got a Crush on You," 33
Ivey, William, 229
"I Want to Be Happy," 22
"I Won't Send Roses," 140

Jackman, Hugh, 229
Jackson, Josephine, 110
Jacoby, Mark, 211
Jacques Brel Is Alive and Well and Living in Paris, 98, 110–11, 137, 198
Jane Eyre, 206
Japan
    American musicals as overshadowing other musicals in, 4–5
    classic Broadway musicals in, explosion of, 217–18
Jazz Age, 19
Jefferson, Miles, 56
Jekyll & Hyde, 180–82, 206, 213
Jelly's Last Jam, 187–88, 202
Jerome Robbins' Broadway, 178
Jersey Boys, 234–35
Jesus Christ Superstar, 116, 127–29, 131, 153, 157, 158
    built on experiments of *Tommy*, 121
    as commercial success, 170
    community in, 54
    iconic logo as marketing tool, 127
    in Japan, 217
    odd time signatures, use of, 158
    revival, 222
Jeter, Michael, 177
Jiler, John, 195
Jim Henson's Creature Shop, 173
Job: The HipHop Musical, 237
Job II: The Demon of the Eternal Recurrence, 237
John, Elton, 115, 135, 153, 200, 209

john & jen, 199
John Phillip Sousa Band, 72
Johnson, J. Rosamund, 13
Johnson, James, 13
Johnson, Lady Bird, 94
Johnson, Lyndon (president, U.S.), 94, 105
Johnson, Van, 200
Johnstone, Tom, 20
Johnstone, Will B., 20
Jolson, Al, 50, 124
Jones, Allen, 27
Jones, Bill T., 237
Jones, Dean, 119, 120
Jones, James Earl, 28
Jones, Shirley, 73
Jones, Tom, 81–83, 84
Jones, Quincy, 202–203
Jordan, Joe, 31, 32
Joseph, Stephen M., 122
Joseph and the Amazing Technicolor Dreamcoat, 128, 179–80
Journal-American, 89
Journal of Popular Culture, 108
Joyce Dynel, 121
Joy Comes to Dead Horse, 81, 82
Juan Darien: A Carnival Mass, 208
Jubilee, 70
Julia, Raul, 30, 101, 139, 163
Julliard School, The (New York, NY), 72, 139
"June Is Busting Out Over," 54
"Just Leave Everything to Me," 94

Kabuki theatre, 146, 218
Kander, John
    Cabaret and, 104, 179
    Chicago and, 144, 145, 184
    Kiss of the Spider Woman and, 182, 183
    musical theatre as art form of, 6
    The Rink and, 156
    sociological insights from work of, 9
Kapur, Shekhar, 227
Karnilova, Maria, 96
"Kate the Great," 37

Kaufman, George S., 33, 60
Kavanaugh, James, 126
Kayden, Spencer, 219
Kaye, Judy, 126, 211
Kaye, Stubby, 62, 63
Kazan, Elia, 57, 84
Keaton, Diane, 107
Kelly, Gene, 45, 74, 94,
    202–203
Kennedy, John F. (president,
    U.S.), 88, 105
Kern, Jerome, 15, 23, 51, 124
    revues as training ground,
    18
    Show Boat and, 23, 27
    songs for Princess shows,
    14, 15–16
Kerouac, Jack, 77, 78–79
Kerr, Deborah, 65
Kerr, Walter, 69, 83
    Cabaret review, 104
    Company review, 119
    Gypsy review, 80
    on *How to Succeed in
    Business Without Really
    Trying*, 88
    Pacific Overtures review,
    147
    on *Pal Joey*, 46
    *You're a Good Man, Char-
    lie Brown*, review, 110
Kert, Larry, 119
Keystone Kops, 140
Kidd, Michael, 56, 57, 60,
    62, 94
Kiel, Henry W., 16–17
Kiley, Richard, 90, 101
King, Dennis, 60
King, Larry L., 149, 150, 151
King and I, The, 46, 48,
    63–66, 68, 146
    as classic musical, 61, 64
    community groups per-
    forming, 7
    emotional response to the
    love story, as demand-
    ing an, 61
    foreign director, 64
    as frequently revived, 44
    in Japan, 217
    politics in, 5
    racism in, 58
    revivals, 65–66, 179
    as Rodgers and Hammer-
    stein's last great work,
    65

King David, 208
King Lear, 156
Kirkeby, Marc, 113
Kirkwood, James, 141, 142
Kismet, 66, 176
Kissel, Howard, 157
Kiss Me Kate, 5, 44, 57,
    176, 226
Kiss of the Spider Woman,
    29, 103, 105, 182–84
Kitt, Eartha, 69
Kleban, Ed, 141
Kleinsinger, George, 68–69
Kline, Kevin, 139
Knighton, Nan, 205
Kopit, Arthur, 163–64
Kotis, Greg, 218–19
Krakowski, Jane, 164
Kretzmer, Herbert, 159
Kreuger, Miles, 27
Krieger, Henry, 161
Kronenberger, Louis, 56
Krulwich, Sara, 124
Kwamina, 91
Kwan, Nancy, 90

La Bamba, 152
La Bella Confusione, 163
La Bohème, 189, 190
La Cage aux Folles, 167–68,
    173, 195, 217
LaChiusa, Michael John,
    214, 223–24
Lady, Be Good, 20–21
"Lady, Be Good," 21
Lady in the Dark, 23, 47,
    50–51
"Lady's Got Potential, The,"
    153
Ladysmith Black Mambazo,
    188
Lahr, Bert, 37, 60
Lahr, John, 118, 211, 224,
    230, 231
Lambert, Hugh, 89
"La Misère," 159
Landau, Tina, 203–204,
    205, 217
Landesman, Fran, 77–78, 79
Landesman, Heidi, 187
Landesman, Jay, 77–78
Landon, Margaret, 63
Lane, Burton, 55, 124
Lane, Nathan, 224
Lang, Harold, 45–46
Lansbury, Angela, 80, 94, 154

Lantz, Robert, 77–78
"La Nuit," 159
Lapine, James, 185
    Falsettos and, 161
    Faust and, 200
    March of the Falsettos and,
    160
    Passion and, 193, 194
    *Sunday in the Park with
    George* and, 165–67
    *The 25th Annual Putnam
    County Spelling Bee* and,
    233–34
    Into the Woods and, 172
La Revolution Française, 158
Larson, Jonathan, 188–91,
    225
Larson, William, 83
Last Five Years, The, 2, 199,
    221, 225, 235
*Late Show with David Letter-
    man, The*, 191
Latessa, Dick, 229
Latin Americans, stunt
    casting of, 43
LaTouche, John, 46, 67
Laurel, Stanley, 12
Laurents, Arthur, 230
    Anyone Can Whistle and,
    94–95
    Gypsy and, 79, 94
    Hallelujah, Baby! and, 110
    having actors applauding,
    96
    La Cage aux Folles and,
    167
    West Side Story and, 69,
    94
"La valse á mille temps,"
    111
"La Vie Bohème," 37
Lawrence, Carol, 70
Lawrence, Gertrude, 47, 63,
    65
Lawson-Peebles, Robert, 146
Layton, Joe, 89, 90, 91
Leach, Wilfred, 170
Leader of the Pack, 156
Leap of Faith, 73
Leave It to Jane, 15–16
Lebrecht, Norman, 61, 235
Lee, Baayork, 144
Lee, Chin Y., 74
Lee, Gypsy Rose, 79
Lee, Sammy, 21, 23
Legitimate theatre, 5

Legs Diamond, 156
Lehar, Franz, 124
Leigh, Carolyn, 205
Leigh, Mitch, 99, 100
Leitch, Donovan, 193
Lennon, John, 235
Lenya, Lotte, 29–30, 66,
 104
Leonowens, Anna, 63
Lerner, Alan Jay
 Brigadoon and, 87
 Camelot and, 86–88
 Love Life and, 57
 My Fair Lady and, 66, 86,
  87
 Paint Your Wagon and,
  87
Leslee, Ray, 195
Les Misérables, 7–8, 128,
 158–60, 180
 developed in France, 86,
  158–59
 as epic tale, 170
 faux primitivism in,
  206
 finding adequate space
  for, problems, 175
 iconic logo as marketing
  tool, 127
 in Japan, 217
 longevity, 235
 9/11 attacks, response to,
  226
 overhaul of (1996),
  204–205
 as part of British chokehold of musical theatre
  in 1980s, 179–80
 as satisfying, 175–76
 similarities to *Miss
  Saigon,* 175
Les Romanesques, 81, 82
"Lesson No. 8," 166
Let 'Em Eat Cake, 35
*Let My People Come: A Sex-
 ual Musical,* 137–38
"Let's Do It," 37
*Let the Sun Shine In: The
 Genius of Hair,* 108
Levene, Sam, 62
Lewis, Albert, 46, 102–
 103
Lewis, Bert (Bob Fosse
 pseudonym), 103
Lewis, Morgan "Buddy,"
 50

Lieberson, Goddard, 45
Life, The, 112
Light in the Piazza, The, 2,
 222, 230, 235
Like Tomorrow, 77
Li'l Abner, 5
Liliom, 52
Lindsay, Howard, 35, 36
Lion King, The, 205,
 208–10, 211, 225,
 231
Lippa, Andrew, 110, 223,
 224
Lipton, James, 143
Little, Cleavon, 118
"Little Jazz Bird," 21
Little Johnny Jones, 10–11
"Little Known Facts,"
 109
Little Me, 111, 112
Little Mermaid, The, 185
Little Night Music, A, 21,
 98, 171–72
Little Orphan Annie, 148
Little Shop of Horrors, 128,
 159, 163, 164–65,
 216
 Goethe in, 199
 revival, 222
Littlewood, Joan, 80, 81,
 154, 205
Litton, Glenn, 130
Liu, Lucy, 146
"Live, Laugh, Love," 124
Livent, 46, 183, 210, 211
Livingston, Robert, 122
Lloyd Webber, Andrew,
 167
Loesser, Frank, 60–62,
 88–89
Loewe, Frederick, 66,
 86–88
Logan, Josh, 55, 58
Lollipop, 16
"London Bridge Is Falling
 Down," 66
London Critics Circle
 Awards, 160
London Daily Mail, 48
London Evening Standard,
 136
London Evening Standard
 Awards, 51, 143, 183
London Fringe Festival
 (England), 43, 237
Longbottom, Robert, 75

Look Again!, 138
"Look of Love, The," 112
L'Opéra Quat' Sous, 30
Lopez, Priscilla, 213
Lopez, Robert, 231
Los Angeles Drama Critics
 Circle Awards, 143
 "deaf" *Big River,* 227
 The Gospel at Colonus,
  168
 Les Misérables, 160
 Zoot Suit, 152
"Losing My Mind," 124
Lost in the Stars, 58–59,
 97
Louisiana Purchase, 60
Louizos, Anna, 232
"Love, Look in My Win-
 dow," 94
"Love Is Only Love," 93,
 94
"Loveland," 124
Love Life, 57, 110, 216
"Lovely Ladies," 159
Love Me Tonight, 50–51
*Lovers: The Musical That
 Proves It's No Longer
 Sad to Be Gay,* 138
"Love Will See Us
 Through," 124
Lucas, Craig, 230
Lucille Lortel Awards, 204,
 224, 232
"Lucy and Jessie," 124
Luft, Friedrich, 57
Lunt, Alfred, 57
LuPone, Patti
 in *The Cradle Will Rock,*
  42
 in *Evita,* 153
 in *Les Misérables,* 160
 in *Pal Joey,* 46
 in *The Robber Bridegroom,*
  139
 in *Sweeny Todd,* 155
Lyles, Aubrey, 19
Lynne, Gillian, 156

MacDermot, Galt, 130,
 131
Mack and Mabel, 140–41,
 167
Mackintosh, Cameron,
 159–60, 175–76,
 204–205, 226
Mack the Knife, 30

"Mack the Knife," 30
Mad, 207
Madame Butterfly, 175
Madonna, 153
Maguire, Michael, 160
Maltby, Richard Jr., 175–76
Malthus, Thomas, 218
Mame, 94, 140, 161, 167
Mamet, David, 3, 201
Mamma Mia!, 164, 199, 234, 236
Mamoulian, Rouben, 48, 52, 58–59
Mancini, Henry, 180
"Man Could Go Quite Mad, A," 169
Mandel, Baabaloo, 173
Mandel, Frank, 21
Mandela, Nelson, 174
"Man I Love, The," 33
Manilow, Barry, 111
Mankowitz, Wolf, 75–76
Mann, Terrance, 157, 181
Man of La Mancha, 1, 50, 98–101
   in Japan, 217
   as political, 5
   revival, 222
Mantegna, Joe, 107
Man Who Owns Broadway, The, 10–11
Marat, Jean-Paul, 95
March of the Falsettos, 4, 115, 160–61
Marcus, Daniel, 219
Marie Christine, 214
Marion, George Jr., 43
Mark, Zane, 202
Marks, Peter, 204–205, 232
Marquis, Don, 68
Marre, Albert, 100
"Marry Me a Little," 120
"Marry the Man Today," 62
Marshall, Penny, 173
Marshall, Rob, 146, 184
Martin, Barney, 145
Martin, Ernest, 62, 89
Martin, Mary, 93, 217
Martin, Steve, 73, 165
Martin, Tony, 62
Martinez, Julio, 207
Marx, Chico, 20
Marx, Groucho, 20
Marx, Harpo, 20
Marx, Jeff, 231
Marx, Zeppo, 20

Mary Jane Kane, 16
Mary Poppins, 67
Masekela, Hugh, 173
M*A*S*H, 3
Masterson, Peter, 149–50
Matchmaker, The, 91, 92
Mathis, Stanley Wayne, 187
Matsumoto, Koshiroh, 218
Matthau, Walter, 94
May, Deven, 207
May, Elaine, 77, 102–103
"May the Good Lord Bless and Keep You," 72
Mazzie, Marin, 211
McAnuff, Des, 115, 169, 179, 234
McCarthy, Joseph, 16
McCarthy, Joseph (senator), 66
McCaughna, David, 148
McClain, John, 89
McConagha, Al, 105
McDonald, Audra, 211, 223
McGillin, Howard, 184
McGlinn, John, 15, 27
McGrath, Matt, 193
McGregor, Ewan, 63
McNally, Terrence, 46, 182, 183
McPherson, Aimee Semple, 36
McSpadden, John, 138
Mead, Shepherd, 88
Me and Juliet, 73
Me and My Girl, 179–80, 224
Mecchi, Irene, 205
Meehan, Thomas, 149, 224, 228, 230
Mendelssohn, Francesco von, 30
Mendes, Sam, 104, 120, 179
Menken, Alan, 164
Me Nobody Knows, The, 122, 125, 131, 141
Menopause: The Musical, 236
Menschen im Hotel (People in the Hotel), 176
Mercer, Marian, 113
Merchant of Yonkers, The, 91
Mercury, Freddie, 135
Merlin, 156
Merman, Ethel, 50
   in *Anything Goes*, 35, 36, 37

in *Girl Crazy*, 35
Guys and Dolls and, 62
in *Gypsy*, 79, 80
in *Hello, Dolly!*, 94
in movie based on *Anything Goes*, 37
as song style, 35
Merriam, Eve, 147, 148
Merrick, David, 91, 93–94, 110
Merrill, Robert, 92–93
Merrily We Roll Along, 123, 216, 225
Merry Widow, The, 60
MGM (Metro-Goldwyn-Mayer), 27, 70, 176
Michael Koalhaus, 210
Michener, James, 57–58
Microphones, first time use, 112
Midsummer Night's Dream, A, 56
Mikado in Swing, The, 51
Milk and Honey, 92, 97, 140
Miller, Arthur, 140, 234
Miller, Flournoy, 19
Miller, Roger, 168–69
Miller, Tim, 1–2
Mills, Hayley, 65–66
Milton, Edna, 151
Milwaukee Press, 11–12
Minneapolis Tribune, 105
Minnelli, Liza, 145
Miracle on 34th Street, 72
Miranda, Carmen, 43, 70
Mirimée, Prosper, 52
Miscegenation, 25
Miser, The, 91–92
"Mis'ry's Comin' Around," 26, 28
Miss Liberty, 60
Miss Saigon, 17, 127, 128, 175–76
Mitchell, Adrian, 95
Mitchell, Brian Stokes, 101, 184, 211
Mitchell, Elvis, 146
Mitchell, Jerry, 228
Mitchell, John Cameron, 192, 193
Mitchell, Julian, 12
Miyamoto, Amon, 147
Mlle. Modiste, 12, 60
Modern Priest Looks at His Outdated Church, A, 126

Moliere (Jean Baptiste Poquelin), 10, 91–92
Molnár, Ferenc, 52
Monet, Claude, 3
Mongkut (king, Siam), 63
Montevecchi, Liliane, 163, 164
Montgomery, James, 16
Monthly Film Bulletin, 76
Monty Python's Spamalot, 225
"Moonfall," 169
Moore, Melba, 107, 118
Moore, Robert, 111–12
Moore, Tom, 125
Moore, Victor, 34, 35, 36, 60
Morake, Lebo (Lebo M), 208
Moranis, Rick, 165
Mordden, Ethan, 41, 44, 178, 235
More, Julian, 75–76
Moreno, Rita, 65, 71
Morgan, Helen, 27, 124
"Moritat," 30
Morley, Sheridan, 183
Morris, Mark, 212–13
Morro Castle, 36
Morrow, Doretta, 60
Morrow, Lee Alan, 96
Morse, Robert, 89
Morton, Jelly Roll, 187
Mostel, Zero, 17, 96
Most Happy Fella, The, 66, 68
"Motherhood March, The," 92–93, 94
Moulin Rouge, 222–23
Mourning Becomes Electra, 33
"Move On," 165
Movin' Out, 199
"Mr. Cellophane," 12
Munk, Erika, 148
Murger, Henri, 189
Murphy, Donna, 65–66, 194
Murray, Bill, 165
"Musette's Waltz," 189
Music, benefits of, 1–2
Musical Comedy Time series, 22–23, 60
Musical theatre
    as American art form, 4–5
    9/11 attacks, Broadway's response to, 226, 235

Broadway as tourist attraction, 204
classical musical, birth of, 44
cost, current, 221
death of, 2–3, 85
exciting new work now happening away from Broadway, 221
golden age of, debate over, 18, 98, 221
as indigenous art form, 4
invention of, 6
musicians strike (2003), 232–33
no precise beginning for, 5
Open Theater, 105, 107
overview, 1–8
psychological musical, first, 47
Theatre Advisory Council, 204
Musical Theatre Lab, 139, 140
Musical Theatre Works, 237
Music Critics Circle Awards (Australia), 160
Musicians strike (2003), 232–33
Music Man, The, 71, 72–73, 80, 100
    community groups performing, problems with, 7
    community in, 54
    leading men in, 11
    music as character in, 72–73
    revival, 222
Musser, Tharon, 187
"My Best Love," 75
My Fair Lady, 7–8, 66–67, 80, 87
    as first Broadway musical in Japan, 217
    longevity, 86
    longing for shows like, 2
    time-telescoping sequence in, 205–206
My Favorite Year, 183, 210
My Love, My Love, 184
My One and Only, 176–77

Mystery of Edwin Drood, The, 169–70
"My Time of Day," 62

Naked Boys Singing, 221–22
Nashville, 3
Nathan, George Jean, 41
National Alliance for Musical Theatre, 216, 223, 237
National Music Theatre Conference, 223
National Music Theatre Network, 237
National Theatre Conference, 197
Natural Born Killers, 144
Naturalism, 3
Naughton, James, 145
Naughty Marietta, 12–13
Nazario, Ednita, 212
Neagle, Anna, 22
Nelson, Kenneth, 83
Nelson, Novella, 118
Nelson, Willie, 151
"Ne me quitte pas," 111
Neo-Futurists, 218
Nervous Set, The, 7–8, 62–63, 68, 77–79, 83
Nervous Set, The (novel), 77
Neurotica, 78
Neuwirth, Bebe, 46, 145
"Never the Luck," 169
New Brain, A, 1, 2, 180, 199, 214–16
    community in, 54
    traditional structural model, rejection of, 221
New Deal, 39
New Dramatists, 219, 221
Newley, Anthony, 180
New Line Cinema, 193
Newman, Randy, 199–202
Newmark, Judith, 203–204
New Musicals, 182–83, 187
Newsday, 184, 203, 225–26, 234–34
New Statesman, 136
Newsweek, 191
Newton-John, Olivia, 126
New York, 101–102
"New York," 79
New York American, 33
New York City Ballet, 38

New York City Opera, 42, 58, 134
New York Drama Critics Circle Awards, 169
Ain't Supposed to Die a Natural Death: Tunes from Blackness, 130
Annie, 149
Candide, 134
Carousel, 53
A Chorus Line, 143
Company, 120
Fiddler on the Roof, 98
Guys and Dolls, 62
Hello, Dolly!, 93
How to Succeed in Business Without Really Trying, 88, 89
Les Misérables, 160
Man of La Mancha, 101
The Music Man, 73
My Fair Lady, 67
The Persecution and Assassination of Jean-Paul Marat as Performed by the Inmates of the Asylum at Charenton Under the Direction of the Marquis de Sade, 95
Rent, 191
South Pacific, 58
Sweeney Todd, 154
Violet, 197
New York Drama Desk Awards, 170
New York Drama League, 49
New Yorker
    Cats review, 157
    Flower Drum Song review, 74
    Follies review, 124–25
    and *The Light in the Piazza*, 230
    "Pal Joey" stories, 45
    Ragtime review, 211
    The Secret Garden review, 187
    The Wild Party review, 224
New Yorkers, The, 35
New York Herald Tribune, 46, 52
New York International Fringe Festival, 219
New York Musical Theatre Festival, 237

New York Philharmonic Orchestra, 72
New York Post, 49, 93, 137
    Annie review, 149
    The Best Little Whorehouse in Texas review, 151
    The Club review, 148
    Jersey Boys review, 234
    on *Pal Joey*, 46
New York Review of Books, 96
New York Rock, 199
New York Shakespeare Festival, 130, 131, 141, 169, 182
New York Sun, 15
New York Times, The
    Ain't Supposed to Die a Natural Death: Tunes from Blackness review, 130
    Anyone Can Whistle review, 95
    Anything Goes reviews, 37, 38
    Avenue Q review, 231–32
    Bat Boy: The Musical review, 208
    The Believers review, 110
    The Best Little Whorehouse in Texas and, 150
    Bring in 'da Noise, Bring in 'da Funk review, 202
    Cabaret review, 104
    Candide review, 68, 134
    The Capeman review, 213
    Chicago review, 146
    Company review, 119
    The Cradle Will Rock review, 41
    on Disneyfication of Broadway, 180
    Dreamgirls review, 162
    East West Players, article on, 216
    The Fantasticks review, 83
    Faust review, 201
    Flower Drum Song review, 75
    Floyd Collins review, 203
    Follies review, 123, 124
    Frank Loesser interview, 62
    Grand Hotel, story about, 178
    Grand Hotel review, 177–78

Gypsy review, 80
Hairspray review, 229–30
Harold Prince interview, 183
Hedwig and the Angry Inch review, 193
Hello, Dolly! review, 93
Jelly's Last Jam review, 187–88
Jesus Christ Superstar review, 127
John Waters piece in, 229
Les Misérables review, 204–205
Let My People Come review, 137
The Lion King reviews, 208, 209
Love Life review, 57
March of the Falsettos review, 160
The Me Nobody Knows review, 122
The Nervous Set review, 79
Nine review, 163–64
Oh Boy! review, 15
Once on This Island review, 185
Pacific Overtures review, 147
Passion review, 194
The Persecution and Assassination of Jean-Paul Marat as Performed by the Inmates of the Asylum at Charenton Under the Direction of the Marquis de Sade review, 95
on *Phantom of the Opera*, 171
Promenade review, 102
Purlie Victorious review, 118
Rainbow review, 133
Rent articles, 191–92
Rent review, 190–91
The Rocky Horror Show review, 136–37
shinbone alley review, 69
Sunday in the Park with George review, 166–67
Sweeney Todd review, 154–55

Tommy review, 115
The 25th Annual Putnam County Spelling Bee review, 233
Two Gentlemen of Verona review, 131
Urinetown reviews, 219, 220, 226
Viet Rock review, 106–107
West Side Story review, 71
The Wild Party review, 224
You're a Good Man, Charlie Brown, review, 110
New York Times Magazine, 222
"Next Time It Happens, The," 75
Ngema, Mbongeni, 173–74
Nichols, Mike, 77, 167, 213
Nicholson, Jack, 115
"Night People," 79
Nights of Cabiria, 103
Nine, 104, 116–17, 162–64, 176–77
Nixon, Marni, 65
Nixon, Richard (president, U.S.), 148
No, No, Nanette, 5, 21–23, 60, 123, 125
Nobel Prize, 211–12
"Nobody," 12
Noh theatre, 146
"No More," 173
Norman, Frank, 80, 81
Norman, Marsha, 187, 205
Norman, Monty, 75–76
Normand, Mabel, 140
No Strings, 89–91
Noto, Lore, 82, 83, 84
Novak, Kim, 46
Nunn, Trevor, 37, 48, 156–57, 159, 179
Nymph Errant, 35

O, Oysters!, 111
Obie Awards, 122, 143, 223
The Club, 148
The Fantasticks, 84
Floyd Collins, 204
The Gospel at Colonus, 168
Hedwig and the Angry Inch, 193
Promendade, 102

Rent, 191
Urinetown, 219
The Wild Party, 224
O'Brien, Jack, 228, 229
O'Brien, Richard, 134
O'Brien Girl, The, 16
Observer, 159–60
Ockrent, Mike, 224
O'Connor, John J., 35, 108
O'Donnell, Mark, 228
Oedipus Rex, 188
Oesterman, Phil, 137
"Off to the Races," 169
Of Thee I Sing, 33–35, 88, 97, 148, 236
"Oh, What a Beautiful Mornin'," 51
Oh, What a Lovely War!, 75
O'Hara, John, 45, 80
Oh Boy!, 15
O'Horgan, Tom, 107, 108, 121, 127–28
O'Keefe, Laurence, 205, 207, 235
Oklahoma!, 11, 47–51, 57, 58, 65, 73
as choreographic innovation, 19
as frequently revived, 44
in golden age of musical theatre, 98
as integrated musical, 14
Larry Hart declining to work on, 47
less than heroic heroes in, 45
longevity, 51
as proof that audiences like what's good, 28
psychological themes and dream sequences, 47
revivals, 48–49, 179
as revolutionary, 33, 19 50, 54, 120
sex drives explored in, 50
staged as nonmusical, 52
standard romantic couple in, 104
starting of show, 11
use of dance as narrative language, 49–50
Old Possum's Book of Practical Cats, 156
Oliver!, 75, 81, 227
Olivier, Laurence, 63

Olivier Awards, 51, 160, 183, 228
"Ol' Man River," 27, 130
Olmos, Edward James, 152
Once and Future King, The, 86
Once on This Island, 184–85, 210
Once Upon a Mattress, 78, 179
"Once Upon a Natchez Trace," 139–40
One Flew Over the Cuckoo's Nest, 101
O'Neill, Eugene, 33, 49, 80
"One More Kiss," 124
One-step, 19
Onion, The, 207
"On My Own," 159
On the Flip Side, 112
On The Line: The Creation of A Chorus Line, 144
On the Razzle, 92
On the Road, 79
On the Town, 5, 44, 79
On the Twentieth Century, 218
On Your Toes, 19, 38–39, 47, 49, 50–51
Open Theater, 105, 107
Operettas, 19
Orbach, Jerry
in *Carnival*, 145
in *Chicago*, 145
in *The Cradle Will Rock*, 42
in *The Fantasticks*, 83, 145
in *42nd Street*, 145
in *Promises, Promises*, 113, 145
in *The Threepenny Opera*, 83, 145
OrchExtra virtual orchestra, 232
"Origin of Love, The," 192
Orton, Joe, 81
Oscar, Brad, 224
Oscars, 202–203
Carmen Jones, 52
Chicago, 146
The King and I, 65
Mary Poppins, 67
Music Man, 71
Oklahoma!, 51
Oser, Jean, 30

Ostrow, Stuart, 131, 132–33, 139–40
Other Side of Silence, The (TOSOS I and II), 138
"Our Heroine," 58
"Our Little World," 173
Our Town, 81–82
Outer Critics Circle Awards
Annie, 149
Avenue Q, 232
Bring in 'da Noise, Bring in 'da Funk, 202
Don't Bother Me, I Can't Cope, 122
Grand Hotel, 177
Guys and Dolls, 62
Hedwig and the Angry Inch, 193
Les Misérables, 160
Man of La Mancha, 101
March of the Falsettos, 160
Miss Saigon, 175
The Mystery of Edwin Drood, 170
Rent, 191
Over Night, 14
Oxenford, John, 91
Oxman, Steve, 181
Oz, Frank, 165

Pabst, Georg Wilhelm, 30
Pacific Overtures, 74, 146–47, 216, 217
as concept musical, 103
as two-visit musical, 178
Page, Elaine, 153
Page, Ken, 157
Paint Your Wagon, 87
Pajama Game, The, 44, 104, 142, 222
Pal Joey, 11, 44–46, 47, 80
dream ballet, 50–51
as frequently revived, 44
integration of dance in, 49, 50
ironic detachment in, 61
less than heroic hero in, 45
politics in, 5
as proof that audiences like what's good, 28
Palmer, Arnold, 200
Panama Hattie, 70
Papirofsky, Joe, 100
Papp, Joe, 100, 141, 182

Parade, 2, 199, 214
Pareles, John, 115
Paris, 35
Parker, Alan, 154
Parker, Dorothy, 15, 67
Passing Shows, The, 18
Passion, 99, 154, 193–95, 216
Patinkin, Mandy, 124, 153
Patrick, Robert, 121
"Pay Day Pauline," 22
PBS Great Performance series, 168
Peacock, Michon, 141
Peanuts, 109
Peaslee, Richard, 95
Peggy-Ann, 23
Pen, Polly, 223
People in the Hotel (Menschen im Hotel), 176
People's Theatre Workshop, 80, 81
"People Will Say We're in Love," 51
"Perfect Time to Be in Love, A," 84
Peron, Eva, 67, 153
Peron, Juan, 153
Perry, Matthew C., 146
Persecution and Assassination of Jean-Paul Marat as Performed by the Inmates of the Asylum at Charenton Under the Direction of the Marquis de Sade, The, 75, 95–96, 101
Peter, John, 228
Peters, Bernadette, 55, 79, 80, 140–41
Peters, Michael, 161
Petrified Prince, The, 199
Phantom of the Opera, 128, 170–72, 173, 227
Bat Boy laughing at, 206
developed in Great Britain, 86
iconic logo as marketing tool, 127
in Japan, 217
longevity, 235
open-ended run in Las Vegas, 236
organ music opening, 154
as part of British chokehold of musical theatre in 1980s, 179–80
reuse of music, 153

Philco Playhouse, 100
Phillips, Lou Diamond, 65–66
Phylon, 56
"Pick the Winner," 61
"Pinball Wizard," 115
Pinkins, Tonya, 187
Pins and Needles, 16, 42, 44, 97
Pinter, Harold, 61
Pipe Dream, 73
Pippin, 116–17, 131–33, 140
as about America, 88
aware of music, characters as being, 196
The Cradle Will Rock as model for, 39–41
hybrid "Broadway pop" music, as having, 128
as making audience uncomfortable, 144
pieces of, in Jekyll & Hyde, 181
Pippin Pippin, 120, 131
Plain and Fancy, 222
Plato, 193
Playbill, 228
Playboy, 149, 150
Playing Underground, 102
PM, 56
Poor Little Ritz Girl, 16
Poor theatre, 205
Pop operas, 127
Poppy, 16
Porgy and Bess, 46, 50–51
Porter, Cole, 92, 124, 172
Anything Goes and, 35–37
Around the World in Eighty Days and, 57
artistic freedom in New York, 37–38
bawdy songs by, 44
Kiss Me Kate and, 57
list songs, use of, 37
New York setting of shows, 50
patriotism and, 14–15
revues as training ground, 18
The Seven Lively Arts and, 57
song style mastered by, 35
"Posterity Is Just Around the Corner," 34–35
Power, Will, 237
Preminger, Otto, 52

Presley, Elvis, 43, 76
Preston, Robert, 73, 140–41
Price, Jonathan, 164
Prince, Daisy, 198–99
Prince, Harold, 27–28, 91, 147, 165
  Cabaret and, 103–104
  Candide and, 133, 134, 155
  Company and, 118
  concept musicals, making of, 103
  conceptual work, criticism of, 2
  Evita and, 153
  Fiddler on the Roof and, 98
  Follies and, 117, 123–24
  Kiss of the Spider Woman and, 182–83
  musical theatre as art form of, 6
  New Musicals group, 182–83, 187
  Pacific Overtures and, 74, 146, 147
  Phantom of the Opera and, 171
  primary dictum, 139
  Sweeney Todd: The Demon Barber of Fleet Street and, 153, 154
  West Side Story and, 71
Princess shows, 14, 15–16, 24
"Princess Zenobia," 38
Producers, The, 119–20, 149, 220, 224–25, 229–30
Promenade, 102
Promises, Promises, 17, 83, 111–13, 138, 145
Prowse, Juliet, 145
Pryce, Jonathan, 175
Public Theater, The (New York, NY), 107, 130, 142, 202
Puccini, Giacomo, 189, 190
Puig, Manuel, 182
Pulitzer Prizes
  A Chorus Line, 143
  Fiorello!, 146
  The Gospel at Colonus, 168
  How to Succeed in Business Without Really Trying, 88

Oklahoma!, 51, 58
Rent, 190
South Pacific, 58, 62
Sunday in the Park with George, 167
Of Thee I Sing, 33, 88
Purlie, 5, 118, 130, 131
Purlie Victorious, 118
"Put a Curse on You," 130
"Put On Your Sunday Clothes," 92
Pygmalion, 66–67

Queen, 236
Queen Latifah, 146
Queen of Basin Street, The, 167
"Quest, The," 99

Rachael Lily Rosenbloom (And Don't You Ever Forget It), 141
Racism
  in *Finian's Rainbow*, 55–56
  in *Flower Drum Song*, 58
  in The *King and I*, 58
  Lost in the Stars and, 59
  in *No Strings*, 90
  in *Show Boat*, 25, 27, 28
  state laws against interracial marriage, striking down of, 91
  in *West Side Story*, 69–70
Rado, Jim, 133
Rado, Ted, 133
Ragas, 228
Raggedy Ann, 156
Ragni, Gerry, 82, 102, 131
Ragtime, 2, 9, 184, 185, 205, 210–11
  could only have been written by Americans, 203
  as missing from golden age of musical theatre, 98
  as next Great American Musical, 210
  as political, 5
Ragtime musicals, 13
Rahman, AR, 227–28
Rainbow, 8, 133
"Rain in Spain, 205–206
"Rain on the Roof," 124
Raitt, Bonnie, 200

Raitt, John, 60, 200
Ramone, Phil, 112
Rando, John, 219
Rankin, John, 56
Rapp, Anthony, 191
Rasch, Albertina, 47
Ratcliffe, Michael, 159–60
Ravinia Festival (Chicago, IL), 139
Raye, Martha, 60, 93
"Razzle Dazzle," 145
Reader's Digest, 236
Ready to Wear, 3
Realism, 3
Really Rosie, 140
"Real Mike Fink, The, 139–40
Realtime Music Solutions, 232
"Red, White, and Blue, The," 34
Redhead, 116
Red Mill, The, 12–13
Red Moon, The, 13
Reed, Alan Sr., 69
Reed, Oliver, 115
Reefer Madness, 221–22, 226
Reilly, Charles Nelson, 89, 92
Reilly, John C., 146
Reinking, Ann, 145
"Rejection," 79
Remick, Lee, 124
Renshaw, Christopher, 64–66, 179
Rent, 1, 2, 7–8, 50, 188–92, 205, 231
  The *Cradle Will Rock* as model for, 39–41
  development of, 7
  list songs, use of, 37
  as low-tech, 201
  as missing from golden age of musical theatre, 98
  A *New Brain* as companion piece to, 215
  as proving that movie musicals can work, 222–23
  as revolutionary, 235
  spectacles of the 1980s, rejection of, 185
  traditional model of content and themes, rejection of, 221–22

Respect, musical theatre
and, 4
Revenge with Music, 60
Revues, 18
"Rhythm of Life, The," 103
Rhythm of the Pridelands,
208
"Ribbons Down My Back,"
93
Rice, Tim
Chess and, 156, 170
Evita and, 152–53
Jesus Christ Superstar and,
127, 129, 152, 153
*Joseph and the Amazing
Technicolor Dreamcoat*
and, 152
The Lion King and, 209
musical theatre as art
form of, 6
Phantom of the Opera and,
170
Rich, Alan, 101–102
Rich, Frank
Dreamgirls review, 162
Follies review, 123
on Frank Lloyd Webber,
171–72
Grand Hotel review,
177–78
on *Gypsy*, 80
Jelly's Last Jam review,
187–8
March of the Falsettos
review, 160
Nine review, 163–64
Once on This Island
review, 185
Phantom of the Opera
review, 171
on *Rent*, 191
*Sunday in the Park with
George* review, 166–67
Richard, Cliff, 76
Richard III, 153
Richard Rodgers Awards,
84, 216
Richards, David, 180, 194
Rickman, Carl, 32
Riggs, Lynn, 47, 48
Right Girl, The, 16
Rink, The, 156
Rio Rita, 60
Rittmann, Trude, 64
Rivera, Chita, 145, 146,
164, 183

Riverfront Times, 198
*Roar of the Greasepaint, the
Smell of the Crowd, The*,
180
Robb, J. Donald, 81
Robber Bridegroom, The,
139–40, 185
Robbins, Jerome, 84, 178
director-choreographer,
introduction of position
of, 116–17
Fiddler on the Roof and,
70, 96, 97
Guys and Dolls and, 62
The King and I and,
63–64
West Side Story and, 69,
70–71, 72, 97–98, 116
Robeson, Paul, 25, 27
Robin Hood, 16
Robinson, Bill "Bojangles,"
32
Rock and roll, good theatre
and pure, 128–29
Rockefeller, Nelson, 212
Rock musicals, 77, 116
Rockwell, David, 137
Rocky Horror Show, The,
128, 134–37, 151
9/11 attacks, response to,
226
as political, 5
rebellion in, 116
Rodgers, Mary, 65–66, 205,
230
Rodgers, Richard, 26, 49,
73, 92, 124, 221–22
Allegro and, 57, 73
Annie Get Your Gun and,
55
The Boys from Syracuse
and, 42–43, 237
Carousel and, 52–54, 57,
65, 73
The Comedy of Errors and,
42–43
emotion in productions, 9
Fiddler on the Roof in style
of Rogers and Hammer-
stein, 97, 98
Flower Drum Song and,
73–75, 146
as great American theatre
creator, 49
Hollywood, disenchant-
ment with, 37–38

imitations, 55
The King and I and, 46,
63–66, 146
on Larry Hart, 14
leaving of Larry Hart by,
44
The Light in the Piazza
and, 230
Love Me Tonight and, 50
Me and Juliet and, 73
on musical theatre, 223
The Nervous Set, com-
ments about, 78
New York setting of
shows, 50
No Strings and, 89–90, 91
Oklahoma! and, 11,
47–49, 51, 57, 65, 73
Pal Joey and, 44–45
patriotism in, 14–15
Peggy-Ann and, 23
Pipe Dream and, 73
revolution, end of, 83
revues as training ground,
18
romantic and a jazzy
composer, as both a,
165
rule breaking by, 23,
53–54
South Pacific and, 46,
57–58, 65, 73
teaming with Oscar
Hammerstein II, 44,
47–48, 165
Too Many Girls and, 43
Urinetown as fitting
Rodgers and Hammer-
stein model, 218
On Your Toes and, 38–39
Rogers, Ginger, 93, 145
Rolling Stone, 191
Romans, music used in the-
atre by classical, 5
Rome, Harold, 42, 217
Romeo and Juliet, 65, 69, 71,
81
Ronstadt, Linda, 200
Roosevelt, Franklin D.
(president, U.S.), 39
Root, Lynn, 46
"Rosamund's Dream,"
139–40
Rose, Billy, 157
Rose, George, 170
Rose, Philip, 118

Rose Marie, 50–51
Rosenthal, Jean, 40
"Rose's Turn," 228
Rostand, Edmond, 81
Rothschilds, The, 117
Rothstein, Arnold, 61
Roxie Hart, 145
Royal Shakespeare Company, 95, 156, 159
Royce, Edward, 16
Rubenstein, John, 131, 132
Rubin-Vega, Daphne, 191, 201
Ruffelle, Frances, 160
Ruhl, Arthur, 31
Running for Office, 10–11
Runyon, Damon, 61, 62
Russell, Ken, 115
Ryskind, Morrie, 33

Sade, Marquis de, 95
Saibil, Jerome, 237
Saidy, Fred, 55
Salad Days, 76
Salmon, Scott, 167
Salonga, Lea, 175
Sandberg, Carl, 48
"Sandman," 200
Sandy, Gary, 151
San Francisco Chronicle, 152
Sarafina!, 173–74
Saturday Night Fever, 222
Saturday Review, 108
Saturday Review Awards, 101
Saturn Returns, 230
Savage, Mark, 195
Savo, Jimmy, 43
Scarlet Pimpernel, The, 182, 201, 205, 213
Scarlett, 217
Scenes de la vie de Bohème, 189
Schaffer, Louis, 42
Schechner, Richard, 105, 106
Schmidt, Harvey, 82–83, 84
Schönberg, Claude-Michel, 158, 175
School of Rock, 73
Schulman, Susan, 187
Schultz, Charles, 109, 110
Schuman, Mort, 111
Schwartz, Scott, 207–208
Schwartz, Stephen, 120–21, 131, 132, 207–208

Scott, Nancy, 148
Scott, Sherie René, 201
"Seasons of Love," 191
Secret Garden, The, 183, 187, 193
See America First, 35
Segal, Vivienne, 45–46
Segregation
  in audiences, beginning of the end of, 20
  in public schools, outlawing of, 20
Sennett, Mack, 140
Serling, Rod, 100
Sesame Street, 231
Seurat, 165
Seurat, Georges, 165–66
Seven, The, 237
Seven Lively Arts, The, 57
1776, 113, 129, 140, 176–77
"76 Trombones," 73
Sex
  sexual revolution, 135135
  treatment of, in musicals, 44–45
Shabalala, Joseph, 188
Shaiman, Marc, 228, 229
Shakespeare, William, 5, 10, 15, 130
  The Boys from Syracuse, 42–43
  boys playing girls in plays, 135
  reasons why work was special, 106
  Romeo and Juliet, 69, 71
  Taming of the Shrew, 57
"Shall We Dance?", 65
Shapiro, Herb, 122
Shapiro, Mel, 130
Sharman, Jim, 128, 134, 137
Shaw, George Bernard, 66–67
Shea, Jere, 194–95
"She Could Shake the Maracas," 43
Sheedy, Ally, 193
Sheinkin, Rachel, 233
She Loves Me, 85, 217
Shenandoah, 118, 218
Shimmy, 19
shinbone alley, 68–69, 100
Shock musicals, 236
Shoo-fly Regiment, The, 13

"Short People," 199
Show Boat, 7–8, 31, 42, 58, 72
  as beginning of revolution, 19, 33, 44
  as first Great American Musical, 23–28, 210
  as integrated musical, 14
  as issue driven, 97
  less than heroic heroes in, 45
  looking at with fresh eyes, 99
  maturity of, 4
  reality in, 49, 54
  revivals, 44, 179
  as revolutionary, 120
  Sammy Lee and, 21
  script, shortness of, 58
  success, reasons for, 50–51
"Show You a Thing or Two," 205–206, 206
Shubert, J. J., 17, 38, 43
Shubert, Lee, 38, 43
Shubert, Sam, 38, 43
Shuffle Along, 19–20
Shulman, Milton, 76
"Sidewalks of New York," 34
Simon, John, 91
Simon, Lucy, 187, 205
Simon, Neil, 3, 102–103, 111, 112–13, 142
Simon, Paul, 188, 201, 211–13
Simonson, Eric, 188, 212–13
Sinatra, Frank, 37, 46, 62
Sinfonia virtual orchestra, 232
"Singing in the Rain," 202
"Sing Me a Song of Social Significance," 42
Sissle, Noble, 19, 20
"Sitting On Your Status Quo," 42
Six Degrees of Separation, 193
"Slaughter on Tenth Avenue," 38
"Sleepy Man," 139
Sloane, Ted, 11
"Small House of Uncle Thomas, The," 64
Smile, 156

Smith, Cecil, 10, 29
Smith, Michael, 105
Smith, Molly, 3
Smith, Oliver, 93
Smokey Joe's Cafe, 235
Smothers, Dick, 77
Smothers, Tom, 77
Solomon, Alisa, 148
Somes, Asa, 193
"Something Just Broke," 186
"Something Sort of Grandish," 56
"Somewhere That's Green," 164
Sondheim, Stephen, 21, 23, 112, 147, 233
  Anyone Can Whistle and, 94–95
  Assassins and, 25, 94, 123, 184, 185–86, 212, 226
  Bounce and, 2, 123, 154
  Candide and, 133
  on *Carousel*, 49
  Company and, 118–19, 179
  on *Floyd Collins*, 203
  Follies and, 17, 117, 123–24
  A Funny Thing Happened on the Way to the Forum and, 94
  Gypsy and, 79, 94
  having actors applauding, 96
  human complexity in productions, 9
  Merrily We Roll Along and, 123, 225
  musical theatre as art form of, 6
  on *Oklahoma!*, 49
  Pacific Overtures and, 74, 146–47
  Passion and, 99, 154, 193–94
  primary dictum, 137
  realism from, 3
  reuse of material, 153
  Sunday in the Park with George and, 165–67
  Sweeney Todd: The Demon Barber of Fleet Street and, 154–55, 217
  three shows running on Broadway at once, 182

West Side Story and, 69, 70, 71, 94
  Into the Woods and, 49, 172–73
Sondheim Celebration, 120
Song and Dance, 128, 179–80, 227–28
Song of Jacob Zulu, The, 188, 212–13
Songs for a New World, 2, 137, 180, 198–99, 202, 214
  spectacles of the 1980s, rejection of, 185
  traditional structural model, rejection of, 221
Sontag, Susan, 102
"Soon," 33
Sound of Music, The, 7, 74, 78, 100, 234
  in Japan, 217
  music as character in, 72–73
  revival, 179, 213
  as Rodgers and Hammerstein's last show, 89–90
  as terminally bland and sticky-sweet, 80
Sousa, John Philip, 186
South Africa, campaign of resistance in, 174
South Pacific, 46, 55, 57–58, 68, 72
  antiracism in, 58, 64
  complexity of real love in, 65
  emotional response to the love story, as demanding an, 61
  as frequently revived, 44
  as issue driven, 97
  Juanita Hall as Vietnamese in, 74
  politics in, 5
  script, shortness of, 58
South Park, 224, 228
Spelling Bee, 2
Spencer, Elizabeth, 230
"Spring Can Really Hang You Up the Most," 78
"Springtime for Hitler," 225
St. Louis Post Dispatch, 203–204
Stage, 41
Stanislavski, Konstantin, 1
Stanton, Olive, 40

Starlight Express, 156, 170, 179–80
"Stars," 159
"Stars Have Blown My Way, The," 79
"Star-Spangled Banner, The," 11
Star Trek, 91
Star Wars, 3, 157
State Fair, 74–75
Steele, Tommy, 56, 76
Stein, Gertrude, 35–36
Stein, Joseph, 96
Sterner, Steve, 138
Stevens, Tony, 141
Stevenson, Robert Louis, 180
Stewart, Michael, 68, 91, 140–41
Stigwood, Robert, 127
Stilgoe, Richard, 170
Stone, Elly, 111
Stone, Oliver, 144
Stone, Peter, 113, 176–77
Stoppard, Tom, 92, 236
Stop the World—I Want to Get Off, 180
Storch, Larry, 74
Stravinsky, Igor, 224
Streep, Meryl, 153
Streets of Paris, The, 43
Streisand, Barbra, 77, 94, 153, 180
Strich, Elaine, 124
Strike Up the Band, 32–33, 34, 60
Stroman, Susan, 224
Strouse, Charles, 92–93, 149
Student Prince, The, 19
Stuttgart Ballet (Germany), 38
Styne, Jule, 45, 79, 110
Sue, Dear, 16
Sugar Babies, 17
Sullivan, Arthur, 32, 34
Summer, Donna, 107
Sundance Film Festival, 193
"Sunday afternoon on the island of La Grande Jatte, A" (*Un dimanche après-midi à l'Ile de la grande jatte*), 165
Sunday in the Park with George, 1, 98, 165–67, 168, 173

Sunday Times, 228
Sunset Boulevard, 127, 128, 172, 201
Supremes, 76
Sutcliffe, Steven, 211
Suzette, 16
Swados, Elizabeth, 205
Swayze, Patrick, 126
Sweeney Todd: The Demon Barber of Fleet Street, 1, 151, 153, 154–55, 171–72, 216, 217
  as Brechtian, 29
  community in, 54
  grief, story of a man driven by, 211
  as missing from golden age of musical theatre, 98
  pieces of, in *Jekyll & Hyde*, 181
  as pointing blame at audience, 144
Sweet, Jeffrey, 53–54
Sweet Charity, 102–103, 111, 116
  Lovers as having roots in, 138
  as making audience uncomfortable, 144
  pieces of, in *Jekyll & Hyde*, 181
  similarities to *Miss Saigon*, 175
"Sweetest Sounds, The," 91
Sweet Sweetback's Baadasssss Song, 129–30
Swerling, Joseph, 61
Swing!, 112
Swinging the Dream, 51
Swing Mikado, The, 51
Swiss Family Robinson, The, 33
Syal, Meera, 227–28
Sydmonton Festival, 156, 170
Symposium, 193

Takarazuka, 217
Take Me Out, 229
Tales of the South Pacific, 57–58
Taming of the Shrew, 57
Tango, 19
"Tango Maureen," 189
Tap Dance Kid, The, 112, 156, 202

Taubman, Howard, 93, 118
Taylor, James, 200
Taylor, Samuel, 90
Taymor, Julie, 205, 208, 209
"Tea for Two," 22
Tebelak, John-Michael, 120, 121
Teddy and Alice, 156
Teeny Todd, 155
Tenderloin, 146
Terry, Megan, 106–107
Tesori, Jeanine, 187, 197–98, 205, 235
"Thank You So Much, Mrs. Lowsborough-Goodby," 37
That Championship Season, 150
"That Old Devil Moon," 56
Theatre, 13
Theatre Advisory Council, 204
Theatre Arts, 38, 91
Theatre Guild, 47
Theatre Hall of Fame, 84
Theatre L. A. Ovation Awards, 227
The Last Five Years, 225–26
"There's No Cure Like Travel," 37
"There You Are," 169
Thibault, Conrad, 84
Third language, 227
"This Guy's in Love with You," 112
"This Was a Real Nice Clambake," 54
Thomas, Hugh, 83
Thomas, Millard, 32
Thompson, Brian, 137
Thoroughly Modern Millie, 187, 198, 222
"Those Magic Changes," 125
Threepenny Opera, The, 29–31, 66, 83, 145, 216
  as first popular off-Broadway musical, 81
  homage in *Urinetown*, 219
  leading men in, 11
  reality in, 152
  as satire, 144
Threes, 118

Three Sisters, The, 139
Tick, Tick . . . Boom!, 189, 225
Tierney, Harry, 16
Time
  The Best Little Whorehouse in Texas review, 151
  Carmen Jones review, 52
  on *Faust*, 200, 201
  The Last Five Years in "10 Best of 2001" list, 225
  The Producers, article about, 225
"Time Heals Everything," 140
Time of Your Life, The, 139
Times, 228
"Time Warp, The," 135
Tinker, Jack, 134
Titanic, 162–63, 176–77, 193
"Tits and Ass," 142
Today, 130
Tommy, 114–15, 121, 127, 193
Tom Paine, 121
Tonight Show, The, 191
Tony Awards, 1–2, 223
  Ain't Supposed to Die a Natural Death: Tunes from Blackness, 130
  Annie, 149
  Assassins, 186–87
  Avenue Q, 232
  The Best Little Whorehouse in Texas, 151
  Big River, 169, 227
  Bring in 'da Noise, Bring in 'da Funk, 202
  Call Me Madam, 62
  Candide, 134
  Cats, 157
  Chicago, 145
  A Chorus Line, 142–43, 145
  Company, 119–20
  Dreamgirls, 162
  Evita, 154
  Falsettos, 161, 214
  The Fantasticks, 84
  Fiddler on the Roof, 98
  Finian's Rainbow, 56
  The Gospel at Colonus, 168
  Grand Hotel, 177
  Grease, 126

Tony Awards (*continued*)
Guys and Dolls, 62
Gypsy, 80
Hairspray, 229
Hallelujah, Baby!, 110
Hello, Dolly!, 93
How to Succeed in Business Without Really Trying, 88, 89
Jekyll & Hyde, 182
Jersey Boys, 235
The King and I, 65, 66
La Cage aux Folles, 167, 168, 173
Les Misérables, 160
The Light in the Piazza, 230
The Lion King, 209, 211
Mack and Mabel, 140–41
Man of La Mancha, 101, 103
Miss Saigon, 175
The Music Man, 71, 73
My Fair Lady, 67
The Mystery of Edwin Drood, 170
Nine, 163, 164
No Strings, 89, 91
Oklahoma!, 51
Once on This Island, 185
Pacific Overtures, 147
Passion, 194
The Persecution and Assassination of Jean-Paul Marat as Performed by the Inmates of the Asylum at Charenton Under the Direction of the Marquis de Sade, 95–96
Phantom of the Opera, 171, 173
Pippin, 132
The Producers, 119–20
Promises, Promises, 113
Ragtime, 211
Rent, 191
The Rocky Horror Show, 136
Sarafina!, 174
The Secret Garden, 187
1776, 113–14
Shenandoah, 218
Show Boat, 28
The Song of Jacob Zulu, 188
The Sound of Music, 80

South Pacific, 58
Sunday in the Park with George, 167, 168, 173
Sweeney Todd, 151, 154
On the Twentieth Century, 218
The 25th Annual Putnam County Spelling Bee, 233
Two Gentlemen of Verona, 130
Urinetown, 219
West Side Story, 71
The Wild Party, 224
Into the Woods, 173
Zoot Suit, 152
Too Many Girls, 43
Torch Song Trilogy, 167
Toronto Star Sunday Magazine, 148
Townshend, Peter, 114, 115
"Tradition," 97, 98
Trash, 69
Trask, Stephen, 192
Travolta, John, 126, 153
Tree Grows in Brooklyn, A, 222
Trip to Chinatown, A, 6, 16, 91
Trip to Coontown, A, 6
Triumph of Love, The, 205
Trudeau, Garry, 109
Trujillo, Sergio, 234
Tubert, Susana, 212–13
Tune, Tommy
Best Little Whorehouse and, 116–17
The Best Little Whorehouse and, 150
The Club and, 147, 148
conceptual work, criticism of, 2
Grand Hotel and, 116–17, 176–78
in Hello, Dolly!, 94
La Cage aux Folles and, 167
Nine and, 116–17, 163–64
The Will Rogers Follies and, 116–17
Tunick, Jonathan, 112, 164
Tuskegee Institute (Tuskegee, AL), 13
Tutt, Homer, 31
Twain, Mark, 169
Twentieth Century Fox studios, 94

25th Annual Putnam County Spelling Bee, The, 4, 233–34
Twilight Zone, 154
Twitty, Conway, 76
Two by Two, 129
Two Gentlemen of Verona, 116, 130–31
"Two Heads," 139–40
Two Little Girls in Blue, 16
Two-step, 19
Tynan, Kenneth, 74

Udell, Peter, 118
Uggams, Leslie, 110
"Ugliest Pilgrim, The," 197
Uhry, Alfred, 139, 214, 230
Un dimanche après-midi à l'Ile de la grande jatte ("Sunday afternoon on the island of La Grande Jatte, A"), 165
Unionist musicals, 39, 42
United States
as inventing musical theatre, 6
9/11 attacks, response to, 226
Universal Studios, 150, 151
Unsinkable Molly Brown, The, 72
Up from Paradise, 140
Urban, Joseph, 23
Urban Cowboy: The Musical, 222
Urinetown, 2, 4, 218–20, 225, 235
copycats, as victim of, 236
partial victim of 9/11 attacks, 208, 226
traces of Little Shop of Horrors in, 164
traditional model of content and themes, rejection of, 221–22
as unconventional, 224
US, 96
USA Today, 215

Valdez, Luiz, 151–52
Valle, Peter del, 138
Valli, Frankie, 234
Vance, Vivian, 42
Vancouver Sun, 237
Vanity Fair, 191

Van Peebles, Melvin, 122–23, 129–30
Variety, 20, 31, 104, 105
  Bat Boy: The Musical review, 207
  The Capeman review, 213
  A Chorus Line review, 142
  Don't Play Us Cheap! review, 123
  Jekyll & Hyde review, 181
  Little Shop of Horrors review, 164–65
  Ragtime review, 211
  Saturday Night Fever review, 222
Variety Drama Critics Awards, 101
Vaselina, 126
Verdon, Gwen, 145
Vereen, Ben, 107, 131, 132
Very Good Eddie, 14
Vessey, Desmond, 30
Via Galactica, 131
Viagas, Robert, 144
Victor/Victoria, 148, 180
Vietnam War, 102, 125
  innocence, loss of American, 93, 116
  optimism, war as taking toll on American, 75, 105
Viet Rock, 75, 96, 105–107, 108
Village Voice, The
  A Chorus Line review, 143
  Company review, 118
  and *Floyd Collins*, 203
  Polly Pen interview, 223
  on Randy Newman, 201
  Richard Rodgers interview, 223
  Viet Rock review, 105
Violet, 180, 187, 197–98
  National Music Theatre Conference, premiered at, 223
  spectacles of the 1980s, rejection of, 185
  traditional models, rejection of, 222
Virtual orchestras, 232
Vogue, 212
Voices of Sarafina!, 174
Voltaire, 67, 133–34

Waddle, Irving, 136
Wagner, Chuck, 181
Wagner, Richard, 4, 153
Wagner, Robin, 140–41
Waissman, Ken, 125
Wake Up and Dream, 35
Walcott, Derek, 211–12, 213
Waldman, Robert, 139
Walker, Joseph A., 110
Walker, Nancy, 60
Walk on the Wild Side, A, 79
Wallach, Eli, 100
Wall Street Journal, 108, 109–10
Walsh, Thommie, 144, 163–64
Walton, Jim, 155
Walton, Tony, 176
"Waltz Down the Aisle," 37
"Waltz in 1,000 Time, The," 111
Warlow, Anthony, 181
Warner's–Seven Arts studio, 90
Warren, David, 181
Washington Post, 206–207, 232
Wasserman, Dale, 99–100, 101
Wasserstein, Wendy, 215, 233
Wasteland, The, 157
Watch Your Step, 13
Waters, Ethel, 46
Waters, John, 228–29
Waters, Julie, 30
Waters, Daryl, 202
Waterstreet, Ed, 227
Watkins, Maurine Dallas, 145
Watt, Douglas, 124, 133, 162
Watts, Richard Jr., 46, 93
Way Back to Paradise, 223
Wayne, David, 56
Webber, Andrew Lloyd, 81, 227
  Cats and, 128, 156, 157–58, 170, 171
  Evita and, 128, 152–53, 170
  flops, list of, 172
  Jesus Christ Superstar and, 127, 128, 152, 153, 170
  Joseph and the Amazing

  Technicolor Dreamcoat and, 152
  Les Misérables and, 159
  musical theatre as art form of, 6
  Phantom of the Opera and, 128, 170–72
  Starlight Express and, 170
  Sunset Boulevard and, 128
  Sydmonton Festival, 156, 170
  three shows running on Broadway at once, 182
Weber, Bruce, 220, 226
"We Do Not Belong Together," 165
Weekly World News, 206–207
"We Go Together," 125
Weidman, John, 37, 146, 185–86, 212
Weill, Kurt, 124
  death of, 66
  Lady in the Dark and, 23, 47
  Lost in the Stars and, 58–59
  Love Life and, 57
  The Threepenny Opera and, 29, 30, 144, 219
Weinstock, Jack, 88
Weiss, Peter, 95, 96
Welles, Orson, 39–41
Welty, Eudora, 139
"Western People Funny," 64
West Side Story, 68, 69–72, 78, 94, 97–98
  could only have been written by Americans, 203
  creative team from *Gypsy* also worked on, 79
  as a Great American Musical, 210
  hatred and racism in, 69–70
  in Japan, 217
  as political, 5
  as proof that audiences like what's good, 28
  revival, 71–72
  sex drives explored in, 50
  time-telescoping sequence in, 206
  use of dream ballet, 50
We Will Rock You, 236

Whale, James, 27
"What a Joy to Be Young," 37
"What Would You Do?," 103–104
Wheeler, Harold, 112, 123
Wheeler, Hugh, 133, 134, 146
"Where Has My Hubby Gone Blues," 22
"Where Oh Where," 139–40
Where's Charley?, 60
Whistle Down the Wind, 172
White, Onna, 73, 113
White, Sammy, 27
Whitney, Salem, 31
Whitty, Jeff, 231
"Whizzer Going Down," 160
Who, The, 114, 115
Whoopee!, 60
Whorehouse Papers, The, 150
"Who's That Woman," 124
Who's Tommy, The, 115
Wicked, 222
Wilbur, Richard, 67
Wilder, Billy, 111–12
Wilder, Thornton, 91–92
Wildhorn, Frank, 180–82
Wild Party, The, 221–22, 223–24
Wilkinson, Colm, 180
Williams, Bert, 12
Williams, George, 12
Williams, Sammy, 142–43
Williams, Treat, 126
Williams, Vanessa, 184
Willman, Chris, 201
Will Rogers Follies, The, 116–17
Willson, Meredith, 72–73
Wilson, Doric, 138
Wilson, Earl, 90
Wilson, Earl Jr., 137

Wilson, John, 57
Wiman, Dwight Deere, 38
Windust, Bretaigne, 56
Winer, Linda, 234–35
Winninger, Charles, 27
Winokur, Marissa Janet, 229
"Wintergreen for President," 34
Within the Quota, 35
"With You," 132
Wittman, Scott, 228
Wittop, Freddy, 93
Wiz, The, 112, 128, 217
Wizard of Oz, The, 12, 38, 56, 213
Wodehouse, P. G., 14, 15, 36, 45
Wofford, Ted, 59
Wolf, Tommy, 77, 78, 79
Wolfe, George C., 187, 202, 223–24
Woll, Allen, 93–94
Woman of the Year, 176–77
Women's Wear Daily, 113, 151
Woolcott, Alexander, 21
Working, 151
Works Progress Administration (WPA), 39
World, The, 32
"World Take Me Back," 94
World-Telegram & Sun, 79
World Trade Center (New York, NY), 9/11 attack on, 226, 235
World War I, 14–15
World War II, 44, 53, 56, 75
Wright, Robert, 176

"Yankee Doodle," 11
"Yankee Doodle Boy, The," 11
Yankee Doodle Dandy, 11

"Yankee Doodle Dandy," 10–11
Yeston, Maury
  Grand Hotel and, 162–63, 176–77
  La Cage aux Folles and, 167
  Nine and, 162–64, 176–77
  Titanic and, 162–63, 176–77
"You Can't Get a Man with a Gun," 5
Yougrau, Tug, 188
"You'll Never Walk Alone," 53, 54
Youmans, Vincent, 21, 124
Young, John Lloyd, 234
You're a Good Man, Charlie Brown, 109–10, 233
"You're a Grand Old Flag," 11
"You're Gonna Love Tomorrow," 124
"You're the Top," 37
"You've Got to Be Carefully Taught," 64
You've Got to Have a Dream, 2

Zaks, Jerry, 186, 213
Zellweger, Renée, 146
Zeta-Jones, Catherine, 146
Ziegfeld, Florenz, 23, 24, 157
Ziegfeld Follies, The, 18, 20, 24, 125
Zimmer, Hans, 208–209
Zindler, Marvin, 151
Zoglin, Richard, 225
Zondo, Andrew, 188
Zoot Suit, 151–52
Zoot Suit Riots (Los Angeles, CA), 152
Zorro, 81–82